BLACK'S
NEW TESTAMENT COMMENTARIES
General Editor: Morna D. Hooker

THE EPISTLE TO THE EPHESIANS

Black's New Testament Commentaries

THE GOSPEL ACCORDING TO ST MATTHEW
Floyd V. Filson

THE GOSPEL ACCORDING TO ST MARK
Morna D. Hooker

THE EPISTLE TO THE ROMANS
C. K. Barrett

THE FIRST EPISTLE TO THE CORINTHIANS
C. K. Barrett

THE SECOND EPISTLE TO THE CORINTHIANS
C. K. Barrett

THE EPISTLE TO THE GALATIANS
James D. G. Dunn

THE EPISTLE TO THE PHILIPPIANS
Markus Bockmuehl

THE FIRST AND SECOND EPISTLE TO THE THESSALONIANS
Ernest Best

THE PASTORAL EPISTLES
Timothy I & II, and Titus
J. N. D. Kelly

THE EPISTLE TO THE HEBREWS
H. W. Montefiore

THE EPISTLE OF JAMES
Sophie Laws

THE EPISTLES OF PETER AND OF JUDE
J. N. D. Kelly

THE JOHANNINE EPISTLES
J. L. Houlden

THE REVELATION OF ST JOHN THE DIVINE
G. B. Caird

Companion volume

THE BIRTH OF THE NEW TESTAMENT
C. F. D. Moule

A COMMENTARY ON

THE EPISTLE TO THE EPHESIANS

JOHN MUDDIMAN

G. B. CAIRD FELLOW IN NEW TESTAMENT STUDIES,
MANSFIELD COLLEGE OXFORD

CONTINUUM
London and New York

Continuum
The Tower Building, 11 York Road, London SE1 7NX
370 Lexington Avenue, New York, NY 10017-6503

© 2001 John Muddiman

First published 2001

ISBN 0-8264-5202-7 (HB)
0-8264-5203-5 (PB)

British Library Cataloguing-in-Publication Data
A catalogue record for this book is available from the British Library.

Typeset by BookEns Ltd, Royston, Herts.
Printed and bound in Great Britain by
TJ International Ltd, Padstow, Cornwall

CONTENTS

182

102121

PREFACE

When I began this commentary several years ago, at the kind invitation of the then editor of this series, Henry Chadwick, I subscribed to the broad consensus of critical scholarship on Ephesians: that it is not a genuine Pauline letter but a 'catholic epistle' intended for wide circulation, written by a later disciple who knew some of Paul's writings and was particularly well acquainted with Colossians, which served as his model. This standard view had what I then considered to be the added advantage of vindicating the authenticity of Colossians, which was and is increasingly questioned, since a pseudepigrapher would be most unlikely to have chosen to imitate something that was not itself the genuine article. As to the purpose of Ephesians, although I had my doubts about the Goodspeed–Knox theory that it was intended as a preface to the publication of the Pauline canon, I did at least see it as belonging more generally to the sub-apostolic process of 'canonizing Paul', making conformity to his teaching the touchstone of a developing orthodoxy.

I now consider this view to be highly questionable in several respects. As one works through the numerous parallels between Ephesians and Colossians and the other Paulines (conveniently set out in synoptic form by Mitton 1951), one realizes their astonishing variety. There is one almost identical paragraph (6.21–2), which must, on the standard view, have been transcribed directly from Colossians, but elsewhere the parallels take very different forms: just occasionally there are clusters of key words in common, but also the same basic idea may be freely expressed in quite different phraseology; in places Colossians has the neater or more evocative formulation, but almost as often the Ephesians version is better. Why, if the author had the text of Colossians available at the time of writing, did he use it so unmethodically? Furthermore, there are distinctive sections of Ephesians with very few parallels, either in Colossians or in the rest of the corpus, and this material includes some of its finest purple passages: the opening blessing, the hymn to Christ as Peace, the meditation on the Church as the bride of Christ and the exhortation to Christian warfare. But again, there is a great block of rather tedious moral teaching which, apart from its sheer length, is similar to what we find in some of Paul's genuine letters. Most difficult of all to explain, when Ephesians departs in detail from what Paul says elsewhere, it sometimes sounds distinctly post-Pauline – and sometimes even more convincingly Pauline.

These observations raised further doubts about the alleged purposes of the pseudepigraphy. For the author is both far more than a faithful follower and exponent of Paul's teaching, and also far less, for instance in his silence on the question of the Jewish Law apart from one passing allusion (2.15). His motivation seems to be neither imitative nor innovative. Despite the large number of parallels with Paul's letters, Ephesians looks as though it was meant to be read on its own and for itself, not as an introduction to something else. And finally, if the author wanted simply to promote the legacy of Paul in the post-Pauline period, would not forging a letter in his name be a very odd way of going about it? Some other solution to the problem of Ephesians was obviously needed.

In the 1970s, recent full-scale commentaries on Ephesians available in English were in short supply. I used to recommend students to read Houlden and Caird in tandem and make up the rest for themselves by arbitrating between their conflicting positions on authorship. The situation is very different today, with massive commentaries by Lincoln, Schnackenburg and Best. The number of references to these in the following pages indicates the extent of my indebtedness to them. With such riches available, is anything further required? I have ventured now and again to offer new interpretations of problem passages; but more significantly, I have constantly questioned the basic assumption that if Ephesians is not by Paul, it must be wholly accounted for as an example of post-Pauline pseudepigraphy. For there is an alternative: it could be an authentic letter subsequently edited and expanded, with the aim of adjusting the Pauline tradition to the situation prevailing at its time and place of composition. The reasons for believing that this may be the answer to the puzzle of Ephesians are laid out in the Introduction, which should be read first. They are then elaborated in the commentary. I refer to other commentaries that are frequently cited, like those mentioned above, by author's name alone, and to other works by author's name and date of publication (see Bibliography, p. 306).

I am grateful to Henry Chadwick and his successor, Morna Hooker, for many helpful comments, and to Leslie Houlden, who generously worked through an earlier draft in the most searching detail. I have also benefited from discussions with other members of the Theology Faculty at Oxford, especially Christopher Rowland, Robert Morgan and Eric Eve. My former pupil and present colleague, Lynda Patterson, has done most to help me develop this new solution to the problem of Ephesians, not least by actually believing in it. Any errors or misjudgements that remain are, needless to say, entirely my own. Finally, it is a special pleasure to acknowledge the help of the Trustees and contributors to the

G. B. Caird Fund which supports my fellowship at Mansfield College. Principal George Caird was finishing his elegant commentary on *Paul's Letters from Prison* while I was one of his research students in the early 1970s, and I dedicate this work to the enduring memory of a tireless and original scholar, confident that he would agree with approximately half of it.

John Muddiman
The Feast of Christ the King, 1999

ABBREVIATIONS

GENERAL ABBREVIATIONS

AB   Anchor Bible
ABD   *Anchor Bible Dictionary*, ed. D. N. Freedman, 6 volumes
            (New York: Doubleday, 1992)
AGJU   Arbeiten zur Geschichte des antiken Judentums und des
            Urchristentums
AnBib   Analecta Biblica
ANRW   *Aufstieg und Niedergang der römischen Welt*, ed. H. Temporini
            and W. Haase (Berlin: De Gruyter, 1982–8)
ANTC   Abingdon New Testament Commentary
AV   Authorized Version of the Bible
BAGD   W. Bauer, W. Arndt and F. W. Gingrich, 2nd ed by F. W.
            Gingrich and F. W. Danker, *A Greek-English Lexicon of the
            New Testament and Other Early Christian Literature* (Chicago:
            University of Chicago Press, 1979)
BBB   Bonner Biblische Beiträge
BBR   *Bulletin for Biblical Research*
BDF   F. Blass, A. Debrunner and R. W. Funk, *A Greek Grammar of
            the New Testament* (Chicago: University of Chicago Press,
            1961)
BETL   Bibliotheca Ephemeridum Theologicarum Lovaniensium
BHT   Beiträge zur Historischen Theologie
Bib   *Biblica*
BibInt   *Biblical Interpretation*
BNTC   Black's New Testament Commentaries
BZ   *Biblische Zeitschrift*
BZNW   Beihefte zur ZNW
CBQ   *Catholic Biblical Quarterly*
cf.   *confer*, compare
ch., chs   chapter, chapters
CIJ   *Corpus Inscriptionum Judaicarum*, ed. J. B. Frey (Rome:
            Pontificio Istituto di Archeologia Cristiana, 1936–52)
CNT   Commentaire du Nouveau Testament
DBI   *A Dictionary of Biblical Interpretation*, ed. R. J. Coggins and J.

	L. Houlden (London: SCM Press, 1990)
DETS	*A Dictionary of Ethics, Theology and Society*, ed. P. B. Clarke and A. Linzey (London: Routledge, 1996)
DPL	*Dictionary of Paul and his Letters*, ed. G. F. Hawthorne and R. P. Martin (Leicester: Inter-Varsity Press, 1993)
DSS	Dead Sea Scrolls
edn, ed.	edition, edited by
EDNT	*Exegetical Dictionary of the New Testament*, ed. H. Balz and G. Schneider, 3 vols. (Grand Rapids: Eerdmans, 1990–3)
EKKNT	Evangelisch-katholischer Kommentar zum Neuen Testament
ET	English translation
EvT	*Evangelische Theologie*
ExpT	*Expository Times*
FRLANT	Forschungen zur Religion und Literatur des Alten und Neuen Testaments
FS	Festschrift
GNB	Good News Bible
HNT	Handbuch zum Neuen Testament
HR	*History of Religions*
HTKNT	Herders Theologischer Kommentar zum Neuen Testament
HTR	*Harvard Theological Review*
ICC	International Critical Commentary
IDB	*Interpreter's Dictionary of the Bible*, ed. G. A. Buttrick, 4 vols. (Nashville: Abingdon, 1962)
JAC	*Jahrbuch für Antike und Christentum*
JB	Jerusalem Bible
JBL	*Journal of Bible Literature*
JETS	*Journal of the Evangelical Theological Society*
JSNT	*Journal for the Study of the New Testament*
JSNTSup	Journal for the Study of the New Testament Supplement Series
JSOT	*Journal for the Study of the Old Testament*
JTS	*Journal of Theological Studies*
KJV	King James Version of the Bible
LSJ	H. G. Liddell, R. Scott and H. S. Jones, *A Greek–English Lexicon*, 9th edn (Oxford: Clarendon Press, 1996)
LXX	Septuagint (Greek Old Testament)
MS(S)	manuscript(s)
n(n).	footnote(s)
NA^{27}	E. Nestlé and K. Aland *et al.*, *Novum Testamentum Graece*, 27th edn (Stuttgart: Deutsche Bibelgesellschaft, 1993)
NCB	New Century Bible
NEB	New English Bible
NIBC	New International Biblical Commentary

NICNT	New International Commentary on the New Testament
NIGTC	New International Greek Testament Commentary
NIV	New International Version
NovT	*Novum Testamentum*
NovTSup	Novum Testamentum Supplement Series
NRSV	New Revised Standard Version
N.S.	New series
NT	New Testament
NTD	Das Neue Testament Deutsch
NTOA	Novum Testamentum et Orbis Antiquus
NTR	New Testament Readings
NTS	*New Testament Studies*
OCD	*Oxford Classical Dictionary*, ed. S. Hornblower and A. Spawforth, 3rd edn (Oxford: Clarendon Press, 1996)
OT	Old Testament
par(r).	and parallel(s)
PGM	*Papyri Graecae Magicae*, ed. K. Preisendanz, rev. edn A. Henrichs (Stuttgart: Teubner, 1973–4)
PhilR	*Philosophy and Rhetoric*
PNTC	Pillar New Testament Commentary
REB	Revised English Bible
rev.	revised (by)
RB	*Revue Biblique*
RHR	*Revue de l'histoire des religions*
RSV	Revised Standard Version
SBLDS	Society of Biblical Literature Dissertation Series
SCM	Student Christian Movement
SE	*Studia Evangelica*
SJT	*Scottish Journal of Theology*
SNTSMS	Society for New Testament Studies Monograph Series
SPAW	*Sitzungsberichte der preussischen Akademie der Wissenschaften*
SR	*Studies in Religion*
ST	*Studia Theologica*
Str-B	H. Strack and P. Billerbeck, *Kommentar zum Neuen Testament aus Talmud und Midrasch*, 7 vols. (München: Beck, 1922–61)
s.v.	*sub vide*, see under the relevant entry
TANZ	Texte und Arbeiten zu neutestamentlicher Zeitalter.
TBl	*Theologische Blätter*
TBT	*The Bible Today*
TD	*Theology Digest*
TDNT	*Theological Dictionary of the New Testament*, ed. G. Kittel and G. Friedrich, 10 vols (Grand Rapids: Eerdmans, 1964–76)
TU	*Texte und Untersuchungen*

TZ	*Theologische Zeitschrift*
v.l.	*varia lectio*, variant reading
WBC	Word Biblical Commentary
WUNT	Wissenschaftliche Untersuchungen zum Neuen Testament
ZKT	*Zeitschrift für katholischer Theologie*
ZNW	*Zeitschrift für die neutestamentliche Wissenschaft*
ZTK	*Zeitschrift für Theologie und Kirche*

BOOKS OF THE OLD TESTAMENT

Gen.	Genesis	Esth.	Esther	Hos.	Hosea
Exod.	Exodus	Job		Joel	
Lev.	Leviticus	Ps.(Pss.)	Psalms	Amos	
Num.	Numbers	Prov.	Proverbs	Obad.	Obadiah
Deut.	Deuteronomy	Eccles.	Ecclesiastes	Jon.	Jonah
Josh.	Joshua	Song	Song of	Mic.	Micah
Judg.	Judges		Solomon	Nah.	Nahum
Ruth		Isa.	Isaiah	Hab.	Habakkuk
1–2 Sam.	1–2 Samuel	Jer.	Jeremiah	Zeph.	Zephaniah
1–2 Kgs	1–2 Kings	Lam.	Lamentations	Hag.	Haggai
1–2 Chr.	1–2 Chronicles	Ezek.	Ezekiel	Zech.	Zechariah
Ezra		Dan.	Daniel	Mal.	Malachi
Neh.	Nehemiah				

APOCRYPHAL/DEUTEROCANONICAL BOOKS

Tob.	Tobit	Let. Jer.	Letter of Jeremiah
Jdt.	Judith	Song of Three	Prayer of Azariah
Add. Esth.	Additions to Esther		and the Song of
Wis.	Wisdom of Solomon		the Three Jews
Sir.	Sirach (Ecclesiasticus)	Sus.	Susanna
Bar.	Baruch	Bel.	Bel and the Dragon
1–2 Esd.	1–2 Esdras	1–4 Macc.	1–4 Maccabees
		Pr. Man.	Prayer of Manesseh

NEW TESTAMENT

Matt.	Matthew	Acts	Acts of the Apostles
Mark		Rom.	Romans
Luke		1–2 Cor.	1–2 Corinthians
John		Gal.	Galatians

Eph.	Ephesians	Heb.	Hebrews
Phil.	Philippians	Jas	James
Col.	Colossians	1–2 Pet.	1–2 Peter
1–2 Thess.	1–2 Thessalonians	1–2 John	1–2 John
1–2 Tim.	1–2 Timothy	Jude	
Titus		Rev.	Revelation
Phlm.	Philemon		

OLD TESTAMENT PSEUDEPIGRAPHA AND THE DEAD SEA SCROLLS

Asc.Isa.	*Ascension of Isaiah*
2 Bar. (Apoc. Bar)	*2 Baruch* (Apocalypse of Baruch)
1 En.	*1* (Ethiopic) *Enoch*
2 En.	*2* (Slavonic) *Enoch*
Ep.Arist.	*Epistle of Aristeas*
Apoc.Mos.	*Apocalypse of Moses*
Od.Sol.	*Odes of Solomon*
Ps.Sol.	*Psalms of Solomon*
Sib.Or.	*Sibylline Oracles*
T. 12 Patr.	*Testaments of the 12 Patriarchs*
T. Levi etc.	*Testament of Levi* etc.
T. Sol.	*Testament of Solomon*
CD	Damascus Document from the Cairo Genizah
1QS	The Qumran Manual of Discipline

OTHER JEWISH WRITINGS

Philo Judaeus

Alleg.	*Allegoriae*, Allegories
Vita Mos.	*De Vita Mosis*, On the Life of Moses
Spec. Leg.	*De specialibus legibus*, On Special Laws
Vita Cont.	*De Vita Contemplativa*, On the Contemplative Life

Titus Flavianus Josephus

Ant.	*Antiquitates Judaicae*, Jewish Antiquities
B.J.	*De Bello Judaico*, On the Jewish War
C.Ap.	*Contra Apionem*, Against Apion
Vita	*Vita Iosephi*, Life of Josephus

Rabbinic Writings

Exod.R.	*Exodus Rabbah*
Deut.R.	*Deuteronomy Rabbah*
Sifre Deut.	*Sifre Deuteronomy*
Melch. Exod.	*Melchilta Exodus*
Num.R.	*Numbers Rabbah*
bSanh.	Babylonian Talmud, tractate *Sanhedrin*

EARLY CHRISTIAN WRITINGS

1 Clem.	*1 Clement*
2 Clem.	*2 Clement*
Barn.	*Epistle of Barnabas*
Did.	*Didache*
Ign. Eph.	Ignatius' *Letter to the Ephesians*
Ign. Pol.	Ignatius' *Letter to Polycarp*
Pol. Phil.	Polycarp's *Letter to the Philippians*
Hermas	*Shepherd of Hermas*
Iren. Haer.	Irenaeus, *Adversus Haereses*, Against Heresies
Tertullian Bapt.	Tertullian, *De Baptismo*, On Baptism
Adv. Marc.	Tertullian, *Adversus Marcionem*, Against Marcion
Augustine *Doct. Christ.*	*De doctrina Christiana*, On Christian Doctrine
Hippolytus *Ref.*	Hippolytus, *Refutationes*, Refutations
Clement *Protr.*	Clement of Alexandria, *Protrepticus*, Exhortation to the Greeks
Epiphanius *Haer.*	Epiphanius, *Adversus Haereses*, Against Heresies
Eus. *H.E.*	Eusebius, *Historia Ecclesiastica*, Ecclesiastical History

OTHER ANCIENT WRITINGS

Aristotle *Rhet.*	Aristotle, *Rhetoric*
Aesch. *Eumen.*	Aeschylus, *Eumenides*
Demosthenes *Orat.*	Demosthenes, *Orationes*, Speeches
Pausanias	Pausanias, *Description of Greece*
Pliny *Ep.*	*The Epistles of Pliny the Younger*
Quintilian	Quintilian, *On the Education of the Orator*
Soph. *Oed.*	Sophocles, *Oedipus Tyrannus*
Thucydides	Thucydides, *Peloponnesian War*

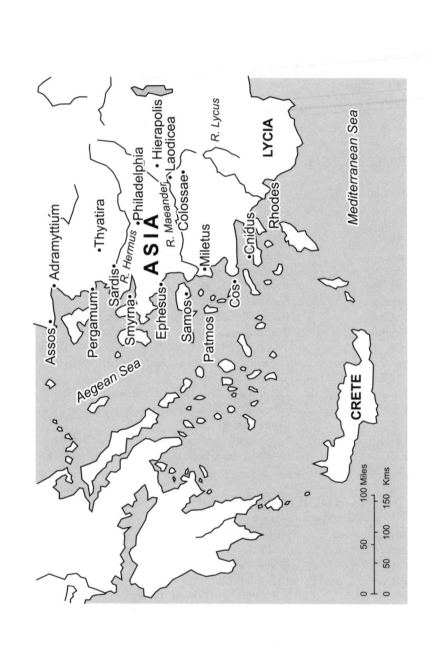

INTRODUCTION

PAUL TO THE EPHESIANS?

The question of authorship inevitably looms large in the introduction to any modern commentary on Ephesians. Although it is difficult to decide whether or not Paul wrote this epistle, one cannot simply suspend judgement, for a decision on the question determines to a large degree the contents and proportions of the commentary itself, why some points are discussed at length and others more or less ignored. The relation between presuppositions about authorship and the special emphasis on certain features of the text creates a vicious circle, of course. What this Introduction will attempt to do is to bring this basic problem out into the open.

If Ephesians is taken to be entirely authentic, then it is a letter sent by Paul to one or more communities from which he was separated, and it needs to be fitted into a plausible biographical and social-historical setting in the apostle's career, and its theological similarities and dissimilarities with his other letters need to be expounded or explained. Its extensive similarities, for example, might imply that Paul wanted to summarize and restate the teaching he had given in a dispersed and *ad hoc* fashion in other letters. In this case, Ephesians will be the indispensable key to the interpretation of the underlying pattern of Paul's faith. Its differences will also be important as indicating those points at which Paul wished to modify his earlier language and re-situate emphases – for example, away from justification by faith and on to salvation, or away from future hope and on to the heavenly and eternal present. If Ephesians is by Paul, it will come into direct competition with Romans as the definitive statement of the heart of Paul's theology.

However, if Ephesians is assumed to be a cleverly restrained *pseudepigraphon* (a document that claims to have been written by someone other than its real author), then we are forced to guess at what sort of historical and social setting it might have had, for no direct references to its actual situation can be included in the document without overt anachronism. On this assumption, it is not even correct to describe Ephesians as a letter. It may have assumed the letter form, but it was never 'sent' anywhere and its readers were not its 'recipients'. Furthermore, its similarities and dissimilarities with the genuine letters take on a different complexion. Some of its similarities may be part of the pseudepigraphical technique, intended to convey the impression of authenticity. But when the author dares to say something not said anywhere else by the real Paul, we should pay particular attention, for his ulterior motive in writing may then be coming to the surface, for example in his idea that Christians are already 'seated in the heavenly realms' or his insistence on the exalted role of the Church. If Ephesians is entirely non-Pauline, it is so convincing an imitation that it has misled centuries of scholarship into thinking that it was genuine.

Two very different sorts of commentary logically follow from the adoption of one or other of these options on the authenticity of Ephesians, though in practice the distinction is often less clearly drawn by commentators. On the one hand, those who defend Pauline authorship resist the radical consequences that their view implies for the interpretation of Paul's thought as a whole. On the other, those who deny Pauline authorship often waver between seeing reverence for Paul and faithfulness to his teaching as the principal motive for writing, and seeing it in terms of novel developments of Paul's views, especially on the Church. But this blurring of the consequences of a decision on authorship has more to do with the hesitations of the commentators than with the logical consequences of posing the question as a stark choice between authenticity and pseudepigraphy.

Hesitation is, however, fully justified, for there are phrases and sentences in Ephesians which, in the judgement of many commentators, Paul cannot have written (cf., e.g., 1.22b–3; 3.5, 10; 4.11; 5.32). Equally, there are phrases and sentences which he could easily have written (e.g. 1.15–17; 4.17–19; 5.18–20), and even some passages which, as we shall try to show in the commentary, he could not but have written (e.g. 3.1–4, 8; 4.20–21; 6.18–22). So the following commentary is unusual in one major respect: it offers a theoretical justification for taking a middle position between authenticity and pseudepigraphy, which others have taken as a practical compromise (cf. Cadbury 1958–9: 93).

We shall begin with a review of the main arguments that have convinced the majority of modern scholars (estimated at 80 per cent by Brown 1997: 620) that Ephesians was not written by Paul, and after each type of argument refer to some of the reasons for lingering hesitation.

Vocabulary and syntax

The argument against authenticity on linguistic grounds has a long history going back even to Erasmus in the sixteenth century. It has been examined in great detail by twentieth-century scholarship (see Percy 1946; van Roon 1974, for thorough presentations and counter-arguments). While not as weighty a factor against Ephesians as it is against the Pauline authorship of the Pastorals, it is not negligible. Even in English translation, the peculiarity of the language, especially towards the beginning, is immediately noticeable; in the second half of the letter, apart from odd patches here and there, Ephesians sounds more like Paul.

There are about 90 words in the letter not used elsewhere in the undisputed Paulines, and 40 of these occur nowhere else in the New Testament. However, raw statistics are, as always, misleading. For instance, Paul never certainly elsewhere uses the word 'water' (Eph. 5.26) in writing, but he could scarcely have passed a day without having it on his lips. Some rare words in Ephesians are simply required by their special contexts, like 'buffeted' (4.14), 'wrinkle' (5.27) or a whole sequence in 6.10–17: 'armour', 'contest', 'girding up loins', 'shield' and 'fiery darts'. Some result from quotations and can also be discounted: 'afar' (2.17), 'capture' (4.8), 'shine' (or 'dawn', see 5.14). Certain of these rarer words become very popular in post-apostolic literature, like 'unity' (4.3, 13) and 'compassionate' (4.32), but this proves little: Christian usage has to start somewhere.

The argument from vocabulary becomes more interesting when Ephesians uses forms of words for which there is a more normal Pauline equivalent, such as 'heavenlies' (e.g. 1.3) for 'heavens'; 'to be allotted' (1.11) for 'to inherit' (the same root in Greek); 'to grace' (1.6) instead of 'to give grace'; variant forms of words for 'gift' (2.8), 'citizenship' (2.12), 'holiness' (4.24), 'salvation' (6.17); and 'the devil' in place of 'Satan' (at 6.11, but see the comment on 4.27).

Secondly, and conversely, there are words that are used both in undisputed Paul and in Ephesians but in different senses: *oikonomia* as the divine plan or 'economy' of salvation (see on 1.10) rather than apostolic stewardship, its regular sense in Paul; *mustérion*, which is the word Paul preferred for the divine plan, appearing in Ephesians with a variety of other referents (see on 1.19); *ekklésia*, not used in Ephesians in the sense of congregation but always of the universal Church; *hagioi*, 'saints', used as an honorific epithet for 'holy' apostles and prophets (see on 3.5 and cf. 2.20). Of course, Paul himself is able to vary the meaning of key words like 'faith', 'law' or 'righteousness' in the space of a few verses, but then we can almost always detect the controversial motive behind his deliberate inconsistency. It is far more difficult to spot the motive in Ephesians.

So this argument is valid, so far as it goes: Ephesians uses slightly different words in the same sense as Paul and the same words in slightly different senses from Paul. Judged by his vocabulary, if the author of Ephesians were an imitator of Paul, he was good, but not that good! Not so much un-Pauline as 'off-Pauline' (in Houlden's apt term, 235).

The oddity mentioned above, that Pauline and off-Pauline usages appear together in Ephesians, can easily be explained on the theory of *de novo* pseudepigraphy. What is more difficult to explain are those words or usages in Ephesians which, though they lack parallels in Paul, are yet wholly in line with Paul's own usage: 'learn' with Christ as a personal direct object (4.20); 'co-bodied' or 'incorporate' (3.6) which, like 'co-spirited' (Phil. 2.2), is *hapax legomenon* (a word that occurs only once in a particular body of literature); the positive word *eutrapelia* or 'wit' turned into a negative, 'facetiousness' (5.4); an unparalleled Greek synonym for the verb 'renew' (4.23); the noun 'ruin' (5.18) and the verb 'to become calloused' or 'insensitive' (4.19). The commentary below will offer arguments in support of the genuine Paulinity of these and several other *hapax legomena*.

As we turn to questions of syntax, the first two chapters of Ephesians particularly, and the remainder more occasionally, are distinguished by a style that is different from that of Paul. There are some excessively long sentences; after the opening greeting, the whole of the first chapter (1.3–14, 15–23) has just two, consisting of 202 and 169 words respectively! They are drawn out by loosely attached participial, relative and causal clauses (see, e.g., on 1.11–14) or adverbial phrases like 'according to the working of the strength of his might' (1.19). This example also illustrates several other recurring features: the over-use of prepositional phrases, redundant synonyms and dependent genitives in place of adjectives. The effect is to produce a style that moves 'gracefully' (or 'ponderously', according to one's taste), and is quite unlike Paul's rapid verbal cascade; more like a 'glacier' than a 'cataract' (cf. Nineham, in Cross 1956: 31).

There are several ways of answering the objection to Pauline authorship on the grounds of differences in vocabulary and style. Paul may have given a co-worker, such as Timothy (van Roon 1974; Bruce) or Luke (Martin 1968), a rough idea of what he wanted to say and allowed him to express it in his own way. Similarly, a secretary (see Rom. 16.22, and Richards 1991) could have been given more than normal freedom in this case. Or again, the prospect of suffering and death may have brought on a more reflective mood in Paul, or the decision to write a circular letter not addressed to any particular church may have inclined him to adopt a more traditional and measured idiom.

The weakness in these counter-arguments is that, while they may explain the differences, at the same time they make the similarities more problematic. The co-worker or secretary has been very free in certain places but in others amazingly intuitive about what Paul himself would have said. The reflective Paul in his death cell or the generalizing Paul writing an encyclical has regular lapses back into his lively, sharply focused old self.

A more plausible explanation of the variations in style within Ephesians is to appeal to different types of source used by a pseudonymous writer. Alongside dependence on the Pauline epistles, the author has incorporated elements of liturgy, like the blessing (1.3–10) or a hymn about Christ (2.14–16, 18), a creed (4.4–6) or a chorus (5.14). The commentary offers arguments in support of these widely canvassed suggestions. But this does not constitute a complete solution, since the elevated style of the opening blessing is maintained in the following material, right up to the end of chapter 2; it begins to fade in chapter 3 and more or less disappears thereafter. It is necessary to posit, in addition to the use of liturgy-type sources, an author who himself prefers, and can reproduce when required, that style of writing.

Several scholars, following the lead of Morton (1978; 1980), have attempted to side-step the inevitably subjective element in judgements about style by employing computer analysis to calculate the incidence of certain features in Ephesians and compare it with those of other Paulines; the results have been disappointingly inconclusive. Kenny (1986: 99) has recently extended earlier researches by comparing the figures for 99 separate indicators of style, and concluded that in the case of the corpus of 13 Pauline epistles, all but Titus pass the test of authenticity! But taking whole books as the basis of comparison assumes, of course, their stylistic homogeneity, which – in the case of Ephesians, at least – is what is in doubt (cf. Best 32).

In short, this is the problem: the writer of Ephesians displays too much independence to be a mere imitator, and yet there is such a high degree of similarity with Paul as to imply that, unless it is by Paul, he must be a subtle and observant imitator. One solution to this dilemma might be to say that there are whole sections of Ephesians that are genuinely Pauline, but that there are also additional comments, expansions and other whole sections which are not.

Form and structure

Another type of argument against the authenticity of Ephesians arises from its peculiar structure, its strange combination of form and formlessness. It has the appearance of a letter but to many scholars its contents seem to be independent of its epistolary framework, so much so that they refuse to classify Ephesians as a letter at all and prefer other terms such as 'tract' or 'homily', 'meditation' or 'liturgy', 'discourse' or 'wisdom speech' (see further below, p. 14).

Paul's genuine letters also incorporate elements of other forms but they are always subordinated to the letter genre; this is true even in the case of disputed letters like the Pastorals, Colossians or 2 Thessalonians, for they are recognizably letters. On the other hand, the New Testament contains so-called epistles, i.e. Hebrews, James and 1 John, whose genre is fundamentally homily and where there is minimal overlap with the letter-form: they are simply 'sermons by mail'. Ephesians sits awkwardly between these two kinds of literature.

At first look, Ephesians is clearly a letter in the Pauline mode. The opening (1.1–2) and closing (6.21–4) sections conform closely to type. The thanksgiving prayer report at 1.15–18 is equally typical and the transition from exposition to exhortation at 4.1 again closely follows the regular Pauline pattern. But Ephesians lacks any references to co-senders or co-workers or specific greetings to those addressed; it includes a general blessing in addition to the first prayer report and throws in a second prayer report for good measure much later (3.14–19). It fails to mark the beginning of the letter-body (see on 2.1); it has two parallel pieces on the readers' pagan past (2.11–13; 4.17–19). It starts a moral exhortation (4.1–3) but quickly interrupts it with credal (4.4–6) and exegetical (4.8–10) material before resuming, and eventually extending to disproportionate length a string of ethical maxims (4.25 – 5.20). It includes a household code (5.21 – 6.9) similar to that in Colossians (3.18 – 4.1), but in the section on wives incorporates a theological and scriptural meditation on the Church.

No letter of Paul is so confused and confusing in its form and structure. The counter-argument that defenders of Pauline authorship plead is that Ephesians is exceptional: it is a circular letter addressed to no one community and is closer therefore to the sermon form. But Galatians, which is an actual example of a circular letter, does not look anything like this. Romans also, because of doubts about the integrity of chapter 16 (Fitzmyer 1993: 55–64), is sometimes said to have been circulated to other congregations, including that at Ephesus, but if so, its differences from Ephesians would raise many problems, for the two circulars are in places at variance with each other (see, e.g., on 2.1–10). Furthermore, at certain points (see on 1.15; 3.3; 6.21) Ephesians becomes rather too specific, despite itself, for this to be the solution.

Several recent scholars have taken the view that Ephesians is basically a sermon later disguised as a Pauline letter, i.e. that the epistolary form is part of the subsequent superstructure imposed when the document was turned into a letter (e.g. Gnilka 27; Kirby 1968: 165). But even within the passages that are, on this view, principally intended to make the document sound like a Pauline letter (e.g. 3.1–13) there are additions (see on 3.5, 10) that move in the opposite direction. So this commentary adopts the more likely assumption, that the epistolary form belongs to the basic substructure which the author's liturgical additions and other expansions have blurred. Schnackenburg and Lincoln, in their commentaries, take a similar view, arguing further that the 'substructure' is Colossians: whether this is the case must wait upon the discussion in the following section.

Relation to Colossians and the rest of the corpus

The similarities between Colossians and Ephesians are much closer than between any other two letters in the Pauline corpus. This fact is often taken as an argument, even the strongest argument, against Pauline authorship, for Paul is never so much like himself as Ephesians is like Colossians!

Both letters start in the same standard way, not surprisingly, but they also end in a very similar way, and at Eph. 6.21–2 (cf. Col. 4.7–8), the commendation of Tychicus, there are 29 identical Greek words in the same order. The subject matter is hardly such as to have warranted careful memorization and the majority of commentators are convinced that this is clear evidence of direct *literary* dependence of one text on the other. If Ephesians is a pseudepigraphon based on Colossians, then the purpose of such an exact transcription must surely have been to lead its readership, who already knew Colossians as Pauline, into thinking that this too came from his hand. (Other, more or less implausible, explanations are discussed in the commentary on this passage.) The only plausible alternative to this view is that Paul wrote both paragraphs himself, or had them written by a scribe, copying one in from the other because the two letters in which they originally stood were in fact both to be delivered by Tychicus.

Apart from this exception, the verbal similarities between Colossians and Ephesians are of a different kind. The letters tap into a distinctive pool of shared vocabulary: there are 22 words in common that do not otherwise occur in the Pauline corpus, and some that occur nowhere else in the New Testament ('alienated', Eph. 2.12; 4.18; Col. 1.21) or in the whole of surviving ancient Greek literature ('eye-service', Eph. 6.6, Col. 3.22). This fact produces, incidentally, a kind of 'domino effect' in discussions of authorship. If Colossians is the model of a Pauline letter imitated by the author of Ephesians, then that *per se* is a strong argument for the former's authenticity (against doubts about it). But when Ephesians is removed from the genuine corpus, Colossians begins to stand out as even more of an oddity in vocabulary and style, and that isolation in turn reinforces arguments against its own authenticity.

The verbal similarity often does not appear concentrated in parallel passages, but rather consists of just a few words in otherwise differently constructed sentences. It is only rarely that there is a 'cluster', but to take perhaps the two best examples:

(1) **Col. 2.19**: 'and not holding fast to the Head, from whom the whole body, supplied and assembled by its joints and ligaments, will grow (with) the growth of God'.
    Eph. 4.15b–16: 'that by telling the truth in love, we should grow up in all things into him who is the Head, Christ, from whom the whole Body, constructed and assembled through every supplying joint, according to the proper activity of each individual part, achieves bodily growth, and so builds itself up in love.'

(2) **Col. 3.16f.**: 'Let the word of Christ dwell in you richly, in all wisdom teaching and admonishing each other in psalms and hymns and spiritual songs, in grace singing to God in your hearts. And whatever you do in deed or word, do everything in the name of the

Lord Jesus, giving thanks to God the Father through him.'

Eph. 18b–20: 'Be filled with the Spirit, speaking to each other in psalms and hymns and spiritual songs, singing and chanting in your hearts to the Lord, always giving thanks for everything in the name of our Lord Jesus Christ to him who is God and Father.'

It is not at all obvious from a careful comparison of these parallels that Colossians must be the source in each case. In (1), for example, it has the more succinct version, whereas in (2) it is more verbose. (The commentary below will argue that Col. 2.19 is likely to be a dependent interpolation into that letter from Eph. 4.16, and that Eph. 5.19f. in context is in several respects 'more Pauline' than Col. 3.16.)

One of the most puzzling features of the verbal parallels between Colossians and Ephesians is that sometimes two distinctive terms are found together in Colossians but apart in Ephesians: e.g. Col. 2.7, 'rooted and built', cf. Eph. 2.20, 'built' and 3.17, 'rooted'; or Col. 1.20, 'reconcile all things whether on earth or in heaven', cf. Eph. 2.16, reconcile' and 1.10, 'all things whether on earth or in heaven'; or again Col. 3.12, 'compassion, kindness, lowliness, meekness and patience, forbearing ... forgiving', which is split neatly between Eph. 4.2, 'lowliness, meekness, patience and forbearing' and Eph. 4.32, 'kind, compassionate, forgiving'. But almost as frequently the opposite phenomenon appears: terms and ideas that are found together in Ephesians appear scattered in Colossians. Take Eph. 1.3–10 as an example: the alleged parallels are in different parts and in a different order in the first chapter of Colossians (thus 1.4, cf. Col. 1.22; 1.6f., cf. Col. 1.13, 14 and 20; 1.8, cf. Col. 1.9; 1.10, cf. Col. 1.20; 1.13, cf. Col. 1.5). But even this list (Lincoln lii) is not exhaustive, for one obvious parallel has been ignored altogether, both because it occurs very late in Colossians and also because it is highly problematic: Col. 3.12 refers to 'God's elect, holy and beloved (*ēgapēmenoi*)' and the ideas of being elect and holy are together in Eph. 1.4, along with the same adjective 'beloved' at 1.6 (*ēgapēmenos*) but turned into a title for Christ, rather than a designation for Christians. Is there any method in this alleged dependency? Is it psychologically credible?

Turning to a brief comparison of the structure of the two letters, we find that there are some significant similarities amid even more striking differences. Ephesians starts with a blessing (1.1–10) in addition to the standard prayer report (1.15–19) which it has in common with Colossians (1.3–14), and later adds another prayer report (3.14–19) without parallel. Colossians has a wonderful hymn to *Christ the Image of the Invisible God* (1.15–20) which is ignored by Ephesians, which has an equally impressive hymn to *Christ our Peace* (2.14–16, 18) with scarcely any trace of it in Colossians. A reminder of the readers' experience of alienation from God (4.17–19), found also in Colossians (1.21–3), is supplemented by an additional reminder (Eph. 2.11–13) of the readers' alienation from Israel. In Ephesians there is no parallel to the main central section of Colossians, the attack on false teaching (2.1 – 3.4), though there are passages that refer obliquely to such a threat (2.2f.; 4.14; 5.6f.). The ethical injunctions about the old and new humanity are far longer in Ephesians (4.17 – 5.20) than in Colossians (3.5–17), as though the writer wanted to emphasize this theme; but in the household code, structurally the same in both epistles (5.21 – 6.9, cf. Col 3.18 – 4.1) but substantially expanded in Ephesians, the emphasis moves away from ethics and on to ecclesiology. There is no equivalent in Colossians to the powerful final exhortation to Christian warfare.

It was not just the ambiguity of the verbal parallels between Colossians and Ephesians, but also these marked differences of structure within an underlying similarity, that led Holtzmann in 1872 to propose that there was a common core to both, Paul's original letter to Colossae, which was first elaborated to create Ephesians and then itself subsequently interpolated with secondary additions. The advantage of this theory (see also, for variations on it, Coutts 1958; Masson 1953 (see Kirby 1968: 9–18); cf. van Roon 1974: 414–26) is that it allows one to admit the occasional passage where Ephesians is more 'primitive'. It is, in other words, by no means as obvious as many more recent scholars have assumed, that the relationship of Colossians and Ephesians is one of direct literary dependence and always and in every case of the latter upon the former.

In order to counter these arguments, defenders of the theory of dependence of Ephesians on Colossians appeal to the broader debt that the author of Ephesians owes to other letters in the Pauline corpus, particularly Romans and 1 Corinthians and, to a lesser extent, Galatians, Philippians, 2 Corinthians and 1 Thessalonians (see Mitton 1951: 98–158). Lincoln, for example, writes (lviii) that Ephesians 'has taken Colossians as its model but further "paulinizes" its fresh interpretation by taking up phrases and themes from the Pauline letters in which the author is steeped'. Notice the implied concession in this statement that in some places Ephesians *appears more Pauline* than Colossians. At other places, of course, as Lincoln with most others would agree, Ephesians appears much *less* Pauline than Colossians (see, e.g., on Eph. 2.6; cf. Col. 3.1–4).

That the writer of Ephesians knew a number of Paul's own letters is taken as virtually certain by the majority of recent commentators. Usually the direction of the dependence is clearly of Ephesians on the authentic Paulines, but there are a few instances that are more questionable. Thus Eph. 2.1–10 looks very much like an attempt to moderate the excesses of Paul's doctrine of justification by faith as expounded in Romans 1–8, but on the other hand, Eph. 4.17–19 could be a straightforward description of pagan darkness such as Paul might have penned before he gave the topic the anti-Jewish twist it has in Rom. 1.18 – 2.24 (cf. also 3.18–19a with Rom. 8.35–9 and see the commentary on these passages).

In conclusion, there is a singularly close relationship of Ephesians with Colossians and with the other letters of the Pauline corpus sufficient to make its authenticity most unlikely, but there are nevertheless some cases where very Pauline-sounding passages in Ephesians may be prior to, and the source for, a parallel in Colossians, and even perhaps to a parallel in the undisputed letters.

Before leaving this discussion of the verbal and structural similarities between Ephesians and Colossians, it is necessary just to note the remarkable *differences* in terms of theological and ethical substance which such similarities belie. If Paul wrote Colossians and also a circular letter to the churches of Asia Minor to be delivered by Tychicus 'in the same mailing', then the Colossians themselves would of course have received both letters; and they would surely have been just as puzzled about the relationship between them as are modern scholars. Was Jewish mystical asceticism with its rules and regulations about food and drink the real danger (Col. 2.16)? Or was Jewish moral teaching and asceticism the hallmark of Christian discipleship (e.g. 4.25; 5.3)? Were the scriptures now redundant or were they still the treasury of sound doctrine and strict behaviour (e.g. 4.26; 6.2; cf. on 5.15)? Were they to practise civility towards outsiders (Col. 4.6) or to have nothing to do with them (5.7)? Were they to shun any kind of syncretism and hold fast solely to the deity of the glorified Christ (Col. 2.9), or were they also to take account of the power of the Spirit (3.16), the dignity of the Church (5.32) and the complementary and necessary symbiosis of Jewish and Gentile Christian views (2.13)? This divergence of content between Colossians and Ephesians, against the background of the undoubtedly close verbal similarities between them, is a major objection to the view that Paul wrote them both. But it is *also* a major objection, though this is rarely noticed, against the view that Ephesians is a pseudepigraphon based on Colossians. For its audience, in that case, would presumably have known Colossians well enough to recognize its verbal similarity with Ephesians (esp. 6.21–2) as authenticating evidence of Pauline authorship, but then they must have been prepared to receive its message in isolation from Colossians, for too close a comparison would have revealed the discrepancies mentioned above. So Ephesians must have been intended to be read on its own and for itself to an audience who did not know – or were at least not interested in the question of how or whether it was related to – Colossians.

Setting and purpose

The trouble with Ephesians can be summed up quite simply: it has no setting and little obvious purpose! The lack of a specific setting and purpose explains the popularity of the 'circular letter hypothesis' among those who defend Pauline authorship. This is the view that the letter was not addressed to one congregation but to several, or to the whole network of Pauline churches (see on 1.1). Paul, awaiting martyrdom in a Roman gaol, would be speaking, as it were, *urbi et orbi*, summoning the universal Church, enthroned with Christ and assured of salvation, to unity and holiness of life. Although attractive in its simplicity, this view yet leaves much unexplained. Why did Paul not choose a literary genre more appropriate to his purpose (cf. 1 Pet. 1.1; Jas 1.1)? By starting this letter in the standard way, with their place name added at 1.1, he would have misled readers in different localities into thinking that he was addressing them in particular. Why does he assume that they will all be personally unknown to him (1.15; 3.2) and all Gentiles (2.11)? If that were so, why does he emphasize the debt they owe to Israel, backed by quotations from Jewish scripture, and not also warn them against the judaising threat, in both respects departing sharply from his other captivity letters, Colossians and Philippians? And why does he not say more about the sufferings of Christ, if he is finally about to gain his share in them (cf. Phil. 1.20f; Col. 1.24)?

Many scholars earlier in the twentieth century continued to hold to Pauline authorship for Ephesians, despite these unanswered questions and despite the mounting linguistic evidence against it, because they just could not see any motive for pseudepigraphy. In a short monograph published in 1933, E. J. Goodspeed believed he had discovered the motive that would clinch the argument. Ephesians was written as a *preface* to the collection of Paul's letters when it was first 'published'. A later follower of Paul, particularly well acquainted with the letter to Colossae because he probably came from that city himself, was stimulated by reading the Acts of the Apostles to go in search of other letters Paul might have written but which had fallen into neglect in the post-Pauline period (a deduction from the observation that Acts does not refer to Paul's writing letters at all). He was rather successful and, having studied the collection of letters and with Colossians as his model, he attempted to distil from them the essence of Paul's teaching, echoing many of his keywords and phrases. Goodspeed accepted the suggestion of Knox that the name of the collector and pseudepigrapher was Onesimus, Philemon's slave and Paul's assistant in prison, presuming that this was the same Onesimus who became Bishop of Ephesus in the early second century (see Ign. *Eph.* 2.1; 6.2).

It should be emphasized here that the Goodspeed–Knox theory is quite different from, indeed incompatible with, the 'circular letter' theory referred to above. For an encyclical would have been intended to be read *on its own* in a variety of locations; but as a 'preface to the letter-collection', Ephesians (whether identified as addressed to one destination or not) would have been meant to be read *along with* the genuine letters.

Goodspeed's basic thesis was adopted, and expounded in minute textual detail, by C. L. Mitton (1951), but it has convinced fewer scholars since, because it has several weaknesses. The speculations concerning the publication of Acts as the stimulus for the collection of the Pauline corpus, and Onesimus as its collector, though not essential to the theory, are doubtful. Acts is quite possibly later in date than Ephesians (so Knox), and Onesimus would surely not have needed Acts to suspect that Paul had written other letters (so Mitton), nor would he have written in Paul's name to Ephesus in such a way as to imply that the Apostle had never been there. More importantly, the collection of the letters at a single stroke after a period of neglect is much less likely than their gradual spread through a process of exchange between the churches of Pauline foundation (Harnack 1926; Aland 1979; von Campenhausen 1972), and that itself implies the *continuing influence* of Paul rather than his neglect. There is, furthermore, no evidence that Ephesians ever stood at the beginning of a canon of Paul's letters, and if it was intended as a summary of Paul's teaching and an introduction to what followed, it fails on both counts. It passes over many themes of importance to Paul, such as freedom or suffering with Christ, even though the setting of the letter, with Paul suffering in chains, ought to have invited the exposition of these themes. It has new, unparalleled material, which is nevertheless impressive and distinctive (e.g. 2.14–18 or 5.22–33), and could even be said to cast some sections of Paul's own letters 'into the shade'. And its irenic tone and lack of controversy compared with Paul, far from diverting attention from those aspects of the genuine letters, might well actually highlight them. More generally, the Goodspeed theory is too 'academic' a conception of the setting and purpose of Ephesians, as though it were an exercise in imitation and synthesis of Paul to be received by an individual reader perusing 'an edition of the collected works'. It also fails to provide a satisfactory explanation of the pseudonymity. Why could the author not come clean and write in his own name, as Polycarp did in similar circumstances in his covering letter to the collection of the epistles of Ignatius (Pol. *Phil.* 16.2)? These objections have considerable weight.

Best (66) concluded his brief discussion of the Goodspeed theory with the judgement that it is now 'almost universally rejected'; it is dismissed by Lincoln (lviii) in a single line and reckoned 'improbable' by Schnackenburg (in a footnote, 36 n. 50). Despite this, one should not underestimate the impact that the theory has had. It encouraged scholars to amass a whole battery of evidence against the authenticity of Ephesians and, although the Goodspeed–Knox–Mitton hypothesis on the purpose of the letter has been largely abandoned, no more plausible theory has managed to replace it (Bruce 243).

A brief survey of some recent proposals, grouped into broad categories, may both illustrate the current disarray on the purpose of the letter and also provide a standard of comparison for the view to be proposed below (pp. 40f).

Liturgical origin

Several scholars have proposed that Ephesians has a liturgical setting and purpose, and that the letter-form is incidental or a later 'disguise'. Dahl (1951; 1978; 1986), for example, understands Ephesians as a homily directed towards Gentile Christians reminding them of the privileges and responsibilities implicit in their baptism. Schille (1965), similarly focusing on the importance of the hymnic material in the letter, understands it as a baptismal thanksgiving and catechesis. Kirby (1968) is even more specific and argues that this sermon on the renewal of baptismal commitment has a life-setting in a Christian celebration of Pentecost and reflects influences from the Jewish liturgy for that festival. Such theories, beguiling as they are, fail to offer a convincing explanation of the epistolary elements that are often more foundational and occasionally more specific than they should be on this showing (see, e.g., 3.2–14).

Early catholicism

Many, especially German Protestant, scholars understand Ephesians against the background of a deutero-Pauline development towards the 'catholicism' of second-century Christianity (Käsemann 1967; Con-zelmann 1976), in its emphasis on the universal Church and the succession of ministries from the apostles, and its loss of eschatological expectation (Lindemann 1975). While they can point to several features of the letter that support such a view, these jostle with other features that make this account of a consistent purpose for the pseudepigraphon more questionable. The lack of any reference to bishops, or the rules for their appointment (contrast the Pastorals) led Fischer (1973) to argue the opposite case: that the 'anti-catholicizing' purpose of the letter is to respond to a crisis of authority in the Church caused by the change from Pauline itinerant missionary structures (defended by the author, see 4.11) to the residential hierarchical organization that is threatening to supplant them.

Anti-pagan polemic

Arnold (1989), taking his lead from the account of Paul's work in Ephesus in Acts 19, with its emphasis on opposition to Jewish exorcism and pagan magic, has seen the references to 'principalities and powers' in Ephesians as the explanation of its setting and purpose. In his view, Paul himself wrote this letter to warn recently converted Gentile believers against the dangers of their Hellenistic religious environment – mystery cults, magic and astrology. Kreitzer (1997), who takes the letter to be pseudonymous, sees it as specifically targeted against the licentious cult of Demeter/Cybele associated with the alleged 'entrance to the underworld' in the city of Hierapolis (see on 4.9; 5.12). Sexual purity and opposition to the wiles of the devil are certainly themes to be found in Ephesians but it is more difficult to see them as the controlling motives for writing. The anti-pagan view is unable to do full justice to the dominant theme of the dignity, unity and universality of the Church, and finds it hard to explain why there are no explicit denunciations of magic or of particular pagan cults.

Political propaganda

Towards the end of the first century (AD 93–6) the churches in Asia were undergoing Roman state-persecution (cf. Revelation) and some scholars have attempted to tie the purpose of Ephesians into such a context. Lindemann (1976) appeals to the military imagery in Eph. 6.10–17 to support this suggestion, and more recently Faust (1993) has argued a similar case based on Eph. 2.14–16. While these theories throw some light on the intention of these sections and could be an alternative explanation (see above) for the emphasis on 'principalities and powers', too much of the rest of the letter is left untouched by them. In particular, Ephesians lacks any call to suffering discipleship on the part of Christians and there is nothing on relations with the state in the section on Christian conduct.

Anti-heretical polemic

The same difficulty afflicts the next kind of explanation, that Ephesians was written to combat 'heresy'. The view that the production of much early Christian literature was provoked by the need to combat deviants of one kind or another is not unreasonable, especially considering the genuine letters of Paul. But when applied to Ephesians it faces the problem that there is no defined group of opponents, unlike, e.g., Galatians, 2 Corinthians, Philippians or Colossians, and some cogent explanation for this reticence would be needed. Cryptic allusions to opponents' views, such as those detected by Goulder 1991, could easily be misunderstood as approval of them, unless their tainted source were explicitly identified. If the letter is pseudonymous, then one might reasonably argue that the post-Pauline writer was inhibited from specificity because of the need to protect his pseudonymity; Goulder, however, believes it to be genuinely Pauline.

Anti-gnostic motivation has often been attributed to Ephesians (Mussner; Schlier 1930; Conzelmann 1976; Pokorný 1965), but at the same time positive influences from gnosticism have been detected, for example in its language of 'mystery', 'aeons', the heavenly 'Man' and cosmic speculation generally, or in the 'sacred marriage of Christ and the Church' in Eph. 5.21–33 (see Sampley 1971, for discussion and refutation). The writer of Ephesians appears confusingly as a 'gnosticizing anti-gnostic', too dependent on its cosmic universalism to attack gnosticism directly on theological grounds and reduced to merely moral objections against it (Koester 1982: 271).

Essene influence, anti-Essenism

Similarities between certain aspects of Ephesians and the Qumran literature have often been noted (e.g. by Kuhn 1968; Perkins 1997), such as 'children of light' (5.8), 'fellow citizens with the holy ones' (2.19), the community as temple (2.21); but they are not distinctive enough (the genuine Paulines and the Johannine literature display similar parallels) to throw much light on the setting of the letter. And it would be difficult to decide whether its purpose was to warn against Essene ascetical mysticism (cf. Col. 2.18) or conversely to attract into Pauline churches displaced Essene Jews, flowing into Asia Minor in the aftermath of the Jewish War of AD 66–70 (Bauer 1972: 86f.; cf. Grundmann 1959).

Jew–Gentile conflict

The relation of Jews and Gentiles in the Church is not only an explicit theme in Eph. 2.11–21, it is implicit and pervasive elsewhere, e.g. in the use of Jewish liturgical forms and scriptural allusions. Some have detected the purpose of the letter here. Chadwick (1960) argued, for instance, that Ephesians is an apologia for the antiquity of Christianity, by appeal to its Jewish roots, against the charge of novelty. Similarly, Fischer (1973: 21–39) argued that Gentile Christians were being warned by this letter not to despise their Jewish origins.

Although ostensibly addressed to Gentile Christians, it is rather too hasty to conclude in the case of a pseudepigraphon that the actual addressees must be exclusively Gentile. Ephesians could be read with equal profit by Jewish Christians who, until they were reassured by this letter, may have suspected Paul of claiming a unique and superior apostolic status (cf. 2.20 and 3.5) and creating an antinomian and anti-

Jewish form of Christianity. Schmithals (1983: 122) comes closest to the view that we shall propose below, when he understands the purpose of Ephesians as 'to seal the acceptance by the Gentile Christians from the Pauline communities of their Christian brothers who came from the synagogue and also at the same time acquaint the latter with the Pauline tradition'. The last part of that summary rightly acknowledges the real possibility, too often ignored, of Jewish Christian readers, and the first part allows also the converse: 'to encourage Jewish Christians expelled from the synagogue to join the Gentile communities of Pauline foundation'. Best (69) points out that with such an understanding of the purpose of the letter 'the paraenesis becomes irrelevant'. But this objection assumes a single consistent purpose that will explain all the material in Ephesians, an assumption that is beginning to look highly questionable.

Deliberate generalization

The 'circular letter hypothesis', popular as an explanation of the generality of the letter among those who defend Pauline authorship (see comments at the start of this section), is also appealed to by those who deny it. Schnackenburg (22–35), for instance, argues that it addresses two main issues of general relevance: the unity of the Church, encompassing scattered congregations; and the need for distinctive Christian conduct that will mark them out from their pagan environment. There is some tension between these two purposes (the one universalizing, the other particularizing) and neither explains why a pseudonymous Pauline letter was required to accomplish them. Lincoln's view better explains the pseudonymous letter-form by reference to what he calls the 'crisis' of confidence and cohesion caused by the death of the Apostle. But if the problem is 'the loss of identity on the part of ... Gentile Christians in Pauline mission churches' (lxxxv) it is difficult to grasp why Ephesians responds to it by emphasizing the debt they owe to Jewish tradition rather than the integrity of their own Pauline inheritance and the legitimacy of their status as *Gentile* Christians.

Theological emphases

We are concerned here only with theological arguments against authenticity, and possible counter-arguments to them. (More general comments on the theological significance of Ephesians will be found on pp. 36–9 and 47–53 below).

Often these arguments turn on the issue of 'development' in Paul's thought. If Paul was someone who changed his fundamental beliefs about Christ, the End or the Church between the earlier and the later letters, in response to varied circumstances or the inner dynamic of his thinking, then it might be possible to accommodate Ephesians as the end point in the series (cf. Dodd 1928). But if Paul's thought remained constant and did not develop substantially during the last third of his career as an apostle (from which period all his letters come), then theological arguments against the authenticity of Ephesians ought to be that much more compelling. And this is surely more likely.

The more realized eschatology of Ephesians (e.g. that Christians are already ascended with Christ and enthroned in heaven, 2.6), or the more cosmic ecclesiology of the equality (3.21) and union (5.32) of the Church with Christ, seem to be 'developments' away from Paul. However, alongside such passages there are others that reflect his position rather accurately and faithfully. The author of Ephesians has not consistently eliminated earlier views whilst incorporating 'more developed' ones. Is this a subtle diversionary tactic, by which he hopes to distract attention from the differences and smuggle in the innovations? Or is he not really concerned with the issue of consistency, but content to live with a certain diversity of doctrine?

The main points of theological difference between Ephesians and the rest of the Pauline corpus are briefly as follows:

(1) The author seems to have combined two ideas that Paul himself kept separate, i.e. that Christ is the head of the new humanity (1 Cor. 11.3; cf. 1 Cor. 15.20–28) and that the Church is the Body of Christ (e.g. 1 Cor. 12.12), and co-ordinated them (see on 1.22f.; 4.15f. and esp. 5.21–32), so that Christ is the head of his body the Church. It could be argued that Paul had already anticipated this development at Col. 1.18a, but that half verse does not fit into its immediate context at all well, and is supported by little else in Colossians, so it may well be an interpolation (see Lohse 1971: 42f. and n. 71; and see further on Eph. 4.15; cf. Col. 2.19). However, in addition to the 'developed' use of head-body imagery in Ephesians, more Pauline undeveloped usages also appear (see on 4.25).

(2) Ephesians speaks of salvation as already achieved (2.5) and insists on the relation of 'saved by grace through faith' to the issue of 'good works'. Pauline eschatology has been more thoroughly realized (cf. 2.6) and his doctrine of justification has been separated from the issue of the Jewish Law and 'ethicized' (see on 2.1–10). However, the emphasis on the need for Christians to grow up into greater maturity (4.14f.) and the references to the 'two ages' doctrine of apocalyptic (1.21) and 'that evil day' (6.13; see also the comment on 'salvation' at 6.17) show that future eschatology has not been eliminated altogether. And the question of the Jewish Law makes a fleeting appearance at 2.15.

(3) Ephesians uses the word *ekklēsia* only in the singular and of the universal Church. The predominant sense of the term in Paul is local (but see 1 Cor. 10.32; Gal. 1.13), and Colossians can also use it in that way (4.15f.). Nevertheless, Ephesians does not consistently remain at the level of abstract ecclesiology; the ethical instructions look as though they are addressed to the concerns of a particular local congregation.

(4) Ephesians uses the terms *mustērion* and *oikonomia* in relation to the cosmic scope of God's mysterious plan of salvation (3.9). But more Pauline usages of these words are also found, even in close proximity to the former (3.2; 3.4).

(5) The author of Ephesians looks back to the historic foundation of the Church upon the first generation apostles and prophets (contrast 1 Cor. 3.11), who are even called 'holy apostles' (3.5), and is concerned with the authority and continuity of ministerial office in the Church (4.11; cf. also comments on 5.21 – 6.9). However, he retains material that shares Paul's own perspective on his work and status as an apostle (3.2f., 7; 6.19f.).

(6) There is no reference anywhere in Ephesians to the problem of continuing Jewish unbelief (in contrast to Paul in Rom. 9–11). It has appeared to many commentators (e.g. Houlden 244; Lincoln xciii) that the Church is viewed as a 'third race', neither Jewish nor Gentile, and that the battle between them is past. But the affirmation that Jews and Gentiles are one in Christ (Eph. 2.11–22) does not necessarily mean that this is already an accomplished fact. On the contrary, it might well imply the opposite. And it is important also to notice that, while the hymn at 2.14–16, 18 speaks of the breaking down of barriers between the races, the surrounding material implies a rather different concept of unity, namely that salvation for Gentiles involves coming closer to Israel (2.13, 17; cf. John. 4.22).

The arguments in this and preceding sections, when taken together, build up into a substantial case against the authenticity of Ephesians, but there are, as we have seen, often good grounds for hesitation as well. Unless one were to write two separate commentaries on the Epistle and simply shuffle the pages, the issue of authenticity has to be decided. To summarize our findings so far:

(a) The vocabulary is a curious combination of the 'off-Pauline' with the convincingly Pauline, sometimes even in passages with no parallel elsewhere; and the style changes from a hieratic sublimity at the beginning (not only in what might be inherited tradition but also in extensions of it) to a leaner, 'punchier' style towards the end.

(b) An epistolary substructure has been obscured through the addition of a more homiletic superstructure.

(c) Similarities with Colossians and other letters, especially Romans, imply the author's acquaintance with Paul's writings and dependence upon them. While the dependence often seems to take the form of a free re-configuration of ideas and keywords, at one point at least it must be direct and literary (6.21–2). And while in most places the *direction* of the dependence is of Ephesians on the other letters, there are exceptions where it is possible to argue cogently for the reverse.

(d) It is not just that scholars have yet to discover the setting and purpose of Ephesians; it appears not to have a single definitive setting or determinative purpose.

(e) Some theological emphases in Ephesians are sufficiently different and later than Paul to require another author, but they sit alongside authentic expressions of Paul's own distinctive emphases.

Ephesians as expansion of an authentic letter

These conclusions, if correct, all point in the same direction, that Ephesians is not homogeneous but composite. It combines in almost equal proportions Pauline and non-Pauline vocabulary, style, forms, settings, purposes and theology.

The difference between expanding a genuine letter and creating a pure pseudepigraphon is basically a matter of intention. The New Testament epistles that are, in the judgement of many scholars, clearly pseudepigraphical (the Petrines, James and Jude) were produced in the name of an authority-figure of the apostolic age from whom no authentic literary remains survived. One might call this 'naïve' or 'innocent' pseudepigraphy. But if Ephesians is a careful, and even reverential, *imitation* of Paul, based upon knowledge of his genuine letters, then it would come into a different category, that of 'imitative' or 'deceptive' pseudepigraphy (in the sense that readers were intended to accept it as genuine, not that it was morally 'deceitful'). If 2 Thessalonians were not by Paul, then it would belong to a third category of 'fraudulent' or 'subversive' pseudepigraphy, for at the same time as imitating a genuine letter of Paul (1 Thess.) it would be trying to discredit and replace it (see 2 Thess. 2.2 and 3.17). This commentary makes an alternative proposal: Ephesians is an expansion of a genuine Pauline letter, and so, although in its finished form it is a pseudepigraphon, it lacks any pseudepigraphical *intention* of the types just described (see further below).

This solution to the problem of Ephesians is not new: it is similar to the one first proposed by Maurice Goguel in 1935. His thesis was generally disregarded as maverick, not only because he found anti-gnostic polemics where others could see only Christian pieties, but even more because he failed to explain how a widely circulated letter of Paul in existence for 20 or 30 years was totally supplanted by an interpolated version; furthermore, the interpolations he detected were not normally extensive (apart from 3.2–13) and he claimed that they were all precisely excisable. In all of these respects, the present proposal is very different.[1]

To state our working hypothesis succinctly before it is elaborated in detail in the following two sections of this Introduction: Ephesians contains within it a genuine letter of Paul that has been edited and expanded by a later follower. Paul's letter was addressed not to Ephesus, his base of operations in the province of Asia during the years AD 53–5 and whose Christian congregations he knew well, but to Laodicea some hundred miles to the east (see map). This congregation, like the neighbouring ones at Colossae and Hierapolis, had been founded by Paul's assistant Epaphras, and Paul had only second-hand knowledge of them (1.15; 3.3). He wrote to the Laodiceans at the same time as writing the letter to the Colossians, along with the personal note to Philemon, from a prison in Ephesus towards the end of his ministry there. And he instructed them to exchange letters with the Colossians (Col. 4.16). An oblique allusion to this exchange may still be found in Ephesians (see commentary on 3.1–4).

The letter to Philemon has been preserved in its original form because it attracted no special attention as a memo addressed to an individual. Colossians, we believe, has been touched up here and there by a later hand, involving some changes in wording and some insertions along similar lines to the editing of Laodiceans. The interpolations into Laodiceans, though more extensive (see below, pp. 29f), involve the reuse of materials, liturgical, scriptural, credal and catechetical, that could have been generally accepted as 'Pauline tradition'. The changes, if they were introduced when the original was copied for 'publication', might well have left no contrary evidence in the manuscript tradition.

In the absence of MS evidence, scholars have been understandably sceptical about 'interpolation' or 'expansion' hypotheses in relation to the Pauline letters. J. C. O'Neill's proposals concerning Galatians (1972) and Romans (1975), for example, have been criticized (or simply

---

[1] M.-E. Boismard has lately revived the expansion theory as the solution to the enigma of Ephesians (1999b). He believes that the letter Paul originally wrote to Ephesus from Rome has been expanded by a redactor who knew Colossians in its canonical form (on this see footnote 2 on p. 25 below). Apart from minor glosses and adjustments, the redactor is chiefly responsible for adding 3.2–7; 4.2–4, 8–10, 20–24, 27; 5.3–4, 6–7, 12–16, 18.20, plus the whole of the household code (5.22 – 6.9) and the final commendation of Tychicus (6.21–2) which has been substituted from Colossians for the original ending of the letter (now to be found in Rom. 16.1–23). Although Boismard's theory is similar to the one proposed below, his criteria for detecting additions, e.g. similarities with Colossians or Luke-Acts, are very different from mine and our results only occasionally coincide; often they are diametrically opposite.

ignored) for failing to see that 'inconsistency' in these letters is Paul's (rather effective) argumentative technique and not evidence of a later hand at work. Nevertheless, in the case of some Pauline letters, especially 2 Corinthians and Philippians, many scholars have adopted a theory of composite origins and some also accept the possibility of smaller interpolations (e.g. 1 Cor. 14.34; 2 Cor. 6.14 – 7.1; and Rom. 16.25–7) with little or no supporting text-critical evidence. If Colossians and Laodiceans each existed only in its single original form (or *autograph*) and if they were for some reason laid aside and neglected (see below), then later edited versions of them could have taken their place, leaving no trace in the MS tradition.

At the moment of its appearance, Ephesians in its present form would have been intended to be received and read on its own and for itself as Paul's letter to the great church of Ephesus. But a subsidiary motive for its expansion might have been to create a suitably impressive work which could eventually be 'bundled' with Colossians and Philemon and produce a scroll of publishable length and quality, consisting of Paul's letters to Asia. It is probably no accident that such a scroll would be almost exactly the same length as that of the Macedonian letters (Phil.; 1 and 2 Thess.), 2 Corinthians and the Pastorals.

The suggestion that Ephesians is a composite document should occasion no surprise; most of the New Testament and much contemporary Jewish literature is of this sort. In addition to 2 Corinthians and perhaps Philippians among the genuine Paulines (see above), the Pastoral Epistles, especially 2 Timothy, have often been taken to be composite, with fragments of notes from Paul himself (Harrison 1921; cf. Miller 1997). Matthew is an expanded version of Mark. Luke explicitly refers to his acquaintance with other sources (1.1–4). John's Gospel is a redacted and expanded version of an earlier text (e.g. ch. 21, esp. 21.24), and similar theories have been advanced with regard to Hebrews (ch. 13) and Revelation (chs. 1–3). Comparable examples from contemporary Judaism would be *1 Enoch* (a compilation of at least five distinct sources), *2 Baruch*, the *Testaments of the 12 Patriarchs*, the Qumran Community Rule, and the *Sibylline Oracles*; and from later Christian writings, the *Didache*, Ignatius' letters, Polycarp to the Philippians and *The Shepherd* of Hermas. The literary techniques and psychological dynamics involved in 'expansions' are very different from those of straight pseudepigraphy (see further below, pp. 41–7).

In English translation, of course, Ephesians does not read like an expanded or edited text. That is largely because its intolerably long sentences have been broken up, missing verbs have been supplied, ambiguities in the positioning of adverbial phrases or participles have been resolved and other grammatical irregularities smoothed over. (What else would one expect from translations intended for reading in public worship?) The Greek text, on the other hand, has many more rough edges.

A commentator naturally has to try to make sense of the final form of a book (though in some of the instances mentioned earlier, e.g. *1 Enoch*, that is a forlorn task), but there is an important distinction to be made between acceptance of the 'integrity' of the final form of the text and recognition of its composite nature. The focus on the former should not lead to a denial, against the evidence, of the latter. Composite religious documents have a peculiarly 'open-textured' quality resulting from the growth of a tradition; they resist unitary literary analysis. But their lack of coherent finish, far from being a defect, is a positive gain, for it creates new interpretative possibilities for the communities that use them.

Some of the immediate advantages of our approach can be pointed out at this stage:

(i)   The passages in Ephesians which are clearly Pauline in thought and expression can now simply be accepted as such. We no longer have to provide explanations of how a later pseudepigrapher can be so convincingly Pauline in one place and so indifferent to Paul's idiom and thought in another. The florid style with which the letter starts is not maintained equally throughout; it is very different from the short ethical aphorisms later. (If you read Ephesians backwards from chapter 6 you get a much stronger impression of its Paulinity than if you read it in the usual direction!)

(ii) The hybrid form of Ephesians – part letter, part homily – is exactly what we should expect if a genuine letter had been turned by various expansions into something more like a homily.

(iii) Eph. 6.21–2 ceases to be the extremely problematic exception to the rule that the writer does not copy in blocks of material from his source. For several other almost pure Pauline blocks have been transcribed: the opening and closing greetings, the two prayer reports, most of chapter 3 and a substantial proportion of the ethical section, including the household code section on slavery.

(iv) It is no longer at all surprising that Ephesians has no particular setting or single purpose, nor that undeveloped and developed theological emphases appear alongside each other.

(v)   The expansion hypothesis allows us to recognize and explain tensions within particular passages: thus in 2.11–22, between uniting separated equals and bringing the alienated home; in 3.1–13, between Paul's unique mission to the Gentiles and the Church's broader foundation upon all the apostles and prophets; in 4.1–13, between horizontal communal solidarity and vertical ministerial authority; and in 5.22–33, between advice to the married and a mystical and allegorical meditation on the Church.

(vi) Finally, it attributes almost all the 'I' passages, and any surviving elements of circumstantial detail (e.g. imprisonment (3.1; 6.19f.), another document soon to become available (3.4) and Tychicus as letter-bearer (6.21)), to Paul himself. The later writer was not intending to create a coherent literary fiction, or he would have avoided the mistake (1.15) of having Paul address the saints at Ephesus as though he had never met them. He has simply shaved off some specifics at the beginning and end of the letter to make it more universally applicable and built on the remainder.

PAUL TO THE LAODICEANS

The evidence of Colossians

Colossians, Philemon and Ephesians are usually grouped together with Philippians as 'Captivity Letters' and the place and occasion of the detention is often assumed to be the same in each case. But this is not necessarily so. Philippians (with or without ch. 3) is still generally thought to have been written from Rome late in Paul's life during a lengthy detention on a capital charge (cf. Phil 1.20; 2.17), but that should not pre-empt judgement on the provenance of the other letters from prison.

The letter to Philemon implies that Paul expects to be released soon and intends to visit his correspondents (Phlm. 22), probably in Colossae. This would support the view that this is a different occasion of imprisonment, not too far distant from there, probably in Ephesus (Duncan 1929; Murphy O'Connor 1997). Colossians was also written from prison (though the fact is not particularly emphasized, Col. 4.18). The similarity between the greetings in Colossians and those in Philemon strongly implies that it was written from the same place at the same time. The main reason for resisting this conclusion is the desire on the part of those who support Pauline authorship for Colossians to explain its differences in theology by taking it to be one of Paul's *latest* letters. But this is questionable on two grounds: it assumes that Paul's theology went through a significant development towards the end of his life; and it ignores the possibility that Colossians may have been 'updated' by a later editor.

Although Acts does not refer to Paul's incarceration in Ephesus, some kind of life-threatening situation while he was there is strongly implied by 1 Cor. 15.32. In addition, 2 Cor. 11.23 refers to 'many imprisonments' (seven according to *1 Clem.* 5.6), far more, therefore, than those referred to in Acts. An early date for Philemon and Colossians is also sometimes ruled out because they do not mention Paul's collection for the Jerusalem church (Gal. 2.10), which supposedly preoccupied him during the mid 50s (see 2 Cor. 8–9). But at Rom. 15.26 Paul does not refer to contributions from Asia, but only from Macedonia and Achaea, so it is possible that the collection was not so strongly promoted among the churches of the Lycus valley, which Paul had not visited personally. In any case, his letters to them may even contain passing allusions to their contributions towards the collection in the phrase 'love for all the saints' (Col. 1.4, and see the comments on Eph. 1.15 and 2.19).

At Col. 4.16 there is a reference to 'the [letter] from Laodicea' which the Colossians are told to acquire in exchange for their own. Some have claimed (see Lightfoot 1884: 274–81) that this formula implies either a letter written by the Laodiceans to Paul or one by Paul from Laodicea. But both options are implausible. Would Paul want the Colossians to read a letter to him from a neighbouring church, presumably of enquiry or complaint, without the benefit of his own reply? And Paul had not visited Laodicea (see Col. 2.1) when he used this phrase.

So, 'the letter *from* Laodicea' must simply refer to the last lap on its journey, for the road from Ephesus passes through Laodicea before it reaches Colossae. And since it was Paul who instructed the exchange, it is most likely that Paul was the author of both letters. Theories that it was a letter by Epaphras (Anderson 1966) or was the Epistle to the Hebrews (Anderson 1975; cf. *ABD* IV, 231–3) can therefore be discounted.

Incidentally, this exchange puts a question mark against one version of the circular letter hypothesis, for Paul clearly did not send separate copies of the same letter to different destinations when they were sufficiently close to one another; it was cheaper for someone to walk the twelve miles between Colossae and Laodicea to make the swap, than to have it duplicated.

So is Paul's Laodiceans entirely lost?[2] John Knox (1935) famously identified it with the letter to Philemon. This involves a complex revision of the usual understanding of the setting of that letter, whereby Philemon becomes a resident of Laodicea and leader of its house-church, while Archippus becomes the owner of Onesimus. However, Knox's view is generally reckoned to be unlikely, for the 'you' (singular) addressed in the letter must surely be the first-named addressee (Phlm. 2) and the owner of the slave (Phlm. 11). More importantly, the letter to Philemon is too much of a private note for it to be appropriate to read it

---

[2] M.-E. Boismard has recently (1999a) argued that Laodiceans can be recovered from the text of Colossians, with which it has been conflated: the lost letter comprises Col. 1.9–14, 21–3; 2.1–3, 8–12, 20–23; 3.8–11, 15–16, 23–5; 4.7–9. Boismard's theory is similar to that of Holtzmann and others (see above p. 10). But there are difficulties with it, not least to explain why the editor of Laodiceans, having conflated it with Colossians, continues to refer to it (Col. 4.16) as though it still existed as a separate document.

aloud to the congregation at Colossae. On the other hand, Knox was surely correct to claim that the behaviour and treatment of Onesimus might well have become a matter of public concern among the churches of the Lycus valley; and it is no accident that both Colossians and Ephesians contain instructions on the treatment of slaves (Col. 4.22–4; Eph. 6.5–9) and also warnings about dishonesty (Col. 4.25; Eph. 4.28). Recently, some scholars (Winter 1987; Wansink 1996; P. Lampe 1985, but cf. Nordling 1991) have disputed the usual view that Onesimus was a runaway slave who may have wronged his master in other ways, and claim that he had simply been sent to serve Paul in prison (cf. Rapske 1991), but Phlm. 18 points clearly to some wrongdoing on the slave's part for which Paul offers compensation (cf. also Phlm. 11, 'he was once useless to you').

What was Paul's letter to the Laodiceans like? Colossians (2.2) appears to be a brief summary of it: 'I want their (i.e. the Laodiceans') hearts to be encouraged and united in love, so that they may have all the riches of assured understanding and know the secret of God, which is Christ.' Each of the elements in this sentence should be compared with statements also made in Ephesians: 'encourage your hearts' (6.22: cf. Col. 4.8), 'united in love' (4.16), 'all the riches (1.18; 3.8) of assured understanding (3.4) and to know (1.17; 4.13) the secret of God which is Christ' (3.3; 6.19). We can further deduce from Col. 4.16 that Laodiceans would have been such as usefully to complement Colossians when the letters were exchanged. It would have been intended to encourage and exhort a particular community to grow together in confidence and unity and to understand their faith better and its outworking in practice. It would probably have mentioned Paul's imprisonment and tried to cast it in a positive light (cf. Eph. 3.1, 13; 6.19f.) and should also have referred to the exchange of letters with Colossae (cf. Eph. 3.4) and alluded to the Onesimus affair (cf. Eph. 4.28; 6.5–9). So we can gain some idea of its original content and purpose, but are left guessing about the detail.

We can at least be certain that Paul's Laodiceans is not the fourth-century Latin claimant to that title (Appendix A). That is no more than a pastiche of phrases culled, probably by memory, from Paul's letters, chiefly Philippians, and its sole motive is to fill the historical lacuna left by Col. 4.16. Despite Harnack's claims to the contrary (1924: 134–49), it is far too inconsequential to be a Marcionite forgery and it is unlikely therefore to be the Laodiceans listed as such in the Muratorian Canon (*contra* Hahneman 1992: 194–200). The Marcionites in any case would not have forged a Laodiceans, since they already had one: it was their version of Ephesians stripped of the interpolations which, they believed, Jewish Christians had introduced into it!

The evidence of Marcion

Support for the view that Ephesians is an edited and interpolated version of an originally Pauline letter addressed to the Laodiceans is to be found in the earliest external evidence about the individual Pauline letters, namely the work of Marcion, who claimed precisely this. Before Marcion, allusions to Paul's writings seem to have been made, in a general way, without identifying particular sources (see Ign. *Eph.* 12.2; 2 Pet. 3.16; cf. *1 Clem.* 47.1; Pol. *Phil.* 3.2).

Marcion was the son of a wealthy shipping merchant from Sinope on the Black Sea coast. He grew up in Christian circles in Asia around the time at which we may suppose canonical Ephesians first appeared. Arriving in Rome around AD 140, he was denounced as a 'heretic' and left the Church in 144. Our knowledge of Marcion's views depends on reports from early Fathers, like Irenaeus (see *Haer.* 1.27.1) and especially Tertullian, who wrote five books attacking him (*Adv. Marc.*). These sources are heavily biased, but there is no reason to doubt that they identify correctly Marcion's basic aim, which was to purge Christianity of its Jewish inheritance in conformity with what he took to be the spirit of Paul, and to replace Jewish scripture with a purely Christian two-part corpus of writings, consisting of the Gospel of Luke in an expurgated version and a collection of Pauline letters (see Blackman 1948).

The letters were listed in Marcion's *Apostolikon* in a peculiar order, which is significant for his theological interpretation of them. He began with Galatians, Paul's sharpest polemic against advocates of Gentile submission to the Jewish Law. Next came the Corinthian letters treated as one, then Romans. There followed the shorter letters, 1 and 2 Thessalonians, again treated as a unit, Laodiceans (Marcion's title for Ephesians), Colossians with Philemon attached; and the collection ends with Philippians, again re-emphasizing hostility towards Judaism. Thus in Marcion's 'canon' there were seven letters to seven different destinations. This is no accident. There are also seven letters to the churches in Revelation, seven apostolic letters of non-Pauline authorship in the New Testament (two Petrines, three Johannines, James and Jude) and seven genuine letters of Ignatius. The numerical symbolism is presumably Jewish, and so unlikely to have originated with Marcion himself; by the early part of the second century such collections seem to have become a convention among Christians in the province of Asia whence all the above parallels derive. If Marcion was using a collection that already existed – which is a probable deduction from this fact – then he may have deliberately changed its order, putting Galatians and Philippians in emphatic positions at the beginning and end.

The most unusual feature of Marcion's collection is the different title, Laodiceans, that he gave to our Ephesians. Tertullian notes that the arch-heretic was most insistent on this point but he clearly had no inkling why this should be so:

> We have it on the true tradition of our Church, that this epistle was sent to the Ephesians, not to the Laodiceans. Marcion, however, was very desirous of giving it the new title, as if he were extremely accurate in investigating such a point. But of what consequence are the titles, since in writing to a certain church, the apostle did in fact write to all? (*Adv. Marc.* 5.17.1).

Modern critics also fail to explain this oddity. It is normally assumed that Marcion had a copy of the letter which lacked reference to the location of its recipients at 1.1 and therefore identified it with the otherwise lost Laodicean letter mentioned at Col. 4.16. But why should Marcion *insist* on such a point, if it were merely an innocent speculation on his part? If, on the other hand, the letter was already generally known as 'to the Ephesians', then Marcion must have daringly retitled it. And we have to ask why, if he were putting himself forward as a reliable exponent of the legacy of Paul, he would expose himself to the charge of blatant interference with the text on a point of no doctrinal significance. The solution to this puzzle that we offer is that, as we know, Marcion suspected Jewish Christians of interpolating the letters of Paul, and Laodiceans was his prime evidence. The longer version of the letter which was in circulation as Ephesians was, he claimed, an imposture. It had clearly been expanded with bits of Old Testament scripture and exegesis, and with echoes of Jewish liturgical forms, to emphasize the unity and harmony of Jews and Gentiles in the Church and the debt that the latter owed to the former. It may even be that Marcion was acquainted with people who were able to confirm his suspicions because they could remember an original shorter letter that Paul had written to the Laodiceans.

It was so easy (and tempting), when documents were being copied by hand, for the copyist to 'improve' them. Ignatius' letters were notoriously subjected to this treatment. And one did not have to be a heretic to harbour suspicions of corruption. Even an honest churchman like Dionysius of Corinth (Eus. *H.E.* 4.23.12) can be heard to complain: 'The apostles of the devil have filled my letters with tares by leaving out some things and putting in others. Therefore it is no wonder that some have gone about to falsify even the scriptures of the Lord, when they have plotted against writings so inferior.' Marcion, the intended object of such criticism, was wholeheartedly of the same opinion.

Even in five books, Tertullian does not comment on *all* the corruptions and omissions allegedly committed by Marcion; he focuses on those small but significant alterations that deal with the doctrine of the Creator God and for which he had a knock-down counter-argument. This is clear from his remark at *Adv. Marc.* 5.18.1: 'Since our heretic is so fond of his pruning knife, I do not wonder when syllables are expunged by his hand, seeing that whole pages are usually the matter on which he practises his erasing procedure.' Tertullian also seems to be suffering from a certain fatigue by the time he gets to Ephesians and has become more selective. So we cannot tell from Tertullian precisely the nature and extent of the differences between Marcion's and the Church's version of the letter.

Criteria for distinguishing tradition and redaction

If Paul's Laodiceans does indeed lie behind Ephesians, it is a difficult and delicate task now to try to recover it. For the writer of Ephesians is no mere scissors-and-paste editor. He has used his main source and other traditions available in his community in a creative and effective way. His work may not be a seamless robe, but neither is it a rag-bag: it has an aesthetic quality similar to that of a mosaic or collage. An analogy might be drawn from Matthew's redaction of Mark's Gospel (which luckily *has* survived!): comparison with Mark allows the interpreter of Matthew to achieve a more intelligent, more 'contoured' reading; and while Matthew has incorporated most of Mark into his Gospel, that does not make him either a devotee or an opponent of his predecessor; the relationship is rather one of 'critical reuse'.

The criteria we have used in an attempt to identify more closely the hand of the editor and to separate redaction from tradition are as follows:

(1) Post-apostolic perspective (e.g. 2.20; 3.5; 4.11).

(2) Jewish–Christian perspective (e.g. 1.12; 2.11–13; 5.15a).

(3) Separable units of liturgical or credal material, especially when they disrupt the underlying letter-form, style, or line of argument (e.g. 1.3–10; 2.14–16, 18; 4.4–6; 5.14).

(4) Citation and exegesis of Hebrew scripture without apology and in a positive sense (e.g. 1.22; 2.17; 4.8; 5.31; 6.2f.).

(5) Significant departures from Pauline style and vocabulary (e.g. 1.19b; 2.12; 3.9; etc.; see above).

(6) Semitic idiom (e.g. 2.2; 3.5; 5.6b, 15a).

(7) Expansive clauses often introduced by a participle, relative pronoun or preposition, especially when they overload sentences (e.g. 1.11f., 13f.; 2.21f.; 3.9–11; 4.13b, 14b; 5.9).

(8) Logical *non sequitur*, i.e. places where one sentence or paragraph fails to follow from what precedes it (e.g. 1.15; 3.12; 4.7; 5.9, 12; etc. – but see comment on 3.2 for a genuinely Pauline, grammatical *non sequitur*!).

(9) A more pronounced ecclesiology (1.23; 3.21; 5.32), including orders of ministry (4.11).

(10) A more muted eschatology (e.g. 1.3f.; 2.6; 4.10; 6.24).

(11) A greater emphasis on the cosmic scope of the Christ-event (e.g. 1.10; 1.21; 2.15; 3.9–11).

(12) An insistence on the theme of unity (e.g. 1.10; 2.14f. 4.4–6; 5.31).

Notice that the criterion that is conspicuously missing from this catalogue is the one that most recent commentators would put at the head of their list, namely 'supposed evidence of dependence on Colossians'. While it is quite likely that the author of Ephesians towards the end of the first century would have known Paul's original letter to the Colossians, one would expect that, if this were the explanation of the similarity between the two works, the correspondences would be more consecutive, and that in passages containing parallels the surrounding unparalleled material in Ephesians would be clearly secondary. But as we have already seen, this is not the case. Thus, similarity with Colossians, far from being a safe criterion for redaction, becomes the first of our tradition-historical criteria for reconstructing Laodiceans (i.e. it belongs to stage one rather than stage two):

(1) Apparent verbal similarities with Colossians (e.g. 1.17; 3.17; 4.2; 4.32; 5.19).

(2) Formal features characteristic of Paul's genuine letter-writing, such as the greeting (1.1–2), prayer report (1.15–19), 'I beseech you' formula introducing an ethical exhortation (4.1) and the final greeting (6.21–4).

(3) Typically Pauline irony and self-depreciation (e.g. 3.2; 3.8; 4.21).

(4) Pauline use of key theological terms like 'secret' (3.3; 6.20) and 'stewardship' (3.2), especially when other senses of these appear elsewhere in the letter.

(5) Unselfconscious variations on ideas spelled out at greater length in other Pauline letters (3.18f.; 4.17–19; 4.22f.).

(6) Indications of a setting different from that of Ephesians (1.15; 3.3).

(7) A less pronounced ecclesiology (e.g. 1.1, 18; 3.8; 4.25; 6.18, 23).

(8) A more vibrant eschatology (e.g. 1.18; 5.5; 5.16).

(9) A heavy emphasis on moral exhortation (e.g. 4.1–3, 22–32; 5.3–5).

(10) A more implicit Christology (e.g. 1.17; 3.19; 4.13).

At this point, it might be appropriate to list the verses or parts of verses where, the commentary will argue, the underlying source is strongly in evidence (1.1–2, 15–19; 3.1–8, 12–14, 16–21; 4.1–3, 7, 13–15, 17–32; 5.3–12, 15–20, 22, 25; 6.1, 4, 5–9, 18–24). But such a list may well tax the patience of the reader. So, at the risk of appearing to claim more certitude than the theory itself either justifies or requires, we have provided a tentative reconstruction, to be found in Appendix B. (Its proximity to Pseudo-Paul to the Laodiceans in Appendix A is intentional and cautionary!)

This letter, as reconstructed, is about the same length as Colossians and opens and closes in a very similar way. Its twin prayer reports are now closer to each other and form a bracket around the relatively brief letter body (3.1–13). The reason for this brevity is stated at 3.3: the letter is to be supplemented by another that will soon become available to the readers. Its language and style are acceptably Pauline, and all the 'I' passages of Ephesians (with the exception of 5.32) are included. As to its contents, there is no special emphasis on the Church, neither its universality nor its cosmic role; its main focus is on the faith and life of a particular congregation. Two short paragraphs mentioning names, including probably that of Epaphras, may have been omitted at the beginning and the end; otherwise most of it has been retained. Its main purpose is the one given in the summary at Col. 2.2, to encourage confidence in Christ on the model of Paul's own confidence despite his current imprisonment, and to exhort the Laodiceans to a communal solidarity in love that is spelled out in an extensive moral catechism.

Some parts of the material that we have excluded from the reconstruction, especially 1.3–10, 20–3; 2.1–22, may have had some basis in Paul's letter but are now so reworked that it is impossible to tell. Furthermore, some parts that we have included, for example within the catena of ethical maxims that forms most of the second half, may be editorial additions, but again it is impossible to tell. These are important caveats. However, it is important also to distinguish between quite legitimate objections to particular judgements about sources and the general plausibility of a source-critical solution to the problem of Ephesians.

There is a comparable case with the Gospel of Luke. We may not be able to tell in particular places whether the Evangelist was using the various possible sources (Mark, Matthew, a Q document or tradition, Proto-Luke, the Johannine Signs Gospel or whatever), but to ignore his debt to predecessors (cf. Luke 1.1–4) and treat everything as homogeneous would be a mistake.

Methodologically it might perhaps be tidier to posit a source that still exists (i.e. Colossians) rather than one that is lost. But we are not in this case positing the existence of something that is unprecedented or unevidenced. We can be reasonably certain, as this section has shown, that Paul did write a letter to Laodicea, probably from Ephesus around AD 54. This letter circulated at least as far as Colossae, but probably not much further afield, because then copies would have been made and it would have survived.

Its disappearance is, nevertheless, a historical puzzle. It may have something to do with the earthquake that rocked Eastern Asia Minor in AD 61 (*ABD* IV, 230). Colossae was wiped off the map, never to be rebuilt. Laodicea, on the other hand, eventually recovered. But the dislocation caused by the catastrophe may have resulted in the loss of a natural home for the Asian letters of Paul. This could explain why they made their appearance before a wider audience quite late, and only in 'edited' versions.

Another factor in the disappearance of Laodiceans might have been the intrinsic quality of the letter. If it was quite short and 'relatively uninspired' – criticisms that could also be made of the letter to Philemon – then 'something extra' would be needed to ensure its preservation. That 'something extra' in the case of Philemon may have been the later eminence of its central character. In the case of Laodiceans, it may have been its expansion and embellishment by the writer of Ephesians.

To speak of Laodiceans as 'relatively uninspired' (in the literary not the dogmatic sense) raises one final issue, which we might perhaps call 'The Rembrandt Commission syndrome', that is, the reluctance of critics to admit into the œuvre of a great master any slightly inferior piece which could damage his reputation for perfection and devalue the assets of collectors. This factor seems to operate, at least at the subconscious level, in critical discussions of the authenticity of 2 Thessalonians. Comparing the reconstructed Laodiceans with canonical Ephesians, one might be tempted *either* to attribute the letter as a whole to the genius of Paul, *or* to credit it entirely to a pseudepigrapher (who would then also have to take the blame for the rather tedious moralizing in 4.17 – 5.20; 6.1–9). But if Laodiceans was, unusually for Paul, hardly worth preserving, that would be a neat explanation of why it was not, as such, preserved.

PSEUDO-PAUL TO THE EPHESIANS

Sources and traditions

The main source used by the writer of Ephesians is the Pauline letter which he took as the basis of his work. Most recent commentators believe that this letter was Colossians. If this is correct, then the author has transcribed only one short paragraph (6.21–2) and elsewhere has 'raided' Colossians for some key ideas and a few key phrases but reconfigured them with words and ideas drawn from his wider acquaintance with Paul's letters. It is not absolutely necessary to this hypothesis that our canonical Colossians is itself authentic, but it must at least be earlier in date than Ephesians and must, by the time of its use as its source, have been generally accepted as Pauline.

Recently, Ernest Best, reflecting widely held doubts about an early date and/or authenticity for Colossians, has concluded that Ephesians cannot be dependent upon it. He has posited instead the existence of a 'Pauline school' in Ephesus (Best 36–40) in which Colossians and Ephesians were produced independently and at about the same time, their authors colluding to some extent and especially on how to conclude their pseudepigrapha. This solution starts from observations that may very well be correct, namely that dependence of Ephesians on Colossians is often problematic and that the relation could even in some places more plausibly be explained the other way round. Nevertheless, it quickly runs into some formidable objections. First, there is no independent evidence of a Pauline 'school' in Ephesus at the end of the first century. Secondly, the purpose of such an institution, if it existed, would surely have been to synthesize and promulgate Paul's teaching, not to encourage imaginative extensions of it in opposite directions: towards Christology on the one hand or ecclesiology on the other, towards a sharper separation from Jewish tradition on the one hand or closer dependence on Jewish scripture and ethics on the other. Thirdly and above all, while Ephesians has multiple parallels with the rest of the corpus, Colossians does not. Apart from Philemon, it would hardly seem to have used them at all.

In addition to the basic epistolary source and other Pauline letters, most scholars believe that other traditions have been used by the writer of Ephesians: liturgical material (1.3–10; 2.14–16, 18; 5.14), and short credal formulae (1.20–3; 2.1, 5, 8; 4.4–6; 5.2). We cannot be sure of the route by which these traditions reached him, but if they were available via his community, then the writer and some of his prospective readers probably believed, and in some cases with good reason, that they derived from Paul's own legacy to his most important church in Roman Asia.

A third resource for the writer's expansion of his basic text was Jewish scripture: he quotes Pss. 110.1 and 8.6 at 1.20–2; Isa. 57.19 at 2.17; a form of Ps. 68.18 at 4.8; Zech. 8.16 at 4.25; Prov. 23.31 at 5.18; Gen. 2.24 at 5.32; Exod. 20.12 at 6.2; and alludes to Isa. 11.4, 5; 52.7; 59.17 at 6.14–17. In a rather surprising contrast to Colossians and the other shorter letters of Paul, the Old Testament is frequently quoted in a positive and non-controversial sense. The longer letters to the Corinthians contain some positive uses of scriptural citations, and Romans and Galatians, of course, very frequently quote the Old Testament, but usually in refutation of judaizing or Jewish opponents, which is clearly not the motive in Ephesians.

Taken together, these different sources and traditions account for the bulk of the epistle, but that does not diminish the achievement of the writer who has selected and woven together his material into an impressive Pauline epistle for Ephesus which was able to bear comparison with anything Paul wrote to any other church.

Date and provenance

If Ephesians, as we have it now, is entirely authentic, then it can be dated no later than the death of Paul (c. AD 64). Advocates of Pauline authorship usually prefer as late a date as possible, i.e. during imprisonment in Rome, in order to allow for the more contemplative mood and more developed theology. However, the relationship to Philemon of both Colossians and Ephesians points to a much earlier date (c. AD 54), as we have seen above. This remains the most natural dating for any authentic letter or letters written by Paul to Christians in the Lycus valley.

If Ephesians in its present form is post-Pauline, then its dating is a problem. The author successfully avoids any grosser anachronisms that might have been helpful to us. The reference to the destruction of the 'middle-wall' at 2.14, if it is not entirely metaphorical, could equally imply a date before or after the Fall of the Temple in AD 70, and even so it would only date the tradition being used and not the whole letter. It must have appeared some time before AD 110 because Ignatius in the Prologue to his own letter to the Ephesians makes several allusions to Eph. 1.3–14, and at Ign. *Eph.* 12.2 the recipients are described as 'fellow initiates (*summustai*) with Paul the Sanctified', recognizably reflecting the emphasis on 'mystery' and on apostles as 'holy' in Eph. 3.3, 5, 9. Whether *1 Clement* (AD 96) knew it is disputed. The claim that the author of Ephesians had read the Acts of the Apostles, an important part of Goodspeed's theory, is also disputable, and of no help, given the even greater uncertainty over the date of Acts.

More helpful perhaps is the argument from the likely dependence of 1 Peter on Ephesians (see below, p. 39). *If* the former was written by Peter himself during the Neronian persecution (AD 64–5) then it would support Pauline authorship and an early date for Ephesians, but its very dependence points rather to a later pseudepigraphical origin for 1 Peter, perhaps as late as the reign of Trajan (AD 98–117). Parallels between Ephesians and the thought (though without clear evidence of dependence on the text) of the Johannine literature, including Revelation, might also suggest a date c. AD 90. Finally, the author of Ephesians almost certainly knew several of the major letters of Paul, especially Romans and 1 Corinthians, but he was probably writing before any of Paul's Asian letters had started to circulate. This does not necessarily push the likely date earlier, for Asia had less 'to write home about', so to speak, as regards letters from Paul and might have been slower off the mark than Rome or Corinth in promoting what it had.

According to the majority of manuscripts, the letter is addressed to 'the saints who are at Ephesus' (see on.1.1) and even those that omit the place name in the text retain it in the title. If it is a genuine letter of Paul written *to* Ephesus, it cannot have been written *from* Ephesus. But if it is a pseudepigraphon, then the destination and the provenance could be – indeed are quite likely to be – the same. The reluctance of scholars to accept the Ephesian address for this letter arises chiefly from the fact that Paul stayed in Ephesus for several years in the early 50s and knew the church he had founded there very well (Acts 19–20) and yet Eph. 1.15 speaks of Paul as 'having heard' of the faith of the recipients of the letter, and 3.3 of their 'having heard' of Paul's mission. Hearsay in both directions, not personal acquaintance.

If the authenticity of Ephesians is to be defended, a non-Ephesian destination is absolutely necessary, by appeal either to the circular letter theory or to a destination in Eastern Asia. But those who deny authenticity also have to explain why a pseudepigrapher, who is normally so astute, has apparently made such a silly mistake at 1.15 and 3.3. For this reason Best argues that the letter was originally addressed generally 'to the saints', and Lincoln 'to the saints at Laodicea and Hierapolis'. Both accept that the provenance of the letter was Ephesus but both find it difficult to explain how it eventually came to be addressed there. They are being forced into this position because of their assumption that the author himself must be held directly responsible for the phrasing of 1.15 and 3.3. If, however, these verses belong to the source he is using, i.e. the letter of Paul from Ephesus to Laodicea, it is much easier (see the commentary on these passages) to explain their retention in the present letter, which was supposedly written from Rome to Ephesus.

Assuming, with the majority of scholars, that Ephesus is the provenance of the letter and that its date is *c*. AD 90, how does this help us interpret it? Ephesus (see Koester 1995) was the third largest city in the Roman Empire, with a population of around 200,000. It was the centre of the cult of Asian Artemis (Oster 1976), whose temple there was one of the Seven Wonders of the World, and pagan idolatry and magic were rife (Arnold 1989) in Paul's day and probably just as much later. The extent of Paul's success in evangelizing Gentiles in Ephesus is disputed; it has recently been claimed (Strelan 1996) that Paul attracted mainly semi-observant Jews into the Christ-movement and that his influence declined soon after his stay there.

Ephesus had a significant minority of Jewish citizens, whose relations with Christians were likely to have been strained (cf. Trebilco 1991). It had been the centre of Paul's mission in Asia but by the end of the first century there were also Christian congregations at Ephesus and Laodicea that could be addressed by the seer of Revelation (2.1–7; 3.14–22) as though they acknowledged his influence and authority. The Gospel and Epistles of John are also normally located in Western Asia Minor at the end of the first century; this is more difficult to prove from any internal evidence, though later church tradition is strong on the point (cf. Iren. *Haer.* 3.1.1). To some extent the issue depends on how close a relationship is conceivable between the clearly Asian Apocalypse of John and the other Johannine writings. The majority view among scholars is that John's Gospel and Epistles were written in Ephesus (see van Tilborg 1996), and the following discussion will assume that this is correct and may even provide extra support for the view. And finally, Asia is among the provinces addressed in the First Epistle of Peter. We shall examine in the next two sections the relations of Ephesians with the Johannine circle and with 1 Peter to see what further light they throw on the motivation behind the letter.

Ephesians and the Johannine circle

We have looked at various different theories about the form, setting, purposes and theological interests of Ephesians, and some of them contain much that is of value for understanding its final form. Ephesians, although it is a letter, functions more like a sermon on the theme of salvation already achieved in Christ through the dignity, unity and universality of the Church, and on the calling of Christians to work out that salvation in unity, love and holiness of living. The unity of the Church and of Christians is therefore the overarching theme of Ephesians, with special emphasis placed on the unity between the Gentile Christians whom Paul is supposedly addressing and their Jewish fellow-Christians, the heirs of God's covenants with Israel (so Patzia 1984).

If the main theme of Ephesians and the key to one of the motives behind its composition is the unity of the Church, it is reasonable to deduce that Christian unity was somehow under threat in Asia Minor at the end of the first century. The Johannine literature fully bears this out: John 13–17 is a powerful call to unity; schismatics are attacked in 1 and 2 John, and the refusal to offer hospitality (and thus take sides) is denounced in 3 John; the letters to the Asian churches in Revelation vilify Nicolaitans (2.6) and other deviants. The Jew–Gentile question, on which Ephesians is so serene, has clearly not yet been solved either. Revelation speaks of 'those who say they are Jews and are not, but are a synagogue of Satan' (Rev. 2.9), and the scars of bitter controversy both with unbelieving Jews and with half-hearted Jewish followers of Jesus are still livid on the skin of John's Gospel. If there was a continuing group of more conservative Jewish Christians who were trying to 'keep their heads down' in the synagogues of Ephesus, their position, as the Gospel makes dramatically clear, was ultimately untenable. Already some radical Paulinists may be moving in the direction that Marcion was to advocate, and be repudiating the Jewish roots of Christianity. On the other hand, Johannine Jewish Christians, after their expulsion from the mainstream Jewish community (cf. John 9.22; 12.42; 16.2), would be wondering whether they could trust Paul's followers. They would have been faced with a choice, either to link up with the majority Gentile house-churches that owed their foundation to him or to continue as a separate isolated group and suffer further disintegration. Such a situation would give a sharp contemporary relevance to the composition of Ephesians, for it is intended to enlist the authority of Paul to enlarge the scope of Pauline Christianity in order to accommodate new members from the Johannine circle.

The tendency of scholarship in recent times has been to keep deutero-Pauline Christianity in a sealed compartment away from other types of early Christianity. But Ephesus, which had been the centre of the Pauline mission, was by the end of the first century the centre also of the so-called Johannine circle, that network of churches which included Laodicea and Ephesus among others addressed in the letters of the Apocalypse, and which are alluded to without geographical specification in the Johannine epistles. It is impossible that the two groups would not have known of each other's existence.

Commentators on Ephesians have been so preoccupied with the question of the continuation of a distinctively Pauline Christianity in the post-Pauline period that they have often neglected or denied any interaction with the Johannine circle. Lincoln's commentary, almost exhaustive as it is, yet seriously neglects this dimension. This is less the case with Schnackenburg's commentary, and in a more recent article (1991), he has begun to underline the continuity of the development from Paul to John in the churches of Ephesus. But already in 1911 Moffatt, after surveying the evidence, concluded that the unknown author to the Ephesians was 'a Paulinist who breathed the atmosphere in which the Johannine literature afterwards took shape' (385). He was more cautious about links between Ephesians and the Apocalypse, but, as we shall see, these also are not inconsiderable.

The following commentary will refer frequently to parallels between Ephesians and the Johannine literature (including Revelation) and they may be checked by consulting the index of scriptural references. So all that is needed here is a short summary. The realized eschatology and cosmic backdrop to salvation in Christ are obvious similarities between Ephesians and the Gospel. The dualism of light and darkness (John 1.5; cf. Eph. 5.8) and of truth and falsehood (John 8.44; cf. Eph. 4.25) is also a marked feature of both. The predestination and election of the Church in Christ (John 15.19; cf. Eph. 1.4f.), the pre-existent Beloved Son of God (John 17.24; cf. Eph. 1.6), his descent and exaltation (John 3.13f.; cf. Eph. 4.9f.) in whom Christians have already experienced resurrection (John 5.21–25; cf. Eph. 2.5–6), the unity of the Church as the divine objective of Christ's sacrifice (John 10.16; 17.20; cf. Eph. 2.14–16), the kingship of Christ (John 18.36; cf. Eph. 5.5), the personal character of the Holy Spirit (John 14.26; cf. Eph. 4.30) and the importance of baptism (John 4.1; cf. Eph. 4.5), sanctification (John 17.17; cf. Eph. 5.26) and indwelling (John 14.20; cf. Eph. 2.22); the language of fullness (John 14.20; 15.4, 8; 17.11f.; cf. Eph. 3.19), measure (John 3.31; cf. Eph. 4.17), glory (John 20.17; cf. Eph. 1.17), confidence (John 16.25; cf. Eph. 3.12; 6.19), faith (John 3.15; cf. Eph. 2.8; 3.12), peace (John 14.27; cf. Eph. 2.14) and love (John 3.16; cf. Eph. 3.19), and the word of truth (John 17.17; cf. Eph. 1.13); and above all, the insistent appeal for unity (John 13–17; cf. Eph. 1.10; 2.14ff.; 4.3–6,13–16; 5.31).

The First Epistle of John shares many of these similarities with Ephesians. It is also structurally comparable, combining in near equal parts (and with a similar tension between them) the assurance of salvation already achieved and the exhortation to walk worthily of it.

Almost as striking are the affinities between Ephesians and Revelation: in both the images of the Church as the bride of Christ and the Christian life as warfare against the powers of darkness are prominent and have a future eschatological reference as well as a realized aspect (see on 5.22–33 and 6.10–17). Ephesians and Revelation also both insist on the importance of preserving Jewish ways of worship and of understanding scripture in the Church. (For further parallels, see the index of scriptural references.)

It is, however, necessary to deal with the objection sometimes made that Revelation is basically anti-Pauline, for this would cast doubt upon the motivation we are suggesting for Ephesians, that of reconciliation between Pauline Gentile and Johannine Jewish Christians in Ephesus, 'thus making both one'. We know from the book of Revelation, written probably in the mid 90s, that some Christians in Ephesus and Laodicea belonged to the circle of the exiled prophet John of Patmos. The Ephesians, according to Rev. 2.2, 'cannot bear evil men but have tested those who call themselves apostles but are not and found them false'. Those who wish to drive a wedge between the Pauline and Johannine branches of Christianity in Ephesus might argue that this is a thinly veiled attack on Paul. They might also point to the question of 'food sacrificed to idols' (Rev. 2.20), which Paul had tolerated in certain circumstances, albeit lukewarmly (1 Cor. 8.4; cf. 8.9f., but contrast 1 Cor. 10.19f.). But if Paulinists were the intended object of the attack, why does Revelation not make it clearer? It is not as though the seer is unwilling elsewhere to 'name and shame' (cf. 2.6). Furthermore, warnings against false apostles are also found in Paul (esp. 2 Cor. 11.13, where the term probably indicates competing Jewish missionaries; 2 Cor. 11.4f.; cf. 11.22). The imagery of the twelve apostles as foundation of the new Temple should not be taken as necessarily exclusive of Paul. Ephesians, after all, uses the same foundation metaphor (2.20 and 3.5) and is careful to include prophets (like the seer himself) along with apostles. A different image of 24 elders at Rev. 4.4 may imply 12 for Israel and 12 for the Gentile world, and along with the 144,000 from the tribes of Israel (7.4) there is also 'a countless number from every nation, tribe, people, and language' (7.9). So opposition to Pauline Gentile Christianity should not to be attributed to the author of Revelation. It is even possible that the description of the two witnesses of Rev. 11.4, 'whose bodies lay in the streets of the great city which is allegorically called Sodom and Egypt' (11.8), refers to the deaths of Peter and Paul in the city of Rome, which is given the additional allegorical name of Babylon at Rev. 18.2. One should not lapse into literalism in interpreting the next clause, 'where their Lord was crucified', as though it necessarily referred to Jerusalem, for Christ is crucified wherever his saints are martyred.

The similarities between Ephesians and the literature of the Johannine circle in Ephesus are more than incidental; they point towards a basic motivation behind the composition of the letter. It offers hesitant Jewish Christians the assurance that unity with the Gentile churches of Paul's foundation will not dilute or compromise their faith or reduce them to second-class citizens. On the contrary, they will contribute more to the union than they receive. Ephesians marks the beginning of that process of re-judaizing Gentile Christianity, the rediscovery of its roots in Jewish salvation-history, worship, scripture and creation theology, that was to preserve it from the threats from Marcionite and Gnostic heresy as the second century proceeded. The author's instinct for unity was the salvation of the catholic Church.

Relation to 1 Peter

There are some remarkable similarities between 1 Peter and Ephesians: both open with a liturgical blessing (1 Pet. 1.3–5; cf. Eph. 1.3–10) and speak of the Church as a spiritual temple with Christ as cornerstone (1 Pet. 2.2–6; cf. Eph. 2.18–22); both relate the death of Christ to redemption through blood and the gaining of access to God (1 Pet. 1.18f.; 2.4; cf. Eph. 1.7; 2.18); both emphasize the heavenly session of Christ above the principalities and powers (1 Pet. 3.22; cf. Eph. 1.20); both contain a household code (1 Pet. 2.18 – 3.17; cf. Eph. 5.22 – 6.9); and both end in a similar fashion with an exhortation to Christian warfare (1 Pet. 5.8f.; cf. Eph. 6.10–17). The conclusion reached by Mitton (1951:

176–97) was that this and other evidence demanded a literary explanation, and it was likely that 1 Peter was dependent on Ephesians. Best once seemed to agree (1971: 35) but has evidently changed his mind (Best 19). In addition to distinctive similarities with Ephesians, there are other Pauline features in 1 Peter, such as the use of the term 'charism' or spiritual gift (absent from Ephesians). There is more emphasis on the death of Christ as the model for Christian suffering and endurance under persecution, and 1 Pet. 2.13–17 offers an interpretation of Rom. 13.1–7 on submission to the authority of the state. Christians are aliens and exiles in this dangerous and godless world (contrast Eph. 2.19; cf. 2.12f.). In some respects then 1 Peter is more Pauline than Ephesians!

Once decide that 1 Peter is a later and dependent text and it could simply be ignored, except perhaps in regard to the dating of Ephesians. But it may have slightly more relevance than this, if its similarities with Ephesians and Paul throw some light on the motivation behind it. Clearly the point of 1 Peter is not to promote a distinctively Petrine theological stance, but to offer encouragement to Christians in danger of persecution through legal proceedings against them. It does this by adopting and underwriting ideas that are in fact Pauline and thereby widens the basis of their support (cf. *1 Clem.* 5.2–7). This could be part of a general programme (to which Ephesians also belongs) to harmonize and unify Asian Christianity, against external and internal threats.[3]

In conclusion, Ephesians as a composite document does not have a single purpose, for it is content in some measure to endorse the purposes of its component parts. Thus it shares Paul's aim in the underlying letter of offering encouragement and moral exhortation to a Christian congregation. Its use of liturgical materials retains some of their original liturgical purpose, to express prayer and praise to God and celebrate salvation through Christ and when read aloud to an assembled group, or even, at appropriate points, sung or chanted (see on 1.3–10; cf. 5.14 and 5.19), these materials could retain their character as contribution to

---

[3] Discussion of the 'Relation to the Acts of the Apostles' has been omitted from this Introduction (though the issue will be raised at appropriate points in the commentary), because neither Asian provenance (but cf. W. Theissen 1995) nor a date earlier than Ephesians is, I believe, likely for Acts. Nevertheless it is strikingly similar in intention to what I have suggested as the motivation behind Ephesians and 1 Peter, irenically uniting different traditions in the early Church and offering a presentation in narrative form of the 'happy apostolic family'. In terms of content, the only really telling cluster of parallels between Ephesians and Acts comes in Paul's speech at Miletus (Acts 20.17–35) with its themes of the plan of God, Paul's apostolic commission, the Church as God's inheritance, shepherding and building. It is possible to believe that the author of Acts knew the letters of Paul (Käsemann 1968) including Ephesians (by that name), and felt it appropriate therefore to echo its contents here in a speech addressed to Ephesian church leaders (contrast Mitton 217–20).

worship. In addition, the writer has purposes of his own. He wishes to preserve and disseminate more widely teaching and traditions from Paul. He may have felt the need, in a period when Paul's major letters to Rome and Corinth had begun to circulate (cf. *1 Clem.* 47.1 and see Trobisch 1994), to provide a comparable literary legacy for the great church of Ephesus. Perhaps he could already envisage the possibility of combining the expanded letter with other surviving documents into a scroll length collection. Given a situation of tension, like the one described above in the Johannine circle, he wanted to emphasize the unity of Christians, to widen and deepen the outlook of Gentile readers, reminding them of their roots in Israel's salvation-history (1.3–14; 2.11–13) and placing Paul in a larger company of apostles and prophets, the historic foundation of the new Temple in Christ (2.20; 3.5). By correcting any possible misunderstanding of Paul's teaching on justification, faith and works of the Law (2.1–22) and by his use of Jewish scripture, liturgical forms and moral principles, he sought to break down the dividing wall and encourage Jewish Christians belonging to the Johannine circle to believe that they would have a welcome and a natural home with the Gentile congregations that owed their origin to Paul.

PSEUDEPIGRAPHY AND THE RHETORICAL SITUATION

The discussions in the previous section of the sources, date and provenance of Ephesians and its affinities with the Johannine literature and likely use by 1 Peter have pushed enquiry into its historical situation about as far as the evidence will permit. To make any further progress, we need to change focus from the historical to the rhetorical situation of the letter, and ask what sort of pseudepigraphy it is, and how this might have affected the way its first audiences would have received it.

Pseudepigraphy was a well-known and apparently acceptable practice in Jewish tradition. The books of Daniel and Ecclesiastes in the Old Testament, and the Wisdom of Solomon and 2 Esdras in the Apocrypha, are obvious examples. Literary imitation of earlier models or writings attributed to the same author played little or no part in this practice. Rather, a figure from Israel's sacred past, when divine truth was more immediately accessible, was invoked to lend authority to a text written in his name. Many examples of Jewish pseudepigraphy belong to the genre 'apocalypse' (see Charlesworth 1983, vol. 1) and this may further help to explain the acceptability of the practice: the later writer, ascending to heaven to receive revelations of God and his eternal purposes, merges his own identity into that of the source of his inspiration (cf. Aland 1961).

In the Greco-Roman world, false attribution of anonymous works to the grand master of a particular genre or the founder of a philosophical school was widespread. In Hellenistic education, the imitation of the style of famous authors was a standard exercise in the art of writing, and produced its own distinctive form of pseudepigraphy (cf. Demosthenes *Orat*. 11). Neither practice was considered fraudulent, unless of course the false claim that a document derived from another person, whether deceased or still living, was intended to secure for its actual author some advantage, legal, financial or political (cf. Pausanias 6.18.5; see further *OCD* 604f., 'Forgeries, Literary', and 1270, 'Pseudepigraphic Literature').

A pseudepigraphical Ephesians can be understood against one or other of these backgrounds (Brox 1975) or some uneasy combination of both. While Jewish pseudepigrapha mainly appeal to characters from the distant past, it is possible that towards the end of the first century the apostles, and Paul in particular, though closer in time, had acquired a comparable status for Christians. But if so, meticulous imitation of his existing letters would not be appropriate, for it would conflict with the basic idea in Jewish pseudepigraphy that one was being privileged to hear 'the living voice' of a classic hero of the faith. While the Hellenistic model is better able to explain the 'imitative element' in Ephesians, it is in other ways more problematic, since that practice was essentially literary and antiquarian. Ephesians cannot be described simply in these terms; as we have seen, it has contemporary religious purposes and, if it is entirely non-Pauline, it would begin to slide into the category of a deliberate forgery aimed at achieving some ideological advantage for its author.

Is there a way out of this dilemma? Extra-canonical Jewish writings are not all pseudepigrapha in the strict sense, despite the scholarly convention of referring to them as such; they include some texts that are genuine but too recent, or written in the wrong language, to be included in the developing Hebrew canon; some that are simply anonymous, with secondary pseudonymous attributions in their titles; and some, finally, that are expansions of older tradition or additions to earlier works (see Charlesworth 1983, vol. 2). Indeed, expansions are perhaps the most common type, found already in the canonical Old Testament, e.g. the book of Isaiah (Meade 1986), and continuing in later 'mainstream' Rabbinic Judaism in the targums (paraphrasing Aramaic translations) of the Hebrew Bible and midrashim (homiletic expansions of it). What is produced by an expansion may in the end be considered pseud-epigraphical in content, but the process is not pseudepigraphical in intention. To take a modern analogy, reproduction furniture and genuine antiques are sold and bought knowingly as such. But there is a grey area in between, ranging from the out-and-out fake that may reuse a few pieces of period timber to the extensive restoration aimed at making something usable. It is not just a question of the *extent* of the alterations involved but also of their *intent*. Thus, both the reproduction and the genuine Chippendale were intended to be sat on; but the fake, however sturdy, was made for a different purpose; and the renovated antique could still be meant for sitting on, but only with a certain reverence and caution. Applying this analogy to a documentary artefact like Ephesians, we could say that if approximately half of it is Paul's letter to the Laodiceans, and if the writer believed that most of what he had added also derived, by another route, from Paul, and if, furthermore, he was intending to make it reusable, the resulting epistle could in good conscience be offered to the public as a genuine article. No intention to deceive would be involved.

The product of the expansion process, however, is bound to create certain tensions not only within the text itself, as we have already observed, but also between the text and its rhetorical situation, and it is to these we now turn.

Rhetoric, the art of persuasion, is a highly relevant factor in the interpretation of almost every act of speaking or writing. To take a trivial example, even a remark like 'It is raining' could be said to have a 'rhetorical situation': it involves, for instance, a decision about the amount of rain required for this verb to apply (rather than, say, 'it is spitting'); it also involves a basic belief system, at least in the ancient world, as regards the identity of the subject of the verb (cf. Matt. 5.45, lit. 'God rains (*sic*) on the just and the unjust'); and it often implies some value-judgement like 'Thank God!' or 'More's the pity!' In any kind of speaking that is more than merely passing the time of day, the techniques of persuasion, perhaps especially in the writing of letters, become the main object of interest for the interpreter. In the case of the New Testament documents, which are after all religious propaganda in the proper sense of the term, this is so much so that a whole new method of enquiry – 'rhetorical criticism' – has developed in recent years (*DPL* 822–6, with bibliography up to 1993, to which may be added the works by Porter 1993, Stamps 1993, Porter and Tombs 1995, Anderson 1996, Porter 1997 and Weima 1995).

Or to be precise, two new methods have developed that are distinct, if not at loggerheads with each other. There are those who, following the pioneering work of H. D. Betz on Galatians (1979, but see Kern 1998), seek to analyse Ephesians in categories drawn from ancient rhetorical theory (e.g. Lincoln xliiif.): *exordium* (c. 1), *narratio* (c. 2), *digressio* (c. 3), *exhortatio* (cc. 4–5) and *peroratio* (c. 6). Such terms give the impression of a technical precision and explanatory force which their application to the text, however, often fails to deliver (see pp. 98, 146 and 282 below). The one key element that is missing from Ephesians, in contrast to Galatians, is the *probatio* (or 'proof of the argument'), and Lincoln (xli) explains this omission by arguing that Ephesians is not apologetic but 'epideictic' rhetoric, i.e. it is congratulatory (like a speech at a funeral) rather than argumentative (like a speech in a law court). But there are several objections to the application in this way of classical rhetoric to the letters of Paul: first, they are letters and not speeches; secondly, it is unprovable and unlikely that Paul had any formal training in rhetoric; and thirdly, the handbooks, like that of Quintilian, from which the above terms are derived are not descriptive of what actually happened but are ostensibly theoretical and idealistic (Porter 1993). In reply to these objections, one might claim that the Ephesian pseudepigrapher has converted the letter into something more like a speech and that he may have had a better education than Paul and be working on theoretical models. But a fundamental objection then arises: a pseudepigraphon cannot be an exercise in direct persuasion because both its apparent author and its apparent audience are 'fictive', i.e. editorial constructs. So the way the rhetoric functions will be *indirect* and mediated through the fictive situation.

The second kind of rhetorical criticism takes its lead from modern or 'New Rhetoric' (see Kennedy 1984; Botha 1994: 121–37). This seeks to interpret the message of a text by means of the situation in which it is conveyed. 'Rhetorical situation' is a term easily misunderstood. A 'rhetorical question', for example, is not a real question at all but a literary device. A rhetorical situation, on the contrary, is indeed a real situation that both requires and is created by the persuasive discourse. As defined by Lloyd Bitzer (1968), a rhetorical situation consists of three elements: exigence, audience and constraints, i.e. what needs to be done, who is being persuaded to do it and what are the obstacles – persons, events, objects or relations – that have to be overcome in order to succeed. Applying this to Ephesians, we might say that church unity is the primary exigence, the audience are those who are being persuaded to bring that unity into being, and the constraints are whatever barriers or suspicions stand in its way.

However, in a pseudepigraphical letter there are likely to be disjunctions between the fictive situation and the rhetorical situation. Thus, the letter may purport to address Gentiles but rhetorically have a Jewish Christian audience chiefly in mind. It may represent Paul as its author and *rhetor*, but actually be negotiating him as one of the constraints. It may present the exigence in one way: 'Gentiles must come near to Israel to be saved', while rhetorically advocating the opposite movement: 'Jewish Christians must throw in their lot with Gentile house-churches if they are to survive.'

We shall attempt to illustrate these complexities by referring to the reception of a pseudepigraphical letter, the nature of its audience, and the way it 'constructs' its author.

If Ephesians is post-Pauline, then it was almost certainly not 'sent' from one place to another. Imagine that it arrived one day from outside the community; that would have invited very awkward questions, such as why its delivery had been delayed for more than thirty years, why Tychicus was not the bearer despite 6.21, and where the actual bearer got it from. A pseudepigraphical letter is not sent; it 'comes to light' or is 'discovered', and for this reason its provenance is likely to be the same as its destination (see above). The logistics of 'publishing' a pseudepigraphon are inevitably obscure. But we can safely assume that the author did not consider his work to be fraudulent, i.e. that he believed that what Paul had once written to the Laodiceans and had instructed to be read elsewhere could also legitimately be read in Ephesus and expanded with other traditions. He may have intended the letter to be read aloud in congregations that identified themselves as Pauline in a post-Pauline age. But it is also possible that he intended the letter to establish itself first among Jewish Christians who had less acquaintance with Paul and might be suspicious that closer association with the congregations he founded would involve a lowering of moral standards and assimilation to the pagan environment. If so, Ephesians is well adapted to allaying those fears.

We do not know how many Christians there would have been in Ephesus towards the end of the first century, but an educated guess would be about 500, i.e. a dozen or so house-churches. Concerned by the question of whether closer unity between them, and especially between Jewish and Gentile congregations, was possible, they might have been pleased to learn that Paul had written so impressively on this very theme and had not omitted to write to their great city (cf. Ign. *Eph*.12.2: 'Paul ... in every epistle makes mention of you'). Even those old enough to have met Paul personally may not have doubted that he could have written like this. Only suspicious-minded snoops with an anti-Jewish axe to grind, of the type of Marcion, would have voiced any objection to the welcome 'discovery' of Paul's letter to the Ephesians.

The process of 'discovery' leads into the question of historical immediacy. Those with whom Paul actually corresponded naturally expected to recognize themselves and their current or very recent concerns in his letters to them. But the post-Pauline readers of a newly 'discovered' text would have no such precise expectations. A pseudepigraphical letter is in this respect more like a stage-play: the audience is not directly included as one of the actors within the text. They could well have understood themselves to be 'overhearing' what Paul wrote once upon a time to the Ephesians. To what extent they would identify more closely with the fictive addressees might depend on a number of other factors like their age, ethnicity and theological sympathies. This needs to be borne in mind when considering certain referential problems in Ephesians, especially the confusing variation between 'we' and 'you' (see esp. on 1.11–14 and 2.1–5): 'we' can mean the historic Paul and his associates (cf. 6.22), or Jewish Christians in contrast to Gentiles (cf. 2.3), or first generation Christians in contrast to later readers (cf. 1.12), or all Christians without distinction (cf. 1.4; 2.10; 2.14); 'you', on the other hand, can mean those originally addressed by Paul (cf. 3.1; 6.22), or Gentile Christians more generally (cf. 2.11), or post-apostolic Christians (see the discussion of the retention of 1.15 and 3.3f.), or all Christians without distinction (cf. e.g. 4.30).

The same issue is raised when a specific genuine letter of Paul is re-read in the post-Pauline period: there is both identification and distancing (1 Clem. 47.1–4, cf. v. 5). Any modern reader of Paul, of course, is doing this all the time. As long as the main point is still relevant, and the insistent call to unity was certainly relevant to the church at Ephesus by the end of the first century, as it is today, then minor irrelevancies can be 'read round'.

Although rhetorical criticism of the second type was developed deliberately to detach texts from too biographical a concern with authors and view them simply from the perspective of their persuasive effects, it is necessary finally to comment on the question of the author. How are we to understand the references to 'I, Paul' and the details of his biography in a pseudepigraphical letter? Although, as we have argued above, in this case they are probably not pure invention but elements retained from an underlying source, they nevertheless contribute to a picture of Paul that has indeed been 'constructed' by the unknown real author of Ephesians. For example, Paul's special status is highlighted by the omission of the names of co-senders or co-workers (but cf. 6.21) and by the description of him as '*the* prisoner of Christ'; but at the same time his place within a larger group of founding apostles is emphasized (2.20; 3.5). It is as though the editor wants to say two rather different things, that Paul was especially important but not uniquely so.

To bridge the gap between Paul and a later author writing in his name, Lincoln (lx–lxii) borrows from narrative criticism the notion of the 'implied author' (see Powell 1993: 5f.). But this term can cause some confusion. 'Implied author' is a concept well suited to narrative, and particularly to anonymous works like the Gospels, where the author so to speak 'hides behind' his story. But an epistle is not a narrative, and Paul is not the implied author of Ephesians but its explicitly stated author. However, the point is important, even if the terminology is flawed: the actual author has constructed a 'Paul' who is not merely an idealization from the past, but someone who has relevant things to say to the present.

The concept of the 'rhetorical situation' has been applied to several Pauline letters (see e.g. N. Elliott 1990; Pogoloff 1992; Geoffrion 1993;

on Rom., 1 Cor., and Phil. respectively). It enables contentious issues like the reconstruction of the historical situation and the use of sources to be set on one side (at least initially). The approach adopted in this commentary is, by contrast, unashamedly historical and source-critical. If Ephesians was indeed written in Western Asia Minor towards the end of the first century by a follower of Paul, who was basing his work on materials that he believed were genuinely Pauline, then the issues of historical context and sources cannot be ignored for long. However, the rhetorical-critical method, with appropriate modifications, can usefully be applied to a pseudepigraphon like Ephesians, and it cautions us not to think of the letter as an exercise in imaginative fiction but as a text with contemporary persuasive aims.

Further exploration of the nature of the pseudepigraphy and of the rhetorical situation of Ephesians is very much needed, but this discussion has advanced our earlier enquiry and confirmed its findings at certain points. The expansion hypothesis permits us to see Ephesians against the background of a legitimate Jewish literary procedure that is consistent with the character of the epistle as a whole. And the attempt to apply new methods like rhetorical criticism helps us to recognize its multi-layered and open-textured composition.

CONTRIBUTION TO THEOLOGY

It is not possible to write a 'theology' of Ephesians, if by that we mean a systematic presentation of its author's religious beliefs, both because it is too short and because it is too composite a document. Even with the Pauline corpus as a whole, where we can test any proposition by cross-referring to different letters, that task is extremely difficult. Moreover, genre (understood as a set of expectations that readers bring to a particular kind of literature) does not include, in the case of a letter, the expectation of theoretical balance or comprehensiveness. And there is still enough of the letter about Ephesians for this to apply. It is particularly hazardous to deduce from any obvious gaps in Ephesians compared to genuine Pauline letters – for example, in regard to the pre-existence of Christ (1 Cor. 8.6; Phil. 2.6; Col. 1.15, but see on Eph. 1.4), or to the importance of the Eucharist (but see on 5.20, when taken with 5.4, 18 and 29) – that our author somehow opposed these ideas. The same could be said of the lack of emphasis in Ephesians on future eschatology or the death of Christ. Along with the obvious gaps, there is a certain lack of proportion in Ephesians. The ethical section is far too long and repetitious (cf. 4.2 and 4.32; 4.19 and 5.3; 4.26 and 4.31) and may even be felt to undermine by its very length the assurances of salvation already achieved that predominate in the first two chapters. So three different sorts of fragmentary theology might be deducible, whether from the underlying Pauline text, the various traditions used to supplement it, or the final redaction.

While it is for these reasons inappropriate to try to construct a theology of Ephesians, we can in this concluding section at least offer a few observations on the contribution that the letter might make to Christian theology today. (For the history of its influence down the ages see the masterly account of Schnackenburg, 311–42.)

The Church

More than any other book in the New Testament, Ephesians makes much of the Church. It has become for this author an object of reflection and of faith. As the 'one Body' it is included in the credal statement at 4.4–6 alongside the 'one Spirit, one Lord and one Father'. The Church is not only one (4.4), she is holy (5.27), catholic (2.19) and apostolic (2.20). At 1.23, the Church is the 'fullness of the all-filling Christ', that part of the cosmos that already acknowledges his headship; she is heir to the promises to Israel (2.12) and has a role as mediator of revelation (3.10); she is the Body of Christ (1.23; 4.16), his new Temple (2.21) and his future bride (5.32).

The glorification of the Church in Ephesians has sometimes been explained, especially by German scholars (e.g. Käsemann 1968; Schlier 1930; but cf. Schlier's commentary, 1963), with reference to post-apostolic 'early catholicism', the provision of ideological justifications for an increasing emphasis on the importance for salvation of church membership, authorized hierarchy and valid sacraments. However, recent studies of Paul's self-understanding as an apostle and the roots in Jewish apocalyptic (cf. Baumgarten 1975; Beker 1982; Rowland 1982) of his own exalted view of the Church as the Body of the risen Christ and the 'Jerusalem above', show that 'early catholicism' is not simply a post-apostolic phenomenon.

These claims for the exalted glory and eschatological destiny of the Church were, we need to remember, originally counter-cultural. Their earthly referent was a small, marginal and quite often persecuted network of house-churches in certain cities of the Roman Empire. The doctrine starts to mean something very different when applied to the Church today, a multinational conglomerate with 'branches in every high street', a quarter of the world's population on its books, paid dignitaries, a massive publishing arm and a controlling interest in many spheres of politics, education, health and social welfare. In the modern world, then, we may be better served by different images and claims than those in Ephesians, like the Church as pilgrim people of God, or the Church as the servant and refuge of the poor.

It is also important in another way not to read Ephesians anachronistically. While it is true, for instance, that Ephesians, unlike Paul, uses *ekklēsia* only in the universal collective sense of Church, it is unsafe to deduce that it is for the writer a purely heavenly notion separable from the actual meeting together of Christians. It probably retains for him much of the concrete and local sense it usually has for Paul. His point, therefore, is not to subordinate the local to the universal, but to enhance the dignity and fullness of being the Church in a particular place by linking it to one heavenly counterpart. And 'heavenly' in this context should not be understood in a Platonic way, as though it referred to a transcendent idea prior to and determinative of its varied manifestations. It is not Greek philosophy but Jewish apocalyptic which is the proper background for understanding Ephesians. The Church is in heaven already because of the predestining purposes of God that are being worked out in salvation-history; and this heavenly reality is at the same time a future hope. The eschatological dimension is a vital corrective to a triumphalist misreading of Ephesians.

But maybe institutional triumphalism is not so much of a danger to the Church today as it once was. Perhaps even more insidious is the modern Western tendency to treat faith as a private matter and to judge the Church by its utility (or otherwise) in lending support to the religious preferences of the individual. Against this Ephesians protests that salvation is essentially corporate; we are saved together or not at all, for salvation consists in breaking down barriers and celebrating a common new humanity in Jesus Christ.

Christian unity

The appeal for unity among Christians is the overarching theme of Ephesians in its final form and provides the chief motive for its composition. We have suggested above some of the particular circumstances that would have made this appeal highly relevant at the end of the first century in Asia Minor. At the beginning of the third millennium, the divided Christian churches spread across the world face a task that is vastly more complex. But the Epistle to the Ephesians may still inspire and inform that effort.

First, it may do so by relating unity to an understanding of God and of salvation. There is one all-embracing God (4.6) whose nature as love (the word is used 21 times in the NRSV of Ephesians) is revealed in the person (1.6) and self-sacrifice (5.2) of Jesus Christ and in the gift of the Spirit (4.4) as the assurance of hope (1.13f.). Human salvation consists in imitating (5.1) the divine unity both inwardly and socially (see on 2.14f.).

The author of Ephesians could no doubt have given more pragmatic arguments for unity than these: there is safety in numbers; pooling resources is more economical; it makes for more effective recruitment etc. But we should be grateful that the pseudepigraphical letter-form made him concentrate on fundamental and enduring truths.

In several other respects, Ephesians offers insights into Christian unity which have only recently and partially been recovered in the ecumenical movement. First, the unity of the Church is not ultimately separable from the unity of all humankind, the summing up of all things in Christ (1.10), and it thus involves the overcoming of all barriers of injustice, enmity and inhumanity that obstruct the peace of Christ (2.14–16, 18). The ethical section of the letter (4.17 – 5.20) is just the beginning – with perhaps too narrow a focus on inner-ecclesial concerns – of a much longer extra-ecclesial agenda on the issues of justice, peace and the integrity of creation.

Secondly, the unity of Jews and Gentiles is a unique and special case. The interpretation of Eph. 2.11–22 is full of problems, which are discussed in the commentary, but to anticipate its conclusion, the author's basic point is that salvation for Gentiles consists in coming near to Israel through faith in Christ (2.13, 17). So there is a basic continuity between the Church and Israel (*contra* Lincoln), as well as a temporary discontinuity because of unbelief and persecution (see on 2.2, *contra* Barth). If we are right to see Ephesians against a contemporary background of sharp conflict between Christians and Jews in Asia Minor (cf. John's Gospel, Revelation), then Ephesians' irenic tone and esteem for the Jewish legacy are a notably rare example in the New Testament of restraint and tolerance.

Finally and more briefly, the substitution of the language of salvation for that of justification (2.1–10) or the co-ordination of head and body imagery for Christ and the Church are two of several examples in Ephesians of 'saying the same thing by saying something different' – an essential insight for ecumenical or inter-faith dialogue. Ephesians asserts in the same breath that salvation is already fully possible, for the Church is already one, and yet that the body has to grow up into Christ, that the new Temple has to be patiently constructed and that the bride has to be made ready by holiness and sacrifice for a union that is still to come. This offers us a third way between catholic and protestant, or visibilist and invisibilist conceptions, of church unity, namely the ultimate visible manifestation of a present heavenly reality. In the same way, Ephesians is not indifferent to the structures that maintain the visible unity of the Church: baptism, an ordered apostolic ministry, common worship and, perhaps by implication, the Eucharist. But this does not constitute rigid 'institutionalization'; ministry and sacraments are not seen as the means of policing the boundaries around the community. On the contrary, they are understood as pointers to the central mystery of union with the exalted Christ through faith and obedience.

Marriage

Ephesians not only provides several fine readings for use in the Week of Prayer for Christian Unity, it also offers a classic text for use at weddings (5.21–33). It is probably a good thing that the following two sections on children and slaves are not normally included, for the subordinationist understanding of the husband/wife relationship would be even more apparent – and to many today distasteful. Any woman who is still willing to promise to obey her husband on their wedding day would surely want to distinguish the quality of that obedience from the sort that arises from immaturity or financial and legal dependence. On the other hand, as the commentary on this passage will try to show, this text is completely misunderstood if it is read as an attempt to transcendentalize marriage, or absolutize the subordination of women. The author is interested rather in glorifying the mystery of the Church and may, like Paul, have believed that celibacy, for all its temptations and difficulties, is the proper vocation for some (see comments on 5.32 and 6.10ff.).

A purely post-Pauline, pseudepigraphical origin for Ephesians has led some interpreters to conflate its view of marriage with that of the Pastoral Epistles, where it is assumed that all women are obliged to marry, that widows capable of child-bearing should remarry (1 Tim. 5.14) and that only 'real widows', i.e. over sixty years old, married just once before and of outstanding virtue, should be allowed to become pensioners of the church (1 Tim. 5.9, 16). If we knew more about the social circumstances of the time to which these rules were responding, that might help to mitigate their apparently gross androcentrism. But there is little doubt that the freedom and equality in Christ that inspired the first Christians was, in the case of women at least, compromised within a generation or so, under pressure of circumstances.

Ephesians, however, should be distinguished from the Pastorals: it still retains something of that earlier vision. 'Let wives submit' at Eph. 5.22 should be interpreted in the greater light of Eph. 2.15: 'in order that he might create the two in himself into one new person, thus making peace'.

While the author of Ephesians cannot properly be blamed, his instructions about marriage and the family have been used to enforce, with theological and moral sanctions, an obligation on all Christians (apart from the clergy and religious, see *DETS* 115–19) to marry and produce new church members, and to reinforce entrenched attitudes towards contraception, divorce and same-sex relationships. But these moral judgements served social needs which are no longer those of today and are increasingly open to question at the practical level, as they have always been at the level of a genuine concern for human flourishing.

The spirit world

Ephesians contains frequent references to what might be called 'the spirit world', beyond the world of ordinary sense perception. This has a bright side and a dark side. The Church is already enthroned (2.6) with Christ in the heavenly realm above every principality and authority (1.20f.) and reveals to them the divine plan of salvation (3.10); and yet these powers are still at work on earth and in the air above (2.2) and even in heaven itself (6.12), attempting to deceive and pervert. Such material contributes to a world-view of cosmic struggle and a mindset of almost impervious self-confidence. But is this a realistic or healthy way of thinking? First, one should notice that, in the first century, Christians shared this outlook with most of their Jewish and pagan contemporaries. It made them normal. Today it does the opposite; it constitutes a programmatic, even belligerent, abnormality that may be used to reinforce a sectarian divide between those who believe in demon possession, exorcism and so forth, and the majority who do not. Secondly, it is also important to remember that in the ancient world appeal to the activity of demons had an explanatory function in relation to otherwise inexplicable phenomena. Today, however, such beliefs pretend to offer alternative explanations to the rational ones that are available.

If this language conveys anything that may still be relevant to us today, it is its insistence on the reality and gravity of evil within human beings and human societies, evils such as promiscuous and predatory sex (a strong theme in Ephesians); anger, violence and blood-lust; and the corruptions of power in the political domain (see on 2.14–18). However, when taken literally, the language of demonology, by prescribing 'spiritual' rather than social–ethical methods of tackling these evils, can feed into a kind of religious fascism. It should also be pointed out that the effect of the belief in demons in first-century society was to place a certain limit on the extent of human responsibility and allow some room, however little, for pity towards those ensnared as the victims of higher powers. In modern secularized societies, this belief often has the very opposite effect of absolutizing moral judgements and demonizing human agents.

There are many other aspects of Ephesians which individual students of the epistle will want to argue with, or weave into their own theology and spirituality. The commentary that follows will only occasionally mention such issues, for its primary aim is to expound the text in a way consistent with the historical origins of the letter. There is a certain intellectual satisfaction to be had in working out a puzzle of the kind represented by the text of Ephesians, but it may be that the real interests of some readers will lie elsewhere, in contemplating the great truths of the Christian faith or the devotional power of Scripture, and they may find the commentary in places too 'analytical'. If so, they should treat it as simply prolegomena to their own synthesis. And in so doing they will have the support of the author of Ephesians, who is himself a supreme synthesizer, one who wanted to see all things in heaven and on earth summed up in Christ.

A NOTE ON THE TEXT

The Greek text used in this translation and commentary is basically that of the 27th edition of Nestlé–Aland, *Novum Testamentum Graece* (1993) and the textual sigla follow the conventions laid out in its preface and appendix. There are just a few variant readings in the MSS of Ephesians which seriously affect the sense (see below), but there is a whole host of others which, though apparently trivial, are nevertheless important because they change the degree to which there is a precise verbal parallel between Ephesians and Colossians (cf. e.g. 1.15; 5.19). The matter is further complicated by similar uncertainties at places in the text of Colossians. When the New Testament writings were copied together as part of a single collection, the scribes, knowingly or otherwise, were inclined to harmonize apparently parallel passages and bring them even closer together: so the reading that resists harmonization should generally be preferred. Critics who emphasize the dependence of Ephesians on Colossians are sometimes inclined, in their attempt to maximize the evidence for their theory, to prefer the harmonizing readings. And it could be argued in defence of this that independent copying of the two documents in the earliest stages of transmission might at first have created greater divergence between them, before the opposite tendency took over later. (On a much greater scale, this particular textual problem is a major headache for scholars trying to explain the interrelationships of the Synoptic Gospels.) The hypothesis outlined above can cope with either view and is free therefore to assess each case on its merits.

The most important textual variants that affect the sense are the following: the omission of 'in Ephesus' at 1.1; the addition of 'first' at 4.9; the substitution of 'spirit' for 'light' at 5.9; the movement of 'strictly' at 5.15 to a position earlier in the sentence, and the omission of 'of his flesh and of his bones' at 5.30. In almost every case these minority readings have the support of P^{46} (the Chester Beatty Pauline codex). In several they also have the support of the most important fourth-century uncial MSS, Sinaiticus (ℵ) and Vaticanus (B).

P^{46} is probably the earliest surviving manuscript of the Pauline letters, datable to around AD 200. It contains Ephesians in the fifth place after Romans, Hebrews (!) and 1 and 2 Corinthians, and before Galatians. Other things being equal, one might expect that the earlier the manuscript the more accurately it would reproduce the autograph. But this is not necessarily the case, for two reasons: an early scribe, like that of P^{46}, may be more incompetent and inattentive than his successors; and secondly, the New Testament manuscript tradition is thoroughly 'contaminated', in the sense that later MSS were regularly corrected against much earlier exemplars that no longer exist, and this means that the original reading may sometimes survive in just a few late witnesses, with all the earlier MSS conformed to some plausible 'improvement'. Much safer, therefore, than external attestation for deciding between variants are 'intrinsic or transcriptional probability' (i.e. the likely intention and style (or styles) of the writer and the likely tendencies and accidental errors of the scribes), and above all the principle that the reading, quite often the more difficult one, that explains the origin of the others is to be preferred. On these grounds, we have in all of these cases rejected the reading of P^{46}, despite its antiquity, though in others, on the same criteria, its text may be correct (see e.g. 6.5).

The standard introduction to the textual criticism of the New Testament is the one by B. M. Metzger (1992), who has also written a commentary on a selection of variant readings (1994). For a rather different approach, see Kilpatrick (1990). For an earlier, still valuable study of the text of the Pauline epistles see Zuntz (1953).

OUTLINE OF EPHESIANS

Title
I Introductory greeting and thanksgiving (1.1–23)
    A   Greeting (1.1–2)
    B   Blessing (1.3–14)
    C   First prayer report (1.15–23)
II Jews and Gentiles (2.1 – 3.13)
    A   Saved by Grace (2.1–10)
    B   One in Christ (2.11–22)
    C   Paul's mission to the Gentiles (3.1–13)
III Prayer and praise (3.14–21)
    A   Second prayer report (3.14–19)
    B   Doxology (3.20–1)
IV Christian integrity (4.1–16)
V Christian conduct (4.17 – 5.20)
    A   Old and new humanity (4.17–24)
    B   Rules for community (4.25 – 5.5)
    C   Light in a dark world (5.6–14)
    D   The wisdom of praise (5.15–20)
VI Christian obedience (5.21 – 6.9)
    A   Husbands and wives, Christ and the Church (5.21–33)
    B   Parents and children (6.1–4)
    C   Slaves and masters (6.5–9)
VII Christian warfare (6.10–20)
    A   The armour of God (6.10–17)
    B   Request for prayer (6.18–20)
VIII Concluding message and grace (6.21–4)

COMMENTARY

Title

To the Ephesians

The titles of the documents in the New Testament canon are later additions designed, among other things, to help users of the collection to find their way around (see Metzger 1987). The books are regularly identified by author, with one important exception – the letters of Paul. First and Second Peter were manageable, but First up to Thirteenth (or Fourteenth) Paul would not have been! So the letters attributed to Paul were mainly classified instead by the place of residence of their addressees.

As soon as the letters of Paul began to be copied and exchanged between different centres of the early Church, some means of distinguishing them would have become necessary. So even if the actual text of Ephesians lacked any reference to its geographical destination (see on 1.1), that information would have been supplied in a title in the process of forming the corpus. It should be noted that MSS which omit the place name (see below) nevertheless still identify this work as 'To the Ephesians' in the title. While it is not impossible that Paul himself for some reason wrote a letter that did not identify its recipients by location, a disciple of Paul, who was acquainted with several of his letters and was writing during the period when the collection was being formed, would *ex hypothesi* have been well aware of the need to do so.

There is no evidence that Ephesians was at first identified by the title 'To the saints' and the suggestion is improbable (*pace* Best 100) because it would fail to meet the need which titles serve of distinguishing one letter from another. Ignatius, *c*. AD 110, knew a letter of Paul to the Ephesians (see Introduction p. 34) almost certainly by that name. Marcion, according to Tertullian, knew a form of Ephesians which he called 'To the Laodiceans', but his very insistence on the point implies that he disputed a different title already attached to the document in his day, early in the second century (see Introduction, p. 28). Furthermore, if 2 Timothy is pseudepigraphical, as most modern scholars believe, then its reference to Tychicus being sent from Rome to Ephesus (cf. 2 Tim. 4.12) is probably a deduction from Eph. 6.21 and implies that the writer already knew this letter as addressed to the Ephesians. The author of Acts may perhaps also have known it by that name (see Introduction p. 40, n. 3). If Ignatius, Marcion, 2 Timothy and Acts attest an Ephesian destination for the letter, their evidence is much earlier than any MS reading that casts doubt upon it. Thus, the most likely explanation of the title 'To the Ephesians' is that it arose from the information given in the first verse of the text.

I Introductory greeting and thanksgiving   (1.1–23)

A Greeting   *(1.1–2)*

(1) From Paul by God's will an apostle of Christ Jesus to the saints who are in Ephesus, even the faithful in Christ Jesus, (2) grace to you and peace from God our Father and the Lord Jesus Christ.

This opening greeting is quite typical for a letter written by Paul. It is an adaptation of the prescript of the Hellenistic letter-form, with the sender and recipients being defined in Christian terms: 'apostle' to 'saints'. The conventional secular greeting (*chairein*; cf. Jas 1.1) has become the similar-sounding, theological concept **grace** (*charis*) to which is added the equivalent Jewish greeting, *shalom*, **peace** (see Dunn 1993: 31, who refers to 2 Macc. 1.1. for a similar cross-cultural combination).

1 Only Paul's name occurs in the greeting. In most other Pauline letters, the names of co-workers also appear: Sosthenes (1 Cor.), Timothy (2 Cor., Phil., Col., Phlm.), or Silvanus and Timothy (1 and 2 Thess.). There are, however, exceptions: Romans mentions Paul alone, but reserves the names of four other well-wishers, including Timothy, to 16.21; in Galatians Paul is alone in sending greetings, but he is alone in other ways too in that defensive letter. If Ephesians is based on a captivity letter of Paul (whether Colossians, Philemon or Laodiceans) to Christians in Eastern Asia Minor, then it is very likely that the name of his co-worker Timothy (cf. Col. 1.1; Phlm. 1) has been omitted in order to focus more exclusively on the special witness and authority of Paul.

The origin of the title **apostle** (*apostolos*) in early Christianity is obscure. In classical Greek, prior to the New Testament, the word was used as a collective noun for a group of people, e.g. colonists, sent on a sea-voyage or mission. In Paul, the term is used in two ways: of representatives or delegates sent from one congregation to another ('apostles of churches', 2 Cor. 8.23); and of representatives of the risen

Christ, sent by him to preach the gospel (1 Cor. 15.8–10; 1 Cor. 1.20). 'Apostle' in this exalted sense seems to incorporate elements of a role equivalent in the new dispensation to that of the Old Testament prophets (cf. Gal. 1.15f.). Another facet of the term may be traceable back to the thought of Jesus himself, who applied the Hebrew concept of 'plenipotentiary agent' (the rabbinic *shaliach*), in a kind of ironic parable, to the ineffectual disciples (Matt. 10.40) and children (Mark 9.37) who were his personal 'agents' for the proclamation of the Kingdom (see Rengstorf, *TDNT* 1.407–47; *DPL* 45–51).

In Jewish Christian circles, *Apostolos* seems also to have been used as a christological title, to describe Christ himself as God's primary representative (Heb. 3.1). In John's Gospel similarly, Jesus refers frequently to the Father as 'the one who sent me' (4.34; 5.23; cf. also e.g. 6.57; 10.36; 17.3). Although this development could well have inhibited the technical use of the term for the inner group of disciples in John's Gospel (cf. John 13.16), it should not be taken to imply that the Johannine circle was hostile to the usage (cf. Rev. 21.14) or opposed to Pauline tradition on this point.

The title 'apostle' may have continued to be used in the post-Pauline period in certain localities (perhaps in Syria, see *Did.* 11.3) but it was becoming restricted exclusively to the leaders of the first generation. And this seems to be already the case for Ephesians, which looks back to the age of the founding fathers (cf. 2.20), who are honoured as 'holy apostles' (cf. 3.5). The exclusive identification of the apostles with the Twelve caused a further restriction of the meaning of the term to witnesses of the historical ministry of Jesus (see Acts 1.21–6; cf. Luke 6.1, contrast 1 Cor. 15.5, 7). If this development had already occurred, it would have posed a problem for the author of Ephesians, who clearly believed that Paul was an apostle in the fullest sense. One solution, apparently also adopted by the author of Acts (cf. Acts 14.4), was to treat the Twelve as a kind of 'baker's dozen': Twelve Apostles for the New Israel plus Paul as the Apostle to the Gentiles (see on 3.1 and 3.5).

Against opponents who accused him of being a second-rate apostle, or even a self-appointed upstart, Paul was wont to insist that he had been called to his office **by God's will** (cf. 1 Cor. 1.1; 2 Cor. 1.1) and not by any human agency (see Gal. 1.1). But the phrase would probably not have been heard with any kind of 'edge' by the later audience of Ephesians; they would have seen here an allusion to the classic ministry of the apostle as part of God's saving plan (cf. 1.5, 9, 11) and Paul himself as a model servant of the divine will (cf. 5.17; 6.6).

Paul regularly refers to his correspondents as **the saints** or 'holy ones', employing the term in the sense of the redeemed community of the end time (cf. Dan. 7.22) and making thereby a claim on behalf of the Christ-movement to be the fulfilment of that hope. In Rom. 1.7 and 1 Cor. 1.2

Paul underlines the eschatological orientation of the title in the phrase *'called* to be saints'; but at Phil 1.1, as here, it is unornamented (cf. also Eph. 1.15; 3.8, 18; 4.12 and 6.18). However, other, non-titular uses also occur later in Ephesians: the moral connotation of the word is more fully exploited in the adjectival form at 1.4 (cf. 5.3); and some argue that it may even refer to angelic beings at 1.18 and 2.19. Furthermore, for the editor of Ephesians it is becoming a special epithet designating distinguished first-generation Christian leaders (see on 3.5).

The addressees are the Christians **who are in Ephesus**: on Paul's missionary activity there and developments after his time, see the Introduction (p. 35f.).

The greeting continues with a further description of those addressed, in the normal Pauline manner, **even** (*kai*) **the faithful in Christ Jesus**. In Greek *kai* is not always the conjunction 'and'; it can be emphatic or explanatory (epexegetic) and be translated 'also' or, as here, 'even'. Colossians offers a near parallel (1.1): 'to the saints at Colossae, even faithful brethren in Christ'. The author of Ephesians normally avoids the technical term 'brethren' to describe members of the Church (but see on 6.23), since he has a more 'hierarchical' understanding of church order than that implied by the term (see 4.11 and the comments on 6.2 and 4 below).

Faithful (*pistoi*) occurs frequently in the Pauline corpus in the passive sense of 'trustworthy' (cf. the description of Tychicus at 6.21); but it can also have the active sense of 'believing', as here (cf. Gal. 3.9).

2 Grace for Paul is principally God's free gift of redemption through the death of Christ (Rom. 3.24; cf. Eph. 1.7). It is often set in contrast to the demands and condemnation of the Law (Rom. 6.14), a contrast largely smoothed over in Ephesians. **Peace**, similarly, is peace with God that results from the work of grace through Christ (Rom. 5.1). The good wishes, then, are not just from Paul to his addressees; they have a deeper source, as by implication does the rest of the letter. The actual greeting is identical with those in other letters (Rom.; 1 Cor.; 2 Cor.; Phil.; and Phlm.) but differs from that in Colossians, which lacks the concluding reference to 'the Lord Jesus Christ'. Thus far, there is hardly anything out of line with the normal start of a Pauline letter.

A note on the text of 1.1

Because it has become a topic of extensive scholarly debate (see Lincoln 1n. and Best 1997b: 1–24, with the literature cited there), it is necessary to consider other ways of reading the phrase in the first verse: 'to the saints who are at Ephesus, even (*kai*) the faithful'. If the *kai* is taken as a true conjunction it would produce the translation 'who are at Ephesus *and* are faithful'. This would be, technically speaking, a *zeugma* (the yoking together of two disparate points); but such a stylistic conceit is unlikely in a conventional opening greeting. Faithfulness surely characterizes the saints everywhere; it is not linked in ironic contrast to their place of residence.

The main problem arises over uncertainty in the text. There are two variants in the MS tradition: the omission by P^{46} and D of the article (*tois*) before the participle (*ousin*, translated 'who are' above), and the omission of 'in Ephesus' in P^{46} and several other early witnesses (א* B* 424^c 1739, but not D). Some of the wider questions that these omissions raise for the purpose of Ephesians have been discussed in the Introduction (pp. 12, 53f.).

The omission of the article in P^{46}, coupled with the omission of the reference to Ephesus, has the effect of turning 'saints' into an adjective, possibly under the influence of the usage at 1.4. Thus the text of P^{46} should be translated: 'those who are holy and faithful in Christ'. It should be noted that this combination of readings is unique to P^{46} and, as the easiest of the variants, should be set aside. Indeed, the presence of such a secondary reading in P^{46} ought to warn us against over-reliance on this early but somewhat erratic manuscript, whose singular readings include many that are simply errors.

However, the omission of the words 'in Ephesus' has more widespread support in the MS tradition. Origen knew this reading and it was accordingly reproduced in the great Alexandrian uncials (א B) and a few derivative minuscules. This shorter reading, whichever way it is construed, is preferred by many recent scholars but their case is weaker than it may at first appear.

The participle with the article 'those being' can hardly stand on its own without a completing complement. Origen's explanation of it, that it means 'those really existing', who share in the being of the Existent One, tells us a lot about Origen, but nothing about the origin of Ephesians. The defence of this reading offered by Foakes Jackson and Lake (1920: 1.56), followed by Schnackenburg (40), arguing that it means 'local' or 'neighbouring', cannot be supported by any comparable usage in the Pauline corpus or the rest of the New Testament (Acts 5.17; 13.1; 14.13 are probably *not* examples of this idiom). If 'in Ephesus' is omitted, the participle has to be taken with what follows. Three possibilities may then be considered.

First, it could mean 'the saints who are also faithful'. But that formula might imply that there were some saints who were not faithful, which would be a strange notion. And the participle would be redundant, adding nothing to the sense.

Secondly, on the hypothesis that Ephesians was a circular letter, a gap might have followed in the autograph into which a variety of geographical destinations was intended to be inserted, as occasion demanded. It is important to note that this is a *conjectural* emendation by modern scholars, for no extant witness to the shorter text actually has a lacuna after 'who are'. Furthermore, there is no parallel (see Roller 1933) in ancient literature for a circular letter of the type proposed here. In the New Testament, Galatians, 1 Peter, James and possibly also 1 John provide different examples of circular letters addressed to more than one community, but they either specify a province or group of provinces, or are deliberately unspecific in their address. Although Ephesians is very general in tone, at certain points it becomes specific about the situation of its addressees: namely 1.15, that Paul has heard of their faith (implying that he did not know them personally); 3.3–4, that he had written an earlier brief document that they will soon be able to read; and 6.21–2, that Tychicus has been sent with the letter to add a verbal report about Paul. These facts are unlikely to be true of all the possible destinations of a circular letter.

Thirdly, and partly in response to the objection just made to the second option, the original text could have read one or two place names other than Ephesus after 'who are': Laodicea (Harnack 1910: 706–8; Goulder 1991); Laodicea and Hierapolis (van Roon 1974: 72–85; Lincoln 3) or Hierapolis (Kreitzer 1997: 31–40). According to these scholars, the place name or names were subsequently excised, producing the shorter text, and then 'in Ephesus' added, producing the majority text. Again one should emphasize that these are *conjectural* emendations, lacking any MS support. Combined with a defence of Pauline authorship (Harnack; van Roon; Goulder), this third option is rather attractive. But if Ephesians is indeed pseudepigraphical (Lincoln; Kreitzer), it is highly problematic. On that view, it would have been the mention of a 'letter from Laodicea' at Col. 4.16 which stimulated the writing of 'Ephesians' in the first place; but then why is the writer not more explicit in his reference to the exchange of letters with Colossae (see on 3.3f.) and why does he not refer anywhere to Epaphras, 'who has worked so hard for . . . those at Laodicea and Hierapolis' (Col. 4.13)? Moreover, if the destination to these two small churches in Eastern Asia Minor indicates the actual location of the post-Pauline readers of the pseudepigraphon (as Kreitzer), they would be in a unique position, remembering the letter that Paul had actually written to them, to detect the forgery. If, on the other hand, the stated destination was purely fictional and the actually intended readers were located in Western Asia Minor around Ephesus (as Lincoln lxxxiii), then why did the pseudepigrapher not develop the fictional framework more convincingly after 1.1, since he could do so with relative impunity?

Normally it is those who argue for Pauline authorship of Ephesians as it stands who dispute the longer reading with its geographical reference to Ephesus. Those who see it as composed later, around the time of the formation of the corpus, ought to accept the argument that some specified destination would be needed.

It only remains, then, to explain how the place name ever came to be omitted from certain early MSS. The following factors might contribute to a solution to that continuing problem. (1) Second only to the Epistle to the Romans in the Pauline corpus, Ephesians is a letter of the most general interest and application and a generalizing motivation could have produced the omission of the reference to a specific destination within the text (it would still remain, of course, in the superscription) in the same way that G and Origen omit the place name at Rom. 1.7. (2) A close reading of the letter, especially the implication of 1.15 (see above), may have raised doubts about Ephesus as an appropriate destination for it, since Paul worked there for more than two years and was personally well known to the Ephesians (Acts 19.10; 20.38). (3) The misconstrual of the epexegetic *kai* in the first verse (see above) as a genuine conjunction could have led to the excision of the place name. (4) Tertullian's comments on Marcion's view concerning the original destination of the letter (Introduction, p. 28) were made around the same time as the appearance of the earliest witnesses to the shorter text (P[46] and Origen) and their omission may reflect Tertullian's response, i.e. that the destination of any epistle is a matter of indifference, since what Paul says to one church he says to all.

B Blessing (1.3–14)

(3) **Blessed be the God and Father of our Lord Jesus Christ, who has blessed us with every spiritual blessing in the heavenly realms in Christ,**

(4) **just as he elected us in him before the creation of the world, to be holy and blameless before him**

in love (5) having predestined us for adoption as his own through Jesus Christ, as he was pleased to will, (6) – praise be to the glory of his grace with which he graced us in the Beloved One! –

(7) **in whom we have redemption through his blood, the remission of trespasses, according to the riches of his grace (8) which he lavished upon us**

in all wisdom and understanding (9) making known to us the mystery of his will, as he was pleased to determine in him (10) to advance his plan for the fullness of time –

that he might bring all things to summation in Christ, things in heaven and things on earth

in him (11) in whom we have gained our allotted portion, having

been predestined by the intention of him who accomplishes all things by the determination of his will, (12) so that we might be those who first hoped in Christ, to the praise of his glory; (13) in whom you also, who heard the word of truth, the gospel of your salvation, – in whom, you also, when you came to faith, were sealed with the promised Holy Spirit, (14) which is the guarantee of our inheritance, so that God may redeem what belongs to him, to the praise of his glory!

After the opening greeting Paul's letters usually continue by adapting a fairly common pattern in Hellenistic letters, expressing gratitude to the gods for some favour received and a report of the writer's prayers for his correspondents. This is the case with Ephesians also, but the expected 'thanksgiving prayer report' is delayed until 1.15–18. In the interval there appears an actual example of a prayer of blessing (in Hebrew, *berakah*), a form familiar from Jewish and Jewish Christian literature.

The Old Testament examples of blessings are often quite brief (e.g. 1 Kgs 8.14–16; Ps. 41.13) but in Jewish synagogue worship (e.g. the Eighteen Benedictions) and at Qumran (e.g. the Hodayoth; see further Kirby 1968: 84–9) they can be quite extensive. As direct address to God, they are usually phrased in the second person: 'Blessed art thou, O Lord etc'. The New Testament reflects this liturgical tradition. There are short benedictions such as Rom. 1.25; Rom. 9.5 and 2 Cor. 11.31 and longer ones, the best known of which is the *Benedictus*, or Song of Zechariah, Luke 1.67–75. One other Pauline epistle starts with a blessing (2 Cor. 1.3–5) but there it substitutes for a thanksgiving prayer–report, while in Ephesians it is in addition to it (see further on 1.15, and Introduction, p. 35).

The *berakah* in Ephesians is composed in an exuberant and lofty style. In the original Greek, vv. 3–14 are one long sentence, extended by participial, purpose and relative clauses, with a succession of repeated phrases and ideas. Although sentence length varies considerably in the undisputed Pauline letters (van Roon 1974: 105–10), there is nothing to rival this monster. It is far too long, one might reasonably suppose, to have been conceived as a single thought, and it is likely to have grown by expansion. Verses 11–14 in particular, though they share the same style, depart from the blessing form. This is often acknowledged with regard to verses 13–14 (e.g. Lincoln 16, who calls them an 'additional statement addressing recipients') but it is equally true of verses 11–12 (see below).

The *berakah* proper (vv. 3–10) blesses God for four or five spiritual blessings: eternal election, predestination to sonship, redemption through sacrifice, secret revelation and hope for the consummation of all things in Christ (the last two being closely related). The arrangement of the translation above attempts to reflect this sequence of ideas. It is difficult to go further than this and separate the material neatly into stanzas, because of the continuousness of the grammar. Different structural elements like the prepositional phrases or participles, clause length or syllable count, or repeated features like 'to the praise of his glory' have been taken as clues for the various attempts at reconstructing an underlying hymn (see Lincoln 13f., who reviews the analyses of Innitzer 1904; Lohmeyer 1926; Masson 1953; Coutts 1956–7; Schille 1965; and Fischer 1973; to which may be added those of Grelot 1989 and Thomson 1995) but consensus among the scholars has not been achieved and, given the nature of the material, is probably impossible.

In the above translation it is at least possible to discern a certain chiastic structure in verses 3–10. The reference to 'heavenly realms' in verse 3b corresponds to 'the things in the heavens' in verse 10b. Similarly the time reference in verse 4, 'from the foundation of the world', parallels 'the fullness of time' at verse 10a. The second and fourth blessings (vv. 5 and 9) are both expressed in participles and both are 'according to good pleasure' (vv. 5a and 9b); and the central motif of redemption is preceded and followed by references to God's grace (vv. 6 and 7b). Verse 10 forms a satisfactory closure to this liturgical prayer, comparable with but clearly not derived from the triumphant endings of the hymns at Col. 1.20 and Phil. 2.11. The structure and symmetry of verses 3–10 point therefore to an original, probably pre-formed *berakah* which has been expanded with verses 11–14 (so also Thomson 1995: 46–83).

The material in verses 11–14 is very loosely connected with what precedes it: the only function of the redundant 'in him' at the beginning of verse 11 is to make that connection. The addition consists of two distinct parts. In verses 11–12 Paul and his fellow (Jewish) Christians, including the writer ('we'), are described as those who, having priority in salvation-history, have taken possession of their special inheritance and are defined as those 'who first hoped in Christ'. In verses 13–14 the readers are directly addressed and identified as those who have 'heard the gospel' and been 'sealed' by baptism in the promised Spirit. Both parts of this addition break away from the form of a *berakah*, in which the mighty works of God are celebrated, and describe instead the respective status of the supposed writer and readers. As far as their content is concerned, verses 11–14 echo many points made previously: predestination (v. 11; cf. v. 5), God's determination (v. 11; cf. v. 9) and will (v. 11; cf. v. 9), 'all things' (v. 11; cf. v. 10), redemption (v. 14; cf. v. 6) and the repeated phrase 'to the praise of his glory' (v. 12 and v. 14; cf. v. 6). The new elements like 'the gospel of salvation' and 'sealed with the Holy Spirit' reflect emphases that will reappear later (see below on 2.5 and 4.30). Verses 11–14 seem to be the writer's own composition.

The origin of the *berakah* itself is more difficult to determine. It contains one or two elements, like 'in the heavenly realms', which are characteristic of this writer, but in view of the weak juncture at the end of verse 10 and the new direction of verses 11–14, it is unlikely that he composed the blessing *in situ* himself. More probably, it was available to him as a liturgical piece circulating in his community. If so, it might well have already been attributed to the inspiration of Paul, their founding apostle. And its incorporation into this letter may have been intended partly to elicit recognition and provide assurance of the letter's authority.

The occasions on which such a blessing for the privileges of salvation in Christ could be used would be many and varied, but the suggestion that it originally had a baptismal setting deserves serious consideration (Dahl 1951: 263f.; Kirby 1968). The strongest argument for this view is the combination, in verses 5–7, of references to 'sonship', God's 'good pleasure', the title 'Beloved' and 'the remission of sins', which strikingly recall features of the Synoptic narrative of the baptism of Jesus (see Mark 1.4, 11), though the lack of reference to the gift of the Holy Spirit or the use of the metaphor of washing tell slightly against it. The editor may have seen in the *berakah* a description of the status of baptized Christians, since his 'additional statement' at 1.13 includes a reference to the readers' being 'sealed with the Spirit'. For later allusions to baptism, see on 4.5 and 5.26. Other liturgical passages in Ephesians (cf. 2.14–18 and 5.14) may have a similar origin, though all of them are now used in the letter with a wider application.

Finally, could Paul himself have written this blessing and even decided to start his letter to the Laodiceans with it? This is not at all impossible, but perhaps unlikely, for the language is more general and verbose than is usual for Paul. The broad sweep of salvation-history offered here lacks his characteristic focus on the cross and resurrection of Jesus. And normally Paul has a definite point when he uses liturgical material or forms: Christ's headship over the powers was the point of using Col. 1.15–20; Christ's humility (Phil. 2.6–11) or poverty (2 Cor. 8.9) were examples of immediate relevance to his argument in those letters. To be sure, he began 2 Corinthians (1.3–7) with a *berakah*, praising the 'God of all *comfort*', using the word ten times in the space of five verses; but that was precisely his point – 'comfort' was what he wanted from the Corinthians and what he painfully had not been getting! It is much more difficult to spot the point of Eph. 1.3–10. Lastly, the intrusion of this blessing delays the prayer report until 1.15 (see below); Pauline letters that include a prayer report invariably start with it.

3 If there is pre-formed liturgical material in verses 3–10, then we should be careful not to 'over-exegete' the passage. The language of praise is not always theologically precise; its sublimity and redundancy are intended to create an emotional response of religious fervour, and to analyse each word or phrase in turn, as one is expected to do in a commentary, is a procedure somewhat alien to the character of the piece. Furthermore, if it is a real hymn, the words would, in any case, be only part of its meaning; the tune (see on 5.19) is now lost to us, but may have been familiar and evocative to some in the first audiences of Ephesians.

The one who is blessed is **the God and Father of our Lord Jesus Christ** (cf. 2 Cor. 1.3). He is both the God of the prophet Jesus of Nazareth, who upheld Israel's monotheistic faith, and also the Father of Christ, in a distinctively Christian reformulation of that faith (cf. John 20.17). The God who is blessed has already **blessed us with every blessing** (a semitic pleonasm). The generosity of God is prior: it arises from God's own nature as 'one who blesses', to which human beings are bound to respond by blessing him in worship. The blessings God bestows are described as **spiritual**. This term may be used in an anthropological sense, referring to the inner life of the human person (so Caird 33); or in the strictly theological sense, referring to the work of the Holy Spirit (so Lincoln 17). But in view of the following phrase, 'in the heavenly realms', the word is probably intended simply to denote other-worldly or non-material.

The frequent language of 'riches' in Ephesians is entirely spiritualized (see on 1.7; 2.7; 3.8). The material prosperity of Christian communities in Asia Minor at the time of writing no doubt varied (compare Smyrna, Rev. 2.9: 'I know your poverty, but you are rich', with Laodicea, Rev. 3.17: 'For you say, "I am rich . . .", not knowing you are poor'), and the writer of Ephesians, like Paul and the seer of Revelation, glories in earthly poverty because it secures a rich reward in heaven.

The author uses here for the first time a phrase, **in the heavenly realms** (*en tois epouraniois*), that will recur in four other places (1.20; 2.6; 3.10; 6.12). It is an adjective used in place of a noun, probably neuter and spatial, the equivalent of 'in heaven' (rather than personal, 'among the heavenly ones'). Its importance is that it indicates the exalted place not only where Christ is, but also where Christians are, through incorporation into him (cf. 2.6). In order to receive the spiritual blessings promised, believers need to understand themselves as mystically transported in faith and worship into the highest heavens.

This favourite phrase is distinctive of Ephesians; it appears nowhere else in the Pauline corpus, Colossians included, though the adjectival form is used by Paul to describe the risen Christ as the '*heavenly* man' in 1 Cor. 15.40, 48. The prefix *ep-* (on to or over) may imply for the writer the 'upper heavens' (cf. Eph. 4.9, where Christ is said to ascend 'far above all the heavens'; cf. also 'in the highest' at Mark 11.10) in contrast to the intermediate zones of the sky in which evil powers are still at work (cf. 2.2). But if so the distinction is not rigidly maintained (see 6.12). Speculation about successive heavens was characteristic of Jewish apocalyptic (see the note on 2.6), from which, in a de-judaized and de-eschatologized form, and with the help of a misreading of Paul, it entered second-century Christian Gnosticism. While the spatial metaphor of heaven and earth predominates in Ephesians, as it does in the Fourth Gospel (see John 3.12, where the same word 'heavenly things' occurs with its opposite 'earthly things'), in neither is the temporal axis completely denied (see John 5.28f. and below, on Eph. 1.21).

The Pauline **in Christ** formula, with its variant 'in him', appears repeatedly in verses 3–14, as it does in the rest of Ephesians (see e.g. 1.20; 2.6, 10, 13; 3.6, 11f., 21 etc.). The exact meaning of the preposition 'in' here is open to discussion (see Best 1955; Wedderburn 1985). Agency is often all that is implied (Allan 1958). Houlden (1973b: 272) points out that 'It is . . . remarkable that a writer who can see the Church in terms of such splendour and speak of her so mythologically, should withdraw from the more internal aspects of the Christ-mysticism in Paul.' But Ephesians is not consistent on this matter; occasionally the more profound (Pauline) sense of incorporation into Christ can hardly be denied (cf. on 3.6). If the latter is present here, the first of God's blessings is bestowed on Christ himself (cf. the christological referent of 'Blessed be he who comes in the name of the Lord' at John 12.13 and parallels), and only thereafter on Christians insofar as they are united with Christ (see further on v. 4).

4 The idea of divine blessing leads naturally to the idea of Israel's election (see e.g. Deut. 30.11–20, esp. v. 19), here reapplied to the Church. In Gal. 3.8, 14 Paul had similarly appropriated the blessing of God upon the seed of Abraham (Gen. 12.3) for his Gentile Christian converts.

God's foreknowledge of those who would eventually respond to the gospel may be all that is meant by this verse. But if the emphasis falls on 'in him', then the election of the pre-existent Son **before the creation of the world** is itself the election of those who are to become incorporate in him. This 'christologization' of the doctrine of election is present in Paul (Gal. 3.16); it is even clearer in the Fourth Gospel, where the very same phrase is used of the Father's eternal election of the Son (John 17.24; cf. v. 26; and see also 1 Pet. 1.10). Thus, it is not so much that Christians claim to be an elect race apart from ordinary humanity, but that they are those who believe in the one who is the unique object of God's elective love.

The free grace of election in Christ is set in balancing tension with the moral demand laid on Christians **to be holy and blameless before him**. Similar phrases appear in Paul, e.g. at 1 Thess. 3.13: 'unblamable in holiness'; Phil. 1.9: 'pure and innocent'; Col. 1.22: 'holy, blameless and irreproachable'. The context of all these examples is that of appearing before God at the last judgement, and this is probably also the implication in the words 'before him' (*enōpion*, 'in his presence', 'before his face'; see also Eph. 5.27 and the comment there). The attempt by some (esp. Lindemann 1975) to remove all such future temporal references from the theology of Ephesians is generally reckoned to be unconvincing. However, as Phil. 2.15 indicates, 'that you may be blameless and innocent *in the midst* of a crooked and perverse generation', Paul believed that the qualities required for an ultimate favourable judgement at the End ought to be acquired in this life, well in advance. The writer of Ephesians is of the same mind (see e.g. 2.10 and 5.24).

The adverbial phrase **in love** is ambiguously placed between two clauses; it should probably be taken with the next verse (so RSV text (cf. RSV marg.); Caragounis 1977: 84–6; Best 123), since 'holy and blameless' sufficiently describes the qualifications needed for ultimate salvation (see above). 'In love' would then start a new clause and receive special emphasis. The same words are connected with a following participle at Eph. 3.17. Ambiguities like this would have to be resolved by phrasing when the text was read aloud or sung in worship. For the emphasis on God's love in Christ in Ephesians see also 2.4; 3.19; 5.2 and, above all, the nuptial imagery in 5.25–33.

5 The *berakah* moves on from election to predestination for **adoption**, in the same way as Paul does at Rom. 8.29: 'For those whom he foreknew he also predestined to be conformed to the image of his Son, in order that he might be the firstborn within a large family'.

At Rom. 8.15, 23 and Gal. 4.6 adoption is particularly associated with the Spirit, but that link is not made explicitly here, though it does appear in the additional material later (see v. 13). It is interesting to note that in Colossians, by contrast with all the other letters of Paul, the Spirit plays hardly any role; the focus there is exclusively on Christ. The reason for this, Schweizer suggests (1982: 38 n.19), is probably the nature of the opponents in Colossae, with their appeal to mystical experience. He comments (39): 'In Christology, the criteria for distinguishing between true and false teaching are more readily available.' The *berakah* is similarly christocentric, but the author of Ephesians himself (closer in this respect than Colossians to the Paul of the other letters) has no hesitations about referring to the Holy Spirit elsewhere (see 1.13; 2.18, 22; 3.16; 4.4, 30).

Adoption (*huiothesia*) was a well-known institution among the upper classes of the Roman Empire (less so in Judaism). The overtones of the word here should be understood not as legal or dynastic, but as religious and metaphorical (see Lyall 1969; Byrne 1979; Scott 1992). Because this word seems to do duty in Greek for the much rarer word 'sonship' (*huiotēs*), we cannot be certain whether a sharp distinction is being made between the status of believers as merely adopted children and the uniquely begotten Son (cf. Rom. 8.29). The seeds of the later patristic doctrines of the eternally generated Son by nature and of the sonship of believers by adoption and grace may be implied in some New Testament passages, like the prologue of John (1.12): 'To all who received him, he gave power to become the children of God'; but it is noteworthy that the relation between the only Son and the Father is described, even in the Fourth Gospel, in terms of grace ('full of grace', 1.14; 'from his fullness have we all received grace upon grace', 1.16) and in the remainder of the Gospel in terms of the union of love. The associations of both sonship and adoption in the New Testament are chiefly those of paternal affection and filial obedience.

The phrase at the end of this statement which has been rather freely translated **as his own** (following Lincoln 9) is literally 'unto him', and it could refer either to God or to Christ as the ultimate aim to which adoption is directed; but it does seem rather redundant. If it is not a very early corruption – and there are no variants in the MSS – it could be an attempt on the part of the editor to qualify the idea of sonship already achieved with the idea of further growth; one might compare the same phrase in 4.15: 'that we should grow up in all things *into him*' (cf. also 4.13: 'attain to the knowledge of the Son of God, *to* a perfect Man').

The voluntary and gracious initiative of God continues to be emphasized, **as he was pleased to will** (lit. 'according to the good pleasure of his will'). The pleonasm suits the liturgical context and style. It does not of itself tell against a Pauline origin. But the sheer concentration of synonyms in this sentence is exceptional: 'good pleasure' (vv. 5, 9), 'will' (vv. 5, 9, 11), 'determination' (vv. 9, 11), 'plan' (v. 10). This emphasis on the divine purpose, along with the corresponding emphasis on divine grace (e.g. v. 6f.), may have an apologetic function (see Chadwick 1960). As a Christian appropriation of Jewish salvation-history, the *berakah* would strain credibility, for all the glowing confidence of its expression, unless it was able to appeal to an extraordinary divine providence. Numerically and culturally insignificant and late-comers on the religious scene, nevertheless early Christian communities believed themselves to be in Christ at the very centre of God's design for the universe from all eternity.

6 This thought provokes a doxological outburst, **praise be to the glory of his grace**, which is echoed twice in the added material (vv. 12, 14). This favoured phrase has no parallel in Colossians but Phil. 1.11 is similar, 'to the glory and praise of God'.

The echoing of noun and verb, **his grace with which he graced us**, is a semitic idiom like that at 1.3; it will appear again later (cf. 1.19f.; 2.4; 4.1).

In the form of the perfect participle, **the Beloved One** as a title for

Christ occurs only here in the New Testament, though in its adjectival form it is used in the Synoptic accounts of Jesus' baptism (see Mark 1.11 and parallels) and transfiguration (Mark 9.7; Matt. 17.5). In pre-Christian Judaism, it was a title, not so much for the Messiah, as for the covenant people as a whole (e.g. Isa. 5.1 (cf. Mark 12.6) and Rom. 9.25). But the corporate Christology of the Pauline and Johannine traditions made the transferral of such titles to Jesus entirely natural (cf. e.g. Christ as the last Adam in 1 Cor. 15, or Christ as the true vine in John 15). In addition to pointing to the relationship of love between God and Christ, the title may carry an undertone of the extent of that love in the sacrifice of the cross (cf. v. 7), typologically modelled on the binding of Isaac, the 'only' and thus specially 'beloved' son of Abraham (see Gen. 22.2 LXX). Col. 1.13 has a similar association of ideas, though it uses a different formula, 'the Son of his love' (contrast Col. 3.12, see Introduction, p. 9).

7f. The blessing continues uninterrupted with a relative clause that points up the connection between Beloved as a title for Christ and his unique atoning work, **in whom we have redemption through his blood, the remission of trespasses**. The wording is almost identical to a clause that appears at the end of the prayer report at Col. 1.14, apart from 'through his blood' (though some MSS of Colossians (see NA^{27}) have added it, probably from Col. 1.20) and 'trespasses', for which Colossians has 'sins'. There are nevertheless eight identical words in the same order, a phenomenon that calls for an explanation, one might reasonably suppose, in terms of literary dependence. But if so, it is equally possible that Colossians is dependent on Ephesians; in other words, that Col. 1.14 is a later gloss added either from Eph. 1.7 or the material it was using. For, first, this clause in Colossians interrupts the flow of the sentence and separates the following relative pronoun (Col. 1.15) from its antecedent (Col. 1.13). Secondly, the version in Ephesians sounds more, not less, Pauline than that in Colossians, inasmuch as it puts redemption into parallel with adoption (cf. Rom. 8.23) and qualifies it as 'through his blood' (cf. Rom. 5.9). (Lincoln (27), who consistently maintains the dependence of Ephesians on the present text of Colossians, argues that our author here has conflated Col. 1.14 with the reference to blood at Col. 1.20, but he concedes that the result is to make Ephesians sound more typical of Paul.) Thirdly, Ephesians, while extracting these fragments from the Col. 1.14–20, has to be supposed to have ignored the main themes, so brilliantly expressed in that passage, namely Christ's work in creation and resurrection, which are conspicuously missing here. Verse 7 in fact contains the only significant point of contact with Colossians in the whole *berakah*, which is otherwise free-standing and independent.

This is the one verse in 1.3–10 (in sharp contrast to the addendum vv. 11–14) where God is not grammatically the subject ('we have'), though of course God remains the subject conceptually: redemption is entirely his doing (cf. on v. 14), achieved by Christ 'while we were still helpless ... and sinners' (Rom. 5.6, 8).

Redemption has a commercial connotation in classical Greek, the payment for the release of a hostage or slave. But for this writer, steeped in the Jewish tradition, the more important background is the salvation-historical motif of Israel's deliverance from bondage in Egypt (cf. e.g. Deut. 7.8), here reapplied to the new Exodus in Christ. In Col. 2.14 Paul exploits the commercial sense when, referring to the 'forgiveness of trespasses' (see the comment above), he uses the metaphor of release from slavery: 'he cancelled the bond which stood against us'. If Colossians were the source for Ephesians, it would be natural to assume (*contra* Lincoln 28) that this meaning would be to the fore at Eph. 1.7, but without that hypothesis, the Jewish use of the term is more likely to be the determinative one, fitting as it does with all the other 'covenantal' blessings listed in this *berakah*. The later patristic doctrine, that the ransom of Christ's atoning death was the payment due to the devil to secure the release of condemned humanity, is inconsistent with the picture of the demonic world which is found in Paul and equally in Ephesians, where the powers are subjected and ultimately vanquished, not just bought off by a commercial transaction. When nuances from the Greek use of the term 'redemption' do appear in the New Testament, they are to be understood as of a limited kind, signifying the personal cost of Christ's work and suffering.

The original 'redemption' of Israel from slavery in Egypt was through the blood of the Passover lamb (Exod. 12.13), which Pauline (and Johannine, see John 19.36) Christians reinterpreted in relation to the death of Christ (1 Cor. 5.7), re-establishing a 'new covenant' (1 Cor. 11.25). Strictly speaking, the Passover is not a sacrifice for sins, but first-century Christian Jews seem to have merged the different types of sacrifice into one composite and general idea (cf. John 1.29 and Heb. 9.11ff.). Any readers of this text with a background in Judaism would almost certainly have made the connection between **through his blood** and some kind of sacrificial offering. For Gentile readers the association may not have been so inevitable (cf. Rom. 5.9 and Rom. 5.7).

Redemption is defined further as **the remission of trespasses**. Surprisingly perhaps, the word translated 'remission', or forgiveness (*aphesis*) occurs only here and at Col. 1.14 in the whole of the Pauline corpus. Even extending the search to the rest of the New Testament epistles, we find it only in Hebrews (9.22 and 10.18); otherwise it is confined (13 examples) to the Gospels and Acts. The explanation of this neglect is probably that the word has Jewish covenantal associations.

'Trespasses' (see further on 2.2 below), i.e. offences against the revealed law of God, can be *remitted* through the offering of sacrifice. Paul, on the other hand, was normally addressing Gentile readers who were formerly outside God's covenant with Israel (see Eph. 4.17–19), so that the sacrificial means of remission were not available to them. (While the word forgiveness is hardly used by Paul, the idea is, of course, everywhere implicit in his writings.) Additional support for this interpretation may be drawn from Rom. 3.25f., where a similar word, 'the passing over (*paresis*) [of former sins]' appears in a passage that also reflects a Jewish-Christian perspective (Käsemann 1980: 95–101).

For the second time (cf. v. 6) the *berakah* emphasizes grace, **according to the riches of his grace (8) which he lavished upon us**. Before, it was the grace of election; here it is the grace of forgiveness. The order of these ideas is worth noting. It is not that forgiveness comes first and election follows, for that would give priority to the problem of sin; election comes first and itself uncovers the extent of human sinfulness, and that gives priority to divine love.

On the language of riches in Ephesians, see on verse 3 above. Paul refers to the riches of God's 'goodness' (Rom. 2.4), 'glory' (Rom. 9.23), and 'wisdom' (Rom. 11.12). The associated verb 'lavished' or 'abounded' is also distinctively Pauline (28 times in the Pauline corpus, see e.g. 2 Cor. 9.8 and Rom. 5.15).

The arrangement of the text above links the clause **in all wisdom and understanding** with the following participle,'making known to us the mystery of his will' (so also RSV; Best 135), for these capacities seem to be appropriate to the apprehension of God's secret plan of salvation. The word order, however, is ambiguous and the ancient MSS largely lack the punctuation marks that could help to resolve the issue. So the phrase might be taken with what precedes it and refer to the wisdom of divine redemption and grace. Schnackenburg (57) and Lincoln (17) both prefer this option (so also REB) despite the fact that the similar phrase at Col. 1.9 ('in all wisdom and insight'), which they hold to be the source for Ephesians, must clearly be taken as attributes that allow Christians to know God's will. This parallel in Col. 1.9 has 'spiritual insight' (*sunesis*) meaning human insight into spiritual things; Ephesians uses a synonym 'understanding' (*phronêsis*) which occurs only here among the Pauline letters (though the verb or compounds of it are very common). The same basic sense is conveyed by both formulations: the mystery of salvation is made known through a special divine enhancement of the human powers of insight and understanding.

9 Making known to us the mystery of his will. 'To make known' (*gnôrizein*) is used of divine revelation in five out of its six uses in Ephesians (6.21 is the exception, where Tychicus will 'make known' how Paul is faring). In the undisputed Pauline letters, the pattern is reversed: it is normally used of human information (six times) but the verb is used with God as the subject at Rom. 9.22f. (cf. Rom. 16.26). The referent of 'to us' would depend on the reader's interpretative standpoint, whether historicizing, particularist or inclusive. Thus, it could be taken to refer to Paul himself as the one to whom the secret plan of God had been revealed; or to Jewish Christians who occupy the central place in salvation-history; or to all Christians, especially as they are instructed in gatherings for worship.

Mystery (*mustērion*) is derived from the verb (*muein*) which means to 'shut' the eyes or the mouth, and thus 'to keep a secret'. In the Greco-Roman world there was a whole range of mystery cults and private religious societies about whose rituals initiates were sworn to secrecy, as a way of creating the impression of profundity and drawing the initiate deeper into the club. Paul was no doubt aware of such groups in his own day, especially in Corinth, and his frequent references to 'mystery' or 'mysteries' in 1 Corinthians (2.1 (*v.l.*); 2.7; 4.1; 13.2; 14.2; 15.51) seem to play upon the idea. Paul, as though trumping the mystery religions, preached the folly of the cross and faith in the risen Christ as a more profound mystery than anything the pagan world had on offer, available to all who were mature enough to receive it (1 Cor. 2.6f.).

In addition to this reactive use, Paul was more positively influenced by the tradition of Jewish apocalyptic, which developed the older prophetic idea (Amos 3.7) 'that the Lord God does nothing without revealing his *secret* to his servants the prophets'. The book of Daniel contains several references to 'mysteries' in chapter 2 (vv. 1, 18f., 27f., 47) and even a *berakah* (see vv. 20–3) which is closely comparable with this passage. The mystery of God's plan for the future history of the world is revealed to the seer through the interpretation of dreams and visions. In later apocalyptic texts closer in time to Paul (*1 En.* 51.3; 2 Esd. 14.5; *2 Bar.* 81.4 and the DSS; see J. Coppens 1968) the mysteries are broadened out to include not just the future but present mystical and liturgical experiences and insights into the nature of the created universe and the invisible world above. Paul may be using the apocalyptic concept at 2 Thess. 2.7 to refer to the puzzle that God could allow evil to flourish temporarily before its final defeat, and at Rom 11.25 to explain the temporary resistance of God's people, the Jews, to the preaching of the Christian gospel as part of the mysterious, indeed paradoxical, plan of salvation.

The term 'mystery' has provoked extensive discussion (see esp. Caragounis 1977; Bockmuehl 1990) not least in connection with the Pauline authorship of Ephesians. Some scholars argue that the word, which appears particularly frequently in this letter (six times) and Colossians (four times) and always in the singular, has a more all-embracing and 'mystical' meaning in deutero-Pauline circles than it had for Paul himself. Others argue that the concept in Ephesians differs markedly from that in Colossians – either by remaining closer to authentic Paul, or the opposite, by going beyond not only Paul but even Colossians and identifying the mystery of Christ with the doctrine of the Church. Mitton (1951: 86–91), for example, argues that Ephesians, though reflecting Paul's own apocalyptic understanding of the 'mystery' of the gospel, has developed it ecclesiologically: the Church is a mysterious unity comprising Gentiles and Jews (3.6), united with Christ in a mystical marriage (5.32), and is a sign of the cosmic union of heaven and earth (1.10). He does not deny that Paul might have been 'capable of originating the further interpretations which we find in Ephesians' but claims that 'it is unlikely that they would appear so fully developed, so explicit and so distinct in a writing simultaneous with Colossians'. For Colossians, according to Mitton, has a completely different view that identifies the 'mystery' exclusively with Christ. More recently, scholars who similarly take Ephesians to be pseudepigraphical and dependent on Colossians (Schnackenburg 58; Lincoln 31) have rejected this sharp dichotomy between the ecclesiological and christological interpretations of mystery in Ephesians and Colossians respectively, and emphasized the similarity between them in the cosmic scope which they attach to the idea. Best, however, who denies the dependence (36ff.), argues that the authors of Colossians and Ephesians, who both belong to a post-Pauline school, represent simultaneous and in some respects divergent developments of Paul.

The main reason that those who have studied this letter in close detail can yet reach such widely differing conclusions is that the meaning of 'mystery' in Ephesians is simply not homogeneous. In its 'salvation-historical' occurrences at 3.3, 3.4 and 6.19 it is entirely in line with undisputed Paul. Here at 1.9 it is cosmic and christological and thus in line with, but not dependent textually on, Colossians. At 3.9 it is cosmic and ecclesiological (the Church is not just the privileged recipient of the mystery but the means by which it is disclosed to the powers); and at 5.32 it is probably allegorical and ecclesiological (referring to the hidden meaning of Scripture). The expansion hypothesis is capable of explaining this otherwise extremely puzzling variety in usage.

The refrain, **as he was pleased to determine in him** (lit. 'according to his good pleasure which he set forth in him'), echoes verse 5, though here with a verb 'to determine' instead of the noun 'will', which has, in any case, just been used. This modification allows the grammar to continue with a following subordinate clause.

Exactly when and how the mystery of God is 'set forth' or 'determined' in Christ is not specified. Was the resurrection of Jesus the moment when the divine plan was revealed (see Eph. 1.20)? Or was

it revealed to the Apostle Paul directly and specially (see Eph. 3.3f.)? Or
did Jesus' preaching of the gospel of peace in the context of his earthly
ministry reveal the mystery of God (see Eph. 2.17)? Or is there an even
fuller revelation of its final out-working which is still to come (Eph. 2.7)?
This indeterminacy is due not only to the generality of the expression,
but also to the different backgrounds and levels of reference for readers of
a pseudepigraphical letter (see on 'to us' above).

10 The sentence continues with another adverbial clause, literally 'unto
the economy', translated here, with the preposition taken as implying
purpose, as **to advance the plan**. The word 'plan' (*oikonomia*) actually
means 'household management' or 'stewardship'. It is used by Paul at 1
Cor. 9.17 to refer to his office and rights as an apostle and the related
noun is used at 1 Cor. 4.1, where apostles are described as 'stewards of
the mysteries (plural) of God'. The office of steward is also the meaning
at Col. 1.25 and Eph. 3.2 (see below). However, the meaning here (and
at 3.9) is quite different: it is not the apostolic office that is denoted, but
the abstract idea of stewarding or managing the universe, hence 'the
plan'. In later Christian usage, this term acquired the technical sense of
the master plan of God or 'the economy of salvation', and that sense may
have its origin in this verse.

Since, in literal usage 'stewarding' is done by someone other than the
owner of an estate, often by his eldest son, it may be that Christ is the
subject of the implied verb (see below).

The phrase **for the fullness of time** is almost identical with Paul's
reference at Gal. 4.4 to God sending his Son 'when the fullness of time
(*chronos*) had come'. Here the word for time (*kairoi*) is different, meaning
'times, seasons or opportunities', but the two terms are nearly
synonymous (cf. 1 Thess. 5.1). Fullness refers to the fulfilment of Jewish
expectation for the coming of the Messiah after times and periods of
oppression (which may be why the article is used in this verse, literally
'the Christ'). This is an idea familiar from Jewish apocalyptic (Dan. 2.21;
2 Esd. 4.37; and see also Mark 1.15). A very different, non-temporal
sense of fullness will be discussed at 1.23 below.

The *berakah* finally reaches its climax and conclusion, **that he might
bring all things to summation in Christ**, or 'that he might sum up all
things in Christ'. Although some dictionaries (LSJ; *TDNT*) treat the
verb 'to sum up' as a middle deponent in Greek (i.e. a verb which does
not occur in the active form but carries an active sense), others (BAGD;
EDNT) rightly recognize that the active (*anakephalaioun*) does exist (see
Barn. 5.11) and that this is therefore a genuine middle, meaning that God
sums up all things 'himself' or 'for his own benefit'. It is a rare technical
term in classical rhetoric (Quintilian 6.1), meaning to recapitulate an
argument at the end of a speech by referring to its main 'headings'

(*kephalaia*). The only other example of it in the New Testament, at Rom. 13.9, is not too far from this: according to Paul, the commandment to love one's neighbour 'summarizes' all the other laws. This meaning is possible here also: in the work of Christ God has summed up, or intends to sum up, as it were, his whole *argument* in the plan of salvation. Clearly, though, with God as the subject of the verb the reference ceases to be 'rhetorical': the whole history of the universe becomes the divine oration, finally articulated in Christ. The Prologue of the Fourth Gospel (John 1.1–18) might be thought of as commentary on this idea.

Because the context stretches the ordinary meaning of this keyword, some commentators (notably Schlier 65 and Barth 89ff.) have sought to relate it to 'head' (*kephalē*) and make a connection with Christ as head over all things for the Church at verse 22 (cf. also 4.15 and 5.23) or, alternatively, to emphasize the significance of the prefix *ana-* ('again'; so Mussner 66) as indicating the notion of restoration to an original unity. One might even add that, given its proximity to a managerial metaphor, the word could be understood as a technical term drawn not from rhetoric but from accountancy, for its root can also mean 'capital', i.e. a large sum of money; in other words, God would be adding up all the resources of the universe in Christ. These extra nuances are not impossible, and to allow for them we have translated above 'to bring to summation'; the depths of meaning in this phrase were to be exploited by Irenaeus at the end of the second century in his doctrine of recapitulation (*anakephalaiōsis*). If the *berakah* ended at this point, as it may originally, it would have been followed by a pause for reflection by its hearers, allowing some of the many implications of this grandiloquent claim to sink in (see Kitchen 1994: 35–42).

All things are not just all that has preceded the coming of Christ along the temporal axis, but, as the following explanation makes clear, **things in heaven and things on earth**, on the spatial, cosmological axis. The hymn at Col. 1.20 similarly ends with the reconciliation of all things in Christ 'whether things upon the earth or things in the heavens'; and Phil. 2.10 also speaks of every knee 'in heaven, on earth or under the earth' acknowledging the lordship of Christ.

11 Arguments have been given earlier for the view that verses 11–14 are additions by the editor to the liturgical *berakah* he has adopted; they will not be repeated here, except to note that 'in him' at the end of the previous verse has no function other than to allow the extra material to be added. The connection, **in him in whom**, is awkward and ragged. While at verse 5 it was predestination that was said to be 'in him', here the phrase is more likely to go with the indicative verb, i.e. **in whom we have gained our allotted portion**, rather than with the reference to predestination in the following participle. The difference is slight but perhaps not insignificant. Earlier, God has been praised for blessings that apply equally to all Christians. Here distinctions start to be made: between 'we' and 'you' and between those who 'inherit' as of right and those with whom they share the privileges of the gospel (see further below). The verb translated as **gain our allotted portion** (*klêrousthai*) occurs only here in the New Testament. In the passive it means 'to be allotted something', 'to obtain something by lot'. It shares the same root as the more common Pauline verb 'to inherit' (*klêronomein*); the related noun (*klêros*) is used at Col. 1.12, where 'God has qualified you [*v.l.* 'us'] to share in the *inheritance* of the saints in light' (RSV). Whichever of the variant readings is preferred at Col. 1.12 ('you' or 'us'), it is still clear that there the inheritance is common to all Christians. But this is not so clear in Ephesians, where the contrast with 'and you also' at verse 13 points rather to the idea of Israel's special destiny to inherit the promises of God (cf. also Caird 40).

The claim continues **having been predestined by the intention of him who accomplishes all things by the determination of his will**. This is an astonishingly verbose formulation. It has usually been explained by the writer's peculiar tendency to use three words when one would suffice, but the heavy emphasis may be particularly motivated by the desire to correct any misunderstanding of Paul's polemical downplaying of Israel's salvation-history in the course of his controversy with Jewish opponents (see Rom. 5, where sin, death and the law characterize the time between Adam and Christ). Paul did, however, go on in Romans to acknowledge Israel's privileged position (see Rom. 9.4–5). Thus, 'we' (i.e. Paul representing Jewish Christians) have been given, the writer insists, our own duly allotted portion in God's plan by his predestination, intention, accomplishment, determination and will. After such a sequence one will scarcely dare to dispute the point!

12 'We' are defined further as **those who first hoped in Christ**. This is another verb (*proelpizein*, 'to hope before') unique to Ephesians in the New Testament. Since hope inevitably precedes its realization, the prefix cannot simply mean that 'we hoped before we experienced' but must mean 'we hoped before others did'. This prior hope may be Israel's historic expectation of the coming of the Messiah, or the fact that Paul and the first generation are the spiritual predecessors of the present readers. Both ideas may be implied. The nearest parallel in Colossians (1.5) speaks of 'the hope laid up for you in heaven', which is a very different idea, to do with the content of what is hoped for rather than, as here, the activity of hoping.

The majority of translators and commentators assume that this phrase is attributive and take **to the praise of his glory** as the complement, supplying the missing verb 'to be', i.e. 'that we *who first hoped* might *be* to the praise of his glory'. This could be correct, though it would be awkward after verse 6 and before verse 12, in both of which the final phrase is adverbial. The NRSV translation 'that we ... might *live* for the praise of his glory' adds something that is not in the Greek. (Schnackenburg (63) discusses the issue.) The privilege of priority is the point that is being made emphatically, and our translation is the more natural one.

13 The *berakah* form celebrating the mighty deeds of God has already been distorted by the references to the precedence of Jewish Christians in verses 11–12; here the form is completely abandoned. Thus Lincoln (38): 'the more general liturgical style has shaded over into address to the readers'. The grammar is slightly loose: the relative 'in whom' is repeated unnecessarily half-way through this verse, but to try to tighten it, by understanding yet again the verb 'to be', i.e. ' in whom you are', would be pedantic; the material is simply being expanded with extra clauses strung together.

In the fictive situation of the letter, **you also** will be Paul's converts in Ephesus, a mixture of Greeks and Jews (cf. Acts 19.9f.). The first actual readers of this letter, however, would have had other options for understanding 'you also'. They might, for instance, have identified with the writer and distinguished themselves from those he was addressing; or they might have identified with the 'you also' as being either Gentiles or second-generation Christians. The 'we'/'you' distinction in a pseud-epigraphical letter is rather subtle, including the following possible distinctions: *we* (Paul, and any who identify with him) and *you* (all other Christians); or *we* (Jewish Christians like Paul) and *you* (Gentiles); or *we* (first generation) and *you* (our successors). These possibilities merge, as can be seen from what follows, where what is said about 'you' in 13b applies equally to all believers in Paul's own day and subsequently, who share 'our' inheritance (v. 14).

The phrase **the word of truth, the gospel** is also used at Col. 1.5 but the remainder of verses 13–14 is completely different. 'The word of truth' echoes Paul's emphasis on the truth of what he preaches (cf. Gal. 2.5, 'the truth of the gospel', and Gal. 5.7, 'obeying the truth') and his use of 'the word' to refer to the Christian message (1 Thess. 1.8 and Phil. 2.16, 'the word of life'). 2 Tim. 2.15 adopts the same formula and so does Jas 1.18. For the word as truth, see also John 17.17. Paul regularly uses 'gospel' as a shorthand near-technical term for the good news of salvation through the death and resurrection of Jesus (see Beker 1982); this author, however, feels it necessary to explain it more fully.

In Ephesians **salvation** (see also on 2.5, 8) is used to describe what has already been achieved; so the sense here is probably the 'good news that you *have been* saved'. Paul, however, preferred to use the word of a present process (1 Cor 1.18) or, more commonly, a future hope (Rom. 5.10; see further below, on 'guarantee').

For the absolute use of the aorist participle **when you came to faith** (lit. 'having believed') to refer to conversion, see Rom. 13.11 and Acts 19.2. This faith was confirmed when **you were sealed with the promised Holy Spirit** (lit. 'with the Holy Spirit of promise'). The phraseology is Paul's, drawn from 2 Cor. 1.22: God 'has sealed us and given us the guarantee of the Spirit in our hearts', which comes after references to God's 'strengthening' and even 'anointing' of believers (2 Cor. 1.21). The mention of the Holy Spirit, missing earlier (see on v. 5), completes in terms of theological content what has been said before about the Father and the Son, even though in literary terms verse 12 probably belongs to material appended to the *berakah* form.

A seal is a mark of ownership, often attached to official documents. In Revelation the scroll of the future is sealed with seven seals (5.5) and this idea is subsequently transferred to believers (see Rev. 7.3) as those who are predestined and assured of salvation. Pilate's seal is used at Matt. 27.66 to ensure that the tomb of Jesus is not tampered with; and the word occurs twice in John's Gospel: at John 3.33 of believers who acknowledge the truth of the testimony of the one from above, and at John 6.27 of Christ himself as the one whom the Father acknowledges. The writer of Ephesians will emphasize later, in an ethical context (4.30), the irrevocable commitment to the Christian way implied by their sealing in the Spirit.

While it is generally agreed that 'sealing' is a metaphor for Christian assurance, the further question of whether it is an allusion to baptism, or some part of the rite of baptism, in the early Church is more disputed. The seal of the Spirit was certainly understood in this way by some of the Apostolic Fathers, not too distant in time from the author of Ephesians (e.g. *2 Clem.* 7.6; *Hermas* 8.6.3; see further G. Lampe 1951). Paul refers to Abraham's circumcision as 'the seal of his justification by faith' at Rom. 4.11, and Col. 2.11f. interprets baptism as Christian circumcision, so it is possible that baptism itself was known as 'the seal'. The analogy with circumcision of male children shortly after birth is significant because it enabled the early Church uncontroversially to adopt the practice of infant baptism in the course of the second or third generation (Tertullian, *c.* AD 200, *Bapt.* 18, is the first to object to the practice). While Acts makes a distinction in a number of incidents (e.g. Acts 8.16; 10.47; 19.2) between the administration of the rite and the reception of the Spirit, this is not the case with Paul. Just as all the Israelites, according to him, were 'baptized into Moses and drank the same supernatural drink' (1 Cor. 10.2f.), so also all members of the true Israel are 'baptized into the one body of Christ and made to drink of the one Spirit' (1 Cor. 12.13). There is, therefore, no reason to exclude a possible reference to baptism here as the moment of sealing and commitment (cf. also on 4.5), though the author's interest is not in the ecclesiastical rite as such but its inner significance.

14 The Holy Spirit himself, or perhaps the sealing in the Spirit, is described as **the guarantee of our inheritance**. 'Guarantee' (*arrabôn*) is a semitic borrowing into Greek (cf. Gen. 38.17 LXX); it means pledge or first instalment towards the payment of a larger debt. What is implied is not so much the certification that the inheritance is true, but the sure promise that it will be delivered. Paul uses this metaphor to describe the Spirit at 2 Cor. 1.22 and 5.5 and, with a comparable metaphor drawn from the sacrificial cult, calls the Spirit 'the first fruits' at Rom. 8.23. These metaphors are attempts to explain the relation between present salvation and its future completion.

Paul speaks of 'inheritance' frequently, especially in Galatians 3 and 4 and Romans 4, where he claims that Gentiles have inherited the promises to Abraham, but his own references to salvation tend to refer to what is still awaited in the future (see comment on previous verse). Thus Paul himself would probably have preferred to call the guarantee of the Spirit a *present* inheritance (shared equally by Gentiles and Jews) pointing to a *future* salvation, whereas Ephesians inverts the time reference of the two terms (see Hammer 1960).

One would expect 'you were sealed' to continue with 'your' rather than 'our inheritance', but the writer reverts to the first person plural, perhaps because the inheritance is Israel's own privileged possession (see on v. 11), graciously extended to non-Jews. That would point to a Jewish Christian perspective for the writer, somewhat more conservative than that of Paul himself (see next clause also). But the switch from 'your' to 'our' can also be explained by the complexity of reference that these pronouns have in a pseudepigraphical composition.

The idea of inheritance is now filled out: **that God may redeem what belongs to him** (lit. 'unto the redemption of the possession'). Every part of this compact phrase is ambiguous. 'Unto' could indicate purpose (so that), or time (until). 'Redemption' could be God's action in the cross of Christ (as at v. 7) or it could refer to believers who are to buy back or 'acquire' what belongs to them. 'Possession' could be God's possession of his people, or Christians' possession of their inheritance. The RSV takes the second option in each case and translates 'until we acquire possession of it'; but commentators usually opt for the first (e.g. Lincoln 9: 'vouching for God's redemption of his possession') or take redemption at least to be God's doing, even if the possessing of it is ours (so Schnackenburg 45 and Best 104). It seems awkward suddenly to change the implied subject in mid-clause, so Lincoln is probably right (cf. also 1 Pet. 2.9: 'a people for his (i.e. God's) possession.')

As a final flourish the doxological phrase of the *berakah* at verse 6, already used once at verse 12, is repeated yet again: **to the praise of his glory.**

C   First prayer report   (1.15–23)

(15) For this reason I also, when I heard of your faith in the Lord Jesus and your love for all the saints, (16) have not ceased to give thanks for you, making mention of you in my prayers, (17) that the God of our Lord Jesus Christ, the Father of glory, might give to you the spirit of wisdom and revelation through knowledge of him, (18) with the eyes of your mind enlightened so as to know what is the hope of his call, what are the riches of his glorious inheritance among the saints, (19) and what is the excellent greatness of his power towards us who believe, according to the working out of his mighty strength, (20) which he worked out in Christ by raising him from the dead and seating him at his right hand in the heavenly realms (21) over and above every principality and authority and power and dominion and all the other names they are known by, not only in this age but in the age to come (22), and 'he has placed all things under his feet' and given him to be head over all things for the Church, (23) which is his body, the fullness of the one who is filling everything completely.

Apart from 2 Corinthians and Galatians, Paul's letters usually begin with a report of his thanksgiving and prayers for his readers. The formal characteristics of these opening sections (first analysed by Schubert 1939; cf. also O'Brien 1977; Stowers 1986) are almost all reproduced in Eph. 1.15–18, as follows: the fact of Paul's thanksgiving, its constancy, its object, its grounds, its occasion and its content. The structure and substance of this first person singular material is so similar at every point to Paul's way of writing that it is hard to think of anyone other than Paul as its author. An imitator who had carefully studied the opening paragraphs of Paul's letters might just possibly have been able to imitate them so precisely, but then such an observant imitator would surely also have noticed that his letters normally *begin* with a prayer report and that the only one that begins with a *berakah*, i.e. 2 Corinthians, lacks a prayer report altogether (cf. O'Brien 1999, 15). If the editor has made any changes in 1.15–18, they are difficult to detect: he may have added the title 'Father of glory' at verse 17 and filled out the content of Paul's prayer in verses 18–19, but the expansiveness could equally well be Paul's own.

However, the second half of the paragraph, beginning with the change from the second to the first person plural at verse 19, exhibits features distinctive of the editor's own style and special interests: the verbose 'according to the working out of his mighty strength' (v. 19b), the phrase 'in the heavenly realms' in verse 20 and, most importantly, the emphasis on the heavenly session of the glorified Christ in verses 20–3. The difference between this and Paul's thanksgivings is notable: his prayer is normally for his readers to persevere until the eschatological Day of Christ (cf. 1 Cor. 1.7 and Phil. 1.6). Here, on the contrary, the eschatology is thoroughly realized (though see the comment on 'the age to come' at v. 21). The prayer seems to have been expanded with certain scriptural and credal formulae (see below) in order to emphasize Christ's cosmic lordship, to which the editor has made a further slight but highly significant addition in verses 22–3, namely 'for the Church, which is his body', introducing his first mention of the Church but incidentally creating thereby an almost insoluble problem in the interpretation of verse 23 in the present form of the text.

15 The strong connective and emphatic first person pronoun, **for this reason I also**, is difficult to explain in its present context. 'For this reason' ought to refer *backwards* (as REB) and, if so, it is either generally to the whole of the preceding paragraph, or particularly to the fact (v. 13) of the acceptance of the gospel by the readers (though the intervening verse with its reversion to the first person plural, '*our* inheritance', blurs that connection). Given this difficulty, it has sometimes been taken to point *forwards* (so NRSV) to the mention of the readers' faith and love at verse 15 as the reason for the writer's unceasing gratitude. The other feature hard to explain in the present form of the letter is the emphatic first person singular, 'I also': why '*also*'?

Although Col. 1.9 is almost identical, those commentators who usually emphasize the importance of such parallels refrain from doing so in this case (see Schnackenburg 72; Lincoln 54). Presumably they are reluctant to admit that the writer of Ephesians has carelessly incorporated into his text wording from the earlier letter that fits perfectly its original context but is at odds with its present one. In Col. 1.9 Paul has just referred to Epaphras' report of his work among the Colossians and their 'love in the spirit', so he can continue quite naturally: '*For this reason* we (Timothy and I) *also* (as well as Epaphras) from the day we have heard of it have not ceased to pray for you.'

The statement, **when I heard of your faith in the Lord Jesus**, is also surprising. At Col. 1.9 'from the day we heard' is appropriate, since Paul had on his own admission not met the Colossians face to face (Col. 2.1). But if, as we have argued, this letter identified its recipients at 1.1 as 'the saints who are at Ephesus', then Paul should not merely say that he has *heard* of the faith of the Ephesians, but remind them that he was the one who brought them to faith and spent more than two years among them nurturing it.

The alternative hypothesis that Ephesians is an expanded version of Paul's letter to the Laodiceans is able to explain both the similarity to and the difference from Colossians here. At the beginning of his original letter Paul would naturally have referred, as he does in Colossians, to Epaphras his co-worker who had brought the gospel to all the churches of the Lycus valley (see Col. 4.13) and mentioned his report of their continuing faithfulness. 'For this reason I *also*' would then smoothly follow such a mention. But the editor redirecting the letter to Ephesus has had to omit any prior allusion to Epaphras' mission in Eastern Asia Minor, since that would have conflicted with its new destination. Nevertheless, he has still retained the wording of his source in this first person singular passage, verses 15–18, as he does in later passages of the same sort (see comments on 3.1–4, 7–8, 13f.; 4.1, 17; 6.20f.).

The difference between our view and that of Lincoln and Kreitzer (see on 1.1 above) should be noted. For them, Eph. 1.15 is intended to reflect the fictional destination (Laodicea and/or Hierapolis) of what they claim to be a homogeneous pseudepigraphon, but they fail to explain why, on that hypothesis, it is so inexplicit. We are claiming, on the contrary, that this verse contains a vestige of the original setting of the genuine Pauline letter that the author has edited, precisely so as to be less explicit.

However, the question remains how an editor could have retained even this vestigial hint of a different setting for the present letter. In response, it is instructive to compare what Paul says at Philemon 4, using a variant of the same phrase 'hearing of your faith' when addressing Philemon. For he must have known Philemon personally (see Phlm. 1, 22f.), perhaps from visits and support to Paul in prison. This may help to explain why the editor left Paul's wording unchanged at this point. That Paul has only 'heard' of the Ephesians' *recent* progress would not necessarily imply that he was not their founding apostle. A further factor that might have allowed this phrase to stand is that the actual audiences of Ephesians towards the end of the first century would have had few members who had known Paul personally.

Faith in the Lord probably means faithfulness on the part of those who are in the Lord (cf. on 1.1), rather than belief in Jesus as Lord. It is the news not of their conversion but of their perseverance that provokes Paul's thanksgiving.

The addressees' **love for all the saints** might have been an allusion in the original letter to the Pauline collection as a concrete act of charity (see further on 2.19), or to loving, personal assistance towards other Christians, not least to Paul in prison. A post-Pauline readership would have taken it more generally, to refer to the obligation to love one's fellow Christians, principally by remaining united in fellowship with them (on the imperative to church unity, see on 2.16; 4.1–6).[4]

16 The typically Pauline hyperbole, **I have not ceased to give thanks**, is to be found also at 1 Thess. 1.2; 2 Thess. 1.3; 1 Cor 1.4 etc. Lincoln's comment (55) that 'there is no reason why this should not reflect the actual prayer life of the writer as much as other letters did that of Paul himself' reveals the uneasiness of some supporters of the purely pseudepigraphical hypothesis in face of 'personal' notes such as this. Even if pseudepigraphy *per se* is not deceitful, the claim that the historic Paul had always remembered the recipients of this letter in his prayers would be disturbing if untrue, Lincoln seems to feel, unless someone else standing in for the apostle, namely the writer, actually did so!

17. The content of Paul's prayer is now summarized. The parallel in Colossians (1.9, but see already above on Eph. 1.8) is worded differently, except for the common use of the terms 'all wisdom' and 'knowledge', but the gist is the same.

The phrase that attracts particular attention in this verse is **Father of glory**. It recalls the language of praise in the Psalter, 'the God of glory' (Ps. 29.3) and the 'King of Glory' (Ps. 24.7). However, this exact formula is unique. It is found nowhere in Paul or the rest of New Testament (though cf. 'God of glory', Acts 7.2 and 'Father of lights', Jas 1.17). One might have expected 'the God and Father of our Lord Jesus Christ' again (as 1.3) but, for a change, 'Father' has been postponed and given an additional qualifier. The genitive 'of glory' could simply be adjectival, 'glorious Father'; or it could imply origin, 'the source of glory'; or it could even be christological, 'Father of the one who is himself the Glory of God' (cf. 2 Cor. 4.6 – an idea developed further in the Fourth Gospel (see e.g. John 1.14 and 17)). The meaning of the Hebrew word for glory, *kabod*, as 'weight', 'influence' or 'power', is coloured in New Testament usage by the overtones of the Greek equivalent, *doxa*, namely 'light', 'radiance' and 'splendour', as the next verse shows (see further Caird 1969). The author of Ephesians frequently refers to 'glory', and may have added the word here.

The request for **the spirit of wisdom and revelation** is reminiscent

---

[4] Some MSS omit 'your love' (P[46] ℵ* A B & Origen), and that would produce the rendering: 'faith in the Lord and [faith] towards all the saints'. If this is the correct reading – and it has the advantage of being the more difficult one – then the longer form of the text will have arisen from secondary harmonization to Col. 1.4. But 'faith towards the saints' looks too difficult a reading to be possible, and the shorter form is probably to be explained either by accidental omission or by harmonization to Phlm. 4 (through misconstruing the grammar there; see Moule 1957: 141).

of 1.8, 'all wisdom and understanding', where, however, Christians were said to be already in possession of these gifts (though see the comment on that verse). It is similar to Col. 1.9 where Paul prays that the Colossians may 'be filled with the knowledge of his will in all wisdom and spiritual insight'. The Colossians version is a neater formulation that avoids the limping and inconsequential adverbial phrase 'in the knowledge of him'. Conscious alteration of Colossians by Ephesians seems therefore unlikely.

As not infrequently in the Pauline letters, it is difficult to decide whether to spell spirit with an initial capital, referring to God's Spirit, or with lower case as a quality or capacity of human beings. (Paul sometimes deliberately exploits the overlap between these referents, e.g. at Rom. 8.16.) That the spirit of wisdom is paired with the spirit of revelation does not foreclose the question in favour of the former view, because Paul can speak of 'a revelation' (1 Cor. 14.26) as an explicitly human contribution to worship (comparable to 'a hymn, teaching, tongue or interpretation'), inasmuch as they come from 'the *spirits* (*sic*) of prophets' (1 Cor. 14.30, 32). Col. 1.9 speaks of 'spiritual insight', which is less likely to be 'insight imparted by the Spirit' (*pace* Lincoln 57) than insight into spiritual things. Here Paul prays for the whole community to acquire the gift of revelation; it is not, therefore, reserved to an élite of apostles and prophets (contrast 3.5, and see the comment there).

18 The grammar of the sentence becomes a little obscure as the content of the prayer begins to be spelled out. One might expect the participle **enlightened** to be in the dative case, agreeing with 'to you' in verse 17; but it is in the accusative. So this is either an adverbial accusative, as reflected in our translation (lit. 'as to the enlightened eyes of your heart'), or alternatively it could be an anticipation of the accusative construction to follow ('that you, having been enlightened as to the eyes of your heart, might . . . '). The phrase explains what was meant by having 'the spirit of wisdom and revelation' and is comparable to the metaphor of 'girding the loins with truth' (6.14; cf. Luke 12.35). Since it is a gift that is prayed for, it is not as such a reference back to some earlier event in the experience of the readers. But a secondary allusion to baptismal illumination is not necessarily ruled out.

The constituents of the knowledge of God (v. 17) are elaborated in three specific points: hope, inheritance and power. Each is echoed in other parts of the letter and they are close to the heart of the writer's own interests, as indeed they were of Paul's. Triple interrogations like this are not untypical of Paul's own style (see Rom. 10.6–8; 11.34 (LXX); 1 Cor. 4.7; 9.7; 1 Thess. 2.9) but the writer of Ephesians is also fond of triplets himself (see on 4.12). It is difficult to tell where the source ends and the editing begins.

The reference to **the hope of his call** also completes a different triad, when taken with the references to faith and love at verse 15 (cf. 1 Cor. 13). In the second half of the letter (4.1, 4) the moral exhortation will be set under the keyword of the Christian *calling*, in a way that implies that 'calling' means not just the initial call but the whole shape of subsequent discipleship. So here also, the readers are to know not just the hope to which they have been called, but the hope which is an integral part of their vocation (cf. also on 4.4).

The hope in view is chiefly that of resurrection life in Christ, already made certain by Jesus' own resurrection from the dead (see v. 20), but it may also include that hope in the Creator God which Gentile Christians now share with the Jews (see 2.12).

The second item is **the riches of his glorious inheritance among the saints**. The phrase 'riches of glory' appears at Rom. 9.23f. in a similar context of Gentiles being grafted on to the people of God (and cf. Col. 1.27). The inheritance is here said to be God's (contrast 1.14, 'our inheritance') in the sense that it is God who reaps a rich harvest consisting of saints. The thought is close to that of John 17.10 where Jesus is 'glorified in those whom the Father has given him from the world'. There are many examples of this idea in the Old Testament (see e.g. Deut. 9.26), from which it has been taken over and reapplied to the Church. Paul used the term 'saints', in the same way as it is used here, to describe all Christians, whether Jewish or Gentile; the writer of Ephesians gives it a more specialized sense elsewhere (see on 2.19).

Some commentators (Gnilka 91; Schnackenburg 74; Best 168) argue that 'the saints' (or 'holy ones') in this verse denotes angels. Examples of the term used with that meaning are not uncommon in the Old Testament, see e.g. Job 15.15, and appear among the DSS (see e.g. 1QS 11.7). But this interpretation is unlikely (so also Caird 45; Lincoln 60 (correcting his earlier view, 1981: 144); and, though tentatively, Houlden 275). It has arisen partly from the influence of the parallel at Col. 1.12: 'who has enabled us to share the lot of the holy ones *in light*'. But without the qualifying phrase 'in light', which may possibly imply supernatural beings, the readers of Ephesians would surely have assumed that 'the holy ones' referred to human beings. This view is supported by the fact that when angels are explicitly mentioned below (v. 21) they are not the kind that belong to God's 'inheritance' at all, but are insubordinate rulers and powers (1.21; cf. 2.2) that have to be subjected.

19 The third item is the **excellent greatness of his power towards us who believe, according to the working out of his mighty strength**. While most of the words for power here are frequent in Paul, this dense concentration of terms is remarkable, and 'greatness' (*megethos*) is *hapax legomenon*. More significant as an indicator of editorial intervention is the change from the second person plural, natural in a report of Paul's prayer for his correspondents, to the first person plural, 'to us who believe' (cf. on 2.3).

The contrast between the power (*dunamis*) of God (v. 19) and the heavenly powers (v. 21) is to be a recurring topic in Ephesians (see on 1.21 and cf. also 2.2; 3.10; 3.20; 4.10; 5.5f. and 6.10–17). The celebration of the power of God no doubt compensates for a sense of powerlessness and political marginalization in early Christian communities and explains the emphasis in Ephesians on the need for the strength that comes from unity in the Church. True power *(dunamis)* belongs to God and not to any of the competing claimants for it, whether cosmic, astrological or political.

20 The power of God is exemplified above all in his **raising** Jesus **from the dead**. Paul also associates power with resurrection at 1 Cor. 6.14 and Phil. 3.10. With a connecting link consisting of a relative pronoun and a verb derived from its antecedent, **the working out ... which he worked out** (cf. also e.g. 1.6), the report of the prayer leads into a series of general statements of belief in a rather different, more aphoristic style than the earlier part of the sentence. This is explicable on the assumption that the writer is beginning to draw upon credal or hymnic formulae. Among several attempts to reconstruct more precisely the underlying source (see Lincoln 51 for references) is that of J. T. Sanders (1965: 220–2) who proposes a pair of parallel couplets, the first two beginning with participles, the second with main verbs, thus:

Having raised him from the dead
And seated him at his right hand,
He also put all things under his feet
And made him head over all things.

This is an attractive proposal in its balanced simplicity. The main objection to it is perhaps the omission of any reference to Christ's exaltation *over the powers*. The famous christological hymns, Phil. 2.6–11 and Col. 1.15–20, both include this motif (Col. 1.16 and Phil. 2.9), but it has been excluded from Sanders' reconstruction (contrast that of Fischer 1973: 18f.). The third and fourth lines speak of the subjection of all things to Christ (citing Ps. 8.6) but, in the absence of verses 21 or 23, the referent of 'all things' is left unclear. It is, then, easier to be confident that credal, scriptural and liturgical affirmations of some kind have contributed to the composition of verses 20–23 than to specify precisely their original form.

Direct borrowing from Colossians, however, is unlikely, for while Eph. 1.20a is admittedly close to Col. 2.12b, 'the power of God that raised Christ from the dead', this is the most commonplace of the statements in the whole passage. The less frequently mentioned 'heavenly session' of Christ (Eph. 1.20b) is not found in the Colossians parallel, but appears in a quite different, ethical context later at Col. 3.1. The writer of Ephesians seems to be especially interested in the vision of Christ seated in heaven, as is clear from the claim later in the epistle (2.6) that Christians too have been made to sit with him in the heavenly realms. It is less clear whether he thought of this as a separate event from that of the resurrection, in the manner of Luke-Acts (see further on 4.9 below). The soteriological application at 2.6 implies that he did not, since the resurrection and enthronement of *believers* can hardly be two distinguishable events.

Being seated at the **right hand** of God is a motif drawn from Ps. 110.1: 'The Lord says to my lord, "Sit at my right hand until I make your enemies your footstool".' This was an early Christian proof-text for the resurrection of Christ (cf. 1 Cor. 15.25; Rom. 8.34; Acts 2.34f.), and was developed with greater emphasis on its christological implications at Heb. 8.1 (cf. Mark 12.35–7). It should be noted that the psalm speaks about 'the enemies' (of the Israelite King) being 'made the footstool'. When Eph.1.22 says that 'all things are put under his feet', the allusion is no longer to Ps. 110.1 but to Ps. 8.6, 'You have put all things under his feet', which refers to the primal dominion of Adam (cf. 'the Son of man' at Ps. 8.4). Nevertheless, the similarity between these two psalms invited conflation, given current Jewish methods of exegesis, and Paul had indeed combined them already in his discussion of the resurrection at 1 Cor. 15.25–8 (on the use and influence of these psalms in the early Church, see further Hay 1973). While the text-form is the same, its use is quite different. For Paul the destruction of the powers (1 Cor. 15.24), including death (v. 26), is not complete until the parousia; the past tense of the psalm text is understood to have future reference (v. 28). Here in Ephesians, however, the formula is taken straightforwardly as a description of the completed work of the exalted Christ.

On the phrase, **in the heavenly realms**, as distinctive of Ephesians, see on 1.3 above.

21 The enthronement of Christ at the right hand of God puts him **over and above every principality and authority and power and dominion**. The second term in this list is usually translated 'power' in the standard designation of Paul's doctrine of fallen angels ('principalities and powers', *archai kai exousiai*). But 'authority' has been substituted in our translation, reserving 'power' (*dunamis*) for the third item, in order to retain the parallel and contrast with the true 'power' which is God's, mentioned already in verse 19. Although this list is similar to the one at Col. 1.16, the dissimilarities should also be noted. In Colossians three of the titles are the same, but in the plural, in a different order, and the list begins with 'thrones' – a concrete and vivid metaphor used instead of *dunamis*. Ephesians is actually closer to 1 Cor. 15.24, where 'power' appears to be normal Pauline terminology (see also Rom. 8.38). While 'thrones' as the term for a type of angel is not unknown from Jewish sources (*2 En.* 20), it is not found anywhere else in the Pauline corpus and in the present context would, in any case, have created a conflict with the metaphor of enthronement: the insubordinate angels are not to be sat on, but stamped on!

Modern scholars, who are perhaps unlikely to share Paul's belief in fallen angels opposed to the power of God needing to be overcome and subordinated if harmony is to be restored to the universe, are tempted to look for some kind of contextual justification for such a peculiar idea. Influence on Ephesians from Colossians, where Paul may be combating a Jewish Christian 'deviation' that put Christ alongside others in the category of an angel, provides one such justification. Other possibilities are anti-pagan polemic or political apologetic. But, as the relatively unprovoked references to the idea in e.g. 1 Cor. 2.8 and 15.24 and Rom. 8.38 demonstrate, this was simply part of the 'mental furniture' of Paul and was shared by the writer to the Ephesians.

The doctrine of fallen angels, supernatural beings who inadvertently obstruct or deliberately oppose the rule of God, is an ancient Jewish idea (Gen. 6.1–4) which comes into major prominence in later apocalyptic (cf. Dan. 12; *1 En.* 6–9, 15). The armies of Yahweh, under Michael the loyal archangel, are pictured as ranged in heaven against an equivalent force in the devil and his angels. This 'cosmic conflict' idea helped first-century Jews to explain various kinds of counter-evidence to their monotheistic belief – the apparent attractiveness and influence of idolatrous pagan cults, all kinds of magical manipulations of the physical environment, the self-divinizing Roman state, the dread sense of God-forsakenness in certain people and places, the fear of death and the underworld, the vagaries of fate and the arbitrariness of disease and misfortune, and any other little gremlins in the system. Neither Paul nor the writer of Ephesians needed any special reason to refer to this perceived reality behind the world in which they lived (contrast Arnold 1989; Faust 1993; see further on this topic Odeberg 1934 and Wink 1984).

The purpose of the motif of Christ's exaltation above the powers is the assurance it gives that ultimately the Church will share in his victory: the exalted Christ has attained the position of God's vicegerent so that the continuing resistance of the powers is useless, even if they are still active among the sons of disobedience (2.2) and capable of assaulting believers (6.12). The author of Ephesians is less clear than Col. 2.15 that the powers have already been shown evidence of their own defeat (cf. further on 3.10), but the difference is merely one of expression and does not indicate a fundamental difference in theology between them. Other New Testament authors maintain a similar tension between the 'already' and the 'not yet' of the defeat of Satan (compare Luke 10.18 with Luke 22.53; and John 16.11 with John 13.27).

Finally, it is probably no accident that Colossians and Ephesians, in spite of their differences, both agree on including four items in their lists (cf. also Eph. 6.12). The powers that are to be overcome are the dark side of the universe, the radiant heart of which is the four dimensions of the all-embracing love of Christ (see on 3.18). One might compare also the four beasts (now reformed and obedient, contrast Dan. 7) in Rev. 4.6–8, and the four horsemen of the Apocalypse (Rev. 6.1–8); and, when Satan is released from the abyss for one last fling, devastation will be caused in all four corners of the earth (Rev. 20.8; cf. Mark 13.27).

We have taken the view, in agreement with the majority of commentators, that the 'powers' represent malign opposition to God's plan of salvation or at best blind obstruction. Carr (1981), however, has argued for a different interpretation, seeing them as good angels and Christ's exaltation over them as intended merely to emphasize the uniqueness of his share in the sovereignty of God. This view, however, owes more to the conception of Hebrews (1.1 – 2.10) than to that of Paul (cf. 1 Cor. 15.24–6), and Eph. 6.12 (see below) is decisively against it.

The preceding list was not exhaustive, so the author continues **and all the other names they are known by** (lit. 'and every name that is named'). It is unlikely that this is merely dismissive ('whatever they are called'), given that four names for them have already been listed; or that 'calling upon the name' has the connotation of worship (as at 1 Kgs 18.24), since some disapproval of the idolatry involved would be expected. Nor is God the implied subject of the passive verb 'named', as though by naming them in the first place he showed his authority over them, for that would detract from their necessary subjection, and unlike the (expurgated) list of abstractions in Ephesians, some of the names that fallen angels arrogate to themselves are distinctly blasphemous. The phrase therefore simply indicates that the writer is aware of other ways of referring to 'principalities and powers', such as 'death and life, angels, things present, things to come, height, or depth' in Paul's memorable doxology at Rom. 8.38. (For the superiority of the name of Jesus above the names of the powers, see also Phil. 2.10.)

The explicit assertion here of the 'two ages' doctrine of Jewish apocalyptic should be noted, **not only in this age but in the age to come**, because although Paul clearly subscribes to it (see his references to 'this age' in Gal. 1.4; 1 Cor. 1.20; Rom. 12.2; cf. also Rom. 8.38: 'things present and things to come'), he nowhere expresses it in quite so unqualified a manner. For Paul, the age to come has already begun (cf. e.g. 1 Cor. 10.11) with the resurrection of Christ. The writer of

Ephesians, of course, should not be taken to deny this (certainly not after 1.20), but the need from the context for an expression of comprehensiveness evokes from him this traditional Jewish formulation.

The largely realized eschatology of Ephesians and its preference for spatial rather than temporal categories is a major point of similarity with post-apostolic and especially Johannine tradition (see Introduction, pp. 37–8). But the outlook of Ephesians and the Fourth Gospel is constructed on a foundation of apocalyptic; it does not arise from its abandonment. The idea that there are even worse powers than those which are active now, who will only emerge later at the arrival of the age to come, is found also in the references to 'the lawless one' at 2 Thess. 2.7f., and 'the beast from the sea' with a blasphemous name upon its heads at Rev. 13.1–10.

22 On the citation from Ps. 8.6, **and 'he has placed all things under his feet'**, see above on verse 20. The wording is slightly different from that in the LXX (and Heb. 2.8), in that it uses a finite verb and has 'under' (*hupo*) for 'underneath' (*hupokatô*). It is, however, identical with the form of the text used by Paul at 1 Cor. 15.27, and this had probably become the standard way of quoting this testimony in Pauline circles. Although some connection with 1 Corinthians 15 is likely, the central point there, the identification of 'the power' as 'death, the last enemy', is not made explicitly here. 'All things' in the text of Psalm 8 originally meant the whole created order subject to the reign of God's human viceroy. But in its present context, following verse 21, 'all things' must refer mainly, even if not exclusively, to the powers in the invisible heavenly realm. On the combination of the themes of the restoration of the dominion of Adam and the subjection of the powers, see further on 3.10.

The formula being used continues with **and given him to be head over all things**. If the writer were drawing directly upon the Old Testament, he might have chosen to fill out the meaning of the citation of Ps. 8.4 by continuing with its next verse: 'and crowned him with glory and honour'. That would have rounded off the thought in a way congenial to someone interested in the enthronement and present kingship of Christ (see 5.5) at the right hand of God. But instead, the psalm text is left behind, and the author inserts **for the Church**, introducing the first explicit reference to his dominant concern in the letter, the Church as the body of which Christ is head. This key idea will be developed in later passages.

Before we comment further on this, the grammar of the clause requires some explanation. Normally, a dative after 'he gave' would indicate the indirect object: 'he gave Christ *to the Church*'; but theologically that would be a startling notion. It would be more fitting to say that God gave the Church to Christ (as at John 17.9) or at least that Christ gave himself for the Church (5.2, 25) or took the Church to himself (5.31). For this reason, the possibility that 'he gave' is a minor semitism for 'he *appointed* Christ as head for the Church' has commended itself to some commentators (see also on 4.11 for this sense of the verb). The cosmic lordship of Christ would then be 'for the benefit of the Church'; and the allusion to 'appointment' would constitute a further echo of Psalm 110, 'Sit thou at my right hand'. This may well be what the writer intended to say, but he has expressed himself in a way that is open to misunderstanding. The explanation of this ambiguity proposed by some (e.g. Sanders 1965 above) is to take 'for the Church' as an addition by the writer of Ephesians to the traditional formula he is using. That neatly solves the problem. In any case, the translation **as head over all things** is inevitable; for the writer cannot mean that Christ is given to the Church as 'its supreme head' (*pace* Barth 157f.), since 'all things' must surely have the same sense here as it does in the first half of the verse.

The immediate reason for describing Christ as 'head' is probably the preceding reference to feet – an obvious contrast to make (see 1 Cor. 12.21). But in the Bible, and elsewhere, 'head' is a common metaphor for leader or ruler (see Deut. 28.13; 2 Sam. 22.44) and the idea of Christ as the head over the powers is emphasized in Col. 2.10, as it is here. A second, less obvious connotation of 'head' is 'origin' or 'source'. Paul seems to employ both senses simultaneously in 1 Cor. 11.3–12, where God is the head of Christ, Christ of man, and man of woman (v. 3; compare v. 8, drawing upon Gen. 2.23 and 3.16) – an argument that is also to be used by the author of Ephesians at 5.23. What we do not find in Paul (until Col. 1.18 and 2.19, unless these references are later additions) is any co-ordination between the ideas of Christ as head (ruler/source) and the Church as body. These two ideas, intimate incorporation into Christ and the sovereign lordship of Christ, are both vital constituents of Paul's thought, but when the images of head and body are combined, they begin to fight with each other. If the Church is the Body of Christ and Christ is its head, then Christ becomes merely a member, albeit the most important one, in something, the Church, which is larger than himself. The author of Ephesians will later propose an ingenious solution to this problem, when he speaks of the Church and Christ as two whole and complete bodies joined together 'in one flesh' on the eschatological wedding day (see Eph. 5.22–33 and cf. Rev. 21.9–11).

The word **Church** (*ekklésia*) is used nine times in Ephesians. It is the ordinary Greek for an assembly or meeting (lit. 'a calling out'), often in political contexts. But the biblical concept of 'the assembly of the Lord' (e.g. Num. 20.4), the covenant people assembled for worship, has clearly coloured its Christian use. The early Church gradually adopted this term as its standard self-designation over against that of the 'synagogue' (a Greek synonym, lit. 'a coming together') to describe both local congregations of believers meeting in private homes, and the whole network of such congregations ('the Church of God', see 1 Cor. 10.32; Gal. 1.13; cf. Phil. 3.6). The tension between these concepts of the Church, the local and the universal, did not become so apparent until structures of organization and control developed at the international level in the third and later centuries. When that happened, of course, it became a major source of internal controversy and dissent in the history of the Christian Church.

In Colossians, the word is used in both senses of the local community (4.15f.) and of the whole company of believers (1.18, 24). But all the references in Ephesians are to the universal Church, for this epistle is not, in its present form, addressed to the local concerns of any one congregation.

It is unlikely, however, given the root meaning of *ekklēsia* and the ordinary secular use of the word for a public meeting, that the writer of Ephesians has entirely moved away from understanding the term *per se* in reference to the concrete reality of Christian communities, to some kind of transcendent, heavenly and invisible entity; when he wants to develop those aspects of his ecclesiology he turns to other terms and images like the temple (2.20–1) and the bride (5.27), in contexts which at the same time imply the idea of further development towards a glorious future reality.

23 The relative clause **which is his body** looks very much like part of the same parenthetical gloss, to be taken with 'for the Church', because its insertion creates a massive problem of interpretation in the last phrase of the sentence.

The image of the Church as the Body of Christ is one of the Apostle Paul's most creative and profound contributions to theology. Various explanations of its origin have been proposed, Stoic, gnostic, eucharistic etc., but it seems most likely to be derived from Paul's fundamental belief in the resurrection of Jesus, whose glorified body anticipated the general resurrection of the dead. Christians were enabled to share in that anticipation by corporate union with the risen Christ, just as in Jewish apocalyptic 'the saints of the most high' (Dan. 7.22) were understood to be incorporated into their heavenly representative, the 'one like a Son of Man' (Dan. 7.13). In 1 Corinthians Paul appeals to the body image constantly in a variety of applications: the Church as Christ's body entails purity and ethical exclusivity (1 Cor. 6.15), sacramental fellowship (1 Cor. 10.17) and an eschatological inclusivism (1 Cor. 15.22). The developed analogy for congregational life of different parts of the body working together co-operatively in 1 Corinthians 12 (cf. Rom. 12.4) is, therefore, only one part of a much grander conception. (On the body of

Christ in Paul see Davies 1967: 36–57; J. A. T. Robinson 1952; Moule 1977; cf. also D. Martin 1994.)

Paul also uses other images to describe the Church, including temple (1 Cor. 3.16) or building (1 Cor. 3.9) and bride (2 Cor. 11.2), but it remained to the author of Ephesians to start to bring these varied images into coherent relation with each other (see below on 2.20–22 and 5.32). The claim, however, that the writer has distorted Paul's teaching on the body of Christ, moving it from a metaphor into metaphysics, abandoning the local reference altogether and replacing it with a cosmic one, is questionable. For if Paul's concept is based on his eschatology, as we have just suggested, then already, in its earliest formulation, it was no mere metaphor. It involved a metaphysical dimension, inasmuch as the resurrection of Christ anticipates the final reconciliation of all things in him (1 Cor. 15.21f., 27 and 45).

Those who see Ephesians as dependent on Colossians face a certain dilemma in regard to the similar co-ordination of head and body images and emphasis on the universal Church in the two letters (cf. Col. 1.18 and 2.19). Lincoln, for example, concludes his discussion of the relation of Ephesians to Colossians by allowing one of two options (lxviii): either 'the writer of Ephesians considered Colossians to have come from Paul himself' or 'he may have believed Colossians to be Pauline in the sense of being the product of another follower of Paul, possibly while Paul was still alive, and therefore treated Colossians as the model of the sort of writing that could be done in the Apostle's name'. On the other hand, in his discussion of the body concept at Eph. 1.23, Lincoln speaks of a development of the Pauline image that had occurred '*by the time of* Colossians and Ephesians' (71, my emphasis). On literary grounds, Lincoln has to give temporal priority to Colossians; but on the theological question, he abandons it. It may be easier to see Col. 1.18 and 2.19 as secondary expansions of Colossians along the same lines as the development in Ephesians (see Introduction, p. 9, and below on Eph. 4.15).

The interpretation of the notoriously difficult phrase **the fullness of the one who is filling everything completely** depends on the resolution of a number of ambiguities. The main ones are: (1) To which of five previous ideas does 'fullness' (*plērōma*) refer? Is it 'body', 'him' (i.e. Christ), 'Church', 'head', or, generally, the whole of the preceding sentence? (2) Does *plērōma* mean 'that which fills' (the contents), 'that which is filled' (the container), or the quality of 'fullness'? (3) Is the present participle (*plēroumenou*) middle or passive, 'filling' or 'being filled'? (4) Is the subject of the participle masculine or neuter, 'the one who' or 'that which'? (5) Are the words translated 'everything completely' (lit. 'all things in all ways') the object of a middle verb, i.e. 'the one who fills the universe in every way', or an adverbial phrase after a passive verb, 'the one who (or that which) is being filled entirely'?

We shall not consider all the possible permutations in this list of ambiguities, but only those that are reasonably likely.

(1) In the present form of the text, it is almost inevitable that *plêrôma* will be taken to refer to the Church. However, if the words 'for the Church which is his body' are taken in parenthesis, as a comment by the editor, comparable to 4.25 and 5.30 (so, de la Potterie 1977 and others), then the original referent is more likely to have been Christ. In Colossians, the christological referent of the word *plêroma* is beyond question: 'in him the fullness of God was pleased to dwell' (Col. 1.19) and, emphatically reasserted using the present tense, 'For in him the whole fullness of deity dwells bodily' (Col. 2.9). Similarly, in Ephesians – though in expressions that owe nothing to Colossians – to know the love of Christ is to be 'filled with all the fullness of God' (3.19) and 'the stature of the fullness of Christ' is what Christian maturity aims to achieve (4.13). Nowhere else in undisputed Paul or Colossians does fullness refer to the Church. Nevertheless, the addition has created an ambiguity which the editor was presumably willing to live with. For the Church is to become what Christ already is (compare the parallelism between them at 3.21: 'to him be glory in the Church and in Christ Jesus').

(2) The Greek word *plêrôma* means 'the result of the action of filling'. It can refer either to the 'contents' of something that has been filled (or in a temporal sense, as at 1.10, to 'fulfilment') or else to the resulting abstract quality of 'fullness'. *Pace* Robinson 255–9, there are no indisputable examples of the word meaning 'that which is filled' in the *true* passive sense, i.e. that which is available to be filled, viz. an empty container. The few examples that Lincoln is able to provide (75) are to be understood as cases of transference, from the substance that fills to the thing that is full. This happens in English too: 'he drank a full glass of beer' does not imply that the glass itself was consumed. Furthermore, the 'passive' sense of *plêrôma* cannot refer to something which is in the process of being filled; it must mean that which is already full, including, and without distinguishing it from, its contents. Therefore reference to Col. 1.24, where Paul says 'I am filling up in turn (*antanaplêrô*) what is lacking in the sufferings of Christ' is not relevant here. It is safest to conclude that the term originally referred to Christ (see above) and that an editorial insertion has created a statement that implies an even more realized eschatology in relation to the Church than the writer expresses elsewhere.

'Fullness' is the sort of word that lends itself to hyperbolic religious use (cf. Rom. 15.29). So to search for some technical allusion behind it is probably unnecessary. Stoicism did use the word technically to refer to the omnipresence of the divine spirit (see Ernst 1970), in opposition to the Epicurean doctrine of the void. It was also picked up by the second-century gnostic Valentinus, who used it to refer to the pantheon of paired aeons that emanate from the supreme deity (see Stead 1969). It is sometimes claimed that Paul was himself confronting a 'proto-Valentinian' heresy in Colossians and borrowing and 'disinfecting' the vocabulary of his opponents. But that would be a dangerous manoeuvre, since it would at the same time concede the seriousness of the heretics' views and afford them the compliment of reinterpretation. Paul's tactic in Colossians is more confrontational: the error is 'vain deceit' (2.8), with vacuous and petty rules for inducing visions (2.18) which are, in fact, no more than 'fleshly self-indulgence' (2.23). Whatever is the case in Colossians, however, there is nothing in Ephesians so far, and hardly anything later, to imply a hidden set of inverted commas around the word *plérôma*.

(3)–(5) The last three ambiguities are interrelated and may be taken together. The participle in the present tense can be passive, 'that which is being filled', only if it refers either to the Church or to the cosmos. It can hardly refer to Christ 'being filled with God' (*pace* Best 185), for that is not a process but a completed fact, from all eternity indeed. Nor can it refer to the Church if, as in the present form of the text, *plérôma* has already done so. Therefore, if the verb is passive, it must mean that the Church is the fullness of the *cosmos* which is gradually being filled up. This is quite plausible as an interpretation of the phrase: the Church is that part of the universe where the summing up of all things in Christ (1.10) has happened already as a sign and foretaste of its future completion (cf. Col. 1.6: 'the word of the Lord has come to you, as indeed in the whole world it is bearing fruit and growing'). However, to conclude such a paragraph with a reference to the cosmos being filled would be to end on something of an anti-climax. The related discussion of the subjection of all things under the feet of Christ in 1 Cor. 15.20–8 ends on a high point, 'that God may be all in all' (1 Cor. 15.28). Unidentified participial forms in doxological contexts similar to this almost always refer to God: see Phil. 1.6, 'the one who began a good work in you'; 1 Thess. 5.24, 'the one who calls you is faithful'; and Rom. 16.25, 'to the one who is able to strengthen you'. Thus to take the verb as a middle is preferable (so also Lincoln 76) and the subject as God or Christ, who is 'filling all things completely'. This has the added advantage of allowing 'all things' to be understood in the same sense as it is in verse 22, of the cosmos. (See further, in addition to the major commentaries, Overfield 1978 and Dawes 1998: 236–50.)

In conclusion, then, whereas the traditional material that is being used to expand Paul's prayer probably spoke of Christ as the fullness of the all-filling God, the present text of Ephesians is patient of another meaning, that the Church is the fullness of the all-filling Christ. Both are acceptable to the writer of Ephesians, and indeed for him, in the end, scarcely distinguishable (see on 5.31f.).

II Jews and Gentiles (2.1–3.13)

A   Saved by grace (2.1–10)

(1) You also being dead to your trespasses and sins (2) in which you once walked according to the aeon of this world, according to the powerful ruler of the air, that is the spirit now at work in the sons of disobedience, (3) among whom also we all once lived in the desires of our flesh, doing the bidding of the flesh and the mind, and we were children of wrath by nature like the rest – (4) but God, being rich in mercy, because of his great love with which he loved us, (5) has made us, dead as we are to trespasses, alive together with Christ, (by grace you are saved!) – (6) and has raised us up together and made us sit together in the heavenly realms in Christ Jesus, (7) so that the excellent riches of his grace in his kindness towards us in Christ Jesus might be demonstrated in the aeons to come (8) (for by grace you are saved through faith! – and this does not come from you, it is God's gift, (9) it does not come from works lest anyone should boast), (10) for we are his handiwork, created in Christ Jesus for good works that God has prepared us in advance to walk in.

According to the conventions of Hellenistic letter-writing (see Doty 1973; Aune 1987), after the greeting and prayer report, the body of the letter should be indicated with a new beginning and a statement of the main purpose in writing. Philippians is a good example of this structure: greeting 1.1–2, prayer report 1.3–11, followed by the letter body, 1.12ff., 'My brothers, I want you to understand . . . ' (cf. also 1 Thess. 2.1; 1 Cor. 1.10; Rom. 1.16).

Ephesians, by comparison, is very confusing. The initial *berakah* was expanded with a description of the sender and addressees; the prayer report was similarly extended with statements of basic doctrine; but there is nothing to mark the transition to the letter's main theme. This passage could therefore be treated as still part of the prayer report (so Ramasoron 1977). But, if so, where would it stop? The whole of the first half of the letter, down to the second prayer report (3.14–19) and doxology (3.20–21), might be reckoned as introduction. The concluding moral exhortation starts already at 4.1 and constitutes the whole of the second half. Ephesians would then be a letter with a head and a tail, but no body at all! And that analysis might be correct, if Paul or his imitator had no particular reason for writing and nothing in particular to say to whomever the letter was directed. A more plausible explanation could be that the letter structure has been obscured by the process of editing an underlying source, expanded with the help of extra traditions.

Paul's letters were intended not just to be read, but to be heard, as they were read aloud in the context of meetings for worship (see the comment on 3.4), so the conventions of public speaking, rhetoric and homiletics, are not irrelevant factors in their interpretation (see Kennedy 1984; Johanson 1987). The picture of Paul in Acts as an accomplished orator who can conduct his own defence (Acts 22.1; 24.10; 26.2) or deliver a speech in the Athenian Areopagus (Acts 17.22) is obviously exaggerated, but then so are Paul's own denials of his competence in this field (1 Cor. 1.17–21). His critics had to acknowledge the power of his letters, and their dismissive comment about his oral performance (2 Cor. 10.10) is probably based on an isolated incident (2 Cor. 2.1). The apostle must have heard speeches in the law-courts, eulogies of the great and the good and political debates in the assembly – the three main types of Greek rhetoric – and been affected by them, at the very least subconsciously.

Another and rather different source of influence on the structure and style of Paul's letters was the Diaspora synagogue, with its conventions of preaching, prayer and exegesis. Elements of each of these forms can be detected in Paul's genuine letters, combined in a highly idiosyncratic way. If Ephesians were a purely literary construct, closer to a speech or homily than a letter, then one would expect its architecture and rhetoric to be more formal and sharply defined. But this is not the case (*pace* Lincoln, and see Introduction, pp. 6–7). The genre of Ephesians is even more mixed, indeed confused, than that of the genuine Paulines.

Appeal to past experience, in the form of a distinct narrative section (*narratio*) at the beginning of a speech, is a feature of Greco-Roman rhetoric (and indeed of Jewish homiletics). But this passage, 2.1–10, bears very little resemblance to that form. True, touches of 'narrative' have appeared in the preceding paragraph (1.20), and the Gentile past of the supposed readers will be recalled again in a similar way in two later passages (4.17–24; 5.8–9). This 'once/now' pattern is a recurring motif in Ephesians (as it is in Paul's letters generally, see Tachau 1972). But these elements do not constitute the formal principle of its literary construction.

Defeated by the problem of entitling this section according to its form, we find almost as much difficulty describing it in terms of its content. So many themes are packed into these few verses. We have chosen to highlight the idea that does at least occur more than once, 'saved by grace' (vv. 5 and 8); but 'dead to sin' is also a repeated phrase (vv. 1 and 5) and other topics, e.g. demonic powers, the lusts of the flesh, new life as co-resurrection and co-session, the kindness of God, faith and works, could claim to be equally important.

The passage is built up around two slogans that may have been common in Pauline circles, expressed in the second person plural:

> And you being dead to trespasses,
> God has made alive together with Christ.

and

> By grace you have been saved through faith!

These represent respectively the salvation-historical and existential poles of Pauline theology. The writer seems to be providing a commentary on these traditional formulae. 'Trespasses' ('transgressions' or 'lapses', see below on v. 1) are explained as the sins of disobedience (v. 2) in a Jewish Christian way that retains a positive function for the Mosaic Law. These sins involve both the devil (v. 2) and the flesh (v. 3). They deserve divine retribution, but God is merciful (v. 4), gracious (v. 5) and kind (v. 7). He has in Christ given life to the dead, which means that believers already share in his resurrection and heavenly reign. It is this christological faith, and not virtue, which is the opposite of sin and brings salvation. Thus boasting is excluded (v. 9) and good works flow naturally from the grace and providence of God (v. 10).

The theological purpose of this section, if not the structure and process of its composition, is reasonably clear. It is to provide a restatement, from a Jewish Christian point of view, of Paul's doctrine of salvation (so Becker and Luz 1998: 134; see also Luz 1976; Lincoln 1983; Gese 1997: 146–70), stripped of its controversial elements. For Paul himself, when formulating his doctrine, had daringly adopted the key term of his Jewish critics, 'righteousness' ('justification'), and twisted its meaning against them. God's righteousness is not, he had claimed, the satisfaction of the Law's demands; it is the power and forgiveness of God demonstrated and enacted in the eschatological events of the death and resurrection of Jesus. The grace of God is to be received on the basis of faith in Christ, not of membership through circumcision of ethnic Israel. The transforming effect of grace will produce in believers the fruits of the Spirit as a free response, in contrast to what Paul as a Christian saw as the slavery of the Law. Paul's protest against the sustained harassment of his mission by Diaspora Pharisees (Phil. 3.2), such as he once was himself (Phil. 3.5f.), provoked from him some extremely polemical statements that seemed to put the whole of the Sinaitic revelation into question and gave rise to accusations that he was promoting a corrupt form of libertine Judaism for non-Jews (Rom. 3.8).

This bitter controversy continued to reverberate in the post-Pauline period, as many of the later documents in the New Testament testify.

The Epistle of James takes the opposite course to that taken by Ephesians and repudiates Paul's teaching: 'You see that a person is justified by works and not by faith alone' (Jas 2.24). 2 Peter adopts a middle position, blaming the 'error of the lawless' on 'ignorant and unstable' interpreters of what Paul in his wisdom really meant (2 Pet. 3.15–17). Luke-Acts and the Pastorals are also sensitive to the possible misunderstanding of Paul's doctrine (e.g. Acts 13.39; 1 Tim. 1.8). But of all the writings in the New Testament it is the Johannine corpus that comes closest to the view of Ephesians, which uses realized eschatology, christological faith and ecclesial union with Christ to reconcile the Jewish Christian and the Pauline understandings of salvation.

This whole paragraph, like the preceding two (1.3–14 and 1.15–23), consists of a single, heavily overloaded and ungrammatical sentence in which participial, relative, purpose and causal clauses with explanatory asides are strung together in a way that makes analysis difficult. Both the wandering syntax and the cross-currents of thought may point, as before, to the phenomenon of editing and expanding traditional materials. The sentence starts abruptly with the object 'you also', but the subject 'God' does not appear until verse 4, and the verb not until verse 5, with the object there repeated but changed from the second to the first person plural. Without the intervening and following elaboration, the core of the paragraph is 'you being dead to sin, God has raised together in Christ Jesus' – a slogan which is authentically Pauline (see on 2.1 below). In addition, there are two interjections, 5b and 8, which are bracketed in thought as well as grammar and stand apart from the rest of the sentence, and again express a Pauline commonplace: 'By grace you are saved through faith', although Paul would probably have used the word 'justified'.

1 You also. The preceding paragraph has referred to the saving act of God in Christ; it is now applied to believers. 'God raised Christ (1.20) ... and you also (2.1) ... he has made alive (2.5) and co-resurrected' (2.6). The intervening verses, however (i.e. 1.21–23 and 2.2–4), largely obscure this sequence of thought. Most new paragraphs in Ephesians are clearly marked with a 'therefore' or some such phrase (see e.g. 2.11; 3.1; 3.14). This is an exception, with its abrupt 'You also'. If it is intended in its present form to be linked with what immediately precedes it (see the discussion above), one might have expected an adversative conjunction, contrasting the glory of the Church with the sinful past of believers. But the theme of the Church, as stated in 1.23 and central as it is in Ephesians, surprisingly does not appear at all in this passage.

The variation in this section between the second person plural (vv. 1–2, 5b, 8) and the first (vv. 3, 4, 5a, 7, 10) is a phenomenon we have already encountered. This could be simply a literary device, oscillating between the pointedness of direct address and rounded expressions of solidarity. Or it could be that some differentiation is intended between 'you' (Gentile Christians of Paul's original mission church in Ephesus) and 'we' (Jewish Christians like Paul and the editor himself). With which group the actual readers of the letter would identify is not so clear-cut. Gentile Christians of the post-Pauline church at Ephesus may have associated themselves with those the author is addressing, while Jewish Christians may well have aligned themselves more with the author himself. The following passage, 2.11–13, explicitly emphasizes the Gentile identity of those addressed, and here also the domination by world powers (v. 2) may imply the typically Gentile sin of idolatry. But the 'you' of verse 1 has, by verse 5, become 'us' and the aside 'by grace you have been saved' cannot be directed only to Gentiles. Furthermore, when an explanation of that phrase is offered in verses 8–10 it is in terms more relevant to the debate between Jewish Christians and Jews.

Kreitzer (1997: 41–8) has argued that the second person plural refers to the church addressed (which he locates at Hierapolis, 31–40), while the first person refers either to its mother church at Colossae, from which the pseudepigrapher is writing (as at 2.3), or is inclusive of both communities (as at 2.4). But it is difficult to discern any indication in the text of such a switch in geographical referent and the theory fails to account for the similar phenomenon when it appears in the letter to the Colossians (see Col. 2.13).

Attempts to explain the variation between the first and second person plural in this section in a consistent redactional way are generally unconvincing. It is caused, in part at least, by the fact that the Pauline traditions which are at its core are retained in their 'you' form, while the editor expounds them in the 'we' form.

The phrase **being dead to your trespasses** is ambiguous. It could, taken on its own, describe either the positive condition of believers now or their negative situation in the past. The participle is in the present tense, though the tenses of participles in Greek do not necessarily have temporal significance. At 2.13, 'being once far off' clearly means 'having once been' and, by parity, we could translate here 'having once been dead (in) your trespasses', along with the majority of translations and commentaries, influenced probably by the parallel at Col. 2.13: 'And you having been dead in trespasses and in the uncircumcision of your flesh, God has made alive with him.' But when Ephesians is read without presupposition from our knowledge of Colossians, 'dead to trespasses' is more naturally understood to be a positive idea, i.e. delivered from them through union with the crucified Christ. The closer parallel to this thought would be Rom. 6.11: 'Consider yourselves then to be *dead to sin* but alive to God in Christ Jesus.' Thus, what at first appears to be a striking similarity between Ephesians and Colossians has been caused by the use in both of the same formula, but its context and development in each of the letters are very different.

The author here speaks of **sins** in the plural and he will include a long passage describing them in detail later on (4.25 – 5.20). Although he understands Christians to be engaged in a continuing struggle with sin and temptation, he is also aware, as the next verse demonstrates, of the idea of the once-for-all transfer from the dominion of the devil. If he wanted to refer to the past as the state of being 'dead in sins', he should have said, 'having *once* been dead' rather than delaying the adverb to verse 2, 'in which you *once* walked', where it could imply a contrast with verse 1 rather than a continuation of the same line of thought. Commentators who translate 'You were dead through your sins in which you once *lived*' unwittingly further compound the difficulty! There are in fact very few passages in Paul where a sinful life is equated with a living death. But when the idea does occur unequivocally (in Rom. 7.9, 10, 13) it is in the context of an argument against the Jewish Law.

The terms **trespasses** and **sins** appear to be treated as synonyms (see on 1.7). That is less clearly so in genuine Paul, for whom 'trespasses' means acts of disobedience to known commandments, while 'sins' are intrinsically evil acts which can be committed even in the absence of law (Rom. 5.13). Paul uses both these terms more often in the singular than in the plural. Trespass (*paraptóma*) in the singular often denotes the fall of Adam (six times in Rom. 5.15–20). But it is also used in the singular of a forgivable offence committed by a Christian (Gal. 6.1) or of Israel's lapse from election (Rom. 11.11f.). The plural references (Rom. 4.25 and 2 Cor. 5.19) are exceptional and formulated under the influence of the LXX. Similarly, sin is usually singular in Paul and as such has a more menacing and dramatic sense, referring to the power that dominates unredeemed humanity. It is used only rarely of particular sins (Rom. 7.15; 1 Cor. 15.17).

The effect of identifying the two terms 'trespasses' and 'sins' is to bring back into Christian currency the Jewish understanding that defines sin as lawlessness (see 1 John 3.4) and disobedience to commandments (see 1 John 3.24).

2 The relative pronoun that introduces the next clause, **in which you once walked**, is actually feminine, agreeing with 'sins' as the nearest antecedent, but it is probably intended to include 'trespasses' as well (but see further on v. 3). The wording invites comparison with Col. 3.7: 'among *whom* (viz. the offspring of disobedience) you once walked', but while the wording is similar, the meaning is different. Furthermore, this parallel is widely separated from the parallel to the previous verse (Col. 2.13). If Colossians were the source for Ephesians, one would have to suppose a conflation of these two verses, ignoring the context of each and all their intervening content. A preferable explanation of the similarity is probably that these phrases represent standard parlance in Pauline circles (see also Best 1997b: 69–85) which has been reused in different contexts and senses.

'Walking' is a semitic idiom for conduct or ethical behaviour and is frequent in Paul (e.g. 2 Cor. 4.2) and John (John 8.12). It will figure prominently in the ethical section of the letter (see on 4.1). We should note here especially the contrast between once 'walking in sins with the sons of disobedience' (cf. also 5.6) and now 'walking as children of light' at 5.8.

According to the aeon of this world. Aeon is a Greek word that we have transliterated because of the controversy surrounding its meaning. It is usually rendered 'era' or 'period of time'. In the New Testament it often refers to 'this present age' or 'world order', with or without the demonstrative adjective, and stands for the Hebrew *'olam*, which can mean both 'world' and 'age'. Behind this usage is the distinction in Jewish apocalyptic between this age of sin and disobedience and the coming age of judgement and salvation (see *TDNT* 1, 202–4; cf. on 1.21 above). Seen against such a background the construction would be a pleonasm typical of the editor, 'according to this world age'. This is indeed the way the word is used elsewhere in Ephesians (see below on 2.7). And Paul himself speaks strikingly of 'the god (*sic*) of this aeon' (2 Cor. 4.4) or 'rulers of this aeon' (1 Cor. 2.6, 8) (cf. John 12.31; 14.30; 16.11).

Given the parallel with the following clause, an alternative interpretation has been offered that draws on Hellenistic and gnostic backgrounds. This takes 'Aeon' as a proper name for a supernatural being. The cult of a deity bearing this name is known from pre-Christian times (see Nock 1934). Ignatius writing to the Ephesians (Ign. *Eph*.19.1f.) also understands aeons to be supernatural beings. On this reckoning Eph. 2.2 would be a rare occurrence in the New Testament of the technical personified sense of Aeon which is quite common in later gnostic texts (see J. M. Robinson 1988: e.g. 108, 279, 514). It would then be possible to explain this as a rather indirect polemic. Aeon, as the name for a lesser deity, would have been downgraded in the cosmic hierarchy and identified with the devil. However, unlike Colossians, where the polemic against deviants is overt (see Col. 2.8ff.) and the technique of polemical reinterpretation of their terminology has often been claimed, in Ephesians it is almost entirely muted (but cf. on Eph. 5.6–13). And if the intended audience of Ephesians were mainly Jewish Christians they would inevitably have taken 'aeon' in its temporal sense and were unlikely to have been aware of any other. It is preferable therefore to take the first phrase in that way, and the following two as elaborations of it, to produce a sequence of complementary but distinct ideas, i.e. according to this sinful world-age, its transcendent evil ruler and its immanent spirit in the heart of unbelievers.

Our translation **according to the powerful ruler of the air** assumes that 'powerful' (lit. 'of power') is adjectival, qualifying 'ruler', though it is possible to take it as a separate noun and translate 'the prince of the power (i.e. domain) of the air'. The realm of evil for this writer is not subterranean but the lower reaches of the upper world, the no-man's-land between heaven and earth (see Eph. 3.10; 6.12; and compare *Asc.Isa.* 7.9, 13), where evil forces reign in a malevolent and/or arbitrary way over the lives of human beings on earth and try to hinder their ascent to the presence of God. This does not mean, however, that the author could not have conceived in addition of an underworld as the resting-place of the dead (see on 4.9). Paul's tripartite view of the universe (Phil. 2.10) is not necessarily at odds with what Ephesians says here.

The preoccupation with astrology and magic in the writer's pagan environment may help to explain what is meant (see Arnold 1989). But a multi-layered upper world is also a feature of Jewish apocalyptic. This schema both enhances the sense of divine transcendence and also offers an explanation of the existence of the devil and his angels, who, though fallen away from God, still remain superior to, as well as enemies of, the human creation (see Meeks 1993: 111–29). The Christian way of salvation eliminates the intermediate barrier between heaven and earth by allowing believers to ascend through it in union with Christ, just as the Son ascended to the right hand of the Father (cf. 1.20; 4.11).

The evil ruler in the heavens has a counterpart on earth, **the spirit now at work in the sons of disobedience**. 'The spirit' is in the genitive here, and the most natural construction grammatically is to take it in apposition to one of the preceding nouns, either the air or the power of the air. The overlap in meaning between air and spirit (wind) might support this. The ruler of the air would then also be the ruler of the spirit in the disobedient (so e.g. Lincoln 96). But the writer's point is to warn against the insidious activity in which this 'spirit' is currently engaged ('now at work'), not to emphasize its subordination to some nameless superior power. So it is better to explain the peculiar genitive less precisely as an attraction into the case of what precedes it, but not grammatically subordinate to it.

This 'spirit' could, then, either be a supernatural personal being, another way of describing the evil ruler in some earthly manifestation, or a facet of depraved human character, equivalent to 'the spirit of disobedience'. It is difficult to decide between these two options. At 6.12 the word 'spirituals' (*pneumatika*) rather than 'spirits' (*pneumata*) is used, and this might indicate some hesitation on the part of the author in ascribing fully personal attributes to the powers of darkness. In Paul, the spirit normally refers to the activity of God himself rather than to an angel or devil, but there are exceptions, e.g. 1 Cor. 2.12: 'the spirit of the world'. In the rest of the New Testament, 'unclean spirits' is a regular way of referring to demons in the Synoptic Gospels, and the Johannine Epistles are particularly insistent on distinguishing good from evil spirits, like 'the spirit of antichrist' (1 John 4.3) who is 'the spirit of error' (1 John 4.6).

The Hebrew idiom **the sons of disobedience** means those 'characterized by' rather than literally 'born from' disobedience. It should not be taken to imply that certain people are congenitally incapable of obedience. It is the equivalent term to 'children of wrath' in verse 3, indicating disobedience as the basic human sin and wrath as the divine reaction to it. Here it could either reflect the Jewish way of speaking about pagans or the Jewish Christian way of speaking about non-Christian Jews. There are so few overt references to the contemporary situation of the writer – naturally enough – that we cannot tell whether it is Jewish or pagan opposition to the gospel that he has in mind. Paul speaks at 1 Thess. 2.16 of God's wrath in connection with persecuting Jews who oppose his message of salvation for the Gentiles. Similarly John 8.44 refers to Jewish opponents as 'children of the devil'. This could well be included within the meaning of the phrase here (see on v. 3 below). When the author repeats it at 5.6, it will be in reference to people who are in close enough contact with the community that it needs to be warned not to be deceived by their empty arguments.

3 After the emphatic 'you' which has dominated the first two verses, it is slightly surprising to find an admission in the first person plural, **among whom also we all once lived**. 'Among whom' could also be translated as 'in which' – they are indistinguishable in Greek. If we do so, it could refer back to the trespasses of verse 1 (so Robinson 155). In support of this suggestion each of the terms, 'sins' and 'trespasses', would then have its own relative clause, sins being defined as Gentile idolatry and trespasses as offences against Torah. But in the present form of the text, that antecedent is so distant that the translation 'among whom' is almost inevitable.

The word for 'we lived' (*anestraphêmen*) can merely indicate 'dwelt among' (cf. Matt. 17.22); or it can have the added connotation of behaviour (2 Cor 1.12) and would then be parallel to 'you walked' in verse 2. Taking the adverb 'once' (*pote*) with it, the statement implies that 'we' once lived among and consorted with the sons of disobedience but have now separated ourselves from them. The 'we' is ambiguous: is it inclusive, 'all of us Christians, we and you together' or does it differentiate the writer (and those who identify with him) from 'you'?

'We *also*' surely points to the latter. If that is correct, the situation implied may be one of a recent separation from 'the sons of disobedience' on the part of (Jewish) Christians – which is precisely the situation of the Johannine community (see John 9.22). 'The sons of disobedience' would then take on an added meaning, not only the pagan idolaters 'among whom *you* walked' but also the hostile Jews 'among whom *we* once lived'. For further discussion of the situation implied, see below on 5.6–14 and Introduction, p. 36f.

That former association is described as having been **in the desires of our flesh, doing the bidding of the flesh and the mind**. 'The flesh' here, emphasized by repetition, has a negative moral connotation typical of Paul's usage, e.g. Gal. 5.16 (see below on 2.14). It is natural to think of carnality and sexual desire as the besetting sin of pagans (see below on 4.19), but the addition of 'and the mind' (lit. 'of the thoughts') may be intended to include other, more intellectual, vices. The word (*dianoia*) does not occur in the undisputed letters, though it appears in the gospel version of the great commandment to 'love God with all the mind' (Mark 12.30). It is used in the singular at Eph. 4.18 of former Gentiles, as 'darkened in their understanding'. But here it may refer also to the attitude of non-Christian Jews. For the 'flesh' has wider connotations than merely sex. In particular, it is possible to represent Jewish opposition to the gospel as caused by a fleshly, unspiritual mind, a heart (the seat of the will and intellect) veiled to the truth (see 2 Cor. 3.15). At Phil. 3.19 Jewish opponents (cf. Phil. 3.2) seem to be the ones attacked with the phrase 'whose god is their belly' (cf. Col. 2.18) and in the same way Jewish scepticism about the Christian doctrine of rebirth, represented by Nicodemus in the Fourth Gospel, is called 'that which is born *of flesh*' (John 3.6). Pagan sensuality and Jewish unbelief may both equally be described in terms of 'the desires of the flesh and the mind'.

Like 'sons of disobedience' in verse 2, **children of wrath** is a Hebrew idiom. It is the way Cain is described in *Apoc.Mos.* 3.2 (cf. Jude 11 and 1 John 3.12). Wrath is divine judgement (not human anger) and this formulation has much the same sense as 'child of perdition', the description of the eschatological anti-Christ at 2 Thess. 2.3, embodied already, according to John's Gospel, in the figure of Judas Iscariot (John 17.12). These parallels point to the conclusion that 'children of wrath' refers to hostile opponents of the Christian message. **Like the rest** shows that it is not just former Gentiles who are in view. On the contrary, the contrast between 'we' and 'you' implies that it may be non-Christian Jews who are particularly under God's wrath (cf. 1 Thess. 2.16 and see below on verse 4).

The children of wrath are so **by nature**. It is illuminating to compare and contrast Gal. 2.15, where Paul says of himself and Peter 'we who are Jews *by nature* and not Gentile sinners' with Rom. 2.14f, where good

Gentiles 'do *by nature* what the Law requires'. In the first, 'by nature' means by race or birth; in the second, something like 'by instinct' or intuition. (Self-evidently, neither passage implies the later Christian doctrine of natural or original sin; not even Rom. 5.12–21, the standard proof-text for that doctrine, refers to an inbuilt human tendency to sin, for what Adam bequeaths to his offspring through his primal disobedience is not sinfulness but mortality.) The reference to 'nature' in the present context is similarly ambiguous: Gentiles may be 'children of wrath' by the circumstances of birth; non-Christian Jews by an evil instinct.

4 The subject of the sentence begun at verse 1 finally appears: **but God, being rich in mercy, because of his great love with which he loved us**. A grammatically redundant 'but' has been added to point up the contrast between 'wrath' (verse 3) and 'mercy' (verse 4).

The contrast between wrath and mercy is particularly important in Romans 9–11, where Paul reflects on the mystery of predestination (see esp. 9.15–23 and 11.30–2). There he compares 'vessels of wrath' with 'vessels of mercy' (9.22f.). But since the former have been 'hardened' by God himself (see 9.15, for Israel's rejection of her Messiah was foreseen in the divine plan), God will also eventually have 'mercy on all' (11.32) and embrace his recalcitrant chosen people once again. The author of Ephesians, despite his vision of universal reconciliation (cf. 1.10), does not seem to hold out much immediate hope of the conversion of unbelieving Jews to faith in Christ.

The editor is fond of duplicate expressions for the sake of emphasis, such as **because of the love with which he loved us** (see similar uses of a verb with its cognate noun at 1.6, 19 and 20). It is a common idiom in the Hebrew Bible and lends a solemn scriptural quality to the expansion here. The unnecessary repetition, however, invited alteration by the scribes: and P[46], with a few allies related to the Latin version, substitutes a different verb: 'with which he pitied us'.

5 At last the sentence is completed with the main verb **has made us, dead as we are to trespasses, alive together with Christ**. In the Greek the clause starts with an 'and' which could make it another relative: i.e. 'with which he loved … *and* made us alive'. But this way of construing the text would create even more chaos in an already hopelessly chaotic sentence, for there would be no main verb at all! The 'and' must be taken as 'also' or 'as we are', qualifying the participle (lit. 'us being *also* dead'). The compound verb 'make alive together with' (*sunzōopoiein*) occurs in the Pauline corpus only here and at Col. 2.13; but the simple form is not uncommon, referring to the future resurrection of the dead (e.g. Rom. 8.11 and 1 Cor. 15.22) and also to the present activity of the risen Christ (1 Cor. 15.45). It is followed, after a parenthesis, by two similarly constructed verbs (see 'co-resurrected', 'co-seated', v. 6). Paul is particularly fond of compound verbs with 'co-': 'co-buried' (Rom. 6.4), 'co-crucified' (Rom. 6.6), 'co-live' (Rom. 6.8) etc., and Ephesians reflects that preference here.

No doubt this 'making alive' becomes a conscious experience for Christians when they decide to be baptized, but theologically – and this is the overriding interest in this passage – it has already taken place prior to that decision, when Christ was raised from the dead (cf. 1.20), just as election before the foundation of the world (cf. 1.4) obviously precedes its realization on the part of believers. This explains the emphasis on grace in the interjection that follows (rather than faith, which is included in the formula only at its reprise in v. 8).

The change back from the first to the second person plural in the bracketed exclamation **(by grace you are saved!)** is unexpected and is probably the result of using a stock formula.

Paul uses the verb 'save' in the present or future tenses but not, as here, in the perfect, of the state that follows from an accomplished fact. (Rom. 8.24 is not really an exception, for 'saved in hope' there is obviously conceptually future.) When speaking about that aspect of salvation which has been achieved, Paul prefers to use 'justified' (Rom. 5.1; 1 Cor. 6.11) meaning 'acquitted' (the forensic equivalent of 'reconciled', see Rom. 5.10). By this Paul did not mean to exclude belief in a future justification or judgement at the end time according to good works (see Rom. 14.10 and 2 Cor. 5.10). He was simply turning his Jewish opponents' objection, that his teaching failed the test of 'righteousness', back against them. However, his language was open to a misunderstanding that the writer wishes to correct.

6 Romans (6.1–11) implies the doctrine that this verse makes explicit, that Christians in a sense share in the resurrection life of Christ: **and has raised us up together and made us sit together in the heavenly realms in Christ Jesus**. But Paul was careful to distinguish what is possible now, 'walking in newness of life' (Rom. 6.4), from what is still to come, 'we *shall be* implanted into a likeness of his resurrection' (v. 5). Because resurrection involves the body (see 1 Cor. 15.35ff.) and not just the spirit, Paul nowhere actually says that Christians have already been raised with Christ, except at Col. 3.1, assuming it is from Paul's hand. But even that reference still retains the Pauline eschatological reserve: 'If you have been raised with Christ, seek the things above where Christ is seated at the right hand of the Father'; Christians cannot be so elevated already if they can still be instructed to 'look up'!

The writer underlines the assurance of salvation with one of his favourite phrases, 'in the heavenly realms' (see on 1.3), and this leads to the further addition of 'in' before 'Christ Jesus'. But this expansion introduces a slightly different sense for the preceding compound verbs, not merely 'raised and seated *with* Christ' but 'raised and seated *with each other* in Christ'. The vertical relation *with* Christ, expressed in Paul's 'co-' vocabulary, is complemented with a horizontal relation with other Christians *in* Christ. To be one with Christ, Christians have to be united with each other.

The nearest parallel to this realized eschatology of the resurrection of believers is John 5.25: 'The hour is coming and now is when the dead will hear the voice of the Son of God, and those who hear will live.' But in John, as in Ephesians, the still remaining future hope is not entirely discounted. The passage just quoted continues with a literal, futurist statement: 'Do not be amazed at this, for the hour is coming when all who are in the tombs will hear his voice and come out.' Resurrection in John's Gospel is both present already in Christ (11.24f.) and still future (e.g. 6.39f.). This sacramental and charismatic assurance of the present possession of salvation did, however, lead to premature claims to moral perfection in the Johannine community (see 1 John 1.10) and to a consequent schism (1 John 2.19).

The unique feature of verse 6, absent from Colossians, is the idea of 'sitting together' with Christ in heaven. The future role of sitting in judgement promised by Jesus to his disciples at Matt. 19.28 (Luke 22.30, see further on 2.21 below) is echoed by Paul at 1 Cor. 6.2: 'Do you not know that the saints will judge the world?' The image is further developed by the seer of Revelation: 'He who conquers I will grant him to sit with me on my throne, as I myself have conquered and sat down with my father on his throne' (3.21), where the link between resurrection and session is made explicit. That this is not a purely future hope in Revelation is hinted at in the following vision, for 24 elders are *already* seated on heavenly thrones (4.4; cf. 11.16, 12 for Israel perhaps and 12 for the Gentiles). In a similar way Ephesians is referring to an eschatological hope as though it were already an accomplished reality. However, resurrection and enthronement with Christ, when translated into an ethical and exclusivist perfectionism, soon became a problem for sub-apostolic Christianity (see 2 Tim. 2.18).

7 The purpose of salvation is not already achieved; it still has a future and cosmic aspect. This is brought out in the next verse: **so that the excellent riches of his grace in his kindness towards us in Christ Jesus might be demonstrated in the aeons to come**. The thought of a final universal demonstration of divine grace in Christ was implied at 1.10, 'the plan for the fullness of time, that he might bring all things to summation in Christ'; and the wording here should also be compared with earlier references to 'the riches of his grace' (1.7) and 'the riches of his glorious inheritance' and 'the excellent greatness of his power' (1.18f.). We might also refer forward to chapter 3, where similar phrases recur: 'the unsearchable riches of Christ' (3.8) and 'the love of Christ that surpasses knowledge' (3.19) in the same context as the important parallel to this verse, 3.9–10.

At 3.9–10 'past ages' (aeons) during which God's plan of salvation was hidden are mentioned, but here the ages are still 'to come' (lit. 'the aeons that are on-coming'). The later passage will emphasize the Church's role in mediating knowledge of the varied wisdom of God to the principalities and powers. Attracted by this parallel and by the possible use of 'aeon' in a personal sense at 2.2 (see above), some (particularly German) scholars who detect an interaction with gnostic ideas in Ephesians (Conzelmann 1976: 97; Schlier 112f.) propose to translate 'demonstrated among the hostile aeons'. They take the participle 'on-coming' to mean 'hostile', 'coming upon' or 'against' (a meaning it can sometimes have, see Luke 11.22). But the combination of 'ages' with a present participle of a verb of movement is so common (e.g. Luke 18.30; Matt. 12.32; Heb. 6.5) and has already appeared in Ephesians at 1.21, right next to a clear reference to principalities and powers, that it is unlikely that anything other than a temporal sense can be intended here.

The fact, however, that the verse can and has been misunderstood as a reference to the revelation of the divine plan to the heavenly powers is itself significant. It shows that the editor is not sensitive enough on the point to put his meaning beyond doubt. This in turn effectively rules out direct opposition on his part to such deviant beliefs, whether astrological and pagan or mystical and pseudo-Christian.

8 The exclamation of verse 5b is repeated in almost the same words: **for by grace you are saved through faith!** But this time the slogan is extended with a reference to faith. Christians were referred to as 'faithful' at 1.1 and 'believers' at 1.20, and their faith in the Lord Jesus was commended at 1.15. Now the great Pauline watchword, faith (*pistis*), comes into even greater prominence. **Through faith** (or even more frequently 'from faith') occurs regularly in Paul; see especially Rom. 3.30, where both formulae appear together. Faith is there contrasted with 'works of the law' and sharply distinguishes the offer of salvation to all, whether Jew or Gentile, from the exclusive claim to salvation for law-abiding Jews alone, a claim such as Paul the Pharisee would once have made. This distinction is missing from Ephesians and the use of 'saved' in preference to Paul's term 'justified' (see on v. 5 above) also helps to smooth over a controversy in which Jewish Christians had serious reservations about Paul's polemical polarization of faith and law.

The subject of the qualifying clause, **and this does not come from you, it is God's gift**, could be either the whole idea of salvation by grace through faith (as Lincoln 112 and many others) or just the immediately preceding word, 'faith' (as Caird 53). The latter view has some merit, for it avoids the apparent platitude that salvation is the gift of God – a point that hardly needs making – and corrects a possible misunderstanding of 'faith' as the meritorious virtue of faithfulness. This interpretation, however, raises the further question, which Ephesians nowhere else addresses, as to how God decides, unless by arbitrary decree, to whom to grant faith and from whom to withhold it. An even stronger argument against Caird's view is that it requires verse 8b to be ignored when verse 9 is interpreted, even though they contain the parallel formulations 'not from you' and 'not from works', for the meaning of the latter must be that it is *salvation* that is not from works.

The question remains, then, why the author should think it necessary here to stress such an obvious point and say that salvation is a gift of God and not a human achievement. The closest parallel in Paul, in both grammatical construction and content, is Phil. 1.28, where the threats of persecutors are said to be 'proof of their destruction, but of your salvation – which is, of course, really of God!' (lit. 'and that from God'). What makes the qualification apposite in the Philippians passage is the ambiguity, in context, of the word 'salvation'; for in face of persecution it can have a this-worldly, material sense of escape or avoidance of a threat to life (see Mark 13.20). The addition of the phrase 'and that from God' is needed to make it clear that religious salvation is meant (which, indeed, is not inconsistent with actually losing one's earthly life in time of persecution, see Mark 8.35).

Surprisingly, the common Greek word for gift (*dóron*) used here is never found in Paul's undisputed letters; he prefers the form (*dórea*), which does appear in Ephesians at 3.7 and 4.7, verses that are more likely to derive from the source.

9 Salvation by faith **does not come from works lest anyone should boast**. Paul drew a sharp contrast between faith and works, meaning not good works (morality) but 'works of the law', the marks of Jewish identity, chiefly circumcision, Sabbath observance and the food regulations. And the boasting that he rejected, in the name of the one God of Gentiles and Jews, was the Jewish boasting of ethnic superiority as God's chosen people (Rom. 3.27). Ephesians has refocused the issue from ethnicity to ethics. Good works (see v. 10) are the result of salvation, not its cause; otherwise human beings could be said to earn their standing with God and that would render grace redundant. While Paul probably considered idolatry the cardinal sin (Rom. 1.18ff.), on this view it becomes pride, i.e. the refusal to acknowledge the need of God's forgiveness. The parable of the Publican and the Pharisee in Luke 18.9–14 illustrates a similar ethicization of the Pauline doctrine of justification (see Luke 18.14).

Hübner (1989: 392–406) has argued that verses 8–9, along with verse 5b, are later interpolations, since they have an epigrammatic, less diffuse style than their surrounding material and can be omitted without disrupting the train of thought. His observations are surely correct, but the absence of any textual evidence for later scribal corruption makes it more plausible to suppose that the writer has himself interpolated them to provide a condensed summary of what he takes to be the main thrust of Paul's teaching.

10 A further explanatory clause completes the section: **for we are his handiwork, created in Christ Jesus for good works that God has prepared us in advance to walk in.** If this depends on the preceding verse (as Lincoln 113) then it is an attempt to explain how human good works, although they are not the basis of salvation, nevertheless flow from it. But it may be better to see this verse as dependent on verse 7, explaining how the kindness of God expresses itself in the re-creation of human beings. And this must be so, of course, if the argument above is accepted, that verses 8–9, as well as verse 5b, are to be put in parentheses.

The noun translated 'handiwork' (*poiêma*) occurs only once elsewhere in Paul (Rom. 1.20), in the plural, referring to the works of the creator God and echoing Old Testament usage (see Ps. 92.5; cf. v. 4). When Paul wanted to refer to believers as made anew by God he used other terms, the new 'creation' (*ktisis*, 2 Cor. 5.17) and the 'work (*ergon*) of God' (Rom. 14.20). But since these two terms are already used up in the phrase 'created for good works', the author needs another synonym and so turns 'handiwork' or 'artefact' into a special term, indicated by its delay in the Greek to the emphatic position at the end of the clause, effectively God's *chef d'œuvre*. An unfortunate consequence of this formulation is that it opens up the possibility, no doubt unforeseen by the author but exploited later by Marcion, that the redeemed are the only true creation, the unique handiwork of the God and Father of Jesus Christ, while the physical creation is the product of an inferior deity.

Three rather different interpretations of **created in Jesus Christ** are possible, depending on whether the reference is to the creation of the world, the historic Christ-event or the present life of believers.

The least likely of these, it might be thought, is the first. Paul makes it clear when he is speaking of the 'new creation' (see esp. Gal. 6.15, and 2 Cor. 5.17) rather than the creation of the world. But our author seems to be less inclined to draw a sharp distinction between the two. He is about to refer to God's 'preparation in advance' of the redeemed for good works, which raises the question: how far in advance? (see below). The idea of preparation from the beginning of time has figured prominently in the opening blessing (1.4); so this first possibility should not be dismissed out of hand; it would parallel the statement at Col. 1.16.

Secondly, taking into account the way the same verb is used at 2.15, where Christ 'created' one new person in himself, the moment of creation referred to might be the historic event of the cross and resurrection: 'in Christ' would then be emphatic, meaning incorporation into Christ as the representative of the new humanity, in Paul's term, the last Adam.

The other use of 'created' in Ephesians points to the third possibility. At 4.24 the author expands the notion of 'putting on' the new human person with the words 'created according to God in the righteousness and holiness of truth' and the context of ethical exhortation shows that the reference is to the present Christian life.

It is conceivable that all three referents are intended and are being run together into a single moment, as they are in the Prologue-hymn to the Fourth Gospel (John 1.3, 9 and 13). These three senses of 'created' are in different ways appropriate to the aim of good works. The original plan of God in creation was that human beings should achieve life through obedience to their creator; Christ's redemption atones for past wrong-doing and provides the example of a life pleasing to God; and the re-creation of believers through faith and baptism enables them to walk in the way of righteousness.

That God has prepared ... in advance (lit. 'pre-prepared'). We should compare Rom. 9.23–4: God 'prepared in advance the objects of his mercy – including us whom he has called not only from the Jews but also from the Gentiles'. This is the only other place that Paul uses the verb 'prepared in advance' and with a personal object.

The grammar of the present clause deserves a comment. The relative pronoun 'that' is in the dative; if it has been attracted into the case of its antecedent, then it is the good works themselves that God has prepared in advance (so Lincoln 115). But it is more likely that people, not what they do, are the object of divine predestination. To achieve this meaning, **us ... to walk in** (lit. 'that (*hina*) we should walk in them') must be understood as the object of the verb (viz. 'our walking in them')[5] and the relative pronoun then becomes an anticipation of 'in them' at the end of the sentence. So what the author intended was 'in which God prepared us in advance that we should walk' (cf. also JB: 'to live the good life as from the beginning he had meant us to live it').

The 'ethicization' of Paul's doctrine of justification (see above on v. 9) requires this final statement; for if salvation by faith is a gift (v. 8), then

---

[5] Although a *hina*-clause normally indicates purpose, it can have a substantival sense; see Moule 1971: 145.

the doctrine of the last judgement will seem arbitrary and immoral unless one adds that, in deciding who is to receive the gift, God foresees the good works they will go on to produce.

B One in Christ *(2.11–22)*

(11) Remember that you were once Gentiles in the flesh, called 'the uncircumcision' by those who are called 'the circumcision' in the literal, human sense, (12) that you were at that time alienated without Christ from the polity of Israel and strangers to the covenants of promise, having no hope and godless in the world. (13) But now in Christ Jesus you who were once far off have become near in the blood of Christ. (14) For,

> **He is our Peace**
> **who has made both one**
> **having dismantled the dividing wall,**
> **the enmity in his flesh,**
> **having abolished (15) the law of commandments in decrees,**
> **in order that he might create the two in himself**
> **into one new person, thus making peace,**

(16) and might reconcile both to God in one body by the cross, having by it killed the enmity,

(17) (and when he came he preached peace to you who were far off and those near)

(18) because through him we both have access, in the one Spirit to the Father.

(19) Surely then you are no longer strangers and sojourners but you are fellow citizens of the saints and members of the household of God, (20) built on the foundation of the apostles and prophets with Christ Jesus as the very cornerstone (21) in whom a whole building fitting together grows into a holy temple in the Lord, (22) in whom you also are being built up together for a dwelling place of God in the Spirit.

The previous section has interpreted salvation by grace in terms of the co-resurrection with Christ of those who are dead to trespasses, including 'you' (v. 1) as well as 'us' (v. 5). We argued above that verses 1–10 were a post-Pauline resumé and reinterpretation of Paul's doctrine of justification by faith, with echoes in particular of Rom. 1–8. The framework of the present section offers a different but complementary angle on salvation, more like that of Rom. 9–11. It stresses the priority of Jewish Christians as heirs of the covenant and the inclusion of the Gentiles to share in their privileges.

Into this framework has been inserted what many commentators take to be a pre-formed liturgical hymn to Christ our Peace (see below on v. 14). It is fitted into its new context by an introduction (v. 13), and possibly by the addition of v. 17 (see below). On closer inspection, certain tensions between the text and the context become apparent: the bringing near of those far off is an image for unity different to that of which the hymn mainly speaks, the breaking down of barriers between mutually hostile parties and between them both and God. The references to the destruction of 'the enmity in his flesh' (v. 14) and 'the law of commandments in decrees' (v. 15) sound more radical than anything in the surrounding framework of the hymn, or indeed than anything else in Ephesians, though they are reminiscent of Paul. These tensions are, however, eventually resolved in the image of the Church as the new Temple of God (vv. 20–22) in which the distinctions, which were reflected in the very architecture of the old Temple, of near and far, Jew and Gentile, God and humanity, are finally abolished.

The similarities between this section and Colossians are superficial rather than substantial: 'circumcision made with hands' at Eph. 2.11 means simply 'literal circumcision', while Col. 2.11 contains the more profound idea of a spiritual 'circumcision not made with hands' through baptism; the same verb 'alienated' is used at verse 12 and at Col. 1.21 but with different connotations ('alienated from Israel'/'alienated from God'); coming 'near through the blood of Christ' (v. 13), 'making peace' (v. 15) and 'by the cross' (v. 16), while separate in Ephesians, are all run together in one phrase at Col. 1.20: 'making peace through the blood of his cross' (see the comments below on these and other minor points of similarity). What is more striking in this passage is its independent liveliness, especially in the hymnic section which is not derived from Colossians and is most unlikely to have been constructed out of bits and pieces from it.

11 Remember that you were once Gentiles. The contrast between the old life and the new now turns from moral (vv. 1–10) to ethnic categories (vv. 11–22). In the preceding section the author was careful to make it clear, by dropping into the first person plural at verses 3, 5 and 10, that Gentiles were not the only ones guilty of sin, disobedience and fleshly desire, for 'all equally have sinned' as Paul himself had said (Rom. 3.23). But in this section the initial focus is on the salvation-historical priority of the Jews, again as Paul had argued (Rom. 11.1–2a).

The supposed audience is told to 'remember' that they were once Gentiles in the flesh and suffered contempt from the Jews. Such a reminder might appear rather unnecessary. Who could ever forget that they were ethnically non-Jewish? Kirby (1968: 129) explains the emphasis on 'remember' as a *liturgical* recalling of the pre-conversion past. But the more natural context for that kind of admonition would be not liturgy but ethics, and indeed a similar passage in an ethical context will appear later (see 4.17–24). More likely, therefore, is the view that the command to 'remember' belongs to that 'long retrospect' (Goodspeed 1933: 35) which reflects the post-Pauline situation of those who had, for some while, lived in a community that claimed true Jewishness for itself. By the time of the writer of Ephesians, Christians may well have thought of themselves as the sole legitimate inheritors of the promises to Israel (cf. Matt. 21.43), having transcended the Jew/Gentile distinction. In that case, such a reminder would take on a different function; it would warn Gentile readers not to think of themselves as superior, as the substitute people of God, and reassure Jewish Christians that they were the holy remnant and the root into which Gentile believers had been grafted. Paul, of course, had made the same point already in Rom. 11.16f., with reference perhaps to a particular situation in the Roman church; here it has become a general principle.

Translators often take 'that you were once Gentiles' in verse 11 as a redundant anticipation of the real object of the verb, which comes only in verse 12: viz. 'Remember that you, once Gentiles in the flesh, [remember I say] that you were at that time alienated' etc. On this understanding, the readers are not being reminded of their racial origins as such, but only of the various disadvantages of not belonging to the elect people (so Lincoln 123; Schnackenburg 104). But that construction is extremely awkward. The length of the description of Gentile status in verse 11 suggests that it stands in its own clause and that 'at that time' in verse 12 adds a new point, picking up 'once Gentiles' and explaining it in more detail.

What kind of situation would be served by this reminder of Gentile origins? It is rather hasty to conclude, with Lincoln (136) and others, that we can deduce from this verse that the actual readers of the letter must have been 'predominantly if not exclusively Gentile'. For in a pseudepigraphon, the actual audience is not the same as the fictive audience. In fact, the wording of the verse points in the opposite direction. It is open to hearers of this text to identify themselves with Paul, rather than with those he is supposed to be addressing; and the apostle is here represented as someone who believed that Jewish Christians and their traditions should be treated with respect by those who – they should never forget! – were once Gentiles. Ephesian Jewish Christians could be 'overhearing' Paul putting the Gentiles of the congregations he founded in Ephesus in their place, and it is they who were being reminded that Paul shared their viewpoint. Such a reminder was very necessary, since Paul was understood as an apostate from his ancestral religion by some at the time, both opponents and enthusiastic followers alike. Ephesians, like Luke-Acts and the Pastorals in their different ways, attempts to put the record straight on this point.

Gentiles in the flesh. Unlike Colossians, the author of Ephesians shows no interest in any deeper connotations of this phrase. The word 'flesh' had negative overtones when it was used earlier (see 2.3; cf. also on 2.14) but here it is neutral. The reference to the flesh simply points to the physical identity mark of male non-Jewishness. In 3.1, 6 and 8, the term 'Gentile' reappears without any qualifier, in the normal Pauline manner, in the sense of non-Jew. But 'Gentiles' by itself can also have a morally negative connotation, as it does at 4.17. The editor is less happy than was Paul (at least in Romans 9.30; 15.9ff.; contrast 1 Cor. 12.2) to describe Christians as Gentiles *tout court*, for the division between Jews and Gentiles has been overcome by the reconciling work of Christ. This new situation is viewed here from a Jewish Christian perspective. Gentiles were formerly beyond the scope of salvation, since they were distant from its only possible source. Now they have been 'brought near' (2.17) and can share in the same privileges as Israel.

Gentiles are those who are **called 'the uncircumcision'**. Jews adopted the physiological term, 'foreskin', to describe by metonymy all races apart from themselves. To non-Jews the idiom would have been deeply offensive, if it were not so ludicrous to dismiss the great cultures of the Orient and of Greece and Rome in such an off-hand manner. They repaid the compliment, despising circumcision as a form of 'mutilation' – a pun which Paul at Phil. 3.2 turned on his Jewish opponents who advocated circumcision (see Bockmuehl 1997: 189f.).

By those who are called 'the circumcision'. The writer distances himself from the standard term by attributing it to others, as he has equally with its opposite. Some commentators prefer to translate here 'the so-called circumcision', implying that the writer would dispute the Jewish claim. Paul certainly does dispute it at Phil. 3.3 ('We are the true circumcision') and this may also be implied by the 'circumcision of Christ' at Col. 2.11 (cf. also Rom. 2.29 and Gal. 6.15f.). But there is no evidence of any anti-Judaic polemic in Eph. 2.11–13; indeed, these verses might fairly be described as anti-Gentile.

It is more useful to compare John 7.22, where the rite of circumcision, deriving from Moses (indeed from the patriarchs), is said to take precedence over Sabbath obligation and justify *a fortiori* Jesus' making a man whole on the Sabbath. The Johannine community, then, had no difficulty with circumcision as a Jewish custom, interpreting it as a ritual symbol of bodily healing. But having themselves been expelled from the synagogue, they would have had no particular interest in imposing their practice on Gentile fellow-Christians. The Judaizing controversy of Paul's day could have happened only while Jews and Jewish Christians were still attempting to live and worship together (Muddiman 1994, *contra* Watson 1986).

The translation **in the literal, human sense** renders rather freely the

Greek 'made with hands' (*cheiropoiêtos*), a compound adjective which occurs several times in the New Testament, often alongside its opposite ('not made with hands'). The contrast is not between 'manufactured' and natural, but between the results of human and divine action, sometimes with elements of another contrast between the literal and the metaphorical.

At Mark 14.58 the temple 'made with hands' is to be replaced in three days – an alleged saying of Jesus understood by the false witnesses at his trial as an attack on the earthly Temple, but by Mark's audience surely as a prophecy of his resurrection (cf. also Heb. 9.11 and 24). At two points in Acts, 7.48 and 17.24, the eternity and immateriality of God are expressed in the form of a denial that he dwells in a temple 'made with hands'. At 2 Cor. 5.1 Paul had described the risen body of Jesus, in which Christians who die before the parousia already share, as a 'house not made with hands, eternal in the heavens'. All of these examples have to do with the contrast between the earthly and the heavenly temple (see Eph. 2.21).

It is striking that the only two places in the New Testament where the word or its antonym is used to describe anything apart from the temple are the references to circumcision at Col. 2.11 and Eph. 2.11. But the similarity ends there. In Colossians, Christian circumcision is 'not made with hands' because it is both non-literal and the work of God, achieved through baptism. In Ephesians, the point is much more straightforward, namely that the ritual of circumcision creates no more than a physical distinction between Jews and Gentiles. It is clear from the references to the 'covenants of promise' in the following verse, which must include the Abrahamic covenant of circumcision, that the writer intended no disparagement of circumcision for Jews.

Rather than suppose Ephesians to have taken a rare word from Colossians, dropped its negative prefix and treated it as just another way of saying 'physically' or 'literally', it would be more plausible to take Colossians as a commentary on Ephesians, unpacking the implications of the term 'made with hands' and elaborating the notion of 'spiritual circumcision', and that remains one possibility. Alternatively, Paul might have used the phrase 'circumcision made with hands' somewhere in his letter to the Laodiceans, knowing that they would have the opportunity to read his deeper reflections on the idea when they read its companion piece to the Colossians, in the context of the refutation of the error which was promoting Jewish legal rituals as the means of obtaining mystical experience. The writer of Ephesians, on the other hand, is concerned not to continue disputes about judaizing practices. On the contrary, he wants to smooth over that old controversy and argue for peace and unity in the Church.

The practice of male circumcision was not, of course, confined exclusively to Jews; it was more widespread in the Ancient Near East, and Paul exploited this fact in Gal. 4.21f., in his reference to Ishmael, the ancestor of the Edomites who, though circumcised and born from Abraham, lacked the freedom and maturity that constitute true sonship. According to Paul, Jews who were so tied to the Law that they rejected the gospel of the Messiah were similarly bastard descendants of Abraham. Ephesians avoids such intemperate polemic.

12 The disadvantages of being a Gentile consist not merely in the physical difference (v. 11) but in spiritual defects that are now listed in two pairs of parallel clauses, the first two longer than the second. These assert that not to belong to Israel and her covenants is to be without the promise of the coming of Christ, and to lack this hope is to be lost in a godless world. Notice how closely the first idea, that to be 'alienated from Israel' is to be without Christ, corresponds to the second, that to be 'in the world' is to be without God. If Paul wrote these words, or something like them (see on 4.17–21), he was probably thinking of the pre-conversion situation of his addressees. In the wider perspective of Ephesians in this passage, it is the situation of non-Jews generally in the long past of Israel's salvation-history that is more likely to be in mind.

This list of disadvantages in verse 12 has often been compared with the nine advantages of the Jews enumerated by Paul in Rom. 9.4–5. Both mention 'Israel', 'covenants' (in the plural) and 'promise' or 'promises'. In addition, Romans has 'sonship', 'glory', 'the giving of the Law', 'worship' and 'the patriarchs'. The final and climactic item in Paul's list is 'the Christ after the flesh' (cf. 'without Christ' here), which evokes from him an outburst of praise (Rom. 9.5).

It is probably the similarity between these two passages that has led many commentators (Robinson 158 being a notable exception) to construe Eph. 2.12 differently and take **without Christ** as an independent complement rather than an adverbial phrase, i.e. 'At that time you were *without Christ*, alienated' etc. This is grammatically quite possible and would simply require a pause after 'Christ' in a spoken version for it to be certain; but one might have expected such an important idea to be expressed more emphatically, as it is indeed in Romans (see above), and at the very least for the name 'Christ' to be given the definite article.

There is a slight but not unimportant difference between these two ways of punctuating the sentence. The first explains the past plight of Gentiles as the result of their alienation from Israel: that is to say, if they had stayed within the covenants that God offered to all humanity, they would not have been 'without Christ' in the sense that they would have shared the hope of faithful Israel for the coming of the Messiah. The second implies that 'being without Christ' in some sense was itself the root cause of the problem for the Gentiles, from which the other deficiencies flowed. If the second punctuation is adopted, Barth's explanation of its implications (256), namely that there is an allusion here to Gentiles rejecting the 'pre-existent' Word (cf. John 1.3), would have some merit (*contra* Lincoln 137). However, there are obvious difficulties with Barth's view: it was by no means only the Gentiles who could be said to have resisted the light of the pre-existent Christ; Israel did so too (John 1.11; cf. 1 Cor 10.4f.); and this interpretation places an excessive burden of extra meaning on a relatively simple phrase that receives no special emphasis.

Whichever way the sentence is construed grammatically, the main theological point to notice is the priority that it strongly claims for old Israel. The difference between this statement and that of the genuine Paul in Rom. 9.4–5 could not be more striking. The tone of the latter in context is not at all congratulatory. Paul says that if he still wanted to belong to Israel, despite all her privileges, he would be 'cut off from Christ' (Rom. 9.3). The failure of his fellow Jews to accept their Messiah has alienated them and made them enemies of God (11.28). It is only through God's mysterious plan (11.25), his 'severe mercy' (11.22), that some ultimate good, through the very successes of his Gentile mission, may result for Israel. There is nothing at all of the irony and paradox of Paul in this passage of Ephesians.

Gentiles were formerly **alienated** (*apêllotriômenoi*) **from the polity** (*politeia*) **of Israel**. The language has political associations. 'Polity' is the term for 'citizens-rights' at Acts 22.28 or 'the state' itself at 2 Macc. 4.11; it does not occur elsewhere in Paul, though a cognate noun, *politeuma*, appears at Phil. 3.20 in the opposite sense to the one here, i.e. 'citizenship in heaven' possessed by all Christians regardless of their race. 'Alienated' is a word that occurs only here and in two other places in the New Testament, at Eph. 4.18 and Col. 1.21. In these other references it has again a very different meaning to its sense here, namely that of alienation from God (cf. e.g. Rom. 5.10) as the common condition of sinful humanity, whether Jew or Gentile. Perhaps the writer of Ephesians has borrowed this term from these more 'Pauline' uses and given it a Jewish Christian twist. Gentiles were once disenfranchised without Christ and alienated from the chosen people. Now, in Christ, they have been 'brought near'. In terms of day to day reality, it was Diaspora Jews who would normally have felt themselves to be excluded from the political process and treated as aliens (though there is some evidence that Jews in Ephesus, exceptionally, possessed the rights of citizenship, cf. Josephus *C.Ap.* 2.4.39; *Ant.* 12.3.2; see Hemer 1986: 38). At the theological level, however, which is the author's chief concern, it was the Gentiles who were excluded – or rather had excluded themselves – from the only possible source of salvation, namely Israel (cf., similarly, John 4.22). Their situation continues to be viewed from a decidedly Jewish Christian perspective.

Strangers to the covenants of promise. For Paul, especially in Galatians 4 and Romans 4, the covenant with Abraham was the covenant of promise *par excellence* and in sharp contrast to the Mosaic covenant of law. The promise to Abraham was specifically inclusive of Gentiles (Rom. 4.17f.). Indeed, Abraham was himself uncircumcised (Rom. 4.10) and theoretically a Gentile when he was justified, and yet he walked with God not as a stranger but as a friend. But in describing Gentiles here as 'strangers to the covenants of promise', the writer of Ephesians is departing from that Pauline position. For him the covenants (in the plural), including those with Noah, Abraham, Moses and David, all promise salvation in the future through Christ.

Reflection on Israel's salvation-history is clearly the main source of this perspective. But it may also have resonated with the writer's situation in Asia Minor after the Jewish War, as Faust (1993) has recently argued. There is a whole cluster of politically charged terms in this passage: 'alienated', 'polity', 'strangers', verse 12; 'unity', 'peace', 'enmity', verse 14; 'aliens', 'citizens', 'household members', verse 19. The destruction of the dividing wall (v. 14) may have included, at least for some readers, an allusion to the Fall of Jerusalem. Furthermore, a critique of Vespasian's post-war peace settlement, the *Pax Caesaris*, may be hidden behind the emphasis on the true peace, which is the empire of the crucified Christ. This theory can find further support from other features of Ephesians, such as the emphasis on 'principalities and powers' (assuming that they have some relation to earthly political structures), and it is not unlike the interpretation given to 2 Thessalonians, especially 2.1–12, by those scholars who take it to be a post-Pauline pseudepigraphon from about the same period.

One might object that the evidence Faust uses is all rather allusive; but it is reasonable to respond that the editor cannot allow himself to be explicit: overt anachronism would expose his pseudonymity. A more serious objection, however, arises from the fact that in the ethical section (4.1 – 5.20), where we should expect the political setting of Ephesians to filter into instructions about practice, there is nothing at all about relations between Christians and the Roman state. If, as Faust clearly believes, Ephesians is a pseudepigraphon written from a consistent viewpoint, this is a near-fatal objection to his theory. But on the supposition that an editor is working with a variety of sources, a political reading of 2.11–20 remains a possibility and we shall refer to it again as the commentary proceeds.

At 1 Thess. 4.13 a similar phrase to **having no hope** occurs: 'we do not grieve as those who have no hope'. There the hope referred to is for life after death. But in this context, having no belief in an after-life can hardly be said to be a distinguishing characteristic of the Gentiles. Indeed, according to the evidence of Josephus and the New Testament, it was a Jewish sect, the Sadducees, who, as a rare exception in the first-century world, rejected belief in life after death. The sense may be that the Gentiles had no hope of entering the age to come until they were included within the promises to the chosen people. If so, their former condition continues to be described in a very Jewish way.

In other passages in Ephesians where hope is referred to, it is closely related to the vocation of Christians (see 1.18 and esp. on 4.4), with no special reference to Israel's historic hope; but see the commentary on 1.12 for an emphasis very similar to the one here, also in a probably editorial passage.

It is most unlikely that Col. 1.27 has contributed anything to the idea of Gentile 'hopelessness'. The wording is very different and makes the opposite point, that the secret imparted among the Gentiles was 'Christ in you, the hope of glory', without any implication that the Jews had a hope which the Gentiles lacked.

Godless (*atheoi*). The word 'atheist' in English is derived from this, but there were very few atheists in the modern sense in antiquity; even the Epicureans, against whom the charge was sometimes levelled, acknowledged the existence of deities, though not the obligation for humans to worship them. It was more often Jews and Christians who were liable to this accusation from pagans, because of their refusal to participate in civic religion.

The word occurs only here in the New Testament or the Greek Bible, but in classical Greek tragedy it refers to deviant individuals who actively exhibit impiety towards the gods (Aesch. *Eumen.* 151) or whom passively the gods have abandoned (Soph. *Oed.* 661). Here all Gentiles as such are called godless, both in the sense that their worship of many gods (1 Cor. 8.5) and excessive superstition (Acts 17.13) are an idolatrous refusal to worship the one true God (Rom. 1.21) and also in the sense that God has accordingly abandoned them to futility (Rom. 1.24).

13 But now in Christ Jesus you who were once far off have become near in the blood of Christ. The pagan past of the Gentiles having been described, the author begins to contrast it with the present Christian life, reconciled to Israel and so to God through the sacrifice of Christ. The coming near in Christ directly parallels the alienation without Christ of verse 12. The 'then and now' temporal scheme is complemented in this verse by its spatial equivalent, 'far and near'. This theme continues in verse 17 and verses 19–22, after the hymnic passage, verses 14–16, 18.

There will be a clear allusion to Isa. 57.19 later ('Peace to the far and the near', see on verse 17 below). But commentators are divided over whether to see an allusion to it already in verse 13. Stuhlmacher (1974), followed by Schnackenburg (112), argues that verses 13–18 should be taken together as a Christian exegesis of a series of texts from Isaiah (Isa. 9.5f.; 52.7 and 57.19). But other scholars are more inclined to see verse 13 as the writer's introduction to a block of traditional, hymnic material (vv. 14–18) built around the theme of peace (see below).

In addition to the allusion to Isaiah in the phrase 'far and near', Lincoln (138f.) detects a reference to the Hellenistic Jewish terminology of proselytism. A proselyte in Greek is literally 'someone who has *come near*' to Israel. However, we cannot be sure that the later rabbinic texts he cites, which interpret Isaiah in this way (*Melch. Exod.* 18.5 or *Num.R.* 8.4), reflect ideas already current in the first century, nor that contemporary Jews were particularly interested in proselytizing (see Goodman 1994). It is more likely that the writer is simply expressing the way he understands the status of Gentile Christians: they were once 'far off' but through their faith in the atoning death of Christ have been 'brought near' to the true Israel and thus to salvation.

The standard formula, **the blood of Christ**, is found frequently in Paul's letters (Rom. 3.25; 5.9; 1 Cor. 10.16; 11.25; see above on 1.7). The idea that access to God is achieved through the blood of sacrifice would be natural to any Jew or Jewish Christian. Within the New Testament it is particularly characteristic of the Epistle to the Hebrews (see e.g. 4.16). But we should also note that access in this passage is achieved through the destruction of barriers between Jews and Gentiles, the clean and the unclean, rather than through the cultic reinforcement of those distinctions.

The theory that verses 14–18 are a piece of early Christian hymnody comparable with Phil. 2.6–11 and Col. 1.15–20 has the support of many commentators (Schlier 122f.; Gnilka 147f.; Barth 261f.; and Lincoln 128ff.). Ephesians refers at 5.19 to the practice of singing hymns to the Lord and is probably quoting the chorus of one at 5.14. This has encouraged widespread acceptance of the hypothesis in this instance.

Although, as we have seen, there are some points of tension between text and context at the literary level, it would be wrong to assume that the basic outlook of the pre-formed material is necessarily going to be very different from that of the writer who chose to incorporate it. He must after all have thought it broadly relevant and consistent with what he wanted to say. So it is a questionable procedure, particularly in the case of Ephesians, to remove from the hymn everything distinctively Pauline in order to leave a residue that says something completely different.

Lincoln's reconstruction, which is by no means the least unconvincing of the many proposed, illustrates this problem. His hymn has eight lines and uses only verses 14–16, removing from them as the writer's glosses the phrases in square brackets:

1 He is our Peace
2 who has made both one
3 and has broken down the middle wall [of partition]
4 having abolished [in his flesh] the hostility [the law of commandments and regulations]
5 in order that he might create the two in himself into one new person
6 thus making peace
7 and might reconcile both to God in one body [through the cross]
8 having put the hostility to death in himself.

Reconstructed in this way the hymn no longer refers to the reconciliation of Jews and Gentiles at all or to the Jewish Law, but to 'cosmic' reconciliation between heaven and earth achieved through the person of a redeemer who unites humanity and divinity in himself.

The controlling motive behind this sort of analysis is usually to uncover evidence for the influence of the so-called 'heavenly Man' myth on the development of early Christology. The scholars of the History-of-Religions School (see Morgan 1988: 124–32; *DBI* 291–2), particularly Bousset (1921) and Bultmann (1956), were convinced that the cosmic Christology of Paul and John could not be explained, given Christianity's matrix in Jewish monotheism, unless some sort of catalyst from oriental gnostic thought were posited. In their view Christians borrowed or imitated gnostic myths and hymns, modifying them with reference to the kerygma of the cross and resurrection. Lincoln is rightly cautious about this theory (129) but he does not seem to recognize how far it is affecting his own reconstruction.

If we ask a simple question: Is the author more interested in cosmic Christology or in the abolition of the Jewish Law? we surely have to conclude from the number of references elsewhere in the letter that he is more interested in Christology. Would he, then, have obscured the original sense of 'he made both one' by placing it in a discussion of the reconciliation of Jews and Gentiles and adding here his only reference to 'the law of commandments in decrees', echoing a battle long since fought and won in Pauline congregations? That is unlikely. It is more probable that the editor has retained the phrase from his source, because it does not have to be read as the complete abolition of the Law (see below). If he deliberately added the phrase himself, it would be necessary to take it as more emphatic.

The commentary below will defend an alternative, ten-line recon-struction, including verses 14–16 but also verse 18, as follows:

1 He is our *Peace*
2 who has made *both* one
3 having dismantled the dividing wall,
4 the *enmity* in his flesh,
5 having abolished the law of commandments in decrees,

6 in order that he might create *the two* in himself
7 into one new person, thus making *peace*,
8 and might reconcile *both* to God in one body by the cross,
9 having by it killed the *enmity*,
10 because through him we *both* have access, in the one Spirit to the
   Father.

In this scheme, the second half of the hymn is a fuller restatement of all
the elements of the first. Christ is the peace that makes both one (lines 1–
2) because he creates out of the two a new person in himself, and so
makes peace (6–7). The dividing wall (3) was dismantled and
reconciliation achieved in the crucified body of Christ (8). The enmity
was destroyed (4) because it did not kill him, he killed it (9). The law of
commandments in decrees was abolished (5), and access was finally
opened in Christ to the Father in the Spirit (10). Furthermore, the first
person beginning ('our Peace', 1) is echoed in the first person ending
('we both', 10) and the hymn achieves satisfactory closure in a
doxological conclusion.

We will discuss the details in the verse by verse commentary that
follows; suffice it to say at this stage that there is nothing in the hymn
which could not have come from Paul himself, or at least from Paul's
own time. The hymn in one respect might imply an origin pre-AD 70, if
it alludes metaphorically to the destruction of just one feature of the
Temple (rather than the whole edifice, see below; but see also Faust's
view, under v. 12 above).

14–15a For, he is our Peace. The addition of the conjunction 'for'
attaches the hymn only loosely to the preceding verse. The sequence of
thought in the mind of the writer may be that for Gentiles ('those afar')
to come near to Israel, there has to be peace between the two groups.
Alternatively he may have thought the tradition appropriate as a way of
picking up and developing his reference to the blood of Christ in verse
13, explaining that this sacrifice was a peace-offering. Peace in the Jewish
tradition (see on 1.2) is a profound covenantal and eschatological
concept: it refers to Israel's relation to God and the promise of her
ultimate salvation. Peace also figured prominently in early imperial
propaganda for Roman rule. Both ideas may be present here, depending
partly on the cultural background of the reader, and to whom 'our' is
taken to refer. Thus Christ is the fulfilment of *shalom* for Israel and the
true alternative to the so-called *Pax Romana*.

Paul's hymns tend to begin allusively (compare Col. 1.15, 'Who is the
image' or Phil. 2.6, 'Who being in the form of God'), rather than with an
explicit identification of Christ as their subject, and the same is true here.
The indeterminacy of the language in this kind of canticle is deliberate: it
excites interest and invites imaginative participation. It might resonate

with the experience of its users at several different levels: peace with God through the sacrifice of Christ, peace between Jews and Gentiles in the Church, and peace in society, yet not that enforced by an imperial tyrant, but true peace, bestowed on humankind by the sovereignty of a loving God.

The equating of Christ with abstract nouns is a Pauline idiom (see 1 Cor. 1.30; 2 Cor. 5.21; Phil. 1.21 etc.). While this precise identification of Christ with Peace is unique here in the Pauline corpus, its sense is not far from that of Rom. 3.25 where God has presented Christ as a *hilastêrion* (meaning either 'peace-offering' or 'mercy-seat'). If so, a cultic context for the word might be implied, again for some readers, and this is picked up by several similarly cultic motifs in the following verses.

Who has made both one. 'Both' is a neuter pronoun here but there is a change at verses 16 and 18 to personal forms. Languages like Greek which frequently use gendered nouns for objects, are conversely freer than English, with its rigid demarcation, to use neuter nouns for persons. It is therefore unnecessary to suppose that the neuter must refer to impersonal entities that have been united, such as heaven and earth. It is natural for the unity that results from reconciliation to be expressed with the neuter 'one (thing)', and 'both' in the neuter then follows appropriately.

This opening line, when the hymn was used at baptisms (which would be one of several suitable settings for it), would express the idea that membership in the Church overcomes the divisive distinctions, not only of ethnicity but also of sex and political status (see Gal. 3.28). The neuter 'both' would further allow this plurality of reference.

The means by which division is overcome in this passage are soteriological; the work of Christ destroys division, enmity and oppressive regulations by breaking down barriers and creating a Church in which peace, reconciliation and common access to God are made available. This is to be developed ethically later in 4.1 – 5.20 and in the household code of 5.21 – 6.9, where mutual love and submission overcome the divisions in families.

The translation, **the dividing wall**, represents a redundant construction in the Greek, literally 'the middle-wall of a barrier'. This is a stylistic feature we have already encountered at 1.6, 19 (twice) and 2.2, but it is not in itself un-Pauline (cf. e.g. Rom. 1.23, 'in the likeness of an image', and see van Roon 1974: 197). The redundancy creates liturgical sonority and special emphasis, and allows extra time for the hearer to register the image and reflect upon it. Lincoln (141) suggests that 'of a barrier' is an addition by the editor, intended to make the hymn refer to the problem of the Jewish Law, but such an important reinterpretation (from a cosmic to a legal barrier) would surely need to be more explicit. So the pleonasm, in this instance, probably belongs to the hymn; it is too ambiguous to be a gloss.

The word 'middle-wall' (*mesotoichon*) occurs only here in the New Testament, but it is an easily understandable compound of its two elements. In classical Greek it normally refers to the shared wall between terraced houses. It could be removed entirely without causing the collapse of the building, or breached by a determined housebreaker from the adjacent property. Any undertone of this kind in the idea of breaking down a party wall would have to be very subtle and ironic, but it may not be impossible: the one who brings true peace and security does so in the manner of a thief in the night; see 1 Thess. 5.2f. (cf. also Rev. 3.3 and 16.15; Matt. 24.42f. and Luke 12.39f.).

The word for a barrier (*phragmos*) is formed from the verb to 'close', 'stop' or 'impede'. At Mark 12.1 it refers to the dry-stone wall encircling a vineyard, and at Luke 14.23 'paths and lanes' (the latter translates *phragmoi*) is a reference to country roads bordered by a stone wall, in contrast (cf. Luke 14.21) to town streets bordered by housing. These are the only other two instances in the New Testament, but it is the standard term, and in and of itself would attract no special attention. However, the combination of middle-wall and barrier is striking and has led to much discussion and speculation about the particular allusion intended.

Two main views are taken. Some commentators are certain that 'the middle wall of a barrier' alludes to the low wall at the far end of the court of the Gentiles in the Jerusalem Temple, mentioned by Josephus (*Ant.* 15.11.5; *B.J.* 5.5.2). It is true that Josephus uses a slightly more technical term for this barrier (*druphraktos*) but it derives from the same root. Two of the notices warning non-Jews not to cross the boundary on pain of death have been found by archaeologists (see *CIJ*, 2.1400). This interpretation fits well with the main theme of breaking down the barrier between Jews and Gentiles, and such a motif in the hymn would be taken up neatly by other allusions to details of the Temple's construction at verse 20. Other commentators (Caird 58; Lincoln 141) are adamant that this view is to be rejected and that the allusion is rather to the rabbinic notion of the Law as a fence dividing Israel from the nations, and this again fits well with the immediate context and with the reference to the 'law of commandments in decrees' in the next clause.

But there are several problems with both of these interpretations, especially the second. The image of the Law as a fence around Israel is mentioned in the *Epistle of Aristeas*, 139 (third or second century BC); this specific function of the Law is to prevent fraternization with Gentiles and preserve Israel from their idolatry. The image is explicitly one of a circular enclosure, like the wall around the vineyard in the gospel parable ('fenced around', Mark 12.1). However, in Ephesians the image is not one of enclosure but explicitly of partition. Furthermore, the rabbinic references in the *Pirke Aboth* (1.1f.; 3.18; see Str-B 3.588) are rather different; they see the oral law as a fence around the Torah, in the sense that the extra legislation of the scribes creates a protective margin, on the precautionary principle, against the danger of inadvertently transgressing any direct commandment of the Law of Moses. There is no reference in Ephesians to the Jewish 'tradition of the elders'; and the notion of oral law as a fence around the Torah cannot be shown to be earlier than the Mishnah (late second century). Moreover, to attribute such a scribal technicality to the writer of Ephesians (or to Paul himself for that matter, Acts 22.3 notwithstanding) is implausible.

An allusion to the partition wall in the Temple may be more likely. Even Gentile readers of the original letter, if this hymn formed part of it, or listeners to the hymn as it may have been used in worship in Pauline congregations, might have been able to pick up such a reference. And the sense of exclusion and inferiority, symbolically represented by the Temple barrier, could well have survived the actual destruction of the Temple in AD 70. Luke-Acts, for instance, assumes that its readers, some time after that event, would still know about the restrictions on access by non-Jews to the inner court (see the particular case of Trophimus, a native of Ephesus and companion of Paul, in Acts 21.28–9). Both Jews and Jewish Christians continued to draw lively metaphors from the layout of the Temple long after its fall. Similar to the image of destroying the dividing wall is the tearing of the veil that separated the Holy of Holies from the outer chamber; it is a motif that appears in the Synoptic accounts of the crucifixion allowing access to God through faith even for a Gentile (Mark 15.38 and parallel), and is developed with great subtlety by the author to the Hebrews (cf. Heb. 6.19; 9.3; 10.20.) A Jewish Christian would no doubt be in a better position than Gentile readers to appreciate the nuance of the barrier image and relate it to other Temple allusions in the hymn, but we have argued that the editor and most of his intended audience have a deeper background in Judaism than Paul's original correspondents. Such a limited and precise allusion is, however, not essential for the understanding of the imagery of the hymn.

Perhaps then, the 'dividing wall' of partition is not exclusively either the barrier in the Temple or the palisade of Jewish Law. It is rather constituted by *all* the expressions of social enmity, familiar to any Jew or Gentile in the Hellenistic world, the differences in place of residence, manner of worship, food and dress, politics and ethics, and above all the blank wall of mutual incomprehension, fear and contempt between the two groups. And this apartheid between Jews and Gentiles is understood here not as a legitimate peace-keeping measure, but on the contrary as the institutionalization of mutual antipathy. For real peace involves the abolition of such barriers (cf. Roetzel 1983).

Early Christians endeavoured to create a bridge between different ethnic groups, emphasizing what was common in human experience and manoeuvring around the continuing minor differences of custom and tradition. They took this stand for several reasons. On the practical level, they were able thereby to attract into the movement not only Jews and Gentiles but also 'god-fearers', Gentile inquirers into Judaism who might well be wealthy and influential members of society (cf. Acts 10.1; Luke 7.5). But the blurring of distinctions was also a matter of deep conviction. Since the Messiah had already inaugurated the beginning of the age to come by anticipating in himself as the last Adam the future resurrection of the dead, that other great eschatological hope, the in-gathering of Gentiles to join the elect people, had also become a possibility, indeed a missionary imperative.

The following phrase, **the enmity in his flesh**, can be taken in several different ways. First, in the wider context of the hymn, 'enmity' might be understood as the hostility between Jews and Gentiles. And a Christian reader of this text after the events of AD 70 could hardly fail to see in the Jewish War an extreme example of that enmity let loose. If the Jews had accepted Jesus as their peace-making Messiah, so Christians believed (cf. e.g. Mark 12.9), that disaster could have been avoided. This connotation of 'enmity' would be further reinforced if the word were taken in apposition to the preceding reference to the middle-wall, as it is in some analyses (see below).

In Paul's own letters, however, there is surprisingly little reference to the theme of enmity between Gentiles and Jews, for he was mainly preoccupied in practice with a different issue, the hostility of Jews towards Jewish Christians. And the way he uses the words 'enmity' and 'enemy' brings two other interpretative possibilities into play.

At 1 Cor. 15.24, death is seen as a personified power, 'the last enemy', due to be destroyed by Christ at his second coming, and here in Ephesians too a personified connotation for **enmity** is not impossible in the light of the idea of 'killing the enmity' in verse 16. This would represent a step further on from Paul in the direction of a more fully realized eschatology: the principalities and powers would have not only been disarmed (see 1 Cor. 2.8; cf. Col. 2.15) but already been destroyed.

Finally, Paul can speak of human beings in their sin and weakness as enemies of God, reconciled through the death of Christ (at Rom. 5.10 and Rom. 8.7f.) and non-Christian Jews as enemies of God for the time being, for the sake of the salvation of the world (Rom. 11.28).

Of the three referents mentioned, enmity between Gentiles and Jews, between the powers and God, and between humans and God, the third seems to be the most likely in the original form of the hymn, given the reference to Christ's work of reconciling humanity to God at verse 16; but the other two are not necessarily excluded and may have added relevance for some later readers. On the difference that the grammatical construction makes to the evaluation of the particular nuances in this vocabulary, see further below.

Paul uses **flesh** in two different senses, one morally neutral, signifying frailty and mortality, the other morally loaded, signifying carnality. At Col. 1.22, which is rather similar to this passage (see on v. 16 below), the second sense is clearly excluded: 'he has reconciled us by the body of his flesh through death'. But unless that parallel is taken as determinative for the meaning in Ephesians, the negative sense cannot be entirely dismissed. We should then need to compare instead Rom. 8.3, where the Son is sent 'in the likeness of sinful flesh'. The flesh of the incarnate Christ is the point at which the hostility, even 'warfare' (see Rom. 7.23), between the spirit and the flesh was overcome. This would allow the two elements in this phrase, 'enmity' and 'his flesh', to be taken together, though they are usually divided by commentators, who connect them respectively with what precedes and what follows. It is not just the vocabulary but the syntax that makes interpretation so difficult here. Without the assistance of a spoken or sung rendition of the hymn, the ambiguity of the grammatical construction of this part of it remains an almost insoluble problem.

For the sake of clarity, it may be useful to list the various possibilities:

(1) 'having dismantled the wall, the enmity, by his flesh; having abolished the law' (so Best);
(2) 'having dismantled the wall, the enmity; having abolished by his flesh the law' (so Schnackenburg);
(3) 'having dismantled the wall, having abolished in his flesh the enmity, the law' (so Lincoln);
(4) 'having dismantled the wall; [having destroyed] the enmity in his flesh; having abolished the law' (see below).

The main difference is that the first three possibilities allow for only two (differently assembled) assertions, while the last detects three. Perhaps it is unnecessary to reach a final decision on this question; the grammar may be deliberately loose-textured in order to allow the hearers and users of this material to fill out its meaning from their own situation and perspective, but a few general comments may help to evaluate the different options.

To put 'enmity' into apposition to the 'dividing wall' (as in options (1) and (2)) fails to give due recognition to the structural importance of the term in the hymn as a whole. It is, after all, the opposite of peace, which is its controlling motif, and the destruction, indeed the killing, of the enmity is a dramatic idea to be repeated at verse 16. Neither destroying a wall by flesh (1) nor abolishing law by flesh (2) is a particularly obvious association, whereas enmity and flesh are often linked by Paul (see above). Lastly, while options (1) and (2) produce longish lines, option (3) in its present form is excessively overloaded. Lincoln naturally prefers this because it then supports his contention that 'the law of commandments and regulations' should be removed as an editorial gloss, but this analysis attributes to Ephesians an even fiercer polemic against the Law than that of Paul himself, who saw it as a form of slavery (Gal. 5.1) or a foothold for sin (Rom. 7.8), but never as an enemy of God.

In view of all this, option (4), in which the phrase 'enmity in his flesh' goes together and stands on its own, deserves consideration. The participle that governs it ('having dismantled or destroyed', *lusas*) has to be understood from the previous line; perhaps it has been left unexpressed in order not to anticipate and weaken the climax of line 9, 'having killed the enmity', or perhaps the original contained a separate participle which the editor, for the same reason, decided to omit. If this is correct, three claims are being made: Christ our peace puts an end to the dividing wall, to the enmity in his flesh and to the law of commandments in decrees.

This arrangement has several advantages: it brings the peace/enmity contrast into greater prominence and creates a connection between the opening of the hymn and its echoing phrases later (see the analysis above). It also allows the destruction of 'enmity in his flesh' to be construed along lines, well attested in Paul, of the hostility towards God of the carnal human will which Christ overcame by sharing the human condition and yet remaining obedient even unto death. And it would then provide the anthropological counterpart to the abolition of social and legal divisions mentioned before and after it, but it would be distinguishable from them as a separate and important assertion. The writer of Ephesians is elsewhere (see 2.3; 4.22–4; 5.7f. etc.) more concerned with the moral question than with the social or legal effects of salvation in Christ.

Marcion also thought that this was what Paul must have meant, and he secured his interpretation of this text by the expedient of omitting the pronoun and reading 'enmity in *the* flesh'. As Tertullian commented (*Adv. Marc.* 5.18): 'Marcion erased the pronoun His, that he might make the enmity refer to flesh, as if he spoke of carnal enmity.' But was Marcion so obviously wrong? Was this not what Paul (and the author of Ephesians) actually believed?

It has to be admitted, finally, that the grammar, in the present form of the text, is so loose and ambiguous as to allow several constructions. If 'by his flesh' is taken as a reference to Christ's death on the cross and connected closely either with the dismantling of the dividing wall (option (1) above) or with the abolition of the law (options (2) and (3)), then different political nuances could be implied, whether anti-Roman or anti-Jewish. Thus, on the first option, the hymn could be read as claiming that the cross of Christ was not to be understood as just a case of enmity between Jews and Gentiles (the persecution of yet another innocent Jewish victim by an oppressive Roman state) but as an act of peace-making between them, because it resulted in the Church as the eschatological community of reconciliation. Alternatively, under the second and third options, the cross could be understood as the moment when the law which formerly kept humanity divided was abolished: for Jesus, though apparently handed over to die by Torah-observant Jews angry at his rejection of their law-based exclusivism, was, so the hymn would assert, actually destroying the law of separate existence itself. Thus, the political 'colouring' of the hymn would vary according to the background and agenda of its users, as well as the way its syntax is construed. We find the same sort of variation, incidentally, in the political complexion of the gospel passion narratives, in their attribution of blame for, and account of the consequences of, the death of Jesus.

Following the destruction of the dividing wall and of the enmity in his flesh, the final idea in the sequence is **having abolished the law of commandments in decrees**. Law and commandments are regular terms in the Pauline corpus, especially Galatians and Romans, but decrees (*dogmata*) occurs only here and at Col. 2.14. The word does not necessarily have the pejorative connotations of its English derivative, dogmas. In Hellenistic Jewish texts, 3 Macc. 1.3, Josephus *C.Ap.* 1.42, Philo *Alleg.* 155 etc., it is used as a synonym for laws, on the analogy of the edicts of a Hellenistic monarch or Roman emperor, and this usage is reflected in Luke-Acts (Luke 2.1; Acts 17.7); at Acts 16.4 it is applied to the decrees of the Apostolic Council. Col. 2.14 is unlikely, however, to be the source for Ephesians at this point since the context and meaning of the word there are so different. In Colossians it is used to elaborate the paradoxical metaphor of the death of Christ as the pinning up of a notice of slave release, a motif absent from Ephesians. Similarly, Colossians uses the cognate verb at 2.20 in reference to the ascetic regulations of opponents, again absent from view in Ephesians. We have another instance (see above on 'made with hands', v. 11 and 'alienated', v. 12 and below on 'reconciled', v. 16) of a superficial similarity of vocabulary with no real agreement in substance.

P[46], the earliest papyrus of the Pauline letters, omits 'in decrees' but the omission may be accidental, or an attempt to reduce the verbosity. Does this build-up of synonyms serve to emphasize or to tone down the sense in which Christ's work abolishes the Law? Those who see the origin of Ephesians wholly from within a continuing Pauline community, quite separate from Jewish Christianity, treat the formula as emphatic. On this supposition, while Paul himself strongly protested against the allegation that his preaching abolished the Law (see Rom. 3.31), the post-apostolic Pauline Church was willing to concede even this point. But apart from this one verse, the attitude towards Old Testament Law elsewhere in Ephesians is much more affirmative (see e.g. 6.2f.).

So, alternatively, one could take the phrase 'of commandments in decrees' as intended to *tone down* the sense in which the Law is abolished, in a way not dissimilar to the more balanced statements which one finds alongside polemical exaggerations in Paul's letters. As revealed Scripture and prophecy of the coming of Christ, the Old Testament Law still has an important place (see Rom. 3.21); it also provides moral guidelines of continuing validity (1 Cor. 10.11); it is only in its regulative and statutory aspects, the element of external compulsion, that it is no longer needed, because the spirit of freedom in Christ achieves the same end by other means and without the cost of creating division between Gentiles and Jews.

15b In order that he might create the two in himself into one new person, thus making peace. This is the first of two purpose clauses, both of which conclude with a participle. The change of syntax may be for the sake of stylistic variety, as the hymn begins to recapitulate earlier ideas. Or it may be intended to indicate that Christ's objectives have not yet been fully achieved, even though they stem from his finished work on the cross. 'New creation' here and 'reconciliation with God' at verse 16 do seem to have an unfulfilled future aspect.

The second part of the hymn starts to echo in reverse order its beginning: 'Christ our Peace made both one'. 'He made' is now the more specific 'he created' (for this variation, see above on 2.10) and evokes the theme of the new creation familiar from Paul, especially at Gal. 6.15, where the new creation replaces the old 'circumcision–uncircumcision' distinction; and at 2 Cor. 5.17, where being in Christ as new creation is contrasted with living and thinking 'according to the flesh'. The source of this idea, that the end time would see a recapitulation and renewal of the creation, is Jewish apocalyptic (see esp. Isa. 56–66; *1 En.* 51.4–5; 2 Esd. 7.25; *2 Bar.* 73–4). Paul took it over and gave it a christological interpretation: Jesus the Messiah had effected salvation by becoming the last Adam at his resurrection, the 'man from heaven' freed from the natural constraint of mortal flesh (1 Cor. 15.22, 45–9), and by reversing on the cross, through an act of God's grace, the disobedience of the first Adam which had imprisoned all his descendants in the unnatural tyranny of mortality and sin (Romans 5). Paul's Adamic typology is very flexible, based on the widely differing views of the origin of death and the significance of Adam's creation and fall current in first-century Judaism. Its one constant feature is that it works backwards from salvation in Christ to find partial and varied parallels in the rich legacy of Israel's creation mythology.

The verb 'to create' is less common in Paul's undisputed letters (only twice, Rom. 1.25 and 1 Cor. 11.9) than in Colossians (three times) and Ephesians (four times), but the distribution of the cognate noun swings the other way (nine times in the undisputed letters, twice in Colossians but not at all in Ephesians). Were it not for the continuation into verse 16, the unexpressed subject might almost be God, a possibility which some witnesses (D G Marcion) prevent by clarifying the pronoun 'in him' to 'in himself'. Christ is both the subject of the verb and the one in whom the new creation takes place. The emphasis on Christ as creator is clearer here than elsewhere in Ephesians (see 1.10; 2.10; 4.24) or in the Pauline corpus as a whole. But that Christ is not only the pattern but the author of the new humanity is the key to the otherwise very differently worded Christ hymn in Col. 1.15–20, and it is implied already in 1 Corinthians, where Christ is not simply the recipient of new life but its bestower (1 Cor. 15.45: 'the last Adam became life-giving Spirit'). These ideas would be particularly congenial to those familiar with Johannine thought (see John 1.1–18; 5.17, 26; 9.5f.).

The inclusive form **one new person** (*anthrôpos*) is used here (as also at 4.24) and Paul is careful to employ this term when he is speaking about universal salvation. It should be contrasted with the 'perfect Man' (*sic*) (*anêr*) at 4.13 (see comment there). In its immediate context the main focus is on the one new person replacing the distinction of Jew and Gentile, but the hymn, especially if it was used liturgically in other contexts, could carry other associations, the overcoming of all divisions including those of sex and political status (see on 2.14). The editor will, for instance, later expand the household code section on husbands and wives with reference to the creation texts (Gen. 1.27 and 2.24), to show that in Christ even the division between the sexes could be transcended (see below on 5.21–33).

16 The hymn continues to expound its first half (see analysis above, pp. 125f.) as follows: **and might reconcile both to God in one body by the cross, having by it killed the enmity**.

The movement of thought from new creation (v. 15b) to the idea of reconciliation (v. 16) is highly distinctive of Paul in both Romans 5 and 2 Corinthians 5 (see esp. 2 Cor. 5.17f.). But the verb that Paul uses there for 'reconcile' (*katalassein*) has been extended here with an extra prefix (*apokatalassein*), indicating the completeness of the action. This minor linguistic difference from Paul's normal usage is not a particularly strong argument against an origin in Pauline tradition, for in other places too he can vary in his use of simple or compound forms of the same verb (compare the words for 'await' at 1 Cor. 11.33 (*ekdechesthai*) and Rom. 8.19 (*apekdechesthai*)). However, the issue is complicated by the fact that the longer form also occurs twice in the first chapter of Colossians (1.20, 22). At Col. 1.20, 'reconcile' is found in conjunction with the two other phrases that also appear in this passage of Ephesians, namely 'making peace' (v. 15b) and 'the blood of his cross' (v. 16). So are we dealing here with a preformed hymn or with a new composition from the writer himself, based on his knowledge of Colossians and other letters of Paul? If the latter, of course, any attempt to distinguish between the original meaning for the underlying hymn and its edited meaning (*contra* Lincoln above) would be unsustainable.

But what makes the view that this passage of Ephesians has been constructed from hints in Colossians so unlikely is the stark differences, aside from the three verbal similarities just mentioned. To be precise, peace is the controlling theme in Eph. 2.14–18 but a subordinate one in Col. 1.15–20, which by contrast is dominated by the idea of Christ as the firstborn of creation and resurrection. Furthermore, the opposition between peace and enmity is the key to Eph. 2.16, but it is an almost incidental juxtaposition in Colossians (cf. 1.20 with 'hostile' in 1.21). So the similarities between the two epistles are to be located at the level of the phrasing of common earlier tradition rather than at the level of the final literary redaction of Ephesians. This passage is one of several that expose the difficulty of the direct dependence theory, namely that when the evidence for it becomes more abundant, the theory itself becomes more problematic.

Does **one body** refer to the person of Christ or to the Church? In favour of the former, this phrase could act as an echo of 'in his flesh' in v. 14 and 'one new person' in v. 15b, effectively conflating the two together. Both the bodiliness and the oneness of the reconciler are essential to his work of reconciliation: the beloved Son is one and unique and the body he assumed was necessary, if he was to die for humankind. The proximity of the reference to the cross supports this view.

Most commentators, however, take the alternative view and prefer to see an exclusively ecclesiological reference in the phrase. This is supported by the description of the Church as the body of Christ at 1.23 and especially the credal statement at 4.4, 'one Body, one Spirit'. That the Church is central to the divine plan of unity in Christ in Ephesians can hardly be denied. Nevertheless, assuming that the mention of the cross is integral to the hymn (see below), the christological referent cannot be excluded. Indeed, a certain porosity between the doctrines of Christ and the Church is one of the distinguishing features of the thought of Ephesians and one of its points of closest affinity with the Johannine literature. The hymn the editor is using may have been meant to refer to the one body of Christ in his atoning death: but he and his readers may well have discerned a second meaning, the one united body of Christians, the Church.

In line with similar alleged additions at Phil. 2.8 and Col. 1.20, **by the cross** has often been treated as an editorial gloss, conforming the hymn more closely to the central motif of apostolic preaching. Whatever may be the case with the other passages mentioned, it is unlikely to be so here, for several reasons. First, it cannot be neatly excised, for it is closely related to the 'killing of enmity' that follows and the two together echo the destruction of enmity in his flesh in v. 14. Secondly, the writer of Ephesians can speak of salvation as resurrection and ascension with Christ without even referring to the cross, as he does at 2.6, so he would not necessarily have felt the need of a reference to it here if it was lacking in the original hymn. And in any case, thirdly, the material he is using is already thoroughly Pauline, as we have shown; he did not have to paulinize it himself.

The earlier reference (v. 14) to destroying 'the enmity' is picked up and underlined in **having by it killed the enmity**. 'By it' (i.e. the cross) might also be translated 'in himself'. If the latter, it would be a reference to the enmity between the flesh and the spirit, which Christ overcame through his obedience unto death (see on v. 14 above). Furthermore, we shall see below that the hymn may have continued with v. 18 as its conclusion, and 'through him' there would pick up 'in himself' here. But in the present arrangement of the text, with v. 17 intervening, the intended referent of the pronoun is uncertain.

'Killing the enmity' is a striking paradox. Normally it is enmity that does the killing! Comparison with 4.8, 'he captured captivity', is relevant here. And the thought in both cases is close to the paradoxes that Paul loved: that the weakness and folly of the cross were in reality the wisdom and power of God (1 Cor. 1.22–5). On the range of meanings of 'enmity', see above on v. 14. It might include all or any of the following: the devil, the flesh, the law, Jew–Gentile antipathy, and the Roman state. If the hymn not only reached its theological climax but were also thought to come to an end at this point, then it has to be admitted that it finishes in a rather negative and ambiguous way, describing salvation as the killing of whatever opposes it. One might have expected it to return to its positive corollary and conclude on a note of doxology, like Col. 1.20 and Phil. 2.11. Verse 17 interrupts the sequence, by reverting to the terms of the author's introduction at v. 13, but v. 18 provides what is needed in terms of satisfactory closure.

17 (And when he came he preached peace to you who were far off and those near). The argument that the editor has interpolated this verse in order to tie the hymn in with his introduction (v. 13) is reinforced by several further considerations. The idea of 'preaching peace' weakens the image of Christ as the actual embodiment of peace in v. 14. It also breaks the chronological sequence of thought, since it comes *after* the reference to the cross in v. 16. It slips back into the second person form of address in a way inappropriate to the hymnic form. And finally, it conflicts with the idea of a fundamental equality between formerly divided parties by reverting to the notion that the

Gentiles, as 'those far off', need to be reconciled *more* than those who are already near, the Jews. The editor reiterates here the more conservative Jewish Christian view. The Old Testament allusion is to two texts from Isaiah combined together. Isa. 52.7 speaks of 'the messenger who preaches the good news of peace' (a text also used by Paul in Rom. 10.15), and Isa. 57.19 reads 'Peace, peace to those far off and those near'. The combination of these two texts by the word link 'peace' is an example of the standard practice in Jewish exegesis, known technically as *gezerah shewa*.

The original meaning of 'those far off' and 'those near' for Second Isaiah was Jews in both cases, either in exile or still in Judah. Later rabbinic texts (e.g. *Num.R.* 8.4) take those 'far off' to be Gentile proselytes, and this idea may be present (according to Lincoln 147). But the scriptures themselves are probably sufficient as source for the author of Ephesians. He has identified 'those far off' with Gentile Christians at verse 13 and here he reasserts the privilege of Jewish Christians as those who are already 'near', correcting any implication in the hymn that they should be seen as entirely equal. He is not being unfaithful to Paul in doing this, for the apostle also on occasion granted priority to Israel, even if on other occasions, especially in the heat of controversy, he appeared to deny it. However, the reference to the historic ministry of Jesus, 'who came', and to its content, 'he preached peace', is quite untypical of Paul.

Sensitive to these points, some have interpreted 'when he came' as a reference to his coming via apostolic preaching (Gnilka 146; Caird 60; compare Caird's similar view of 'he descended' discussed at 4.9 below) or to his coming and ascension into the heavenly realm to preach peace to the hostile powers (Schlier 137f.). But the natural referent, indeed inevitable without any indication to the contrary, is to the preaching and public ministry of the *earthly* Jesus. The Cornelius episode in Acts 10 illustrates in narrative form the meaning of verse 17 – the god-fearer joins the people of God through faith in Christ – and Acts 10.36 in particular summarizes Jesus' earthly ministry in terms very similar to those used in this verse: 'You know the word which he sent to Israel, preaching good news of peace by Jesus Christ'.

18 Because through him we both have access, in the one spirit to the Father. The connection of verse 18 with verse 17 is unclear. The preaching of peace would not in itself effect access to God, unless some response to the preaching followed. Furthermore, 'we both' picks up 'the two' in verse 15 and 'them both' in verses 14 and 16 and allows the inclusion of all the divisive polarities in human experience, not just those between 'the near and the far' of verse 17. The near, after all, are always in a better position as far as access is concerned! For these reasons and others mentioned above (on vv. 13f.) verse 18 may be part of the hymn, which verse 17 has briefly interrupted.

After the opening statement, the series of participles and the two purpose clauses, we arrive at last in verse 18 at the ultimate goal, the gift of 'peace' in its fullest sense of access to God. These terms, peace and access, are also found together in Rom. 5.1–2. It is worth pointing out that there is a slight difference between the writer's earlier, more 'realized' assertion that Christians are already seated with Christ in heaven (2.6), and the image that concludes the hymn of approach into the throne room of God.

Access to a monarch in virtue of the full rights of citizenship may be part of what is meant (cf. the political metaphors, esp. in 2.12–13). But this merges into a primarily cultic reference, approach into the presence of God through worship with all the barriers of ethnicity and law removed. This is often the connotation of the idea of 'coming near' in the Old Testament (see 1 Kgs 8.41–3; Isa. 56.6–8; Zech. 8.20–3). In the New Testament it is Jewish Christian writings like Revelation and Hebrews that develop most thoroughly this cultic imagery for the goal of human existence. For a possibly different sense of 'access' see below on 3.12.

The verse is a natural conclusion to the hymn in other ways also. It ends on the note of praise and refers to Christ ('through him'), to the Spirit and to the Father, in a triadic pattern that is reflected also in 2.22, 4.4–6 and 5.18, 20.

19 Surely then you are no longer strangers and sojourners but you are fellow citizens of the saints and members of the household of God. After the hymn, the tone changes from doctrine to exhortation, from first- or third-person statements to second-person address; and there is also a shift in perspective from the theme of peace and reconciliation between two parties, both of whom equally need it, back to the emphasis on Gentiles acquiring the status that the Jews already enjoy.

The terms recall those of verse 12: 'alienated' and 'strangers to the covenants' become 'strangers and sojourners'. The words in Greek (*xenoi* and *paroikoi*) are very nearly synonymous. But in Jewish usage, strangers and sojourners mark a technical distinction between Gentiles living in their own lands ('foreigners') and Gentiles living in the land of Israel ('resident aliens'). The wording is likely to have been influenced by Gen. 23.4, where Abraham describes himself as a stranger and sojourner (*parepidēmos*), a phrase that is picked up in other New Testament epistles (Heb. 11.13; 1 Pet. 2.11) as the basis of an appeal to Christians to live as citizens of heaven. The writer may be aware that the use of the term *paroikoi* (lit. 'dwellers near') introduces a middle category between 'the near' and 'the far', namely 'Gentiles who dwell near', i.e. god-fearers who have one foot in Judaism. While the Jewish community treated them as second-class citizens, in the Church they had achieved full rights of membership (see above on Acts 10).

The opposites of strangers and sojourners are those who belong and are at home, as **fellow citizens** (*sumpolitai*) and **members of the household** (*oikeioi*). There is a clear difference between these two terms. A citizen is one who has voting rights in a Greek *polis*; members of the household include not just those who are related by birth but also the clients of a patron. In Hellenistic society, these two systems, democracy and patronage, operated alongside and in some tension with each other. Here both are given a theological reinterpretation.

Christians are fellow-citizens **of the saints**. There has been much discussion about the exact meaning of this reference to 'the saints'. The standard Pauline usage is that the term describes all Christians viewed as the eschatological community of salvation. This is reflected in the greeting at Eph. 1.1 and in a series of other passages that probably derive from the original Pauline letter (1.5; 3.8; 5.3; 6.18) or from traditions preserved in the Pauline communities (4.12). But standard Pauline usage does not necessarily determine the meaning of the word in the final form of our text. If all that was meant was 'fellow citizens with all other Christians', the emphasis in the phrase would have to fall on the word citizens; however, the following description, 'household members *of God*', implies that some emphasis at least must fall on the second limb of the phrase. All the alternative interpretations follow from this basic observation.

Paul appears to deviate from his own usage when he refers to the Jerusalem church as 'the saints' in contexts concerned with raising money for them (e.g. 1 Cor. 16.1; cf. 2 Cor. 8.4; Rom. 15.25). But he may have substituted his normal term for their preferred self-designation, 'the poor' (cf. Gal. 2.10), not in order to indicate a special status for Jerusalem (as 'saints' *par excellence*) but – exactly the opposite – to indicate that they were just saints like any other Christian community.

Allowing that the writer may have a different understanding of 'the saints' from Paul's, we can consider other possibilities. The saints (lit. 'holy ones') could be good angels (Schlier 140; Gnilka 154; Gärtner 1965: 63f.), as in several Jewish texts (e.g. Job 15.15; cf. above, p. 86): citizenship of heaven along with angels is the supreme privilege of a Christian (cf. Heb 12.22) and one could also compare members of God's household with the reference to (possibly angelic) 'families in heaven' at Eph. 3.14 (see also the discussion on 1.18 above). However, one would have expected the author to make it clearer if he was referring to supernatural 'holy ones'. Alternatively, they could be Jewish Christians generally, as those with a prior claim to the privilege of salvation (*TDNT*

1.106; Kirby 1968: 168; Faust 1993: 184–8). This fits well with the preceding argument, and the contrast with 'alienated from the polity (citizenship) of Israel' (v. 12) supports that sense of 'fellow citizens' here, i.e. sharing in Israel's citizenship.

But in addition we should remember that, in post-apostolic usage, 'the saints' is coming to mean outstanding dead Christians honoured for their virtue and/or martyrdom. This special use has its roots in Paul himself (see 1 Thess. 3.13 and cf. 2 Thess. 1.7, 10; Col. 1.10). It comes to the fore in post-apostolic texts (Rev. 19.8; cf. Heb. 12.23). That the editor of Ephesians knew this technical use of 'saints' as an honorific title is implied by 3.5 (see p. 154 below) and, as Houlden (292) says, he is looking back at 'the first Christians already seen as a golden generation'. This is surely the most likely view (so also Best 278), even though it cannot be maintained consistently for all the uses of the word in Ephesians. But on our understanding of the origins of Ephesians, consistency in terminology or conceptuality is not a safe criterion for the exegesis of its individual parts (contra Lincoln 151).

Members of the household (oikeioi) is a term used once by Paul, at Gal. 6.10, where he qualifies it with 'of faith' (cf. 1 Tim. 5.8) rather than, as here, **of God**. The underlying idea, though, is well attested in Paul, being implied in the language of adoption as God's children and of fellow-Christians as brothers and sisters, which occurs throughout his letters. The early Pauline churches met in the houses of their wealthier members and it was natural for the institutions of kinship and patronage to filter through into their theological vocabulary (see also 1 Pet. 4.17 and cf. J. H. Elliott 1990). The writer of Ephesians is, however, probably thinking not so much of a series of local household churches which belong to God, as of the one heavenly household, God's temple (cf. v. 21) to which Christians are already privileged to belong (see Merklein 1973: 133f.). The later so-called household code (see on 5.21 – 6.9) will also be edited in the same direction, towards a unified and transcendent concept of the Church.

20 The mention of household members leads naturally into a building metaphor for the Christian community, **built** (lit. 'house-built') **on the foundation of the apostles and prophets with Christ as the very cornerstone**. The building metaphor is common in Paul, see esp. 1 Cor. 3.10–17, where a distinction is made between the once-for-all foundation, the preaching of the gospel of Christ, and the ongoing work of apostolic edification compared to the construction of a building. The distinction is reflected in Col. 1.23, where Christians are 'founded' (past tense) and Col. 2.7, where they are 'being built' (present tense). Here in Ephesians, however, that distinction is eroded (but compare on v. 22 below). Lincoln (152; but contrast 154) explains the referent of 'built' as conversion-initiation; but this may be to harmonize the text of Ephesians too closely to Colossians. It is more likely that the writer means that the Church of the post-apostolic generation, its basis and its structures (see 4.11), depend on the work and witness of the founding fathers. Several other passages in the New Testament of the same period as Ephesians or later reflect this concern for faithful continuity with and succession from the original apostles (Acts 1.25; John 14.26f.; 21.24; Jude 1, 3 and the Pastoral Epistles, *passim*).

Paul makes another distinction in 1 Cor. 3.9–17 (but contrast Rom. 15.20) between the foundation which is Christ and builders upon it, like Paul, Apollos and Cephas. Again Ephesians erodes that distinction; the foundation now is the apostles and prophets of the first generation, alongside and aligned with Christ as cornerstone. Some translations (e.g. GNB, NEB corrected by REB) attempt to harmonize Ephesians with 1 Corinthians by rendering: 'the foundation laid by the apostles'. But it is quite clear that Ephesians believes that the foundation of the Church is not Christ alone, but Christ along with, and rightly interpreted by, authentic apostolic tradition. This is the characteristic view of sub-apostolic Christianity, reflected in the two volumes of Luke-Acts and the bipartite structure of the developing collection of texts that became the New Testament canon. Appeal by deviants to secret words of a living Jesus (see *Gospel of Thomas* 1) threatened to bypass and subvert the Church's traditions and constitution. So the Church began to realize that the Jesus tradition could be dangerously opaque and open to distortions, unless it was officially interpreted in the light of the teaching of apostles, like Paul, James the Lord's brother, Peter and John. Adherence to the tradition of the apostles and their legitimate successors, along with an upright moral life, became the litmus tests of right belief.

The change in Paul's imagery that Ephesians has introduced, seeing the apostles as the historic foundation of the Church, should be compared with the description of Peter as the rock on which the Church is built at Matt. 16.18 and the vision of the heavenly Jerusalem at Rev. 21.14: 'And the wall of the city had twelve foundations, and on them the twelve names of the twelve Apostles of the Lamb'. Paul himself was aware of the claims made by the Jerusalem apostles to be the founding 'pillars' of the Christian Church (Gal. 2.9) but he was rather cautious about them (Gal. 2.6). The author of Ephesians, however, has fewer reservations. As long as Paul can be included in the foundation of the new Temple or the heavenly Jerusalem, he is happy to accept the imagery.

For the reason just given, it is incorrect to think here of only twelve 'Apostles', excluding Paul, along the lines of the otherwise Paul-friendly author of Acts (see Acts 1.26; but cf. 14.4). For comments on the meaning of this term in early Christianity see above on 1.1.

At 4.11 'apostles and prophets' are understood to be the gifts of the exalted Christ to the Church, and Christian prophets are probably also intended here, rather than the prophets of the canonical Old Testament, but some secondary reference to the latter is not altogether excluded (see Rengstorf, *TDNT* 1.44). The very retention of the title prophet for preachers in local Christian communities (1 Cor. 12.28) indicates that the early Church wanted by this means to claim some sort of continuity with Jewish tradition. Whereas for Paul, apostles and prophets are distinguishable as itinerant and resident church leaders respectively, in the post-Pauline period the terms became almost interchangeable (see Acts 13.1; Rev. 18.20; cf. *Did.* 11–13).

If apostles and prophets form the foundation, they do not replace Christ, but are aligned to him **as the very cornerstone**, which is probably to be understood as the carefully squared-off stone determining the right angle at the base of a building. J. Jeremias, however (*TDNT* 1.791–3), has argued strongly that the rare term *akrogóniaios*, unknown from classical Greek literature, should be translated capstone or keystone, not foundation stone, i.e. the last, not the first, to be set in place, the summit of the building. The term occurs at 2 Kgs 25.17 (LXX) where it means the *top* of a pillar. It also occurs in another Greek translation of the Old Testament (not LXX) at Ps. 118.22, where it renders the Semitic expression 'head of the corner' (cf. Mark 12.10). But in Psalm 118 the head of the corner must be taken not vertically but horizontally (see Kramer, *EDNT* 268). It is only later texts like *T. Sol.* 22.7 – 23.3 that provide unambiguous evidence that this word can be used of a capstone. Those who support Jeremias' view (e.g. Lincoln 154) argue that it alone is consistent with the exalted position, elsewhere in Ephesians, of Christ as head over his body the Church. Their reasoning is that, although the Church as building is still under construction, its completion is already assumed in Christ; compare 4.15f. where the body 'grows up into the head'.

However, the arguments for the translation 'cornerstone' are more compelling (see McKelvey 1969: 195–204; O'Brien 1999: 217). Along with Ps. 118.22, the main Old Testament allusion is to Isa. 28.16, where the precious cornerstone is identified specifically as the *foundation* of the New Jerusalem. Furthermore, since Paul described Christ as the foundation (1 Cor. 3.11) it is unlikely that the author of Ephesians would flatly contradict him. Isa. 28.16 was combined with Ps. 118.22 to create an early Christian proof-text for the crucifixion and resurrection of Jesus (see Mark 12.10; Acts 4.11; 1 Pet. 2.6–8); but 'The stone which the builders rejected has become the head of the corner' does not imply that the builders at the beginning of their work rejected a stone as part of the foundation but eventually found it to be ideal as a keystone. The builders' rejection is more complete and its consequences more devastating: their work will be destroyed and replaced by a new building, which is entirely 'the Lord's doing, and marvellous in our eyes'.

21 In whom a whole building fitting together grows into a holy temple in the Lord. The paragraph ends with two appended relative clauses – an obvious technique for amplification and expansion, as we noted in respect of 1.11 and 13. The translation 'a whole building' could equally well be 'every building'. A minority of manuscripts, including $\aleph^c$ and A, add the definite article and thus resolve the ambiguity. Individual, local and universal referents are all possible.

(1) In Christ every individual Christian, understood as a building, grows in holiness as a temple of God. This is apparently the sense of the temple imagery at 1 Cor. 6.19 and we could compare Eph. 4.13, in a context (4.16) which repeats the key terms of this verse – 'building' (in the verbal, i.e. upbuilding, rather than substantive sense), 'fitting together' and 'growth' – though they cluster around the image of body rather than temple. And Ephesians understands the call to holiness in an ethical and individual way later (see 4.24). However, 1 Cor. 6.19 may itself be a collective use of the temple image (notice that the singular 'your body' is used there); and against an individualistic interpretation of Ephesians here is the fact that 'fitting together' implies the idea of co-operation. But the point is not decisive, because the verb, especially if it is in the middle (reflexive) voice, could mean 'fitting in with itself', i.e. developing personal maturity and integrity. On balance, this first interpretation is perhaps not very likely, for it introduces an idea for which there has been little preparation in the preceding paragraph.

(2) 'Every building' (without the article) might mean each local congregation (as Mitton 115), along the lines of 1 Cor. 3.16f. The theory that Ephesians was not addressed to one destination but was a circular letter sent to several could be used to support such a view. While the body of Christ is one and universal, indeed cosmic (1.23), several buildings may be constructed in different places on the one foundation. On this view, the ideas of harmony, growth and holiness would take on a different colouring; divisions within the community which impede growth and evangelism are to be overcome, if necessary by the expulsion of disruptive elements that are incompatible with its character as God's holy temple and refuse to fit in.

(3) Although 'every building' is the natural translation of the Greek, and one or other of the foregoing interpretations might be how the text was heard by some at least of its readers, the intended meaning was probably in reference to the whole Church. Semitic idiom permits the sense 'a whole building' (see Rom. 11.26, 'all Israel' or 'a whole Israel'). This is more likely given the larger context, in which the theme of unity has

dominated. And a Jewish Christian would automatically think of the temple of God as one not many, located in one particular place, whether Jerusalem or heaven. In contrast to the static images of the Church's infrastructure in the preceding verse, the writer here speaks in dynamic terms. The different strands in post-apostolic Christianity in Asia, whether Pauline, Petrine or Johannine, need to be fitted together for the sake of more effective mission and greater holiness of life. This is the overriding aim of the letter to the Ephesians.

22 Another relative clause concludes the section: **in whom you also are being built up together for a dwelling place of God in the Spirit**. The natural antecedent of the relative pronoun is the temple: 'in which' would then be the correct translation. But 'in whom', overleaping verse 21 to Christ in verse 20, is more likely. At 1.13, the writer has constructed a similar sequence of relative clauses; and he ended that section in the same way with a direct address, 'you also'. The use of the second person plural in Ephesians, as we have seen, is very confusing (cf. above on 2.1); it sometimes means 'you Gentiles', in contrast to 'we Jewish Christians', including Paul; but here there is no reason to suppose a racial distinction, as though the whole Church was to be a temple, but all that Gentile Christians could expect to be was a dwelling place. Verse 22 actually adds very little to the content of verse 21; its purpose is simply to drive home the point that what is said there about the universal Church applies also to the readers of the letter. In other words, this use of the second person plural, like that at 1.13, is a momentary lapse from the pseudepigraphical framework of the letter (see Introduction, pp. 45f).

The word 'dwelling place' (*katoiktérion*) occurs in the New Testament elsewhere only at Rev. 18.2 (Babylon as the 'dwelling place' of demons), but in terms of content Rev. 21.3 is nearer, where, as a result of the descent of the new Jerusalem, 'the dwelling (lit. tabernacling) of God is with humankind'.

The final verse of this section echoes the ending of the hymn around which it has been constructed, with a triadic formula – 'in whom', i.e. Christ, 'of God' and 'in the Spirit'.

C Paul's mission to the Gentiles   (3.1–13)

(1) On account of this I, Paul, the prisoner of Christ for the sake of you Gentiles – (2) always assuming you have heard of the mission to you that God in his grace has given to me, (3) that by a revelation the secret was made known to me, as I have already written briefly. (4) As far as that is concerned, you can learn, when you read, the insight I have into the secret of Christ (5) which was

not made known in other generations to the sons of men, as it has now been revealed to his holy apostles and prophets in the Spirit, (6) that the Gentiles should be co-heirs incorporate and shareholders of the promise in Christ Jesus through the gospel, (7) of which I have become a servant according to the gift, which God in his grace has given to me – that is the way God's power works. (8) To me, the least of all the saints, this grace was given to preach to the Gentiles the good news of the unfathomable riches of Christ (9) and to enlighten everyone about the secret plan of salvation, hidden from all eternity in God the Creator of all things, (10) in order that the manifold wisdom of God might be made known now through the Church to the principalities and powers in the heavenly realms (11) according to the eternal purpose which he accomplished in Christ Jesus our Lord, (12) in whom we have boldness and access in confidence through faith in him. (13) Therefore I beg [you] not to be depressed by my afflictions on your behalf: they are your glory.**

Up to this point, Ephesians has maintained a tone and perspective of the widest generality, with the exception of 1.15ff. (the first prayer report), which was expressed in the first person singular. Even that passage avoided mentioning the particular circumstances in the lives of his correspondents for which Paul had cause to be grateful, and moved quickly back to exhortations and statements of faith that could apply to any group of Christians anywhere. Chapter 2 continued in the same vein, with an exposition of the themes of salvation by faith and unity in Christ, referring to the historic division between Jews and Gentiles as a broad generalization, though blurring it somewhat by the statements in 2.3f. that implicated Jews as well as Gentiles in former disobedience. While holding firmly to a Jewish Christian standpoint (see notes on 2.11–13 and 17), the author has affirmed, probably with the assistance of a hymn from the Pauline tradition on Christ as our Peace (2.14–16, 18), the present unity, equality and collaboration between all Christians on the basis of their common foundation, Christ and his apostles.

In sharp contrast to this, chapter 3 is much more specific. The first person singular is used prominently throughout 3.1–8, 13–14. We are informed that Paul is in prison (3.1, the first mention of this fact in Ephesians), that his imprisonment and suffering are 'for the sake of you Gentiles' (3.1, 13), but that they should not be discouraged by it; that they have heard of his mission and will be able to read more about his understanding of it from this letter and also from another document that will soon become available to them (v. 4); and that Paul, though merely a servant (v. 7) and 'the least of all the saints' (v. 8), is specially commissioned to preach the gospel to the Gentiles.

The specificity but at the same time allusiveness of this section (similarly 6.18–22) puts a question mark against many of the current theories on the origin of Ephesians. It is, for instance, incompatible with Kirby's liturgical hypothesis; he has to treat 3.1–13 as 'a long parenthesis' (1968: 129), out of keeping with the style and structure of the baptismal homily contained in Ephesians 1–3 and added as part of the pseudepigraphical framework when the liturgy became a letter (170). It is also a problem for Schnackenburg (128), who cannot accommodate this section of apparent 'historical recollection' within his theory (see above, Introduction, p. 17) and so calls it a 'Paul-anamnesis', by which he means that it 'claims the authority of the Apostle for the author's understanding of the mystery of Christ'. Lincoln (171) draws on the rhetorical category of *digressio* to help with the problem this passage poses to his hypothesis of Ephesians as a consistent and homogeneous pseudepigraphon. The purpose of a digression, in this technical sense, is 'to elicit the good will of the audience towards the speaker by treating a relevant though not logically necessary theme' – the theme here being Paul's mission to and suffering on behalf of the Gentiles. But even on the assumption that it is appropriate to appeal to classical rhetoric in this way (see Introduction, p. 44), this explanation entails that the actual audience of Ephesians (as distinct from its fictive audience) are exclusively Gentiles, which we have had occasion to doubt. Finally, Best (293), whose own view is that Ephesians is the product of a school of Pauline pseudepigraphy at Ephesus, understandably hesitates here:

> If [this passage] were written by Paul, it allows us to view Ephesians as a letter, and not a homily or a theological tractate. But if it is post-Pauline, then the section must be seen as part of the theological argument, indicating how God chose one particular human being to work his purpose out.

The latter explanation is so weak ('one particular human being') that it points strongly towards the former.

Whether one adopts the classic Goodspeed–Knox–Mitton hypothesis of Ephesians as a summary of Pauline teaching (see Introduction, pp. 13f.), or one of its more recent competitors just mentioned, there is a most surprising omission in this section, namely the word 'apostle' in the singular to describe Paul's status and work. Defence of his apostleship against detractors both within and outside the Church is a standard topic in the authentic letters of Paul (Gal. 1.16; Rom. 11.12; 1 Cor. 15.9; 2 Cor. 12.11f.; 1 Thess. 2.7 and many other references). It would be almost impossible, after reading through the major letters, to express Paul's mission in any other way than by appeal to this term. The writer of Ephesians, though he prefers to speak of apostles in the plural (2.20; 3.5; 4.8), yet faithfully transcribes Paul's self-designation at 1.1, where he might, if he had serious reservations about it, have followed other models and used the title servant (Phil. 1.1) or prisoner (Phlm. 1) or just the name alone (1 Thess 1.1). The real Paul, however, did speak extensively about his mission to preach and suffer for the gospel, without ever using the word 'apostle', in just one of his letters, i.e. Philippians. But while Paul himself, confident of the Philippians' loyalty, could there refrain from asserting his apostolic claim, a pseudepigrapher would surely not have been able to resist the combined force of all the other precedents.

The parallels between Eph. 3.1–13 and Col. 1.23–9 are impressive when the verbal similarities are extracted from their contexts and presented in tabular form (as Lincoln 169). But on closer inspection, they become not only inconclusive but, as the commentary below will argue, inexplicable on the theory of the direct dependence of Ephesians on Colossians. For the moment, two points should be noted. First, the echoes between the letters are in a non-sequential, almost random order (thus, Col. 1.23c (or 1.25) is echoed at Eph. 3.7; Col. 1.24 at Eph. 3.13; Col. 1.25 at Eph. 3.2; Col. 1.26 at Eph. 3.4, 9; Col. 1.27 at Eph. 3.8; and Col. 1.29 at Eph. 3.7). Secondly, the parallels mainly (but not entirely, see on 3.4) appear in Col. 1.24–9, which is the immediately preceding paragraph to the mention of Paul's concern not just for the Colossians but also (Col. 2.1.) 'for those at Laodicea and for all who have not seen my face'. So it is not at all surprising, if Ephesians is based on Paul's letter to the Laodiceans, that this passage should include a higher than average number of similarities with Colossians in wording and theme.

Ephesians 3.1–13 presents Paul's explanation of his ministry to the Gentiles. The first sentence breaks off abruptly and is never completed as such. What it was intending to say is represented partly by verse 13 and partly by the opening verse of the next section, verse 14. It is only verses 2–13, therefore, excluding verse 1, which can properly be called a (grammatical) digression or parenthesis (see discussion above).

The obscure reference in verse 3 to a previous writing which will be available to the recipients, the vocabulary and syntax of the passage, the emphatic use of the first-person pronoun throughout, and the improbable complexity involved in any attempt to derive this material from Colossians, put the hypothesis of pseudonymity under enormous pressure in this passage. Second only perhaps to the final postscript, 6.21–2, chapter 3 of Ephesians has the strongest claim to be from Paul's own hand, apart from some minor editorial glosses and one major addition (see below on verses 9–11, *contra* Goguel 276, who views the whole of 3.2–13 as an interpolation).

1 On account of this I, Paul, the prisoner of Christ for the sake of you Gentiles – It is only possible to make this verse a complete sentence by supplying the verb 'to be', as NRSV: 'I, Paul, *am* the prisoner of

Christ'. Two factors make that unlikely. The emphatic 'I, Paul' occurs elsewhere only when the apostle is uttering some solemn request (2 Cor. 10.1), warning (Gal.5.2; cf. Eph. 4.1) or assurance (Phlm. 19 1 Thess. 2.18), and not merely describing himself. Secondly, 'prisoner' has the definite article. In regular Greek usage, when a noun is used as a complement, with the verb 'to be' unexpressed, the definite article is dropped, and to avoid all doubt it should precede the subject. It is therefore almost inevitable that 'the prisoner of Christ' will be read in apposition and the reader will still be waiting for the main verb – a long wait, as it turns out!

Paul describes himself as *a* prisoner (*desmios*) of Christ twice in Philemon (1, 9). Lincoln (173) suggests that the author of Ephesians 'takes up Paul's self-designation but adds to it the definite article and thereby heightens the distinctiveness of Paul's apostolic achievement'. This is an attractive explanation for the presence of the article, but it does not quite work if the pseudepigrapher was, as Lincoln believes, responsible for writing the whole paragraph. For, as we have just seen, this small alteration has thrown the grammar of his own composition into disarray. He ought to have added, as well as the definite article, the missing 'I am', thus avoiding the ambiguity and at the same time making his point about Paul as the prisoner even more emphatically. So while the article may well be the editor's, the untidiness of the grammar already belongs to the material he is using. This grammatical *non sequitur* belongs to the source, not the editing. Paul can and does occasionally write as carelessly as this (see e.g. Rom. 3.2 and 4.16); it is less likely that an imitator would have done so.

The preposition 'on account of' (*charin* with the genitive) is rare in Paul, understandably, since he prefers to avoid the possibility of confusing it with the accusative of one of his favourite nouns 'grace' (*charis*); nevertheless it does occur at Gal. 3.19 and twice in this part of Ephesians (3.1 and 3.14). An imitator might be expected to conform to Paul's normal usage, 'because of this' or 'therefore', which is also the normal way in Ephesians of marking a new paragraph (2.11; 4.1; 4.25; 5.1; 5.15).

If the phrase points back to what precedes, it is hard to see any real connection. Indeed, the unity of Jews and Gentiles in the Church (2.11–22) involved doing away with barriers, enmity and regulations, but Paul as a prisoner would still be subject to all three! If the phrase looks forward to what follows, there is still a problem, for it is only at verse 13 – and fleetingly – that another allusion is made to Paul's suffering in the service of the Gentile mission. Otherwise the theme is not developed or explained.

While the reason for Paul's imprisonment 'on behalf of you Gentiles' is not actually stated, this passing allusion seems to assume a certain awareness of it. A pseudonymous writer might be pretending to know something of which he was in fact ignorant, or he could have his own motive for reticence, for example, if he suspected that certain Jewish Christians had actually been involved in denouncing Paul to the authorities (cf. Rom. 15.31). But in the latter case, he would have been better advised not to mention at all the detail that Paul was imprisoned 'on behalf of the Gentiles', since it raises a suspicion that he was not in a position to refute.

The alternative hypothesis is therefore more plausible, that this is Paul's own allusion to his present circumstances which he here leaves undeveloped because Tychicus has been charged with the task of filling in the details (see below on 6.21–2) when he delivers the letter. Although Paul does not make this claim explicitly anywhere else in his undisputed letters, it is entirely compatible with his own historical situation. For his detentions, like his beatings in the synagogue (see 2 Cor. 11.23), were the result of Jewish hostility aroused by his preaching of a law-free gospel and his rejection of the demand for the circumcision of Gentile Christians. Another, more theologically profound sense in which Paul's sufferings could be said to be 'on behalf of Gentile Christians' at Colossae and Laodicea has been asserted at Col. 1.24: 'I make up in my flesh what is lacking in the sufferings of Christ.' Paul does not explain himself in Ephesians, because he is just about to refer his readers (v. 3) to what he has said there, i.e. in Colossians, on that theme.

Rather surprisingly, in view of Col. 4.18 ('Remember my bonds'), Colossians nowhere actually uses the word 'prisoner' of Paul; Aristarchus is called Paul's 'fellow prisoner of war' (*sunaichmalótos*) at Col. 4.10, but that term must to some extent be metaphorical, and it could be entirely so (in effect 'taken captive by Christ', see further on 4.8 below). The precise parallel is found only in Philemon, where Paul's imprisonment is central to the purpose of the letter. There is no particular reason in Ephesians to stress the fact. Indeed, since it is Paul's apostolic mission to the Gentiles rather than his imprisonment that is the proper subject of this section, we should have expected it to begin 'I, Paul, apostle to you Gentiles'. That would have provided a link back to 2.20 and a suitable introduction for what is to come. Since the fact of imprisonment is of no relevance to what the writer has to say, the most plausible explanation for verse 1 must be that the writer was indeed in prison at the time of writing, i.e. he was Paul. The abrupt, unprepared introduction of the motif here is not picked up again until verse 13, 'Do not be depressed by what I am suffering for you', where it is equally vague and undeveloped.

2 Always assuming you have heard. 'Always assuming' represents the Greek, *ei ge*, 'if at least'. It must be ironic. Of course his correspondents have heard of Paul's mission! For they are themselves the result of it, through the agency of Epaphras. The subtlety of this irony (of which another example appears in Eph. 4.20; cf. Gal. 3.4; 2 Cor. 6.3) tells conclusively against seeing the remark as 'part of the device of pseudonymity' (*contra* Lincoln 173). For it assumes information about the situation of Paul's original correspondents (i.e. their conversion through a co-worker) which would not have been available to readers of the canonical document.

What Paul's readers have hearsay knowledge of is **the mission to you that God in his grace has given to me**. We have translated the words 'stewardship *towards* you' somewhat freely as 'mission to you' in order to bring out the force of the preposition. The Greek word stewardship (*oikonomia*) can mean both the office of a steward, and the plan for stewarding a household (see on 1.10 above). When that household belongs to God (see 2.19) it means the plan for running (and saving) the universe. Of the two meanings, the Pauline usage is demonstrably that of the steward's office (1 Cor. 9.17; 1 Cor. 4.1f.). And this is faithfully reflected both in Col. 1.25 and in this verse. The modification of the term to cover the larger sense of 'plan of salvation' has occurred in the *berakah* at 1.10 and will reappear, also in probably editorial material, at 3.9 (see below).

The wording is very close to that of Col. 1.25 (but see also on v. 7): 'I became its servant, according to the stewardship of God towards you that has been given to us, to make the word of God fully known.' There are some minor differences from this in the Ephesians version: 'grace' (rather than stewardship) has been given (cf. also Rom. 1.5, in relation to Paul's apostleship) and 'to me' (rather than 'to us'). Both versions are consistent with authorship by Paul. If Ephesians were dependent on Col. 1.24–7, we should have to suppose that the other elements of that Colossians passage have been scattered around Ephesians – the suffering moved to verse 13, the reference to Paul as servant to verse 7, the idea of hiddenness to verse 9, and the phrase 'to generations and ages' delayed as late as verse 21; and the idea of 'fulfilling the word of God' dropped altogether.

3 That by a revelation the secret was made known to me, as I have already written briefly. On the meaning of **revelation**, see above on 1.17. Our translation here assumes a particular moment of insight when Paul realized that the Gentiles were to be included within the scope of the gospel, presumably his Damascus road encounter with the risen Christ (as Gal. 1.12, 16; Acts 26.18; so also Schnackenburg 131). Despite Lincoln's protest (175), the preposition used here with revelation, *kata*, has a variety of meanings in koine Greek, and can be translated 'by' or even 'at' (Rom. 2.5; 16.5) and not always 'according to'. Lincoln prefers 'according to revelation' in an attempt to remove the autobiographical allusion that might otherwise authenticate the expression as Paul's. He even goes so far as to claim that 'revelation' has become a more general concept for the writer of Ephesians, which 'underlines Paul's role as receptor of revelation ... and the normative status the writer attributes to Paul's interpretation of the gospel' (175). But this is not the way the word is used at 1.17, where Paul prays that *all* his correspondents may be given 'the spirit of revelation'. It is noteworthy that, although revelation is a thoroughly Pauline concept (occurring 13 times in the corpus as a whole), neither the noun nor its related verb occurs anywhere in Colossians.

The **secret** or mystery of God's plan of salvation was the theme of the opening blessing (see on 1.9 above). In this section, we have preferred to translate *mustérion* as 'secret' because it corresponds better with the ideas of hiddenness (vv. 5 and 9) and revelation (vv. 3, 5 and 10). While the Greek word can have both senses, in English a secret can eventually be told but a mystery is intrinsically untellable. The word is repeated three times emphatically in this one short section (vv. 3, 4 and 9).

In 1 Cor. 1–4, Paul rejects the wisdom of this world in favour of the secret wisdom of God (1 Cor. 2.1). He, Apollos and Cephas are servants of Christ and stewards of God's mysteries (1 Cor. 4.1f.) and the plural occurs again in 1 Corinthians at 13.2 and 14.2, but Paul reverts to the singular at 15.51 to describe the resurrection hope. The inclusion of the Gentiles is referred to as 'this secret' (in the singular) at Rom. 11.25. The closest parallel to our passage occurs in the doxology of Rom. 16.25f.: 'according to the revelation of the mystery kept secret for long ages but now disclosed and through the prophetic writings made known to all nations according to the command of the eternal God'. This passage, for various text-critical and stylistic reasons, is under suspicion of being a later addition to Romans (see Metzger 1994: 533–6, 540), but the way it connects 'revelation' to 'secret', just as Eph. 3.3 does, and to prophecy (see on 3.5 below) is noteworthy. Colossians makes neither connection.

We have already referred to the complexity involved in supposing that Col. 1.24–9 is the literary source for Eph. 3.1–13. Simpler by far is to suppose that it is Paul himself who in this section restates his understanding of his apostolic mission, varying his language slightly from Colossians and referring his correspondents to that other account of it which he knew would shortly become available to them.

I have already written briefly. The verb (lit. 'I have pre-written', *proegrapsa*) cannot be an epistolary aorist (the courtesy adopted in Greek letters whereby the writer assumes the temporal perspective of his correspondents) since 'I have written' according to that idiom would already mean precisely 'I have written earlier'. Nor can the aorist refer back to earlier parts of Ephesians itself, such as 1.9f. or 2.10–22 (cf. NRSV, 'as I wrote above' (*sic*)) since that would make a nonsense of the following clause 'you can learn, when you read'. The readers will have already read those parts of the letter and it is too late now to tell them that they are able to understand, *when they read*. (RSV is also tendentious: 'when you read *this*'; there is no word for 'this' in the Greek.) We can hardly suppose that the individual reader is being encouraged to refresh his or her memory of the earlier passages, even less that the public lector stops at this point and rereads those passages, as Schnackenburg seems to imply (132). Surely, the more reasonable explanation of these words is that they are an allusion to a document already in existence which the correspondents have not yet had access to, but will be able to read in the near future when they do.

It should be noted that this is incompatible with any form of the 'circular letter' theory (see Introduction, p. 12). For a circular letter, almost by definition, has to be self-sufficient, able to be read independently in a number of places and sets of circumstances. The 'preface to the corpus' theory is better able to explain the wording here, for several relevant passages in other letters could be identified as an earlier exposition of the ideas referred to in this section. But in addition to the general problems associated with that theory (see Introduction, pp. 25 and 35f.), yet another is raised by this particular passage. If Ephesians was designed to stand at the head of a collection of Paul's letters, then 'I have written *earlier*' introduces, quite unnecessarily, a problem which the order of the letters in the collection notably fails to answer, namely the relative chronology of their composition.

If the most natural reading of the text is that one specific letter, written earlier than this but not yet available to the correspondents, is meant, then that letter must surely be Colossians (Mitton 1951: 234), which is indeed a brief letter and alludes frequently to the secret of God's eternal plan (see below). An important conclusion follows from this line of reasoning. These words are unlikely to have come from the pen of a later editor or pseudepigrapher, for then Ephesians would have been intended to function as a companion piece to Colossians; but despite all the minor verbal similarities, the present form of Ephesians is at several key points not complementary to but distinctively divergent from Colossians. Thus verses 3–4 are probably an oblique allusion to the intended exchange of letters between the Colossian and Laodicean congregations (see Col. 4.16). If an explicit instruction to exchange once stood in the conclusion to Paul's letter to Laodicea (as it does in the Latin pseudo-Laodiceans, see Appendix A) then it would have had to be excised when the letter was expanded and redirected to Ephesus (see Introduction, pp. 31f.). But the editor has allowed this less specific, but nevertheless tell-tale fragment of evidence about its original setting to stand.

4 As far as that is concerned, you can learn, when you read, the insight I have into the secret of Christ. The noun 'insight' (*sunesis*) occurs only here in Ephesians (a different term, wisdom, *sophia*, is preferred at 1.8 and 1.17). It is used with emphasis at Col. 1.9 (cf. Eph. 1.8 above) and 2.2. But its use here is unemphatic and almost verbal, i.e. 'the way I understand'; and the verb does occur in the undisputed Paulines (2 Cor. 10.2, and twice in Romans in quotations).

For the phrase 'the secret of Christ', Col. 4.3 provides a precise parallel, but its context is very different, in a final prayer request for missionary opportunities to be opened. The content of the secret is illuminated by several passages in Colossians: 1.27, 'to make known what are the riches of the glory of this secret among the Gentiles which is Christ in you, the hope of glory'; 2.2, 'that you may have all the riches of assured understanding and the knowledge of the secret of God, namely Christ'; and 3.3 is also relevant, 'Your life is hidden with Christ in God'. Paul did not feel he was able to improve on the eloquent formulations of his letter to the Colossians, so he referred his correspondents to what he had written there. The relatively underdeveloped and restrained statement of Paul's special commission in Ephesians is neatly explained by this reference to an earlier exposition of the theme. A pseudepigrapher who was intent on glorifying Paul's apostleship and was basing himself on Colossians as his model ought to have been able to produce something much more impressive here.

5 Which was not made known in other generations to the sons of men, as it has now been revealed to his holy apostles and prophets in the Spirit. For the reason given in the previous comment, the wording of this verse bears a close similarity to Col. 1.26, but the differences should also be noted. The Colossians verse reads: 'the secret hidden from ages and generations but now manifested to his saints (holy ones)'. If this is the source, 'hidden from ages and generations' has been changed to 'not made known in other generations' (but cf. 'hidden from ages' which reappears at v. 9, see below), and 'now manifested' has been changed to 'now revealed'. On this view, the wording of Colossians has been altered arbitrarily, while retaining the same overall sense. However, comparison with Colossians at this point does at least help to isolate two elements in Ephesians that are 'alien' in the sense that they find no parallel in Colossians nor anywhere else in the Pauline corpus: the addition of the Semitism 'sons of men' and the addition of 'apostles and prophets', which has the effect of turning the preceding noun 'saints' into an honorific adjective 'holy'. These look very much like the work of the editor.

The sons of men. If we may assume that what Paul originally wrote was 'not made known *to* other generations', varying his language slightly from Colossians, then he might have been taken to imply that there was no previous revelation of God to Israel before the coming of Christ. But according to Jewish Christians, and among them indeed Paul himself (see Gal. 3.8; 1 Cor. 10.4; Rom.1.2), Abraham, Moses and the Prophets had, in some degree, been granted glimpses of the mystery of Christ (cf. also Heb. 11, esp. vv. 13, 26). To avoid any possibility of a proto-Marcionite reading, the editor supplies a new indirect object, 'to the sons of men'. He means by this to emphasize that the ordinary bulk of common humanity in former times (excepting perhaps the privileged few) was left in ignorance. The addition also prepares the way for another addition later in verses 9–11, that the powers also, like the mere mortals of this verse, were ignorant of the divine plan until it was made known to them through the Church.

His holy apostles and prophets (lit. 'the holy apostles of him and prophets'). That this phrase, or some part of it, is an addition to whatever source the author is using is widely acknowledged by commentators. Instead of disclosure to the saints (i.e. all Christians) – which is what Paul would have written (cf. Col. 1.26) – it is made only to '*holy* apostles' like '*Saint* Paul'. The honorific use of the term has been discussed above on 2.19. It strongly implies a post-apostolic perspective on the part of the writer. The founding apostles are now 'Saints', glorified in heaven and honoured on earth. This expression is alien to Paul in another respect also, as Lincoln astutely comments (179):

> It is not only the singling out of apostles as a holy group that makes the sentiments of this verse unlikely to have come from Paul himself, but also the willingness to attribute to the other apostles the reception of the distinctive revelation of the place of the gentiles in the church, which he regarded as his special commission.

But Lincoln fails to appreciate the difficulty for his own thesis that his comment poses. If a later author was willing to give the credit for the Gentile mission to the other apostles as well as Paul, as the writer of Acts was (see chs 10 and 15), then what motive did he have for writing a letter in the name of Paul in the first place, and for composing this section of it in particular? There is, in other words, an unresolved tension between this general reference to 'holy apostles' and the material that surrounds it. For that material focuses on Paul's special role, though in a more restrained way than other passages where Paul, in the face of his detractors, parades his credentials as the Apostle to the Gentiles (Gal. 1–2; 2 Cor. 10–13). It is clear, from the rest of Ephesians, that the expansion of 'holy apostles and prophets in the Spirit' is not evidence of diminishing respect for Paul on the part of the editor, any more than of the author of Acts. On the contrary, he retains the highest respect for him, precisely because the other apostles, so he believed, held the same view as Paul of the Church's universal mission.

'Apostles of him' must mean 'of Christ' as in verse 4 (so Schnackenburg) and not 'of God' (*pace* Lincoln), for it is specifically the exalted Christ who gives apostles to his Church in Ephesians (see 4.11 below). Apostles and prophets are mentioned together in that passage too and this probably also explains their addition as a pair here. The 'prophets' in both passages means principally local Christian preachers. However, since the pronoun 'of him' is supplied only with apostles, the possibility cannot be completely ruled out that the 'prophets' also includes the Old Testament prophets (see also on 2.20 above). Of course, the temporal distinction between 'earlier generations' and 'now' in the underlying material might be urged against this interpretation, but if the other addition of the 'sons of men' is understood in the way explained above, it is not impossible, and the concluding phrase 'in the Spirit' would then be given extra relevance. It is usually translated 'by the Spirit' and taken with the verb 'revealed'. Without the addition of the reference to apostles and prophets, of course, there would be no other way of taking it. It is entirely consistent with Paul's idea of revelation to see it as the work of the Spirit (1 Cor. 2.10), though the connection is not made anywhere in Colossians. However, in the present expanded form of the text 'in the Spirit' could equally well be linked closely with 'prophets' (so Schnackenburg 134) and that would permit an allusion not only to Christian prophets but also to the inspired text of the prophetic writings, i.e. the Old Testament prophets as they continue to speak in the present day as witnesses to the revelation in Christ (see Rom. 3.21; 16.26; cf. 1 Tim. 1.18 and 2 Pet. 3.2).

6 That the Gentiles should be co-heirs incorporate and share-holders of the promise in Christ Jesus through the gospel. The content of the secret is that through the preaching of the gospel the Gentiles should inherit the promise in Christ. Three compound adjectives are used to describe this privilege, each starting with co- (*sun* in Greek). **Co-heirs** occurs in Paul at Rom. 8.17: 'heirs of God and co-heirs with Christ', in a context that derives the notion from that of being children of God, and offers co-heirship on the condition of suffering with Christ. An even closer parallel is Rom. 4.13, where Abraham's seed are all who share his faith in God's righteousness, whether Jews or Gentiles, and are co-heirs together of God's promise. The controversial aspect of Paul's use of the word is missing from Ephesians, but the term itself is retained. There is no parallel to it in Colossians.

The second term **incorporate** (lit. 'co-bodied') is a neologism, i.e. it occurs nowhere else in surviving Greek literature prior to Ephesians. Its innovator was probably Paul, for he coins similar, unprecedented words at Phil. 3.17 (*summimêtês*, 'co-imitator'), 1 Cor. 1.20 (*suzêtêtês*, 'co-seeker') and especially Phil. 2.2 (*sumpsuchos*, 'co-spirited').

The third term **shareholders** ('co-partners', *summetocha*) is more widely attested; indeed, it appears with the different connotation of association with deviants later in Ephesians itself (5.7). So to give it a positive sense here, it is explained as 'shareholders of the promise'. This last phrase **of the promise** cannot qualify all three preceding adjectives; for though it might fit the first, it cannot fit the second. The share in the promise in Christ Jesus makes 'through the gospel' somewhat redundant and the sentence starts to look overloaded. So it may be that 'of the promise' has been added – along the same lines as earlier additions – to emphasize continuity with the hope of Israel; but one cannot be certain. For these earlier references to 'the promise' see on 1.13 and 2.12.

7 Of which I have become a servant according to the gift, which God in his grace has given to me – that is the way God's power works. Paul's unique service to the Gentile mission comes back into centre-stage after the more generalized statements of verses 5 and 6. If the purpose of a pseudepigrapher was to celebrate in this section the historic role of the founding Apostle to the Gentiles, as those who defend a unitary pseudepigraphical view of Ephesians believe, we must ask why he has not described Paul in particular as *the* apostle, instead of using the plural, apostles, at 3.5; and why, after the understated references to Paul as 'servant' (v. 7) and 'least of all the saints' (v. 8), he continues to focus on the content of the message (vv. 9–11) rather than the exalted status of the messenger. This argument is further strengthened if, as the evidence of style and substance implies, these verses (9–11) are the contribution of the editor.

The purpose of chapter 3 cannot be to praise Paul to his admirers in a later Pauline school, or to a generation in danger of neglecting his achievements, for it says too little about him, and what it says is too allusive and in places too disparaging. On the contrary, the basic purpose of this chapter is more consistent with a setting in Paul's lifetime: it seeks to offer humble praise to God for bestowing upon Paul the revelation of his secret plan to save the Gentiles.

Col. 1.23 uses a similar expression, 'the gospel, preached to every creature under heaven, of which I, Paul, became a servant'. But this is not the only possible source; Paul calls himself a 'servant' frequently elsewhere (1 Cor. 3.5; 2 Cor. 3.6; 6.4; Rom. 15.16). An even closer parallel to this verse in Ephesians comes two verses later in Col. 1.25 where Paul refers to himself as 'a servant of Christ's body the Church, according to the stewardship of God which has been given to me'. The formulation in Ephesians, instead of 'stewardship' etc., has **the gift,**

which God in his grace has given to me but the expression is no less Pauline (see Rom. 3.24; 5.15f.; 2 Cor. 9.15). Since the author of Ephesians is profoundly interested in the doctrine of the Church, it is most unlikely that he has deliberately omitted the phrase 'Christ's body the Church' while conflating Col. 1.23 with 1.25. The similarity with Colossians, on the contrary, points to the basic Paulinity of this section of Ephesians so far.

That is the way God's power works (lit. 'according to the working of his power'). If a source for this phrase is sought in Colossians, we have to look four verses further on, Col. 1.29, 'I toil and struggle with all the energy which he energizes in me with power', where the correlation between Paul's labours and divine energy makes perfect sense. In Ephesians there is no obvious reason for the inclusion of the phrase except to provide a buffer between 'given to me' in verse 7, and 'To me was given' in verse 8. And if it is editorial, that may be the explanation for its addition. A similarly phrased liturgical flourish may have been added earlier at 1.19b.

8 To me, the least of all the saints, this grace was given to preach to the Gentiles the good news of the unfathomable riches of Christ. Paul's self-effacing use of the 'servant' title in verse 7 is taken a step further here, with 'least of all the saints'. This should be compared with 1 Cor. 15.9: 'least of all apostles, not worthy to be called an apostle because I persecuted the Church of God'. The grounds for Paul's statement that he is the least of all Christians are left unspoken in Ephesians, but it is surely an allusion to his former career as a persecutor (cf. 1 Tim. 1.13, 15f.). Mitton (125) calls the phrase 'false modesty' without apparently realizing that such a term would, if admitted, authenticate the material as Pauline. For only a genuine speaker can strictly be guilty of false modesty. If a pseudepigrapher constructed the phrase he is likely to have had genuine reservations about Paul. Bruce (53) is surely right: 'No disciple of Paul's would have dreamed of giving the Apostle so low a place.'

The word for 'least' is emphatic, formed from a superlative with an extra comparative ending, i.e. 'less than the least'. The saints, in Paul's own usage, are all Christians (see the discussion on 2.19 and 3.5 above), but for the author and audience of Ephesians, for whom 'saints' is a prize-term for the first-generation heroes of faith, this statement would be tolerable exaggeration, not merely as proof of Paul's humility but also because, in such exalted company as 'the Saints', to be least and a servant is also to possess a certain greatness and primacy (cf. Mark 10.43f.).

The unfathomable riches of Christ. Riches (or 'wealth', *ploutos*; the word is singular) is a characteristic Pauline way of describing the abundant grace of God. It is very frequent in Romans (2, 4; 9.23; 10.12;

11.12; 11.33; cf. also Phil. 4.19). It has been echoed already in Ephesians (see on 1.7f.; 2.7; and cf. 3.16 below). Here, the riches of Christ are described as 'unfathomable' (*anexichniastos*, lit. 'not to be tracked', 'leaving no traces'), a word which does not appear in Colossians and only elsewhere in the Pauline corpus at Rom. 11.33. It is an uncommon word, occurring in the LXX only in the book of Job (5.9; 9.10; 34.24). But it does belong to Paul's active vocabulary. Admittedly, at Rom. 11.33 it is the judgements and ways of God (as in Job), not the riches of Christ, that are unsearchable and inscrutable, but the variation in referent while retaining the same adjective is what we should expect from someone who fancied the word. In the present arrangement of the text, verse 8 is at some distance from the second prayer report, verses 14–19, but it nevertheless prepares the way for it in an important respect, by introducing the idea of the infinite and immeasurable grace of God in Christ (see below on vv. 18f.).

9 And to enlighten everyone about the secret plan of salvation, hidden from all eternity in God the Creator of all things. No sooner has the specific mission of Paul to the Gentiles been restated (v. 8) than the author goes off at a tangent to refer again to the theme of the secret hidden in the past and now brought to light (v. 9) in its cosmic, not merely human aspect (v. 10, contrast v. 5), in fulfilment of the divine purpose (v. 11). There are good reasons for suspecting that verse 10 reflects the author's own idiom and special interests more than those of Paul, i.e. the Church's cosmic role in mediating revelation to the principalities and powers (cf. 1.21) and the distinctive phrase 'in the heavenly realms' (cf. 1.3, see further on v. 10 below). Arguably, the surrounding verses, 9 and 11, display non-Pauline characteristics and should be taken along with it as expansion by the editor, who, as we have seen, is not so concerned to glorify Paul as to explore some of the deeper implications of Paul's teaching about the cosmic scope of salvation.

'To enlighten' (*phōtizein*) has occurred in the development of the first prayer report (see 1.18) in a similar construction: 'with eyes *enlightened* so as to know *what is* the hope', compare here literally, '*enlighten* everyone as to *what is* the secret plan'. The verb occurs only once in undisputed Paul, with the different sense of 'to expose, bring to light the dark secrets of the human heart', at 1 Cor. 4.5 – an idea closer to Eph. 5.8–14 than to the thought here.

Everyone (*pantas*). Several MSS (including ℵ* and A) and early Fathers omit, but the majority include it. It may have been removed because it was too universalist for the tastes of some later scribes to say that *everyone* had been enlightened by the gospel. Whichever is the true reading, the author is moving away from the topic of the mission to the Gentiles to a more comprehensive vision of the divine plan.

The secret plan of salvation (lit. 'the economy of the mystery'). Paul uses the word 'stewardship' ('economy', see above on 3.2) to denote the office of a manager. Here it is used in the 'off-Pauline sense', as at 1.10, of the 'management strategy', the divine plan for the universe.

The wording of verse 9, as of verse 5, should be compared to Col. 1.26: 'hidden from ages and generations'. If that were the source, the author of Ephesians must be assumed to have split it into two, 'not known to generations' (v. 5) and 'hidden from ages (aeons)' (v. 9). This seems unlikely, because one consequence of this repetition is that it fails, unlike Col. 1.26, to exclude decisively the possible misunderstanding that the 'aeons' are not periods of time, but fallen angels, from whom the secret has been hidden (see above on 2.2). Indeed the next verse, with its reference to the principalities and powers, might even encourage such a misinterpretation.

In God the Creator of all things. The earlier uses of the verb 'to create' (at 2.10 and 15) have included some idea of the 'new creation', though the writer does not draw a sharp distinction between creation and salvation (see above on 2.10). Here the reference is clearly to the original creation at the beginning of time. The hiddenness of the mystery, in other words, goes right back to the beginning. The reference to the Creator of **all things** also prepares the way for the reference to principalities and powers in verse 10 who, we are thereby reminded, are themselves creatures and therefore subordinate to God.

The celebration of God as Creator is a standard feature of Jewish Wisdom literature (see e.g. Wis. 1.14), and leads smoothly into the reference to God's varied wisdom in the next verse. But in relation to the idea of a hidden purpose of salvation only lately disclosed, it is Jewish Christian apocalyptic, in which the original creation was the pattern for the world's future restoration, that provides the more relevant parallel; see Rev. 4.11: 'Worthy art thou, our Lord and God, to receive glory and honour and power, for thou didst create all things, and by thy will they existed and were created.'

Notoriously, Marcion (Tertullian *Adv. Marc.* 5.18) omitted the preposition 'in', with the result that it was the inferior deity that created the world who was the one *to whom* the secret remained hidden.

10 In order that the manifold wisdom of God might be made known now through the Church to the principalities and powers in the heavenly realms. The relation of this purpose clause to what has been said so far is not immediately clear. Some commentators (Lincoln 185 and others he cites there) prefer to link it with verse 8: Paul's preaching to the Gentiles was the way God's wisdom was finally made known to the powers, either because it gave them evidence of God's universal sovereignty, or perhaps because, more obscurely, the preaching to the Gentiles also involved the proclamation of the gospel to their angelic representatives (as Wink 1984: 89ff.). This assumes the consistency and homogeneity of the thought in this passage. However, there seems to be quite a leap in thought from the mission to the Gentiles, through the agency of Paul (v. 8), to the role of the Church in making known God's wisdom to the heavenly powers (v. 10); and it is the latter which is more clearly the author's own special interest.

The simpler view, therefore, is to relate verse 10 directly to the previous verse, and see it as providing the purpose of the long-hidden plan of salvation and contrasting 'the ages' past with 'now' and the one creator God with the plurality of the powers. This, then, reinforces our suggestion that the editor is moving off on to his preferred territory in these verses (9–11) in his elaboration of the underlying material. He has, incidentally, made exactly the same move in the first prayer report (see on 1.20–23 above).

The adjective 'manifold' (*polupoikilos*) occurs nowhere else in the Greek Bible. Its natural meaning is 'much-varied', 'multi-patterned', or 'multicoloured' in contrast to 'plain'. In the list of the twenty-one characteristics of Wisdom in Wis. 7.22, the fourth is 'of many parts' (*polumeres*; cf. Heb. 1.1) which is a synonym. But the 'multi-faceted' character of Wisdom there does not prevent her being described also as 'pure' and 'clear'; she is (7.25f.) 'a pure emanation of the glory of the Almighty' (quoted at Heb. 1.3), 'a spotless mirror of the working of God, and an image of his goodness'. One could say, perhaps, in a modernizing idiom, that the pure light of God refracted through the prism of the material creation breaks into all the colours of the spectrum (see on 5.6 below).

The reason that the plan of salvation was not recognized, until it was revealed in Christ, is precisely that it was so subtle and variegated, encompassing all the ambiguities of the natural world and human society, and all the setbacks and false starts of Israel's journey of faith in the Old Testament (Heb. 1.1 and see further in Heb. 11). But now the varied wisdom of God is plain for all to see in the variety of membership in the Church.

Paul also refers to the idea of the hidden wisdom of God at 1 Cor. 2.7, and speaks of Christ as God's wisdom at 1 Cor. 1.24 in a paradoxical way: wisdom is demonstrated in the foolishness of the preaching of Christ crucified. But there is little here to imply such a paradox. Indeed, the adjective 'manifold' forbids it. What is multi-faceted and all-embracing must exclude the polarities that Paul exploits in 1 Corinthians between human wisdom and divine folly.

Commentators who (like Schlier 159–66) see some contact between Ephesians and the gnostic myth of Wisdom go further and explain the use of the term 'manifold' mythologically. Wisdom, like the Egyptian deity Isis, adopts various disguises so that she can slip past the angelic beings that rule over the intermediate heavens and bring saving knowledge to humankind below. This purpose having been achieved, disguise can at last be thrown off and the truth disclosed to all. But to speak, as Ephesians does, of God's wisdom as multi-faceted at the very moment of its disclosure shows that there is no relation with that mythological scheme.

The making known of God's plan to the powers could mean that they are thereby reconciled to it (Caird 67) or, more likely, that they are given the evidence of the victory of God, in the victory of his saints, and therefore of their own inevitable defeat (cf. 1 Pet. 3.19 for a similar ambiguity, which probably should be similarly resolved). If this is correct, 'now made known' is only verbally parallel with 'not made known in earlier generations' in verse 5. In terms of content, they refer to quite different ideas: in verse 5 to the proclamation and acceptance of the gospel by those who through birth or spiritual blindness were formerly ignorant; and in verse 10 to the proclamation of their defeat to supernatural beings, the principalities and powers, whose opposition to God's sovereignty was clear-sighted and therefore inexcusable. This further supports the view that verses 9–11 are an addition, echoing the terminology of Paul's original letter but with a different purpose. On principalities and powers, see on 1.21; on the distinctive expression 'in the heavenly realms', see on 1.3; and on the cosmic role of the Church, which is explicitly mentioned here only for the second time in Ephesians, see on 1.23. Thus, the whole of verse 10 is a summary in the editor's own idiom of the main thrust of his thought.

11 According to the eternal purpose which he accomplished in Christ Jesus our Lord. The Church's role in verse 10, to embody and thus disclose the divine plan, is related by this verse to the role of Christ in the eternal purpose of God. Cosmic ecclesiology and cosmic Christology are correlated in Ephesians (cf. also 1.23) as they are in the Apocalypse (Rev. 14.1) and the Gospel of John (John 17.24).

The eternal purpose (lit. 'the purpose of the aeons'): 'purpose' or determination has been used already at 1.11 (see comment there). It does not occur in Colossians, but appears twice in Romans (8.28 and 9.11) in connection with the doctrine of election. God's purpose is 'eternal', meaning either that it is conceived from all eternity, or that it is directed towards the age to come, or that it is the purpose for which God ordained the unfolding ages of salvation-history. It is clearly not, however, the purpose of the aeons ('powers' as angelic beings, see on v. 9), for that would be something quite different from the purpose of God. And the fact that the writer can use such a formula shows that he is unaware of that peculiar meaning of 'aeons'.

Although it is not apparent in the translation above, the terms 'Christ' and 'our Lord' both have the definite article. This is a departure from usual practice in Ephesians, which retains the article with Christ alone (3.1; 3.8 etc.) but drops it with the combined name Christ Jesus (1.1, 5; 2.13). So it may be that the phrase ought to be translated 'in *the* Christ, Jesus, our Lord', putting the emphasis on the Jewish messianic hope fulfilled in Jesus, the Church's Lord.

12 In whom we have boldness and access in confidence through faith in him. The train of thought here is not at all easy to follow. Lincoln (191) suggests that 'in 3.12 the access can be seen as no longer impeded by the menace of hostile principalities and authorities'. But there are certain difficulties with this explanation. At 2.6 the author has asserted that Christians are already 'seated in the heavenly realms with Christ', which, notwithstanding 2.18, implies an exalted position which is in some tension with the notion of 'access' in the sense of admission into the presence of a king or potentate. Secondly and conversely, the revelation to the 'powers' of their ultimate defeat – if that is what is meant by verse 10 (see above) – does not mean that they are no longer a menace or impediment to human beings; quite the contrary, see 6.12 (cf. Rev. 12.12).

Best proposes only the loosest of connections between this verse and what precedes it: 'the redemption of believers takes place through the same Christ as the one through whom God's purpose has been made known to the aeons' (329). This is a peculiar assertion, given both that Best has previously (327) discounted the personal sense for 'aeons', and that it was the *Church*, not Christ, through whom God's purpose was disclosed to the powers in the previous verse. The commentators are at a loss at this point because there is indeed no logical connection between verses 11 and 12.

The author has previously used the word **access** (at 2.18) in the Old Testament cultic sense of access to the Father in worship, but we need to pause a moment before allowing that usage to predetermine the sense in the underlying material here. The other two terms, boldness and confidence, first deserve a closer look. **Boldness** (lit. 'saying everything one wishes', 'free speech', *parrēsia*) occurs later in Ephesians at 6.19, in connection with the unhindered proclamation of the gospel. This is its regular meaning in Paul (see Phil. 1.20; 2 Cor. 3.12; 1 Thess. 2.2). The other term appended to 'access' is **confidence** (*pepoithēsis*) which occurs particularly frequently in 2 Corinthians, in relation to Paul's confident hope that his recalcitrant church will eventually comply with his wishes (1.15; 8.22; 10.2 and even 3.4, cf. 3.3). At Phil. 3.4 it refers to Paul's confidence in his own Jewish credentials. Neither word then has a necessary cultic association of bold or confident approach to God in prayer or worship. On the contrary, the more natural association of both is the bold and confident preaching of the gospel (to the Gentiles), last referred to in verse 8 (so van Unnik 1980: 277). Indeed, verse 12 would follow on quite smoothly from verse 8 without the intervening expansion, and then the meaning would be unavoidable.

In this light we should reconsider the meaning of 'access' (NRSV, 'access to God' is unwarranted by the Greek). The noun, *prosagōgē*, does not invariably have ceremonial or cultic associations; it may be used simply of movement towards, or of an enquiry, introduction, or even a dose of medicine (see LSJ s.v.). Paul as a prisoner might be thought to be under restricted access both to visitors wanting to see him and to potential audiences for his preaching. But, surprisingly, that was not the case. Though in chains, he was still able to be an ambassador for the gospel (see 6.19 below). In Col. 4.3 he prayed – with a certain irony for someone in prison – that a door for evangelism might be opened for him. In the captivity letter to the Philippians, he remarks that 'what has happened to me has actually helped to spread the gospel' and make it known among the Imperial guard, and inspiring others 'who have been made confident [the verbal form of the noun used here] in the Lord by my imprisonment to dare to speak the word with greater boldness' (Phil. 1.14). Acts says the same about Paul's imprisonment in Rome (28.31: 'he received all who came to him'); it allowed open access and assisted the bold proclamation of the gospel.

The advantage of this view is that it explains the connection with what follows in verse 13. 'Therefore' – that is, because of the continuing opportunities that are offered even in prison to the service of the gospel – 'I beg you not to be disheartened by my trials'; and since they give Paul a greater opportunity for evangelism among the Gentiles, 'they are your glory'. **Through faith in him** (lit. 'through the faith of him', objective genitive) is a regular Pauline idiom; see Gal. 2.16.

In conclusion, verse 12 makes perfect sense as the sequel of verse 8 and the lead-in to verse 13, and it supports all the indications given above that verses 9–11 are an editorial insertion. Otherwise, verse 13 would be very hard, indeed almost impossible, to explain.

13 A precise deduction is drawn from what has just been said (see above). **Therefore I beg [you] not to be depressed by my afflictions on your behalf: they are your glory**. The object of 'beg' and the subject of 'be depressed' are not expressed in the Greek. If the sense were 'I beg God that I may not be depressed' or 'I beg God that you may not be', the extra words would probably need to be included. The absence of the object and the subject of the verbs probably means that they are the same, i.e. 'I beg *you* that *you* may not be depressed.' If verse 8 were followed immediately by verse 12, there would be no difficulty, for the unexpressed 'you' would be the Gentiles to whom Paul is commissioned to preach, including his correspondents.

The implausibility of a purely pseudepigraphical account of the origin of Ephesians is illustrated by this verse, for a later generation of readers would have no grounds – not even human sympathy – to be disheartened by the sufferings of someone who had long since won the martyr's crown. The attempt to derive the wording here from Col. 1.24 also demonstrates the implausibility of that hypothesis. For there Paul says that he rejoices in his sufferings because they make up what is lacking in the afflictions *of Christ*, while in Ephesians the 'afflictions' are all Paul's own. Paul may be allowed to use these terms interchangeably with different referents, but it is hardly likely that a pseudepigrapher who had studied the letter to the Colossians, could knowingly make such a change.

They are your glory is literally a relative clause 'which is your glory'. The relative pronoun is feminine singular, so it has been only partly conformed to its plural antecedent 'my afflictions'. Lincoln (192) understands the 'glory' which is identified as the afflictions of the apostle as that eschatological glory for which suffering is the necessary precondition (cf. 2 Cor. 4.17 and Rom. 8.17f.). This would certainly be a profound, if somewhat elliptical, thought. However, in Eph. 3.13 it is Paul who does the suffering on behalf of (and in place of) Gentile believers (cf. 2 Cor. 1.6 and 4.12).

A simpler interpretation may be preferable: that Paul's correspondents are entitled to exult in their apostle's afflictions on their behalf, since it furthers the cause of the gospel, just as he in his afflictions takes pride in their faith; compare 2 Cor. 7.4: 'I have great confidence in you; I have great pride in you; I am filled with comfort. With all our affliction, I am overjoyed.' The formulation of 3.13 has a brevity and freshness that bear the stamp of Paul himself.

III Prayer and praise   (3.14–21)

A   Second prayer report   (3.14–19)

(14) On account of this I kneel before the Father [of our Lord Jesus Christ] (15) after whom every family in heaven and earth is named, (16) that he grant that you be strengthened with power through his Spirit in the inner person according to the wealth of his glory, (17) that Christ dwell in your hearts through faith, you being rooted and founded on love, (18) so that you may be able to grasp along with all the saints the breadth, length, height and depth, (19) and to know the love of Christ that surpasses knowledge, and be filled with all the fullness of God.

On the form and function of intercessory prayer reports see the commentary on the first prayer report (1.15–23) above. The presence in the same letter of two reports, separated at such a distance from each other, is most unusual (see G. Wiles 1974: 300). In Colossians, there are also two references to Paul's prayers (1.3 and 1.9) but they are adjacent in the introduction to the letter. The structure of 1 Thessalonians provides a more interesting parallel, but the whole of the first three chapters of that letter are 'autobiographical' in tone, and continually remind the addressees of evidence for Paul's concern for them, including his prayers (compare 1 Thess. 1.2 with 2.13). If an original letter of Paul, underlying Ephesians, began with more circumstantial detail (see on 1.15) and lacked those parts of chapters 1 and 2 that have subsequently turned it into a theological meditation on salvation and the Church, then its similarity to 1 Thessalonians would be even closer.

Most of this paragraph sounds like Paul. The themes of his prayer, inward strength through the Spirit linked to the indwelling of Christ through faith, and the paradox of knowing the love of Christ that surpasses knowledge, bear the Pauline imprint. The only points at which one might reasonably hesitate are the relative clause in verse 15 and two phrases in verse 16 and verse 19 (see below). The paragraph consists of one long sentence (91 words; but if the doubtful material is discounted, this reduces to a more acceptable 68).

14 On account of this was the way the previous paragraph began (see the comments on 3.1). If, grammatically, the sentence that started at 3.1 has not yet been completed, it is so at last here. But in terms of the thought, it is the request 'not to be depressed' at verse 13 which explains this connective phrase. Paul's repeated prayer for his correspondents is intended to relieve their depression (see on 3.13 above).

The normal word for 'pray' or 'beg' has already been used in verse 13, directed towards the readers, so now, as we turn to prayer towards God, a more intense way of expressing supplication is used to mark the difference: **I kneel** (lit. 'bend my knees') **before the Father**. The phrase 'bend the knees' has no parallel in Colossians, but it occurs three times in undisputed Paul, at Phil. 2.10, Rom. 14.11 (from Isa. 45.23) and Rom. 11.4 (from 1 Kgs 19.18), and signifies a posture of homage. In Jewish tradition prayer was usually offered standing (see e.g. Mark 11.25) but kneeling, especially in supplication, was not unknown (see Dan. 6.11), and the example of Christ kneeling to pray in Gethsemane (Luke 22.41) may have been influential in eventually forming Christian practice. To pray kneeling was to pray with particular intensity.

Paul's intense prayer is **before the Father [of our Lord Jesus Christ]**. A number of MSS (including אᶜ and D) continue with the phrase in brackets (omitted by P⁴⁶ א* A and B). There are no other examples in the letters of Paul of the use of the absolute term 'the Father' standing on its own. Elsewhere in Ephesians, in most cases though not all (see on 2.18), the title is qualified in some way. While it is true that the divine name is frequently embroidered in scribal transmission, it is also possible to explain the omission of the phrase as an attempt to bring the reference to the Father (*patér*) into closer proximity to the cognate noun for a patriarchal clan or family (*patria*) and to avoid the possible misreading that it is Christ from whom every family is named. Decision between the longer and shorter readings is, therefore, more difficult than recent commentators (Lincoln; Best; Schnackenburg) admit. If the material is basically Pauline, the longer reading might be preferable.

15 After whom every family in heaven and earth is named. In the first prayer report (see on 1.17) the reference to 'the God of our Lord Jesus Christ' may have been expanded with the phrase 'the Father of glory'. A not dissimilar expansion could have happened here.

The Jewish idea of 'naming' implies more than just nomenclature; it involves the notions of determining the character and exercising authority over what is named (see Gen. 2.19; Ps. 147.4; Eccles. 6.10; compare comments on 1.21 above and 5.3 below). The word for 'family' is cognate with the noun 'father' but is used in the ancient sense of the extended family, the clan or tribe, and not in the restricted modern usage of the nuclear family.

Several interpretations of 'every family in earth and heaven' are possible.

(1) 'In earth and in heaven' could merely be an ornamental flourish meaning 'every family whatsoever', without any particular emphasis on the existence of families in heaven (cf. perhaps 1 Cor. 8.5; Phil. 2.10; Eph. 1.10). But the author has shown himself to be more interested in the demography of heaven than this interpretation allows. And it seems too generous an estimate of families in general: would the 'family' of the Flavian emperors, for instance, count as one of those 'named' after the fatherhood of God?

(2) A '*whole* family encompassing (and reconciling) earth and heaven' could be intended, on the model of 2.21, 'a whole building'. But, while at 2.21 a singular collective sense might be appropriate in the context (see above), here the contrast is between the one Father of all (cf. also 4.6) and the plurality of families who are named after him.

(3) A distinction could be meant between every earthly family and every heavenly clan or class of angels (see on 1.21). Admittedly, the different ranks of angels were not seen as formed by descent from a common ancestor, but they could be called heavenly families by extension, as they are in later Jewish texts (e.g. *bSanh.* 98b). The main difficulty with this

otherwise attractive option, however, is the one pointed out by Schnackenburg (147), that it does not make the necessary further distinction between the ranks of good angels and those of evil angels who are in rebellion against the Father (see 1.21; 6.12).

(4) Finally, 'every family on earth' could refer to every genuine 'family', i.e. Christian household church, where brothers and sisters in the Spirit worship a common heavenly Father; and 'families in heaven' would then, by a legitimate projection, refer to departed Christians who are thought of as still organized for worship in the same way (cf. Heb. 12.23, 'the congregation of the first born who are enrolled in heaven'; cf. also John 14.2, 'in my Father's house there are many apartments'). Despite its rejection by some commentators (e.g. Best 339), this remains the most likely interpretation for an author as conscious of 'the communion of the saints' as the writer of Ephesians (see on 2.19).

The universal fatherhood of God is emphasized by this expansion of the beginning of the prayer, but it is not picked up in the rest of the paragraph (except at the end of verse 19, see below), which focuses rather on the work of the Spirit and of Christ. So another motive for the expansion might have been to provide a more balanced 'trinitarian' structure (cf. 2.18 and 4.4–6) by extending the address to the Father.

16 The first petition in the reported prayer is for inward strength, in contrast to the faint-heartedness that the thought of Paul's imprisonment may have induced in his original readers: **that he grant that you be strengthened with power through his Spirit in the inner person according to the wealth of his glory.** Strength through the power of the Spirit is a distinctive and recurring theme in the Pauline corpus (1 Thess. 1.5; 1 Cor. 2.4; 2 Cor. 6.6f.; Rom. 15.13). The notable expression 'the inner person' (*ho esố anthrốpos*) occurs in two other places: at Rom. 7.22, where it is contrasted with 'another law at work in my members', and at 2 Cor. 4.16, where the contrast is with 'the outer person who is wasting away'. These passages involve slightly different nuances attached to the same phrase, fleshly temptation in the first example, and external physical affliction in the second. There is no reason why Paul could not have used the phrase here with yet a third nuance, of the inward power that comes from prayer.

Paul understands the 'inner person' not in a naturalistic or dualistic way of the spiritual essence of a human being but rather of the believer in Christ turned towards and waiting expectantly for the life of the age to come, delighting in God's law (Rom. 7.22), being renewed daily (2 Cor. 4.16) and here being strengthened by the Holy Spirit. Colossians, almost uniquely in the Pauline corpus, makes little of the Spirit (see on Eph. 1.5 above) and it does not use the Pauline expression 'the inner person'.

Barth's suggestion that 'in' should be translated literally 'into' (*eis*) with the result that the phrase becomes a reference to Christ, *into* whom believers are to grow (cf. 4.15f.) is unconvincing, for 'in the inner person' is parallel to 'in your hearts' in the next verse, and refers to the place within believers where the effect of the Spirit of promise is already felt.

The thought is complete as it stands and the additional phrase 'according to the wealth of his glory' adds little to it; it might even be thought to distract attention from it. It is similar to the formula that may have been added to the first prayer report (see on 1.18; and cf. 1.7 and 2.7, and Col. 1.27). The source of the addition could simply be the fulsome language of liturgy, or a reminiscence of Paul's use of the phrase elsewhere, e.g. at Rom. 9.23 and Phil. 4.19. But Paul had good reason in those contexts to refer to 'riches': the mention of different kinds of vessels at Rom. 9.21, some expensive, others cheap (cf. 2 Cor. 4.7); and the mention of the gift of money from the Philippians at Phil. 4.18. Here, on the other hand, the phrase appears to have little point.

17 The first petition is further explained: **that Christ dwell in your hearts through faith**. In a similar fashion, Paul puts 'Christ in you' into parallel with 'the Spirit indwelling you' at Rom. 8.10–11. For other passages in the undisputed letters where Christ and the Spirit are set alongside each other see 1 Cor. 15.45; 2 Cor. 3.17; Gal. 4.6. More often, of course, Paul speaks of Christians being 'in Christ', rather than of 'Christ living in them' (though see Gal. 2.20), but this is itself an argument in favour of Pauline origin for this material: an imitator would be more likely to copy the regular idiom. Paul does not refer to 'the indwelling Christ' as an individual mystical experience; for the corporate and communal aspect is often emphasized. So also here the strengthening of the Spirit in the inner person (v. 16) is a shared experience which can be expressed as 'Christ dwelling in your hearts' (plural), 'being rooted and founded' on the common ground of love (v. 17) and 'knowing *with all the saints* the love of Christ' (vv. 18f.).

The compound verb **dwell in** (*katoikein*) never occurs in undisputed Paul; its simple form (*oikein*), in reference to the Spirit indwelling believers, is also rare, occurring only at 1 Cor. 3.16 and Rom. 8.9, 11. Ephesians has used the related noun 'dwelling place' at 2.22, where, like Paul's more normal usage, it is the Spirit that dwells in believers.

This verb does, however, occur twice in Colossians (1.19 and 2.19) of the fullness of God or of deity 'dwelling bodily' or 'being pleased to dwell' in Christ. If Ephesians was dependent on Colossians for the use of this word, then we should have to suppose that it has dropped its strongly christological sense, of God indwelling Christ, and has taken Christ's indwelling of the heart in a soteriological sense, parallel to being strengthened by the Spirit. But then we should also have to suppose that

Ephesians has reintroduced a christocentric emphasis in verses 18–19, with its reference to the infinite love of Christ which Christians need to comprehend and contemplate. And finally, in verse 19, the writer of Ephesians has to be supposed to have gone back to these passages of Colossians and adopted the expression 'the fullness of God' but reapplied it to believers rather than to Christ. Conscious literary dependence on Colossians is thus very problematic, for the similarity of vocabulary is at a superficial level, and the writer is displaying that remarkable freedom to vary the meaning of certain words and reapply them which is almost an identifying characteristic of Paul himself.

It is **through faith** that Christ is able to enter and indwell the hearts of Christians, both in the sense of belief in his saving work and risen power and also in the sense of trust and the faithfulness that puts belief into practice. The meaning and importance of faith, the watchword of Paul's gospel (see on 2.5 and 8), are assumed here rather than explained, in a way entirely typical of Paul (see on 3.12 above).

Grammatically the plural nominative participles **you being rooted and founded on love**, may be taken either with verse 16, 'that he may grant you to be strengthened' (as a subsidiary prayer-wish, Lincoln 197) or forwards with verse 18, 'that you may be enabled'; or the words may stand alone and form a separate petition.

In the Greek **on love** comes before the participles in an ambiguous position. It could be taken with the previous clause, i.e. 'through faith by love' (as Robinson 175 and NEB; cf. 6.23), or it could be attached to what follows, as in our translation above, following the majority. (It is one of those linguistic ambiguities in Ephesians that a spoken rendering would have resolved.) The latter is more likely because without the reference to love, 'rooted and founded' would be left hanging in the air, so to speak. Nevertheless, the alternative construction, 'through faith by love', would allow faith to be understood as the root and foundation which enables understanding, which is what the parallels in Colossians say (Col. 1.23; 2.7; see below). So one might have expected those who emphasize the dependence of Ephesians on Colossians to support this construction, but they do not (see Lincoln 196; Schnackenburg 144).

Love without further definition could mean the love of believers for God and for each other and, if it were taken with the preceding clause (see above), it would probably have to have that meaning. But it could also be shorthand for 'the love of God in Christ' in anticipation of the explicit reference that is to follow at verse 19.

Rooted and founded is a striking pair of participles, combining organic and building metaphors in the way that Paul does at 1 Cor. 3.9 (cf. above on 2.21). They both occur in Colossians but in separate contexts, the first at 1.23, the second at 2.7. In both places they refer to undeviating adherence to the faith as Paul has taught it, a motif which does occur in Ephesians but later and in a very different context (see 4.20f.). In fact, it would be just as easy to imagine Colossians separately developing the double expression in Ephesians as to suppose Ephesians has conflated two verbs from different passages in Colossians but ignored entirely what they signify in their contexts. Neither explanation is necessary. The editor of Ephesians understands the foundation, in a way very different from either Col. 2.7 or this verse, as 'the apostles and prophets' (see on 2.20). So the phraseology and the thought here are likely to be Paul's.

18 What appears to be the second main petition in the prayer follows: **so that you may be able to grasp along with all the saints the breadth, length, height and depth**. It is probably dependent, like the first (v. 16), on verse 15, 'I kneel (i.e. 'I pray') . . . that'. But this verse might also be a purpose clause dependent on the reference to 'founded on love' in verse 17. The choice between these options depends on the possible meanings of this puzzling text.

A normal Greek verb for 'to be able' is used here with an additional emphasizing prefix (*exischuein*). It occurs nowhere else in the Greek Bible apart from Sir. 7.6. The following verb 'to grasp' (*katalambanesthai*) has the force of precise intellectual understanding. Its only other uses in the New Testament are in Acts, where it means to 'take the point' (10.34; 25.25) or 'take into consideration' (4.13). The strong emphasis on the special ability of intellectual comprehension in the first half of the verse has naturally led commentators, both ancient and modern, to try to find some deeper significance in the four terms in the second half – which are on the face of it a string of abstract nouns so vacuous as to defy precise intelligence.

Among the many interpretations, five different options are worth weighing, in case they offer insights into the way audiences with different interests and cultural backgrounds might have heard this text. If Ephesians is an expanded and reissued letter of Paul, then authorial intention and the context of those addressed will no longer function in the usual way as determinative controls on its interpretation.

(1) *The symbol of the cross.* This allegorical interpretation was favoured by the Church Fathers (Irenaeus *Haer.* 5.17.4; Augustine *Doct. Christ.* 2.4.1). The cross is the symbol of universal divine love, for the saving work of Christ reaches up to heaven and down to hell, and covers the world from East to West in a cruciform shape. The idea of a cosmic cross already appears in early New Testament Apocrypha and figures particularly in Jewish Christian theology (Daniélou 1964: 279–92). A minority of modern commentators (e.g. Schlier 174; Houlden 304) still defend this interpretation, pointing to the reference to the cross at 2.16 in a context of cosmic reconciliation that removes horizontal and vertical

barriers. They detect the related notion of Christ as the cosmic Man behind 4.13–16 (see comment there). This may sound a bit fanciful, but before rejecting it, we should recall how Paul meditates on the cross as the secret wisdom of God in 1 Cor. 1.18–25 and 2.1–13. However, while such an allusion would add profundity to the concept of Christ's love, there is no other support for it in the text. And we cannot even be sure that early Christians would have pictured the cross as having four limbs (the normal Latin cross, or *crux immissa*), and not (Hengel 1977: 8) as a capital T (the cross of St Anthony or *crux commissa*), in which case the allusion would be lost.

(2) *The dimensions of the heavenly Jerusalem*. A spiritualized topography of the Jerusalem Temple may lie behind the symbols of the dividing wall (2.14) and the cornerstone and foundations (2.20). So, 'founded on love' in the previous verse may evoke the New Jerusalem image again here. Rev. 21.16 provides precise measurements for the heavenly city (cf. Ezek. 48.16), using three of the same terms as Ephesians, length, breadth and height, which are all equal and measure 1500 miles in each direction! The significance of this enormous size is that it is capacious enough to contain not only the fullness of redeemed Israel (144,000, see Rev. 7.4) but also a countless number from the Gentile nations (Rev. 7.9). Revelation 21.17 goes on to speak of 'walls' measuring a mere 144 cubits (*c.* 75 metres) which are clearly not defensive but supportive walls, such as old Jerusalem itself was built on. So there are, strange to say, four, not three, spatial dimensions of the heavenly city: it is a perfect cube (like the Holy of Holies, 1 Kgs 6.20), *plus* an underneath layer (a 'depth') of apostolic foundations. If Paul wrote these words he was probably thinking about the present immensity of Christ's love (see (5) below) rather than the ultimate immensity of the Church, but that would not prevent the editor or some at least of his audience, acquainted with the traditions of apocalyptic, from understanding verse 18 with an ecclesiological meaning in such 'New Jerusalem' terms as those here suggested, i.e. that Christians needed to grasp the magnitude, vast though not infinite, of their heavenly inheritance built on the apostolic faith. However, it must be admitted that ecclesiology is not the dominant theme of chapter 3, even though it is never, as it were, very far below the surface (see v. 21).

(3) *The terminology of opponents*. We can consider under this heading a number of theories that offer to explain the terms of verse 18 as the disinfected vocabulary of some opposition group, whether gnosticism (Gnilka 188; Pokorný 1965: 78; cf. also Schlier under (1) above), Jewish Christian mysticism (Goulder 1991: 33–5), or pagan magic (Arnold 1989, *passim*). While not impossible, they all suffer from the same weakness: there is nothing in Ephesians at this point to imply that deviant beliefs are being refuted; and yet the author elsewhere is aware of

the danger of doctrinal controversy (4.14) and warns against associating with those who 'deceive with empty words' (5.6). So such a theory is not impossible in principle. However, without some signal of disapproval, the adoption of the terms supposedly used to describe the cosmic Christ in gnosticism, or in the Jewish Christian Elchasaite sect (as Goulder 1991, who quotes Hippolytus *Ref.* 9.131–3), or in pagan magical texts (*PGM* 4.960–85) to denote the location or the names of spirit powers (cf. Rom. 8.39 but see comment below), would only serve to lend credibility to such views. To suppose that, whatever the opposition, its views were sufficiently well known and understood for the mere juxtaposition of their specialist vocabulary with the reference to 'the love of Christ that surpasses knowledge' or 'the fullness of God' to guarantee recognition, entails the assumption that Ephesians was addressed to one precise and highly particular situation, which the present form of the letter refutes. The author of Ephesians has in any case a quite different strategy in dealing with deviant views from that of baptizing them into orthodoxy. He attacks them directly as the wiles of the devil (6.11f.) and discredits their proponents as immoral (5.11).

(4) *The wisdom of God.* The possible link, in the present form of the text, of verse 18 to the mention of the manifold wisdom of God in verse 10 has led a number of scholars (e.g. Dupont 1949: 489; Dahl 1975: 73–5) to detect here a reference to the cosmic dimensions and functions of wisdom. The relevant Old Testament background would be passages such as Job 11.5–9: 'Oh, that God would ... tell you the secrets of wisdom. It is *higher* than heaven ... *deeper* than Sheol ... its measure is *longer* than the earth and *broader* than the sea.' Paul refers to the 'depth' (but no other dimension) of the wisdom of God at Rom. 11.33, where, however, he has the paradoxes of Israel's salvation-history rather than the vastness of creation chiefly in mind. But for readers particularly attuned to the idea that Wisdom incarnate in Christ was the agent of God in creation (Col. 1.15–20; John 1.1–5), this would be a natural and consistent reading of the text, again in its present form.

(5) *The immeasurable love of Christ.* When taken closely with the following verse, the four measurements probably have one and the same referent, as the fact that they share a single definite article in the Greek implies, namely the love of Christ that surpasses knowledge. The meaning of the prayer is that Christians must make every intellectual effort to measure the immeasurable. This is a paradox with an authentic Pauline ring to it. In 1 Cor. 13.11, Paul says he has put away childish things in favour of a mature faith, but now 'we know only in part, until we know fully as we have already been fully known' by the love that is beyond knowing (1 Cor. 13.8–13). Using similar imagery of childhood (1 Cor. 3.1) and maturity (1 Cor. 2.6), Paul quotes at 1 Cor. 2.9 an unidentifiable

scriptural source to the effect that 'What no eye has seen, nor ear heard, nor the human heart conceived . . . what God has prepared for those who love him.' For human knowledge of spiritual things is divine self-knowledge operating within the human mind (1 Cor. 2.12).

Strong support for this interpretation may be drawn also from Rom. 8.35–9 (so also Lincoln 212 and Best 346), a passage which is strikingly similar both in its ideas and its exultant confident tone. There Paul asks rhetorically: 'What can separate us from the love of Christ?' Persecution cannot, for it makes us more than conquerors (8.37; cf. Eph. 3.13); mortality, angels, time and the devil cannot (8.38); nor can the whole vast created universe, i.e. 'nor height, nor depth nor anything else in all creation' (Rom. 8.39; cf. 8.20). That last sequence is given in Eph. 3.18f. in its full form: 'height, depth, length and breadth'; and instead of being understood as potential separators from the love of Christ, they appear here in a complementary way as its essential descriptors. While 'height' and 'depth' in Romans could possibly be names for supernatural powers, Ephesians, assuming its dependence, must be understood to have deliberately eliminated that possibility, despite its interest in the powers elsewhere. So perhaps we should not assume dependence, but attribute both passages to the independent creativity of Paul himself. If this section belonged to Paul's letter to the Laodiceans, it should be noted finally, then it *preceded* in date of composition the summary and further development in Romans of the theme of the greatness of God's love in Christ.

With all the saints. The usage is Paul's and means 'with all other Christians', like 1.1, 1.15 and 3.8, but unlike 1.18 and 2.19 (see comments on these passages).

19 If the fifth option above is correct, the previous verse is at last explained: **and to know the love of Christ that surpasses knowledge, and be filled with all the fullness of God**. The use of a new verb 'and to know' does not imply a new thought. It simply explicates 'to grasp' in verse 18 in a form that allows the oxymoron: 'to know . . . what surpasses knowledge'.

Paul speaks of the glory of the new covenant that *surpasses* the old at 2 Cor. 3.10 and of the peace of Christ that *passes* understanding at Phil. 4.7 (a different verb but a similar sense). An even nearer parallel is Phil. 3.8, where all his advantages as a Jew are treated as 'loss, because of the *surpassing* worth of knowing Christ Jesus my Lord'. All of these examples, like Eph. 3.19, entail a comparison: the love of Christ surpasses and exceeds human knowledge. The earlier uses of the same verb in Ephesians have been superlative rather than comparative: 'the *exceeding* greatness of his power' (1.19) and 'the *excellent* riches of his grace' (2.7).

The love of Christ is referred to only occasionally but at climactic points in Paul's letters (Rom. 8.35; Gal. 2.20 (cf. Eph. 5.2, 25) and 2 Cor. 5.14). This remarkable passage would certainly count as one such climax. A repeated emphasis on love, whether God's, Christ's or believers', is most distinctive in the New Testament of the Johannine writings, see e.g. John 13.1, 34–5; 17.26; 1 John 4.14–21, and Ephesians elsewhere also shares that emphasis.

There are several variant readings among the MSS for the last clause of the prayer. The majority text reads literally 'that you may be filled *into* the whole fullness of God'. Although 'with' (so RSV, REB) or 'up to' must be what is meant, the construction is awkward and invites emendation. By changing the verb to the third person singular (as P[46] and B) the offending preposition can simply be omitted altogether: 'so that the whole fullness of God might be fulfilled'. This also avoids any implication that Christians can attain to the unique status of embodying 'the whole fullness of God', which is reserved to Christ (see Col. 1.19; 2.9), and this is presumably the motive behind this secondary reading. But the author of Ephesians, unlike Colossians, is quite willing to speak of the Church, collectively and eschatologically (not as individual Christians here and now) on the same level as Christ in relation to God (see the following doxology, 3.21; on 1.23 above, and on 5.32 below; cf. Rev. 22.17). No use of the word 'fullness' in Paul comes close to this (see on 1.23). Since the first prayer report ended with a similar flourish, it may just be that the editor has done the same here. And by ending with a reference to God, rather than Christ, the transition to the doxology is eased.

B Doxology (3.20–1)

(20) To him who is able to do more abundantly, beyond everything that we ask or understand, according to the power at work in us, (21) to him be glory in the Church and in Christ Jesus through all generations for ever and ever, Amen.

Doxologies constructed on a basic three-part pattern ((1) 'to him / to you'; (2) 'be glory'; (3) 'for ever') are found in the Old Testament (e.g. 1 Chr. 29.11) and in intertestamental literature (Pr. Man. 15.2; 4 Macc. 18.24). They are popular among New Testament writers. The simple form occurs at Rom. 11.36; Gal. 1.5; 2 Tim. 4.18 and Heb. 13.21, and with one or more of the three clauses extended, sometimes to considerable length, at Rom. 16.25–7; Phil. 4.20; 1 Tim. 1.17; 1 Tim. 6.16; 1 Pet. 4.11; 1 Pet. 5.11; Jude 25; Rev. 1.6; 5.13; 7.10–12 (cf. also Matt. 6.13, *v.l.*). 2 Peter 3.18, yet another example of an extended doxology, is of particular interest since the ascription is clearly to Christ, rather than the Father, though several of the above examples are ambiguous on this point. If Paul added a doxology to the end of his prayer which was subsequently expanded, the referent might also originally have been unclear. (For a similar problem, compare Rom. 9.5.)

20 To him who is able to do more abundantly, beyond everything that we ask or understand, according to the power at work in us. The doxologies at Rom. 16.25 and Jude 25 also begin 'To him who is able'. His ability to do 'more abundantly, beyond everything that we ask or understand' picks up the idea of the love that exceeds knowledge in verse 19.

More abundantly (lit. 'hyper-abundantly', *huperekperissou*) is used twice in 1 Thessalonians (3.10; 5.13). The cognate verb 'to hyper-abound' occurs at Rom. 5.20 and 2 Cor. 7.14 (and there are 26 other instances of the verb in simple or compound forms in the Pauline corpus). This pleonastic form should not be over-interpreted, as though it could only refer to divine action (*contra* Lincoln 216). The Thessalonians references, for instance, concern human actions. This is why a further phrase, 'beyond everything' etc., is needed. Throughout the first half of Ephesians, the idea of the unimaginable greatness of God's design for the salvation of the world in Christ has been presented time and again, as it is fittingly here.

It is difficult to see the point of the last clause in this verse: **according to the power at work in us**. Comparison with the similar construction at 1.19 implies that it is a reinforcement of the idea of God's surpassing greatness, pointing to its powerful effect in the worship and lives of believers. However, in this context, it creates a certain tension, for after saying that God has the power to do much more than believers ask or understand, to continue 'according to the power at work *in us*' implies a limitation. The solution to this problem, namely to link the phrase to 'what we ask or understand' rather than to what God is able to do, should not therefore be dismissed too hastily (*contra* Lincoln 216). An alternative solution would be to take the phrase as referring not to Christians generally but to Paul's ministry in particular ('in *us*'), as an illustration of the divine power that exceeds all expectations (cf. Phil. 4.13, where Paul says 'I can do all things through him who strengthens me'). On balance, however, it is more likely that the phrase is an addition in the style of the editor.

21 To him be glory in the Church and in Christ Jesus through all generations for ever and ever, Amen. If the first limb of the doxology has been expanded to some degree, the second and third certainly have been. Glory is offered to God **in the Church and in Christ Jesus**. The co-ordination of the Church and Christ and the precedence given to the former is striking and unparalleled in the New Testament. The variants, omitting the 'and' (D^c K L P) or reversing the order (D^* F G), only serve to underline this fact. 'In the Church and in Christ' must be locative (so Best 350) and not (*contra* Houlden 305) instrumental (i.e. 'by the Church and by Christ'), for a doxology cannot, with reverence, instruct Christ to give glory to God. The editor is presumably looking forward to the eschatological consummation of the Church as the bride, the equal and complement of Christ the bridegroom (see on 5.32).

The last phrase (lit. 'to all generations of the age of the ages') is a combination of two traditional formulae with the same meaning: 'from generation to generation' (cf. Ps. 10.6; 85.5) and 'to ages of ages' (Gal. 1.5; Phil. 4.20). For the variation between generations and ages, compare 3.5 and 3.9 above. It is unlikely that there is any special significance in the combination, except to add emphasis and produce a rousing conclusion to the chapter and to the first half of the book.

IV Christian integrity   (4.1–16)

(1) I, the prisoner, exhort you therefore in the Lord to behave in a manner worthy of your proper calling, (2) with total humility and gentleness, and with patience being tolerant with one another in love, (3) eager to preserve the unity of the spirit in the bond of peace.

> **(4) One Body and one Spirit,**
> **just as you were called in the one hope of your calling,**
> **(5) one Lord, one faith, one Baptism,**
> **(6) one God and Father of all,**
> **who is over all and through all and in all.**

(7) But to each one of us grace has been given according to the measure of Christ's gift. (8) As the saying goes:

> **Ascended to the height,**
> **he captured captivity itself**
> **he gave the people gifts.**

(9) What does 'he ascended' mean if not also 'he descended' into the lower parts of the earth? (10) The one who himself descended is also the one who ascended above all the heavens in order to fill everything. (11) And he himself granted some to be apostles, some prophets, some evangelists, some pastors and teachers, (12) for the equipping of the saints, for the work of ministry, for the building up of the Body of Christ (13) until we all attain to the

unity of faith and of the knowledge of the Son of God, to a perfect Man, with a full stature measured by Christ himself, (14) so that we should cease to be infants buffeted and blown about by every current of teaching, devised by human vagary and cunning that promote the great scheme of error, (15) but rather that, by telling the truth in love we should grow up in all things into him who is the Head, Christ, (16) from whom the whole Body, being constructed and assembled through every supplying joint according to the proper activity of each individual part, achieves bodily growth, and so builds itself up in love.

A formal break with the first half of the letter is signalled with 'I exhort you' (*parakalô*), which is Paul's formula for the application of teaching to behaviour. In terms of content, however, the break is less well defined, for the theme of the unity of all things in Christ (1.10; 2.14) is reiterated strongly in this section, and the author's interest in the Church (1.23; 2.21–2) and its foundation in the apostolic ministry (2.20; 3.5) is further developed here, momentarily overshadowing the ethical exhortation (or *paraenesis*) which is resumed at 4.17. The title we have given this section, 'Christian integrity', is an attempt to convey the relation it implies between ethics and Church unity.

The passage may be divided into three parts: verses 1–3 are a personal plea from Paul for the qualities that preserve the unity of the spirit; verses 4–6 are a quasi-credal chant, basing Christian unity ultimately in the doctrine of God; verses 7–16 start from a modified quotation of Psalm 68 and offer an interpretation of it, explaining the gifts of the exalted Christ as various orders of ministry in the Church, and their purpose as bringing about unity in faith, spiritual maturity, and the growth of harmony and co-operation in the Church.

If we are correct in supposing that Ephesians is the expansion of an earlier letter of Paul and therefore lacks a basic pseudepigraphical motivation, when the first person singular is used, as it is here (and at 1.15f.; 3.1–8, 12f.; 6.21f.), it is because these passages come from Paul's own hand (5.32 would be the exception that proves the rule). In 4.1–3 there is no reason to doubt Pauline authorship. These verses echo and complete the earlier appeal to Paul's imprisonment (3.1, 13) and, unlike Colossians but in a manner typical of Paul, they consciously move from doctrine to ethics with the 'I exhort you' formula.

The theory that these verses are drawn from Col. 3.12–15 is complicated by the fact that two other passages in Ephesians (4.32 and 6.10) also echo the supposed source in Colossians. It is more likely that in two letters written at the same time an original author would repeat the sequence 'humility, gentleness, patience, being tolerant with each other', than that an imitator would extract it from Col. 3.12 and leave the rest of that verse, 'compassion, kindness and forgiving each other', until 4.32. This phenomenon, 'dispersal' rather than 'conflation' of sources, is very difficult to understand on the assumption of direct dependence on Colossians.

There are other problems with the theory of literary derivation from Colossians in this passage. In Col. 3.14 love is called the 'bond of perfection', referring presumably to Christ's love, whereas here it is love within the Church that is the 'bond of peace'. The Colossians are told to let 'Christ's peace reign in their hearts' (3.15) whereas in Ephesians the language is plainer: 'behave in a manner worthy of your proper calling'. If Ephesians is derived from Colossians the changes are very strange, for the latter's tight structure is loosened for no obvious reason, and its sharp christological focus is at first lost but comes strongly back into the centre in the credal and exegetical parts that are to follow, which have no parallel in Colossians.

1 The formula **I exhort you therefore in the Lord** is typically Pauline. Apart from the absence of the vocative 'my brethren' (which is not used in Ephesians, see on 6.23), this example conforms closely to the pattern that has been analysed in detail by Bjerkelund (1967: 13ff.) and is present at 1 Thess. 4.1 and Rom. 12.1 (and many other examples). Paul prefers to use **in the Lord** rather than 'in Christ' in contexts of moral exhortation like this. The word order allows the phrase to be taken with the noun, as it is in most translations, i.e. 'the prisoner in the Lord'. It would then be the equivalent of 'the prisoner of Christ' at 3.1; but it is difficult to see any reason for a change that would, if anything, be weaker than that earlier claim, and a reference to the speaker's situation and authority detracts from the appeal to intimacy and mutual trust on which the 'I beseech you' formula rests (so Bjerkelund 1967: 186, who for this reason rejects the whole verse as un-Pauline). It may be preferable, therefore, to take 'in the Lord' with the verb, in conformity with Paul's original formula.

The title **the prisoner**, or perhaps just its definite article, could be an addition by the editor (see on 3.1 above), but undue weight should not be attached to this point as though it were enough to discredit the whole verse as inauthentic. Lincoln (234), for instance, claims that 'it functions here to lend Paul's authority to the writer's pastoral appeal' and observes that 'this explicit feature of pseudonymity begins and ends the paraenetical section of the letter (cf. 6.19f.) but does not surface within it'. But he cannot explain why this should be so, nor why in both 3.1 and 4.1 the passing references are left undeveloped and unintegrated. If a pseudepigrapher wanted to appeal to Paul's unique authority in order to underwrite the exhortations that follow, other more appropriate titles (e.g. 'herald, apostle and teacher', see 2 Tim. 1.11; cf. 1 Tim. 2.7) would have been available to him. The unstated implication is presumably that imprisonment, far from being unworthy of Paul, is the way that for the present he is indeed behaving worthily of his own calling.

The readers are similarly **to behave in a manner worthy** of **your proper calling**. The concluding phrase represents the Greek 'the calling by which you were called'. This pleonasm is echoed by the editor in 4.4 in his attempt to fit verses 4–6 into their present context, but it is not in itself un-Pauline (see 1 Cor. 7.20). The thought is close to 1 Thess. 2.12: 'to lead a life worthy of God who calls'.

2 With total humility and gentleness, and with patience being tolerant with one another in love. Paul speaks of humility as the basic virtue that ensures the unity of the Church at Phil. 2.3 (see also Rom. 12.16). Distinctions of rank and wealth and personal rivalries are to be banished from the community life of Christians. The relative egalitarianism of the early Christian movement must have been one of its most attractive features to those marginalized by the class structures of Hellenistic urban society (Meeks 1983; G. Theissen 1982). In secular Greek, humility (*tapeinophrosunê*, 'humble-mindedness' and *tapeinotês*, 'humility') had negative overtones of servility (see Aristotle *Rhet.* 1384a4, where it is synonymous with *mikropsuchia* or 'small-mindedness'; cf. also Josephus *B.J.* 4.9.2). But in the 30 uses of the noun, verb or adjective in the New Testament, this negative connotation is entirely absent (though in Jas 1.9f. 'humble' means no more than 'impoverished'). The Old Testament and Jewish idea of humble submission to the will of God (see e.g. 1 Pet. 5.5, quoting Prov. 3.34 LXX) has eclipsed the social snobbery of the word's usage in Hellenistic Greek. In addition to its standard New Testament sense at Col. 3.12, Colossians also uses the word technically at 2.18 to mean 'self-humiliation', i.e. fasting, linking it with angel worship, but there is no hint of that peculiar meaning in Ephesians.

The other two terms, **gentleness** and **patience**, also belong to Paul's normal vocabulary of moral exhortation. They are two of the nine fruits of the Spirit in Gal. 5.2. Gentleness is the hallmark of Christ's own character at 2 Cor. 10.1 (cf. Matt. 11.28), and patience (lit. 'long suffering') is frequently commended (1 Thess. 5.14; 1 Cor. 13.14; 2 Cor. 6.6).

Being tolerant with one another in love. The verb 'tolerate' (*anechesthai*) is often used by Paul (especially in 2 Corinthians where he twists it ironically: 'Tolerate a little foolishness from me', 2 Cor. 11.1; cf. also 11.4, 19f.). Its use here is more straightforward and should be compared with the command to 'forgive each other' at 4.32. The moral injunctions that follow, especially at 5.4–5, sound distinctly *in*tolerant (at least to a modern reader) – there are definite limits to what is to be tolerated. Pre-conversion sins may be forgiven (cf. 4.17–22), but perhaps here it is merely the differences of ethnicity, status and sex that are to be 'tolerated' within the community.

God's tolerance in passing over the sins of Israel is mentioned at Rom. 3.25, and it is coupled with his patience at Rom. 2.4. The verb 'tolerate' standing alone can have the sense of 'endure', especially in face of persecution (1 Cor. 4.12; 2 Thess. 1.4). But without that connotation, it calls for more positive reinforcements, which are provided by linking it to 'with patience' and 'in love' as in the above translation. It is, however, possible to take 'in love' with the following phrase instead, i.e. 'eager in love ...'; ambiguities of this kind are frequent in Ephesians, not least in the case of references to love (see on 1.4; 3.17; 4.15), and would only be resolved by phrasing and intonation in a spoken rendition of the text.

3 Eager to preserve the unity of the spirit in the bond of peace. The verb 'to be eager', 'to hasten to' occurs in Paul at Gal. 2.10 and 1 Thess. 2.17, relating to the urgent matter of the collection for Jerusalem and Paul's eagerness to revisit one of his congregations. Its use with 'preserve' implies that the unity of the spirit is something that can be lost unless every effort is made to retain it.

If the spirit here is given a capital letter in English – in the earliest Greek MSS the whole text is written in capitals, so it is impossible to tell the difference – then the phrase means the 'unity in which the Spirit binds you together in peace'. But this translation, popular though it is, is heavily influenced by the proximity of the next verse. Clearly no amount of eagerness on the part of believers will affect the oneness of the Spirit of God in the strict sense of verse 4. However, if verse 3 comes from the source and verses 4–6 are extra material added by the editor, we need to challenge the presupposition that the connection in thought is entirely consistent. Indeed, the change from the oneness of spirit in the community to the one Spirit of God may be taken as an indication that verses 4–6 are secondary expansion.

The same term 'unity' occurs at 4.13 ('until we all attain to the unity of faith'), and this parallel may be another reason not to spell spirit with an initial capital. These are the only two uses of this abstract noun (*henotês*) in the Pauline corpus (cf. the more concrete expressions used at Eph. 2.14–16), although it is taken up enthusiastically by Ignatius of Antioch (see Ign. *Eph.* 4.2; 5.1; 14.1, and five references in his other letters). We cannot safely deduce from the fact that the word is not found elsewhere in Paul that he could not have used it just once or twice in his Laodicean letter, for in a comparable discussion of spiritual gifts in 1 Corinthians 12, the antonym of unity, namely 'diversities', appears just three times, in verses 4–6, but nowhere else in Paul or in the New Testament. Rather than inauthenticating the material, the presence of a

Pauline *hapax legomenon* may even certify its genuineness. An imitator might well have attempted to conform rather than innovate. The editor does, however, find in this phrase, 'the oneness of the spirit', a peg on which to hang the credal formula of verses 4–6.

In tone and thought, verses 4–6 interrupt the exhortation begun in verses 1–3. If we still possess in this chapter of Ephesians the next point that Paul originally intended to make, it is probably contained in verse 7 (see below).

4–6 (4) One Body and one Spirit,
just as you were called in the one hope of your calling,
(5) one Lord, one faith, one Baptism,
(6) one God and Father of all,
who is over all and through all and in all.

The style suddenly changes in verses 4–6 to one of verbless, creed-like aphorisms. The longer phrase at the end of verse 4, 'just as ... calling', is seen by several commentators (e.g. Schnackenburg 162) as an editorial adjustment to context, repeating the pleonasm of verse 1, 'called in ... your calling', and reflecting the editor's earlier interest in the link between vocation and hope (see 1.18). Lincoln (228), on the other hand, argues that the whole of verse 4 is the writer's composition, intended to form the connection with verses 1–3, and that separate credal material is found only in verses 5 and 6. This theory has the advantage of removing the ambiguity that otherwise affects the interpretation of verse 4 (see below), but it fails to take account of the cumulative integrity of verses 4–6. Moreover, it is based on the assumption that the author has derived verse 4 from Col. 3.15 ('called in the one body') and has expanded it with verses 5 and 6 which, since they have no parallel in Colossians, must be drawn from elsewhere. But Col. 3.15 is insufficient basis for verse 4 because it lacks the other key elements, the Holy Spirit and hope. It is more reasonable, therefore, just to remove the final phrase of verse 4 as editorial. The description in verse 6 of God as 'Father of all' might also have been added, but that case is even more difficult to decide (see below). Supposing that both these elements are secondary, we would be left with a clear triple triadic structure:

One Body, one Spirit, one Hope
One Lord, one Faith, one Baptism
One God, over all, through all, in all.

The function of this chant was probably to inculcate solidarity among believers by reference to some of the basic tenets of their common faith. Its use would be particularly appropriate when new members joined the group (see S. Hanson 1963: 159–61) and the mention of baptism in the second line and the formal similarity with other brief, possibly initiatory formulae (cf. Rom. 10.9 and Eph. 5.14) make this suggestion attractive (though the absence of any reference to the resurrection of Christ tells somewhat against it). But the use of such a chant need not be confined exclusively to a baptismal setting. Its stress on the unity of God and on salvation through faith in the one Lord would have many possible applications. Although it is clearly a Christian composition, it displays a certain reticence about the details of the Christ-event and emphasizes the unity of the only God in a way that points to an origin in Jewish Christian circles still in touch with the piety of the Diaspora synagogue.

The build-up of threefold phrases in this chant invites comparison with similar triadic hymnic material in the book of Revelation: the four living creatures, for instance, sing 'Holy, Holy, Holy is the Lord God Almighty, who was and is and is to come' (4.8); and the twenty-four elders echo this in their song, 'You are worthy, our Lord and God, to receive glory and honour and power, for you created all things and by your will all things existed and were created' (4.11) – passages where the element of redundancy is simply intended to achieve these triple patterns. We might also compare the early Christian creeds (Kelly 1960), which probably originated in baptismal professions of faith but diversified into other uses, and whose three-paragraph structure echoes this chant in Ephesians, though in reverse order, starting rather than ending with the one God.

Once a prior and independent tradition behind verses 4–6 is acknowledged, its interpretation becomes more complicated, for phrases which in their present context are reasonably clear could have had other, rather different, connotations when the material was used as a separate liturgical piece, as the comment on verse 4 will illustrate (cf. also above on 2.14).

4 One Body and one Spirit ... one hope. The opening line of the creed-like chant is ambiguous. In isolation from its present context the terms 'body' and 'spirit' could almost be taken as anthropological, signifying the constituents of common human nature. All humanity, descended from Adam, has the same flesh and the same divine breath or spirit (cf. Gen. 2.7; 1 Cor. 15.49). The union of the body and spirit, though dissolved at death, will be re-established in (resurrection) hope, and that would then explain the third element in the line. Anyone who used this text with 1 Corinthians 15 in mind could easily have interpreted it in this way, as laying out an (essentially Jewish) anthropological basis for the Christian doctrine of salvation that follows in the next line.

However, the image of the Church as the one, indivisible Body of Christ had probably become so well established in and beyond Pauline circles that it might well be invoked in this abbreviated fashion (cf. also Rom. 12.4; Col. 3.15) and this is almost certainly how the author of Ephesians understood the material he was incorporating. The ecclesiological sense of the first term then dictates a theological sense for the second and a collective sense for the third. Thus, the Church is a single body infused with the one and the same Holy Spirit of God and living in corporate hope of an eternal inheritance. Anyone who used this text with 1 Corinthians 12 in mind would naturally interpret the words in this way. The parallel with 1 Cor. 12.13, 'For in the one Spirit we were all baptized into one body', is particularly close. (The parallel would be even closer if the chant had referred to baptism in the first line and joined hope with faith in the second.)

The Church as the Body of Christ is 'one' because Christ cannot be divided (cf. 1 Cor. 1.13), though there may be divisions and quarrels within a particular congregation, which were Paul's concern when he wrote to the Corinthians. The threats to unity in the post-apostolic Church were even greater. The writer of 1 John, for instance, was faced with a full-blown schism, the separation of a whole group of Christians from the parent body (1 John 2.19); and the author of Ephesians, writing in the same region of Western Asia Minor and at around the same time, may also have had this problem in mind as he rehearsed this chant on Christian unity. His approach to the problem is more irenic than that of the Johannine writer. Ephesians does not demonize schism explicitly as the work of anti-Christ (1 John 2.18), nor claim that those who have left never belonged to the Church in the first place (1 John 2.19). But this passage is nevertheless similar, inasmuch as it absolutizes the unity of the Church by linking it doctrinally to the one Spirit, Lord and God. By contrast, the emphasis in other parts of this section (vv. 3, 13 and 16) is on the need for Christians to make efforts to preserve their unity and to grow up into a still greater unity. These two perspectives are not incompatible with each other as long as the unity of the Church is understood, as it was by Paul, as an eschatological anticipation of a future reality rather than a present dogmatic fact (see also on 5.32); as something given and yet also something to be striven for.

After Eph. 4.4–6, the passage in the New Testament that is most emphatic about the unity of the Church is undoubtedly John 17. There also it is deduced theologically from the unity of the Father and the Son, which is the pattern and basis for the unity between believers (17.11) and is extended to the unity between the first and later generations ('those who will believe in me because of their preaching', 17.20) united by the same apostolic faith, for the sake of the unity of humankind ('that the world may believe', 17.23).

The theme of the Church's unity is pervasive in the central section of the Fourth Gospel: 'other sheep not of this fold' that are to be brought in so that there will be 'one Shepherd, one flock' (10.10); the gathering together of the 'scattered children of God' (11.52); the drawing of 'all people' to the Christ uplifted on the cross (12.52); the union with Christ through an unrepeatable act of washing (13.10); the faith in God that also entails faith in the Son (14.1 and 10); the ministry of the Paraclete-Spirit through whom faith and knowledge of Jesus as the Son of God are brought together and confirmed (14.26; 15.26 and 16.12); the 'true Vine' in whom Christians are united by remaining rooted in him (15.1). What produced this extraordinary emphasis on unity in the Johannine community, and its multiple parallels with passages in Ephesians, was the experience of disunity, both of severance from the synagogue amid accusations of blasphemy and threats of violence (Martyn 1979; Brown 1979), and of subsequent internal schism on the part of a perfectionist élite (Bogart 1971). Learning these lessons from their recent history, the Johannine Christians at Ephesus were open to a rapprochement with the other traditions (Pauline and Petrine) in Asian Christianity (Brown 1979: 81–8).

5 It goes without saying that the **one Lord** is Jesus Christ (Rom. 10.9; Phil. 2.11). The title (cf. 1 Cor. 8.6) implies believers' exclusive personal allegiance as slaves of Christ and, for this writer especially, the exclusive metaphysical conviction that the whole cosmos is summed up and united in Christ (Eph. 1.10).

One faith. Faith can mean the act of believing, the content of what is believed, or indeed the virtue of faithfulness. The latter can be discounted in this context, but either of the first two is possible. According to Paul, Jews and Gentiles are both equally justified by faith (Rom. 3.30), and faith in this sense, as the act of believing in the gospel, is therefore one. A post-Pauline reader, however, might more naturally think of faith in terms of its content, especially in such a context as this passage, where credal articles are being listed. This is the sense that predominates in later New Testament writings. In the first century, Christianity as a movement was not held together by any recognized central authority or uniform hierarchical structures, nor by a fixed liturgy. It was nationally, ethnically and linguistically diverse (Rev. 7.9). What united this diversity was common faith in the Lordship of Christ, in whom all barriers were removed and all differences reconciled (cf. 2.14–18).

It is less obvious why there should be **one Baptism**, than one Lord and one faith. It may simply be due to the momentum of the chant. But if it is making a new and significant point, then there are several possibilities.

(1) There is one baptism because water baptism for the forgiveness of sins (as initiated by John the Baptist, Mark 1.4) is one and the same as baptism

for reception of the Spirit (following Jesus' example, Mark 1.10). Acts 19.3 refers to some Christians at Ephesus who knew only John's baptism until Paul put them right on the matter. Behind this account in Acts some scholars have detected a critique of the views of later followers of the Baptist, although this is not actually explicit in the text.

(2) The one baptism could be metaphorical, the 'baptism' of Christ as his unique saving work on the cross (see Mark 10.38; cf. Luke 12.50), an idiom with which Paul was also familiar (cf. Rom. 6.3; see further, J. A. T. Robinson 1962: 58–175). But one would have welcomed a little more help if that were the meaning intended.

(3) If these interpretations are too obscure and remote from the concerns of Ephesians, then the one baptism is more likely to be the once-for-all and unrepeatable act of commitment to faith in the one Lord. This is also the view of the Fourth Evangelist, that, 'once washed', the faithful disciple has no need of any further washing except his feet (13.10). Oscar Cullmann (1953: 105–10) has argued that the footwashing in John 13 is a parable on the meaning of baptism (so also Brown 1970: 566f.; cf. 558f.), and he further speculates that it contrasts the single moment of baptism with the repeated moments of eucharistic reconciliation.

The fact that baptism, like circumcision, was performed only once, as an initiation into the redeemed community, could lead to the false deduction that Christians are already morally perfect. It is likely that the schism within the Johannine community, referred to in the comment on verse 4, was in part at least caused by such a perfectionist deduction from the rite of baptism, entailing the denial of the possibility of post-baptismal sin (cf. 1 John 1.8, 10) and also perhaps of the reconciling function of the Eucharist (see John 6.53, where schism is also at issue, and 6.66; and cf. 1 John 5.6). The author of Ephesians will go on to challenge such views himself with his emphasis on the need for growth into Christian maturity and sanctity in the following section, verses 12ff.

The affirmation here in Ephesians of 'one baptism' had a powerful impact on the ecumenical movement in the twentieth century. Whatever their other divisions, sacramental or ecclesiological, separated Christian churches came to recognize that in baptism with water in the threefold name they remained united in an important sense.

6 One God and Father of all. 'All' could be either impersonal, 'all things', or personal, 'all people'. The latter is more likely in association with the idea of fatherhood, for in Ephesians God is the Father of Jesus Christ (1.3, 17) and through him of believers (1.2, and see comment on 3.15). However, the neuter, cosmological reference seems to be required in the following triadic formula 'over all, through all, in all' (cf. 1.10 and 1.23). The tension could be explained by supposing that the author wants either to widen out the idea of the Church towards the cosmos (so Lincoln 240) or, conversely, to narrow down the cosmic activities of God and locate them in the Church (so Schnackenburg 167). Perhaps the solution to this dilemma is simply to see 'Father of all' as an addition by the editor (see also on 1.17), by means of which a tradition celebrating the oneness of the God who generates, sustains and permeates the universe is made to refer to the Church. Any hint of pantheism in the formula would also thus be corrected. A similar explanation is often given for Paul's own additions to the proverb he quotes at 1 Cor. 8.6: ' "There are many gods and many lords in heaven and earth"; but for us one God – the Father – and one Lord – Jesus Christ.'

The underlying material has affinities with Jewish Wisdom speculation tinged with Stoicism, a potent mix in Hellenistic Judaism, whence it infiltrated the piety of early Christianity. The Jewish emphasis on the oneness of God, over against the polytheism of Greco-Roman official religion, is an important background for this material. It was given classic expression in the *Shema* ' (Deut. 6.4): 'Hear O Israel the Lord Thy God is One'. Worship of the only God and the claim to possess a unique revelation of him in Torah was the creed that held Jews in the Diaspora together (cf. Josephus *Ant.* 4.201). The same can be said of early Christianity, which saw both the propaganda advantage of a strong affirmation of monotheism (cf. Acts 17.23f.) with its claim to unique revelation recentred on the person of Christ, and also the apologetic advantage of this move as an answer to the Jewish charge of ditheism (cf. e.g. John 10.30–3).

When read with a Christian hermeneutic, the final formula becomes almost trinitarian (see on 2.22 and 3.15; cf.. 3.20f.). God is transcendent Father ('over all'), the same God in Christ is mediator of salvation ('through all') and in the Spirit indwells believers ('in all').

7 But to each one of us grace has been given according to the measure of Christ's gift. The connection with verses 4–6 is superficial and merely verbal, 'to each *one* of us'. The thought is completely different, for 'each one of us' points towards the idea of the diversity of gifts. This verse would follow on well, both in style and content, from verse 3. Maintaining the unity of the spirit would then be complemented by the variety of graces given to different individuals. Rom. 12.6–8 indicates how Paul himself might have developed the thought. The gifts mentioned there make it plain that the whole community is in view, not just its leaders. And this would also be the natural way of taking Eph. 4.7, were it not for the fact that the present form of the text continues with an exclusive focus on various types of leader (v. 11). Read in the light of what follows, 'each one of *us*' takes on a different meaning, i.e. 'each of us who continue the apostolic ministry as evangelists, pastors etc.'. The scholars are sharply divided on this issue: Merklein (1973: 62) and Mussner (122) argue for a limited reference to the 'hierarchy', Lincoln (241) and Best (376) for a wider reference to the 'laity', while Schnackenburg has admitted to changing his mind on the issue (175, n. 5). There are indeed good reasons for hesitation, for the text taken by itself has a Pauline ring and meaning but, inserted into this context, starts to mean something more exclusive. We are forced here, as elsewhere in Ephesians, to question the assumption of homogeneous composition.

Grace has been given. In the previous chapter (3.2, 7, 8) grace and gift were repeatedly emphasized with reference to Paul's own ministry of the gospel to the Gentiles. This passage will eventually come back to that idea, apostolic ministry as the gift of Christ (see v. 11), after a psalm citation and commentary upon it (vv. 8–10).

The phrase **according to the measure** can be read in different ways, depending on whether 'measure' means a limited amount, i.e. a unit of measurement (Matt. 7.2; cf. also John 3.34), or maximum capacity, full measure (Matt. 23.32). Paul uses it in both ways: at 2 Cor. 10.13 he claims that he has kept within 'set limits' in his mission territory (unlike others!), limits which, however, definitely include Corinth; while at Rom. 12.3 Christians are humbly to reckon others better than themselves 'according to the measure of faith', which can hardly mean varying amounts of faith, which would be grounds for some to congratulate themselves; it must surely mean the full measure possessed by all believers equally (see Cranfield 1975: 615f., for a thorough discussion). The two other references in this passage similarly vary in meaning (see vv. 13 and 16). It is not easy to determine here whether it is the abundance of grace or its allocation in different proportions that is meant. As the passage continues, the latter becomes increasingly more likely.

8 **As the saying goes:**
   Ascended to the height,
   he captured captivity itself
   he gave the people gifts.

This and the next two verses of Ephesians are possibly the most difficult in the whole letter. The reference to 'gifts' in the quotation of verse 8 is the point of connection back to verse 7 and forwards to verse 11, but it is a different feature of the passage that seems to preoccupy the writer's attention in his appended comments, verses 9–10, namely the reference to ascending to the height, which is understood to involve a corresponding descent to the depths. The text also raises other questions.

What is being quoted here? Why does the following explanation comment on words that are not even in the quotation? And how is the ascent/descent theme related to the gifts of ministry? The whole section (verses 7–11) lacks a 'close-knit structure of . . . argument' (*pace* Lincoln 241). It is highly compressed and allusive, as though the author could, given a more suitable occasion, say much more than he has allowed himself to do here. (For a similar case, compare 5.31f. and see commentary there.)

The introductory formula, **As the saying goes** (lit. 'Therefore it says'), is also used at 5.14, where the citation is not, apparently, from Scripture. When Paul is quoting the Jewish scripture, he normally makes it quite clear, even if we cannot always identify the citation (e.g. 1 Cor. 2.9), with a phrase like 'as it is written' (31 times) or 'Scripture' or 'God' or 'David (i.e. the Psalmist) says' (Rom. 4.3; Rom. 9.15; Rom. 4.7). But there is no parallel in Paul to this vague introduction (but cf. Jas 4.6). (Gal. 3.16 and Rom. 15.10 are not comparable, for the former explains words already quoted, i.e. 'this (text) means'; and the latter picks up 'it is written' in the verse before.) Although the text of Eph. 4.8 must ultimately be derived from Ps. 68.18, it may be quoted by the author not directly from Scripture but in a Christianized form from the hymnody of his community. It is clear from the Benedictus (Luke 1.68–79) and Magnificat (Luke 1.46–55) that whole phrases and verses could be lifted from the Old Testament and used in new Christian compositions (compare also e.g. Rev. 18.7f. with Isa. 47.9, and Luke 2.32 with Isa. 42.6). This would help to mitigate the problem of what would otherwise be an astonishingly bold interference with the text of Scripture on the part of the writer of Ephesians (see below). If this is correct, the quotation would have come from a larger whole which may have been familiar to some of the readers and, without the rest of it, it is hard to tell precisely what the hymn originally meant.

Ps. 68.18 reads: 'You ascended the high mount, leading captives in your train and receiving gifts from people, even from those who rebel against the Lord God's abiding there' (NRSV). The LXX translation (67.19) should also be taken into account: 'You have ascended on high, you have captured captivity, you have received gifts.' Notice that in Ephesians (1) the opening indicative 'you have ascended' has been changed into a participle, 'ascended'; (2) the second person 'you have captured' has been changed to the third, '*he* captured', and the LXX has been preferred to the Hebrew (there is no mention of *leading* captives); and (3) both the person and the verb of the last clause have been altered from 'you have received gifts' to 'he gave gifts'.

Psalm 68 originally depicted Yahweh's ascent in triumph to Mt Zion leading a train of previously captured enemies, to receive tribute from the rebels. One implication of the psalm was that Yahweh must have earlier

descended to help fight Israel's battles on earth. The crude anthro-
pomorphism implied would naturally invite reinterpretation. The
Aramaic translation (Targum) of Psalms accordingly obliges with a
radical reinterpretation: 'You have ascended to heaven *that is Moses the
prophet*, you have taken captivity captive, *you have learnt the words of the
Torah*, you have given it as gifts to men *and the Shekinah of the Glory of* the
Lord God dwells also with the rebellious, *if they turn in repentance*.' In this
expanded version, the one who ascends is no longer God but Moses, and
he ascends not just to Sinai but to heaven to have a mystical encounter
with God. (Such an interpretation may have been encouraged by the
allusion in the preceding verse of the psalm (68.17) to 'the chariots of
God', a stock theme in Jewish mystical speculation, following Ezekiel 1.)
Above all, it should be noted that, as in Ephesians, the Targum has
changed 'You received gifts' to 'You have given it as gifts'. While we
have no evidence that this way of reading the psalm was actually current
in the first century AD (the Targum on Psalms is of a much later date; see
Hall Harris 1996: 92–194), Moses-mysticism as such is early and
widespread (see esp. 2 Cor. 3.7 and cf. Philo *Vita Mos.* 1.158; and see
further Himmelfarb 1993), and it is possible that the interpretation was
known in early Jewish Christian circles. This would account neatly for
the alteration of the verb in the psalm text from 'receive' to 'give'. And
Eph. 4.8 could then be understood as a contradiction of the Targumic
interpretation: it was Christ, not Moses, who 'ascended' and his 'gifts'
were not Torah but Christian salvation (cf. John 6.32f.; 6.62). The
Johannine community was particularly interested in portraying Christ as
a prophet like, and superior to, Moses (see Meeks 1967; Brown 1979).
Putting together these observations on the puzzle presented by the psalm
text in Eph. 4.8, we could say that Ephesians is here quoting from an
early Christian hymn that has reused and adapted Psalm 68, transferring
to Christ what some Jews at the time claimed for Moses (cf. also John
1.1–18, esp. v. 15: 'the law was given through Moses, grace and truth
through Jesus', and v. 18: 'No one has ever seen God … ').

Ascended to the height (*anabas eis hupsos*). Making this a past
participle rather than an indicative appears to change the sequence of
events. If the participle has a temporal sense, i.e. 'having ascended', then
ascension must precede whatever is meant by 'he captured captivity'.
However, the past participle in Greek is not necessarily temporal; it can
describe an action that is coincident or identical with that of the main
verb, i.e. 'by ascending he captured'. What is definitely excluded is the
idea that capture *precedes* ascension, and yet surely this would have been
the most natural order to expect in a Christianized version of Psalm 68.
'He ascended, *after* having captured' would have allowed the allusions to
be to the exaltation of Christ *after* his crucifixion.

Nevertheless, when the author comes to comment on this text (v. 9), he will change the verb back from the participle to the indicative. This may imply that he was aware of the Old Testament text and its difference on this detail from the quotation he was using, and perhaps also some hesitation on his part about the order of events. His commentary in verses 9–10 will reintroduce the idea of a divine descent (see above on the original meaning of Psalm 68), which his quotation had obscured, and put ascension and giving gifts back into parallel as they are in the psalm; in the form quoted here that parallel has been subordinated to a different one, that between capturing captivity and giving gifts.

The next part of the psalm text, **he captured captivity itself**, is not explained in the following exegesis and it receives little notice from the commentators. They just refer in passing to Christ's exaltation over the powers at 1.21f. (Lincoln 242; Houlden 311). The thought then would be something like this: Christ's ascension, by subjecting the powers to his rule, allowed his gifts to be given to the Church. But it is surprising that the author of Ephesians, with his interest in the powers, does not make this sequence of thought more explicit when he comes to comment on the quotation. This does not necessarily rule out this reading. Hymnic material can legitimately carry more than one meaning. But there are other ways of taking 'he captured captivity' that are better able to explain this apparent neglect.

The writer and some of his readers might have been sufficiently attuned to Semitic idiom to understand correctly 'he captured captivity' to mean 'he took a large number of captives', and they might have interpreted the phrase as a reference not so much to captured 'powers' as to Christian converts who had been 'captured' and captivated by Christ. This possibility cannot be ruled out just because of the supposed parallel at Col. 2.15, for we should not assume that readers of Ephesians were constantly referring to Colossians, as most modern commentators do, to determine the sense of what they read.

At this point, it is worth remembering that Paul can use the images of capture in war and a triumphal procession in a very different and even more paradoxical way than Col. 2.15. For instance, at 2 Cor. 2.14 he prays: 'Thanks be to the God who always triumphs *over us*'. Paul is calling himself not a fellow-victor, but a victim of the vanquishing God! In the same vein, Paul writes at 1 Cor. 4.9: 'For God has exhibited us apostles as last of all, as though under sentence of death, a spectacle to the world, to angels and humans.' The term 'fellow prisoner of war' (derived from the same root as 'capture' and 'captivity' here) is used to describe apostles at Rom. 16.7; Phlm. 23; Col. 4.10. The description of Paul as 'the prisoner of Christ' (3.1; cf. 4.1) should also be remembered. In Ephesians, although Christ is exalted over the powers (cf. 1.21) and reveals things to them through the church (3.10), he is not said elsewhere to have yet captured or conquered them – indeed, they are still at work (see 2.2; 6.12).

The interpretation that takes apostles *par excellence* as captives of Christ not only fits the context well, it also explains why this part of the psalm text seems to be ignored, for then 'he took captives' and 'he gave the people gifts' both refer to the same thing, i.e. the provision of the apostolic ministry in the Church (cf. v. 11). The lack of any conjunction between these two clauses of the quotation may also imply that they have the same referent. And the order of ascension followed by capture is now perfectly understandable (but see further below), since it is the risen Christ who calls apostles (cf. 1 Cor 9.1; 15.7f.).

So far we have argued that he 'captured captivity' and 'gave gifts to the people' may be taken to refer to the same action at the same moment in time. But before we decide that this is the only possible meaning, we need to take another look at 'he captured captivity': it strongly evokes an earlier formulation, 'he killed the enmity', at Eph. 2.16 and it would be natural to take it in the same way, as an allusion to the reconciling effects of the cross, notwithstanding the other interpretation for the phrase proposed above. But then 'ascended to the height' seems to come too soon, as we have already noted. This oddity leads us to reflect on what other meanings there might be for 'ascended'. The text might be taken to imply that this atonement ('capturing captivity') was achieved not only by Christ's ascension into heaven after death, but also by some other 'ascension' or 'going up', namely his lifting up on the cross, which is of course at the same time his descent into the realm of death (see v. 9). And it was by this action that 'captivity', i.e. sin and death, was defeated in the unique anticipatory case of Jesus himself.

This line of reasoning would be greatly reinforced if an audience in Ephesus towards the end of the first century were aware of the sort of 'passion-mysticism' developing in the Johannine circle. The Fourth Gospel plays on the use of the verb 'to exalt' or 'lift up on high' (*hupsoun*) with precisely this double meaning (at 3.13–14; 8.28; 12.32–4). The first of these passages is particularly relevant to the exegesis that the writer of Ephesians is about to offer for his text: 'No one has *ascended* into heaven except the one who has *descended* from heaven, namely the Son of Man [who is in heaven]. For just as Moses lifted up (*hupsōsen*) the serpent in the wilderness, so also the Son of Man must be lifted up (*hupsōthēnai*).' Notice the use of 'ascended' and 'descended' as correlative terms and that the verb 'lifted up' is formed from the noun (*hupsos*), translated above as 'ascended to the *height*'.

Combination of the two possible meanings of 'he captured captivity' discussed so far, the atoning death of Christ and the calling of apostles, would not be so strange to anyone who knew of Paul's understanding of apostleship as authenticated not just by a call from the exalted Christ but also by conformity to the crucified Christ (see e.g. Gal. 6.14f.; 2 Cor. 4.10f.; 12.9–12).

On this alternative interpretation, each of the three clauses of the hymn could be taken to refer to one and the same moment: the ascending to the height is already Christ's lifting up on the cross, which is also his capturing of captivity in both senses, his atoning death and his appointment of apostles, who are his gifts to the Church. It remains to be seen whether there is any support for such a condensed reading of the quotation in the author's all too brief and enigmatic commentary upon it in the next two verses.

9 What does 'he ascended' mean if not also 'he descended' into the lower parts of the earth? As noted above, the author changes the verb back from the participle to the indicative while retaining the third person form. He seems to be offering here a rather unusual explanation of the meaning of the verb, and not merely deducing descent from the reference to ascent.

Two variant readings should be noted before we discuss this strangely worded question. Several MSS (including ℵ^c and B) and versions have added the adverb 'first', underlining the idea of a temporal sequence: he *first* descended, then he ascended. One interpretation (see (3) below) rejects this reading because it sees the temporal sequence as the opposite, first ascent and then descent. We also reject it, but for different reasons, because it is the easier reading and naïvely resolves what is intended to be a deliberate ambiguity.

Secondly, some witnesses (P^46 D* Irenaeus Origen) omit the word *merê*, translated 'parts' or 'regions', producing the translation 'the lower things of the earth' or 'the things lower than the earth'. There is little to choose between the variants: either could be correct. But the addition or omission of *merê* may be the result of an attempt, albeit unsuccessful, to resolve the ambiguity of whether the phrase refers to the earth itself or the underworld.

There are three very different ways of taking this exegetical comment, and none of them offers an entirely satisfactory explanation of all its puzzling aspects. Different interpreters have understood 'he descended' to refer to (1) the descent into hell or (2) the descent to earth at the incarnation or (3) the descent of the Spirit at Pentecost. Some comments on each of these in turn will highlight their strengths and the problems they leave unsolved.

(1) The first, a reference to the descent into the underworld, is the view most widely adopted by Patristic commentators and some modern commentators (e.g. Robinson 180; Dunn 1989: 186f.; Arnold 1989: 57; Kreitzer 1997: 127). In its favour are the following points. It is the most natural reading of the phrase 'lower regions of the earth' in contra-distinction to 'above all the heavens' in the next verse. It is supported by Rom. 10.6–8, which is also a Christian revision of an Old Testament

text (Deut. 30.12–14); here Christ's death (v. 7) is described in a similar way, as his 'going down into the abyss'. It provides an allusion to the death of Christ which might otherwise be thought to be missing in this passage. And as 1 Pet. 3.19 shows, theological interest in the reason for the three-day delay between the crucifixion and resurrection was growing in the post-apostolic period (see also Matt. 12.40; 27.52; cf. the Apostles' Creed, 'he descended into hell').

However, there are several problems with this view. It fails to explain why a reference to the descent into hell is needed when the main point is the connection between the exaltation of Christ and his gift of leadership in the Church. Furthermore, no other passage elsewhere in Ephesians displays any interest in the effect of Christ's work in the underworld, and the presupposition for such speculation is missing, for in Ephesians malign spiritual forces inhabit the air or the lower reaches of heaven (2.2; 6.12), they do not imprison or torment the souls of the departed in Sheol. Despite these objections, it is difficult to deny that the most natural meaning for 'he descended into the depths of the earth' is indeed a reference to the death of Christ, though perhaps simply to his death.

(2) The second view, that the reference is to the incarnation, is maintained by several modern commentators (Mitton 147; Schnackenburg 178; Best 386). It also has advantages. The descent motif would correspond more precisely to the ascent motif: in other words, since the ascent is from earth to heaven, the descent should be from heaven to earth (and not from the earth into the underworld). And it can appeal for support to Phil. 2.6–11, where Christ's voluntary self-emptying to take human form as a servant is followed by his exaltation and universal sovereignty (Phil. 2.10), described in terms similar to those of verse 10. Even more than the descent into hell, the doctrine of the incarnation preoccupied theological interest in post-apostolic times. The MS tradition that added 'first' to the reference to 'he descended' (see above) may not be the correct reading but it may be an early and correct interpretation. Lastly, the original implication of Psalm 68, that Yahweh must have first descended to help defeat Israel's enemies before he ascended in triumph to Zion, then becomes the model for the descent and subsequent ascent of the incarnate Christ.

However, there are also problems with this second interpretation. While the resurrection to heaven of Christ is indeed emphasized elsewhere in Ephesians (e.g. 1.19f.), there is no other reference to his incarnation, and one might have expected such a momentous idea to receive more than a passing allusion. To use the phrase 'the lower parts of the earth' to mean 'the lower parts of the cosmos, namely the earth' is hardly a natural way of speaking. And to refer to the incarnation simply as a descent to earth does not cover the key point in the doctrine, which is the assumption of human flesh (Rom. 8.3; John 1.14; 1 John 4.2) or human form (Phil. 2.8). Furthermore, the deduction of 'he descended' from 'he ascended' is the opposite of what a statement of that doctrine requires, for it would allow a similar claim to be made on behalf of anyone else (Enoch, Moses, Elijah and Isaiah, for example) who supposedly ascended to heaven; one could argue that they also must have previously descended from heaven! The view taken by the writer of the Fourth Gospel is the exact opposite of this: 'no one has ascended into heaven except the one who has descended from heaven' (John 3.13; see above on v. 8). This passage in John, however, remains remarkably similar to Eph. 4.9, a similarity which is noted by some commentators (Barth 432), though ignored (Lincoln 242) or rejected (Schnackenburg 178) by others. So there may be some truth in the claim that this verse alludes to the incarnation, but it is unlikely to be the whole truth.

(3) The third interpretation, which takes 'he descended' to refer to the descent of the Spirit at Pentecost, is a modern solution to the problems facing the two earlier views. It was first suggested as a possibility by von Soden in 1891 (see Lincoln 246) and developed into a theory by Caird (1964: 536–43), Kirby (1968: 145f. and 187n), and most recently Hall Harris (1996: 235ff.) and is followed tentatively by Lincoln (246f.); it has several points in its favour. First, it begins from the observation, surely correct, that the main thrust of the psalm text and the author's interpretation of it is the relation between the ascension and the giving of gifts. If the descent into hell or the descent to earth at the incarnation were meant, the allusion has been left undeveloped in what follows.

Secondly, Psalm 68 was used at the Jewish feast of Pentecost (Kirby 1968: 145), and the Targum on Psalms shows that it may have been interpreted in Jewish circles to refer to an ascent (of Moses to heaven) *followed* by a descent (to give the gift of Torah to Israel). The text of Eph. 4.8, so these scholars argue, has made the same change to the sequence of events as the Targum; the addition of 'first' (see above) was an early scribal misunderstanding that has skewed the interpretation of this passage ever since.

Thirdly, in the account in the Acts of the Apostles, the ascension of Christ (chapter 1) is followed by the giving of gifts to the Church at Pentecost (chapter 2) and this corresponds to the sequence of events in the quotation, first ascent then descent.

Finally verses 9–10 imply that the Spirit is not to be distinguished from the risen Christ himself (see Rom. 8.9–11 and 1 Cor. 15.45). In Ephesians also the Spirit and Christ are almost interchangeable (1.13, cf. 4.30; 3.16f.; 1.23, cf. 5.18; cf. also John 14.16, 18).

Despite these valuable insights, this view faces several difficulties. First, it is only Luke among the writers of the New Testament who separates the resurrection, ascension and giving of the Spirit as three distinct events. And he has special reasons for doing so. His emphasis on the physicality of the resurrection body (Luke 24.35) necessitates a final departure at a particular moment of ascension. Luke's account of Pentecost as another event, ten days later, is also peculiar to him (contrast John 20.17). It allows him to see the gift of the Spirit enabling world mission as a partial compensation for the delayed parousia. Can we assume that such Lucan idiosyncrasies were widely enough known and accepted in Asia at the time of Ephesians to be presupposed in this exegesis of Psalm 68?

Secondly, the Acts account is at odds with this interpretation of Eph. 4.9 at two key points. Pentecost in Acts is precisely *not* the descent of Christ but of the Spirit in his place, for Christ himself 'will come again in the same way as you have seen him go' (Acts 1.11). And again, while amazing spiritual gifts are indeed given in the Pentecost scene in Acts, apostleship is definitely not one of them, for it depends on knowledge of the historical Jesus (see Acts 1.21–5) and not merely on inspiration. In other words, this interpretation attributes to Ephesians the time-frame of Luke-Acts but then fills it out with a different content drawn from Paul, namely that apostleship is the gift of the risen Christ himself (cf. 1 Cor. 9.1; 1 Cor. 15.8; Gal. 1.6, cf. John 20.21f.).

(4) Is there a solution to this old problem that is able to combine the best insights of the three earlier views? We can start perhaps by accepting from (1) that 'he descended into the lower parts of the earth' is most likely to be a reference to the death of Christ; from (2) that the descent-ascent motif of John 3.13 is too close a parallel to be ignored, especially when it is remembered that it actually continues (v. 14) with a reference to Moses, whose 'lifting up on high' of the serpent in the wilderness is a type for the lifting up of Christ on the cross; and from (3) that, although the peculiar time-frame of Luke-Acts should not be imposed on Ephesians, the main point of the passage is indeed to relate the exaltation of Christ to the gift of ministry in the Church.

While previous theories have assumed that 'he ascended' must either follow 'he descended' as in (1) and (2), or precede it as in (3), the neglected possibility is that the actions are taken as simultaneous. This is, after all, what verse 9 says. There is no justification in the Greek for the RSV translation 'that he *had* descended'; and the text does not say that 'he ascended' implies either a prior or subsequent descent. Rather, it asks, in a question that is not merely rhetorical, whether 'he ascended' does not also mean 'he descended'. On this reading, what might have seemed an almost pedantic verbal deduction in an inconsequential parenthesis becomes instead a profound insight. The crucified Christ 'raised up on high' at that very moment plumbed the depths; his humiliation was his exaltation, as Paul (1 Cor. 2.8) and John (John 12.28) would have agreed (see also Mark 10.37, and Muddiman 1987: 51–8).

John's Gospel is extremely subtle on the descent–ascent motif: it combines in a paradoxical way three different spatial schemes: (1) the Word descended from heaven to earth at the incarnation *before* he ascended back to the Father; but (2) Christ also ascended the cross, which was *at the same time* his descent to death; and (3) the ascent of Christ in another sense was *followed by* his descent in the form of the Paraclete-Spirit in the Church. Unlike Luke-Acts, which is driven by narrative simplicities, the theologian of the Fourth Gospel refuses to string out in a sequence what must theologically be held together – the incarnation, death, exaltation and sending of the Paraclete. This 'concertina' of separate ideas into an 'eternal now' is expressed at John 16.16 with the riddle: 'A little while and you will not see me and again a little while and you will see me'. According to John, resurrection, Pentecost and parousia occur simultaneously (cf. Bultmann 1971: 581). 'The little while' may be a few hours only or many years; Jesus will be seen again in his resurrection, in the gift of the Paraclete and when he comes again at the end of time. In the same way, lifting up and crucifixion happen at the same moment. And indeed, the whole of salvation-history can be compressed into a single day (cf. John 8.56).

Furthermore, in Johannine theology the exalted Christ, crucified and yet glorified, gives gifts to his Church. On the cross he bestows spirit, water and blood as his witnesses (John 19.30, 34; cf. 1 John 5.6) and creates the Church by uniting his mother with his beloved disciple (John 19.26f.; see comment on 5.31 below). At the resurrection, Christ breathes out his spirit (John 20.22) and endows the leaders of the Church with the authority to forgive sins; and finally Christ sends (15.26) or 'comes again as' (14.18) the Paraclete to perform the ministerial functions of remembering, teaching (14.26) and defending the truth (16.8). Thus, if Eph. 4.9 is Pentecostal, it is more like a Johannine than a Lucan Pentecost.

We have seen that the ambiguity created by the alteration of the time sequence in the text of Psalm 68 is almost as important for understanding the writer's exegesis of it as the more dramatic change of 'you received gifts' to 'he gave gifts'. Ministerial office in the Church (v. 11) is to be understood in relation to the indivisible saving event of Christ's death, exaltation and gift of the Spirit. Is this interpretation supported by the way the author proceeds with his next comment?

10 The one who himself descended is also the one who ascended above all the heavens in order to fill everything. It is the emphasizing pronoun 'himself' (*autos*), not the identifying pronoun 'the same' (which would be *ho autos* in Greek), that is used here and it qualifies the first participle not the second, i.e. 'he who himself descended'. Many translations either mistranslate (JB, REB, NRSV) or fail to translate (RSV) the pronoun. This emphasis corresponds to that in

John 10.18: 'No one takes my life from me, I lay it down of *my own accord*' (lit. 'of myself'). It indicates that the descent into death (which was also his lifting up on high) was entirely voluntary. But why is the rest of the sentence needed?

The apparent repetition in this verse of a point which might be thought to have been adequately stated in the preceding one requires an explanation. It might be taken merely as the writer's 'habit of labouring a point unnecessarily' (Lincoln 247). Those who take the 'Descent into hell' view see this verse as emphasizing the exaltation of Christ as simply the reversal of his death. Those who adopt the 'Incarnation' view attempt to find here an exclusion of the error of docetism, through the assertion of the personal identity of the earthly Jesus with the heavenly Christ. Neither explanation is very convincing. Those who prefer the 'Pentecost' view argue that this assertion of the identity of the Spirit ('he who descended') with Christ ('he who ascended') is fully explained by their theory, for verse 10 would be claiming that the Spirit in the Church is the presence of Christ himself. But if the other arguments given above against that view are accepted, then an alternative interpretation consistent with option (4) should be considered. The point of this verse would then be to assert that alongside the paradoxical sense of the crucifixion as 'an ascending on high to capture captivity' there is also a more straightforward, *literal* sense of ascension as the exaltation of the risen Christ to heaven (cf. John 20.17) and his cosmic lordship.

Above all the heavens. Paul speaks of at least three heavens (2 Cor. 12.2); other Jewish writers were not so restrained (see Lincoln 1981: 78–80) and the number of heavens was a topic of lively speculation. The exaltation is **in order to fill everything**. This could be merely a flourish to finish off the section, echoing the earlier reference to the idea of filling everything (see on 1.23) (so Best 388). Or it could be connected more closely with what follows and refer to Christ's filling the whole Church with gifts and powers (Meuzelaar 1961: 135; and see again on 1.23, cf. 4.6). Or again, it could link back to Christ's descent to the lowest depths and emphasize by contrast his ascent above the highest heavens, thus encompassing the whole cosmos, its height and depth (cf. Rom. 8.39 and the discussion at Eph. 3.18f.). The last solution is probably correct.

It may be useful here to summarize the argument. The quotation with its remarkable alteration of the text of Psalm 68 probably came to the author via the worship of his community. The author's comments on it in verses 9f. make three main points:

(1) Since Christ captured captivity on the cross, 'he ascended' does not mean just what it says literally; it also means 'he descended', for his lifting up on high was at the same time his reaching down into the depths of suffering and death.

(2) The captivity he captured was not only the negative overcoming of the powers of sin and death, but also the positive capturing of the hearts and minds of those, his apostles and servants, whom he would give as gifts to his Church.

(3) The paradoxical identification of ascent with descent in verse 9 requires the further affirmation in verse 10 of the literal glorious exaltation of the risen Christ to the right hand of God in order to fill all things.

11 And he himself granted some to be apostles, some prophets, some evangelists, some pastors and teachers.[6] The pronoun 'himself' appears again (cf. v. 10) and is emphatic: it identifies the crucified and exalted one of verses 9–10 as the source of the gifts of ministry. The verb **he granted** (or 'he has given', see the comment on 1.22 above) echoes 'he gave the people gifts' in the quotation (v. 8), but the application is more restricted here than we have been led to expect by verse 7 (but see the comment on verse 8).

On **apostles** and **prophets** as the founding fathers of the first generation, see the comments on 1.1, 2.20 and 3.5. At 1 Cor. 12.28, Paul puts **teachers** next in his list, but in Ephesians they come later, after two new terms, **evangelists** and **pastors**. These titles for church leaders are both rare. 'Evangelist' occurs elsewhere only at Acts 21.8 (of Philip) and 2 Tim. 4.5 (of Timothy himself), and it is not clear that in either case

---

[6] Since Merklein's study of authority in the Church (1973), the translation of this verse has been hotly disputed. The translation above assumes that the titles of church officers are predicative: i.e. 'he granted some *to be* apostles' or 'he appointed some *as* apostles' etc. In a list like this, indicated by the particles 'first' (or 'on the one hand, *men*) and 'second' (or 'on the other hand', *de*), the Greek language normally prefers to use relative pronouns rather than, as here, definite articles (see 1 Cor. 12.28), but it is not a cast-iron rule (see 1 Cor. 7.7). If the articles are taken with the nouns attributively, the following translation would result: 'he gave first *the* apostles, second *the* prophets' etc. (so, adamantly, Merklein 1973: 73–5; followed by Lincoln 249; Schnackenburg, tentatively, 180; and Best, apparently, 389, but cf. 374). However, there are several difficulties with this translation. What is given turns out to be the actual people rather than their appointment to certain roles, and the verb is left without an indirect object indicating *to whom* they have been given (cf. 1 Cor. 12.28). Furthermore, while *the* apostles and *the* prophets are understandable emphasis, given the earlier references to them, it is harder to understand why the definite article is used with the other ministers, who have not been mentioned before. And lastly, the Greek particles referred to above, while they are often used definitely to contrast two articular nouns, when they appear with a longer series the items in that series are usually *indefinite*. The departure from normal usage is perfectly understandable in this instance, if the author felt that in the light of 2.20 and 3.5 'apostles and prophets' demanded the definite article. So, despite the subtle discussions of the commentators, the translation above (in agreement with RSV, REB, and Porter 1994: 113) is still preferable.

it denotes a specific office rather than a function. The use of this term as the designation for a liturgical deacon or a Gospel writer is attested only later (see *DBI* 218–20). 'Pastor' (i.e. shepherd) occurs only here in the New Testament with reference to an order of ministry, though related pastoral metaphors are found at Acts 20.28, 1 Pet. 5.1–4 and John 21.16. It implies care and nurture of the faith of a local congregation. The distinction between itinerant and resident church leaders, which lay behind the terms 'apostles' and 'prophets' for the first generation, is thus maintained in the distinction between 'evangelists' and 'pastors' in the second: evangelists are the missionary successors of the apostles, just as pastors and teachers are the local successors of the prophets (see MacDonald 1988: 133).

By the time of Ephesians, other titles for local church leaders, bishop/presbyter and deacon, were becoming established; compare the Pastorals, *1 Clement* and Ignatius. Fischer (1973: 21ff.) has argued that the avoidance of these specific titles by the author of Ephesians is deliberate and implies his rejection of them and the institutionalizing tendency they represent. But if the author wanted to oppose 'clericalism', he went about it in an odd way, for he has identified Christ's gifts to the Church exclusively in terms of its leadership. It is more likely that he is interpreting the earlier titles, apostle and prophet, by means of these other terms to indicate his understanding of their main functions: to preach the good news and care for Christ's flock respectively; and that he was flexible about the actual titles by which these activities could be duly recognized in the Church. There is evidence in the New Testament of a certain Jewish Christian hesitation about the use of fixed titles for church offices. Matthew rejects those that are being introduced in contemporary Judaism (Matt. 23.8f., 'rabbi' and 'abba'). 2 and 3 John were written by someone who was content to call himself simply 'the Elder' (see Campbell 1994, and the discussion below on 6.4). Hebrews is particularly vague in its reference to 'leaders' at 13.11.

Teachers. Apart from 1 Cor. 12.28, this title as such is not used by Paul (cf. 1 Cor. 14.26; Rom. 12.7). At Acts 13.1 'prophets and teachers' are the titles of the leaders at Antioch, including Saul. Teaching is also described as one of the chief functions of bishops (1 Tim. 3.2) or presiding elders (1 Tim. 5.17) in the Pastoral Epistles.

It is unclear whether teachers are a separate category or should be taken closely with pastors. The 'some to be' formula is missing with this last item in the list, but it may have been dropped as unnecessarily tedious repetition. The question of a distinctive office of teacher in Ephesians can be answered only in relation to the way the functions of ministers are described in the next verse.

12 For the equipping of the saints, for the work of ministry, for

the building up of the Body of Christ. The function of the various leaders is now described. The different types of leaders have been granted, not to enhance their own prestige or power, but to equip, serve and build up the whole community (or, possibly, to equip the whole community to serve, and build *itself* up as Christ's body; see below).

The above translation takes the three prepositional phrases as each equal and separate (so also Lincoln 253; Schnackenburg 182; and see Gordon 1994). This is consistent with the style and compositional technique of Ephesians, piling up prepositional phrases (here, 'towards', 'into', 'into') which are only loosely connected (cf. also e.g. 1.14). The next verse displays a similar structure with, literally, '*to* unity, *to* a perfect Man, *to* the measure', and so does verse 14 ('*in* vagary, *in* cunning, *towards* the scheme of error'). We have taken these parallels to be decisive. The earlier triple pattern of the credal material at verses 4–6 may also have influenced the editor to continue with it in this paragraph.

However, before we discuss the meaning of the three clauses in verse 12, another way of construing it should be considered. The first two phrases could be combined into one, i.e. 'to equip the saints for the work of ministry' (so Caird 76; Mitton 151; Best 396). It is then the whole community that is to do the 'work of ministry' (on the meanings of this phrase, see below). This is possible grammatically (though the motivation of those who support the view may be to try to distance Ephesians from the institutionalized clericalism of a deutero-Pauline 'early catholicism', or any of its modern–day equivalents). If the first two phrases are combined, the third becomes ambiguous: it might be intended either to explain what the word 'ministry' means, as the activity of all the saints, or to explain what 'equipping' means as the activity of church leaders. But this very ambiguity makes the earlier solution of three distinct clauses more likely.

A key factor in the sharp disagreement among the commentators has been whether 'equipping (*katartismos*) the saints' can stand as a phrase on its own. This noun occurs only here in the New Testament but its root verb occurs several times in Paul's letters. At 1 Thess. 3.10 and Gal. 6.1 it has the sense of 'repair' or 'restore'. It can also have the sense of 'equip', as at 1 Cor. 1.10 ('equipped with one mind'), or 'prepare', as at Rom. 9.22 ('prepared for destruction'), and in this latter sense it may be felt to require, as in the examples just quoted, some further phrase, explicit or implied, to complete its meaning.

Comparison with the ambiguity in the sense of the word at Mark 1.19 well illustrates the problem. There John and James are either *repairing* (torn) nets (see also Luke 5.6 and contrast John 21.11) or else *preparing* nets (i.e. arranging them neatly) for a future catch. Accordingly, if it stands on its own, the phrase could mean 'restore the saints', i.e. readmit lapsed Christians into fellowship, and certainly such a function is the prerogative of church leaders (see 2 Cor. 2.6–8), even if there is no other indication in Ephesians that this problem is in view. Or it could mean 'to equip people to be saints', to make them holy and blameless (cf. 1.4; 5.3; cf. 4.24). This adjectival use of saints is sufficiently well evidenced in Ephesians to allow the possibility here.

Ministry (or 'service', *diakonia*) is a word used in the New Testament in the senses both of charitable service and of the work of 'serving the word', i.e. preaching (see Acts 6.2). The decision between these options largely depends on whether the implied subject is leaders or the whole community. Service as works of charity is probably the meaning at Rom. 12.7 (cf. 1 Pet. 4.11); at 1 Cor. 12.5, 'varieties of service' parallels 'varieties of gifts' (*charismata*) and includes all kinds of God-given capacities and functions within the Church; at 1 Cor. 16.15, Stephanas and his household are commended for their 'service to the saints', probably by offering free accommodation to church meetings; and the 'service of the saints' at 2 Cor. 8.4; 9.1 refers to the collection of money for the church at Jerusalem. The other sense, the ministry of the word, is also found frequently in Paul (2 Cor. 3.8f.; 4.1; 5.18; 6.3; Rom. 11.13). But the two are not wholly distinct, as some of the previous references show: there are functions of leadership that involve acts of charity on the part of the leader. It is likely that by the time of Ephesians the word was increasingly used in the technical sense of ministerial office (see 'deacons' in 1 Tim. 3.8–15; cf. already Phil. 1.1).

If there are then three separate clauses in verse 12, following the three titles of post-apostolic ministers in verse 11, it is tempting to ask whether the titles can be co-ordinated with the functions. 'Equipping' is an idea echoed at Eph. 6.15, where the Christian soldier's sandals are identified as the preparation of the gospel of peace, and it could correspond to the missionary work of evangelists. Secondly, the 'work of ministry' could be understood as the task of pastors, for the good pastor has to find pasture for the sheep (John 10.9; 21.15) and the other connotations of 'service' ('waiting on', 'providing food for', cf. Mark 1.31) would be appropriate in this context. And, thirdly, teaching may be seen as the chief means of 'edifying' and building up the community (see Kitzberger 1986). The correspondences may not be absolutely precise, for the function of teaching overlaps with those of evangelism and pastoral care, but they support the view taken above that this verse should, after all, be divided into three distinct members.

13 Until we all attain to the unity of faith and of the knowledge of the Son of God, to a perfect Man, with a full stature measured by Christ himself. As the text is now arranged, this verse states the ultimate goal of ministry (vv. 11–12) as the attainment of unity. But the first person plural 'we all' is noteworthy. It must mean 'all we Christians' and not 'all we church leaders' and it therefore reverts to the perspective of verse 7, which the intervening material has altered (see discussion above). Indeed, verse 13 could directly follow on from verse 7 without any difficulty and take up the earlier phrases, the 'measure of Christ' (v. 7) and 'the unity of the spirit' (v. 3).

By adding the credal section (vv. 4–6) and the christological psalm, interpreted in terms of gifts of ministry in the Church (vv. 8–12), the editor has emphasized the importance of doctrinal and organizational unity and not just unity in spirit. It is reasonable to ask whether some particular disunity has provoked this emphasis. There is little in the present form of the letter to help us give a clear answer to such a question, although in the next verse there is an allusion to deviant beliefs that may disturb the faith of the immature and promote the scheme of error. Various attempts have been made to pursue this issue. The deviant beliefs could be astrology (Arnold 1989), the cult of Demeter (Kreitzer 1997), Jewish Christian visionary mysticism (Goulder 1991), or a vaguer threat derived by the author from his knowledge of Colossians (Lincoln). But none of these suggestions, though they can all draw on support from elements elsewhere in the letter, throws any particular light on the terms in which the author expresses what he most values here. That the ministry of the Church is given in order that 'we all attain to the unity of faith and of the knowledge of the Son of God' implies the need to progress in understanding and not simply to hold fast to the tradition as received. This is the situation which we have posited for understanding Ephesians, the attempt to reconcile the traditions of Asian Gentile Christianity, which holds Paul in the highest esteem, with the teaching of Johannine Jewish Christianity, recently and after a bitter controversy expelled from the Jewish fold. The coincidence of the words 'unity', 'faith', 'knowledge' and 'the Son of God' supports this suggestion, for these are precisely the themes which dominate the Johannine Gospel and Epistles (although they were almost as important for Paul himself.).

The literal sense of the verb, **until we attain**, is to arrive at a place; and it is most frequently used in this sense in Acts. But it can be used figuratively too; see Acts 26.7, 'attaining to the promises to Israel', and compare Phil. 3.11, 'attaining the resurrection of the dead' (cf. also 1 Cor. 10.11; 14.36). The verb is in the subjunctive, which adds a note of purpose to the temporal clause: the ministers are to continue their work until its objective is achieved.

Unity here is not so much something already given (as in vv. 4–6) but something to be striven for (cf. v. 3). It is described as the unity **of faith and of the knowledge of the Son of God**. Several different constructions of this phrase are possible. (1) The unity of faith and the unity of knowledge may be two separate ideas. Unity of faith could then be either objective, believing in the same creed, or subjective, belief as the common means to salvation for Jews and Gentiles alike (see on 'one faith' at v. 5). Similarly, unity of knowledge could be the unified content of what is known, or the common apprehension of it. (2) The unity of faith and knowledge may be taken together as a single phrase. John's Gospel (4.42 and 6.69) and Epistles (1 John 4.16) make a similar apologetic claim that faith and knowledge are one, i.e. Christian faith is not mere belief or opinion but is grounded in sure knowledge. (3) The unity of the faith (the same creed) may be further defined by the following phrase, viz. 'of the knowledge of the Son of God'. This third option is perhaps the most likely construction, particularly if the explanation is an editorial comment on the meaning of 'one faith' (cf. v. 5) as the knowledge that the 'one Lord' is the Son of God.

The actual title **Son of God** is used only here in the letter, though it is implied at 1.5f., 1.17 and 5.1f. 'His Son' occurs quite often in Paul and the full title appears twice, at Gal. 2.19 and 2 Cor. 1.19. For the author of Ephesians and the Fourth Evangelist, and implicitly also for Paul, it has the unique sense of the pre-existent heavenly being who became Jesus Christ, the visible image (Col. 1.15) in human form (Phil. 2.8) of the one invisible God (cf. 2 Cor. 4.4–6; John 14.9). *Knowledge* of the Son of God is a particular emphasis of the Johannine Epistles (see 1 John 5.10, 13).

To a perfect Man. The Greek word *teleios* (perfect or complete) takes much of its sense from context. Here, with a following reference to stature (and to children in v. 14), it probably means 'mature' or 'adult' (as at 1 Cor. 2.6). Grammatically, it connects with the preceding verb, i.e. 'to attain both to the unity of faith' etc. *and also* 'to a perfect Man'. But in sense, the connection is probably with the reference to 'knowledge of the Son of God', offering a further definition of that title; for the revelation of God in Christ is also the revelation of perfect humanity through him. It should be noted that the word for **Man** here is the masculine noun for a male person (*anér*). It is different from the inclusive 'human being' (*anthrópos*) used at 2.15 and 4.24.

The parallel at Col. 1.28 is quite close, 'that we may present every human being perfect in Christ', and may indicate that 'human' was what the writer of Ephesians originally read in his source. If so, his substitution of 'male' changes the sense significantly. It is possible that the gendered noun has arisen simply from the following reference to 'the full stature' of Christ, since the fully grown male is on average taller than the female and thus more suitable as a metaphor for spiritual stature. But it is more convincing to explain the use of the term with some reference to Christology: 'a perfect Man' as the cosmic Christ. This should be compared to Paul's Adam–Christ typology (cf. 1 Cor. 15 and Rom. 5) and the idea that Christ is the model of perfect humanity in the Fourth Gospel (see e.g. John 1.12f.; 19.5). Some have gone further and detected here a connection with gnostic speculations about the primal Man (see

Schlier 1930: 27–37; and see above on 3.18). But this probably reads too much into the phrase, for it should be noted that there is no definite article in the Greek. In short, the author is thinking mainly of Christian growth to maturity, but he has substituted 'Man' for 'human person' under the influence of the preceding reference to the Son of God.

With a full stature measured by Christ himself (lit. 'to the measure of the stature of the fullness of Christ'). For 'measure' in this sense as full measure, i.e. 'maximum height' rather than an actual measurement, see on verse 7. The word translated 'stature' (*hēlikia*) can also mean a period of life, i.e. the prime of life or early adulthood; it then takes on connotations of age as well as size, like the English expression 'grown-up'. It is clearly used of age at Heb. 11.11, but equally clearly of size at Luke 19.3. The saying of Jesus at Matt. 6.27 (cf. Luke 12.25) illustrates the ambiguity: 'No one can by anxious thought add a cubit to his span', which means either grow 21 inches taller or live proportionately longer (presumably one third) in terms of life-span. Although maturity in age is implied by the later reference to children (v. 14), the link with measure may imply that the metaphor of height is intended.

The later gnostic development of this metaphor for the cosmic dimensions of the primal Man (see above) is probably less relevant than the Jewish background, though the evidence for that also comes from later than the first century. The rabbis taught that Adam, who was indeed created 'a perfect Man', measured one hundred cubits in height (*Pesikta* 1b; see Davies 1967: 45f.). After the Fall, however, he was reduced to merely three. This is a neat theodicy, for if Adam had remained the size God had intended him to be, he would have towered over the 'natural evils' of the created world. Understood against this background, here the risen Christ recovers that lofty stature, metaphorically speaking. (For a literal presentation of this mythological point, see the account of the resurrection of Jesus in the *Gospel of Peter* 10.40, see Schneemelcher 1991–2.) The exalted Christ now has everything under his feet (cf. 1.22) and in him the Church attains that fullness intended from the beginning (cf. 1.23). In terms of age, rather than height, one might compare the argument of Irenaeus (*Haer.* 2.22.5), based on John 8.57 ('You are not yet fifty years old'), that Jesus was nearing fifty when he died and had thus 'recapitulated' (see on 1.10) the complete human experience, including full maturity (i.e. 'a perfect Man').

14 So that we should cease to be infants buffeted and blown about by every current of teaching, devised by human vagary and cunning that promote the great scheme of error. Christ's gift of ministries in the Church is intended to enable Christians to achieve a mature faith measured by the full stature of Christ himself (v. 13). This verse goes on to underline that purpose by contrasting it with its opposites, the immaturity of infants, the bewildering variety of views by which people are blown about and various forms of deceit, in contrast to 'telling the truth in love' (v. 15). The images therefore link in well with what precedes and follows, but taken together they are a strange mixture of metaphors. **So that** might indicate a purpose clause ('in order that'), in which case it would follow on from verse 11, ignoring verses 12f. But that seems unnecessarily complicated and the conjunction can be used more loosely in koine Greek to introduce a consequence clause ('with the result that'), and then it would follow on naturally from verse 13. This is more likely.

No longer infants. Infancy or early childhood as a negative image implying a lack of intelligence or seriousness occurs elsewhere in Paul (1 Cor. 2.6; 3.1; 13.11) and the New Testament (e.g. Heb. 5.13f.), though it can also be used positively to symbolize simplicity and innocence, unsullied by adult decadence (see 1 Pet. 2.2 and Matt. 11.25; 18.3; 19.14). And it is so used at Eph. 5.1 of children lovingly imitating their father. The summons to be 'infants no longer' might suggest that before their conversion believers were just immature and ignorant, but Ephesians has described that period in somewhat darker terms at 2.3 ('children of wrath').

More likely, therefore, it implies a reference to growth since conversion with the help of the shepherds and teachers mentioned earlier, who include, of course, the writer of this letter himself. This ecclesiastical use of the metaphor of childhood and parenthood should be kept in mind when evaluating the address to children in the so-called household code (see on 6.1): household and Church are closely related ideas.

Buffeted and blown about. The imagery suddenly changes from the immaturity of infants to wave-tossed and wind-swept instability. If there is a connection in thought, it may be that the child is more likely to be carried away by the latest fashion or idea than the mature adult. The same metaphor is used in Jude 12f., warning about intruders with perverse views who are 'clouds carried along by the winds . . . wild waves of the sea foaming in their own shame'. And mixed metaphors are even more abundant in that passage, which compares the heretics to 'unsightly stains' on the common table, 'fruitless trees in autumn' and 'wandering stars destined for darkness' (cf. also 'accursed children', 2 Pet. 3.14). Invective produces a welter of different images.

The verb **buffet** (lit. 'overwhelm with waves') appears only here in the New Testament; but for the related noun, see Luke 8.24; cf. Mark 4.37. These references in the 'stilling of the storm' pericope may have been understood by the readers of the Gospels as an allegory for doctrinal controversy in the Church. The Epistle of James similarly compares 'doubters' to 'a wave of the sea blown and tossed by the wind' (1.6). The ideal Christian stance is to be 'rooted and founded' on the apostolic faith (Eph. 3.17), not blown about in a disorderly fashion. Compare the emphasis on 'standing firm' in 6.13f. (though there it is in the context of a military rather than a nautical metaphor).

By every current of teaching. Teaching is in the singular and has the definite article, i.e. 'the Teaching'. It is used to denote Christian teaching at Rom. 12.7 and 15.4 and frequently in the Pastoral Epistles (e.g. 1 Tim. 4.13). But what does it mean here? No assistance as to the sense in Ephesians can be derived from Col. 2.22, where the plural 'human commands and teachings' refers to the rules of ascetic opponents in a verse that has no other point of similarity with the present passage (*pace* Lincoln 258).

The problem envisaged may be the sheer variety ('every current') of views among Christian teachers (Schnackenburg 186) or various non-Christian religious philosophies (Lincoln 258). It is difficult to choose, because the author of Ephesians is forced to remain at the level of generality and allusion; explicit denunciation of contemporary opponents would involve him in an overt anachronism. If 'heresy' is the issue, it is reasonable to deduce from the context (v. 13) that it is belief in and knowledge of Jesus as the Son of God that is at stake. The Johannine community certainly saw denial of this as the main threat to its unity in faith (see 1 John 2.18–23). Schnackenburg (186) comments that 'it is *not (yet)* a question of the doctrine of Christology as in the Johannine letters ... but of attitudes detrimental to morals' (my emphasis), and he refers forward to 5.6–13. But the 'not yet' assumes that a pseudepigraphon such as Schnackenburg takes Ephesians to be will consistently reflect the stage of doctrinal development of the date of its publication, which is a false assumption. And in any case, the Johannine Epistles are chiefly concerned about detrimental moral attitudes, as implying the deficient Christology (see e.g. 1 John 2.3–6, 15–17).

It is not necessary to suppose that the errorists of 1 John were themselves consciously advocating a christological 'heresy'. Their schism seems to have been motivated principally by the boast that they had achieved a higher moral perfection than the rest of the community (1 John 1.8, 10; 2.9). But, of course, the Johannine writer explains the schism in christological terms, deducing from their deviant behaviour an implicit deficiency in doctrine. So if the author of Ephesians does have a specific problem in mind, it is not unlike that confronted by 1 John and he expects his readers to take note accordingly. The way the verse continues confirms this view.

Devised by human vagary and cunning that promote the great scheme of error (lit. 'in the dicing of human beings, in omnicompetence, towards the method of error'). As the literal translation reveals, the three nouns that precede 'error' are rather neutral. **Vagary** ('dicing', *kubeia*) appears only here in the Bible. In classical Greek it is used simply of the game of chance played with two or more six-sided dice thrown from a box, with bets laid on the outcome. This author may have disapproved of the associated gambling, or the not uncommon practice of loading the dice, or the addictiveness and sheer waste of time of the activity. He uses the metaphor here presumably to mean reckless or ill-considered actions. The vagary is specified as 'of human beings', either in contrast to God who allows them to be so deluded (cf. 2 Thess. 1.11) or in contrast to the devil who by definition must be an inveterate (indeed hopeless!) gambler. **Cunning** (*panourgia*) is literally omnicompetence 'the ability to do everything'. It is used in 2 Cor. 11.3 of the serpent who deceived and tempted Eve, and at 2 Cor. 4.2 of the trickery of false apostles. It is clearly one stage further on from vagary, from the arbitrary to the downright underhanded. The **great scheme** (*methodeia*) is again a neutral word originally. This is its only occurrence in the Greek Bible, apart from Eph. 6.11 (in the plural), where it refers to the dishonourable tricks of the devil in his assault on the soldier of Christ. Here, the singular denotes the grand design and strategy of evil, not just its base tactics. The sequence rises to a climax with the term 'error' (*planê*) which darkens the neutral shade of the preceding nouns. At 1 John 4.6 'the spirit of error' is contrasted with the 'spirit of truth' and refers to the deviant practices and implicit 'heresy' of those who have left the community (so also Jude 11; 2 Pet. 2.18; 3.17) and this is probably the allusion here. Thus the abstract noun 'error' is almost a term for the devil; cf. also 2 John 7, where deceiver (*planos*) is a synonym for the anti-Christ (and cf. 2 Thess. 2.11f.).

15 But rather that, by telling the truth in love we should grow up in all things into him who is the Head, Christ. The plethora of terms for deception in the previous verse is contrasted with the one simple verb 'to tell the truth', rare in Paul though it does occur (at Gal. 4.16). **In love** is tacked on, as often in Ephesians (cf. 4.16; 6.23), in an ambiguous position (cf. 3.17; 4.2). It could qualify 'telling the truth', thus mitigating the absolute command to speak the truth with the idea of generous and mutual forgiveness; or equally well it could qualify 'grow up', since it is love that builds up the Church (v. 16 and cf. 1 Cor. 6.4).

We should grow up in all things. The verb (*auxanein*) can be transitive, 'to make to grow' (with 'all things' as direct object, see on 1.10; cf. 1 Cor. 3.7); or intransitive, 'to grow up as to all things' ('in every way', adverbial accusative, see on 1.23). It is the Church's own growth, both in the quality of its corporate life and in the number of its adherents (cf. 1 Cor. 3.9), which is the author's chief concern in this passage and the reason for his insistence on the need for unity; so the intransitive is probably correct.

Into the Head. On Christ as head to the Church, his body, see the discussion of 1.22-3 above. In this verse Christians grow up into the head; the opposite idea, closer to ancient ideas of foetal development, is expressed in the next verse, that the human body develops downwards from the head. But, theologically, the two ideas are complementary, for Christ is both the goal and the source of the Church's life.

16 (Christ) from whom the whole Body, being constructed and assembled through every supplying joint according to the proper activity of each individual part, achieves bodily growth, and so builds itself up in love. The similarity between verse 16 and Col. 2.19 is very close: 'the head *from whom the whole body*, supplied and *assembled* through joints and ligaments, will grow (as to) the *growth* of God'. The four words or phrases in italics are identical; two others are almost so, 'joints' ('every joint') and 'supplied' ('supplying'). 'Ligament' may be missing, but it has already been used (in a metaphorical sense) of the 'bond' of peace at Eph. 4.3. Ephesians also uses the verb 'grow' (v. 15) and the noun 'growth' in close relation (v. 16), though not quite as close as the 'grow (with) the growth' of Col. 2.19. Finally, there are two participles qualifying body in both texts: 'assembled' appears in each, while the author of Ephesians repeats the word he has already used at 2.21, 'constructed' or 'fitting together' (in reference to the Church as a building).

Many of the parallels that are often pointed out between Colossians and Ephesians consist of a single word or phrase, but here there is a veritable cluster of similarities. Is this to be explained as evidence that Ephesians is a literary redaction of Colossians? Several obstacles stand in the way of that explanation.

(1) 'From whom' (masculine) makes sense in Ephesians because its antecedent is Christ, but in Colossians 'from whom' is also masculine though its antecedent is the feminine word 'head'.

(2) The context in Colossians fails to explain the emphasis on the Church's growth. The regulations of the ascetics have been attacked as a mere shadow of things to come and not its 'substance' (lit. 'body', Col. 2.17 – a rare, non-ecclesiological use); worship of angels through fasting and visions is contrasted with 'holding firmly to the head' in the sense of 'head over every ruler and authority' (Col. 2.10 – again a non-ecclesiological use of the term). In Ephesians, on the other hand, the whole passage is concerned with the growth of the Church through ministries (v. 11) that build up its life (v. 12) through the attainment of maturity (v. 13), leaving childish ways behind (v. 14) and growing up into Christ its head (v. 15). In short, the verse is entirely at home in Ephesians; it is an intrusion into Colossians.

(3) The anatomical metaphor of 'supplying joints' by which the Church

is brought together makes good sense in Ephesians as an allusion to the work or person of the Church's ministers (cf. v. 11; see Schnackenburg 189; Lohse 1971: 122, n. 65). In Colossians it is if anything even more emphatic in phrasing, with its pairs of synonymous participles and nouns, but for no apparent reason.

(4) 'Grows (as to) the growth of God' in Colossians is a rather abrupt and elliptical finish (God after all does not grow!); the phrase has to be unpacked as 'the growth that comes from God'. The longer version in Ephesians more naturally speaks of the growth, not of God, but of the body, and explains this consistently with the earlier ideas of the Church's upbuilding (v. 12) in love (v. 15).

For these reasons, Holtzmann (1872: 51f.) was quite correct to observe that dependence is more likely to be of Colossians on Ephesians than vice versa. Although there are too few examples as convincing as this one to support the larger theory proposed by Holtzmann (see Introduction, p. 10), nevertheless Col. 2.19 looks very much like an interpolation into that letter by someone who had the same basic view on the Church as the author of Ephesians.

Every supplying joint (or perhaps 'every supplied joint': lit. 'every joint of supply'). The noun 'supply' (*epichorēgia*) occurs in Paul at Phil. 1.19, probably alluding to material supplies sent by the Philippians to him in prison. The related verb occurs, apart from Col. 2.19, at Gal. 3.5, of God supplying the Spirit, and 2 Cor. 9.10, of God supplying seed to the sower (i.e. a spiritual harvest in return for the collection of money). So here also the meaning could be that ministers as joints in the body of Christ are supplied (i.e. given by God). Alternatively, ministers could be said themselves to supply the whole body by their work of co-ordinating each part harmoniously with the whole. Both may be intended by this rather loose phrase.

According to the proper activity of each individual part. As Lincoln (263) correctly comments, this is an expansion by the writer in his own style; the phrase 'according to the activity' has appeared at 1.19 and 3.7 (see on these passages above). **Individual part** (lit. 'measure') is used in the sense of a limited special function (see on v. 7). The purpose of the phrase is to draw attention to the significance of the 'ministerial joints' of the body of the Church and their specialized functions (cf. 4.11f.). But it separates the subject of the sentence so far from its verb, 'the whole body . . . makes growth', that another addition, 'bodily', is needed as a reminder. The last sentence, expanded to tie in with the earlier expansions in this chapter, thus becomes somewhat overloaded. It is intended both to emphasize the collaboration and organic growth in love of all the members of the body, which was Paul's chief concern in Laodiceans (see Col. 2.2), and yet not lose sight of the crucial role of ministers, which is the editor's.

V   Christian conduct (4.17 – 5.20)

The ethical theme announced in 4.1–3 but diverted, because of the additional material, on to the topic of Christian unity and ministry, is now resumed and maintained more or less consistently for the remainder of the letter and particularly in this section, 4.17–5.20. The main features of Pauline ethics (see the works by Furnish 1968 and 1979 Deidun 1981; Meeks 1986 and 1993; Hays 1996) are all well illustrated in this section: the sharp dichotomy between outsiders and insiders (4.17); between the old and the new (4.22f.); darkness and light (5.8); wisdom and folly (5.15); the regeneration of the moral agent through the Spirit (4.23f.) and the consequent ethic of wholeness, naturally producing the fruit of good works (5.9); the concern for solidarity within community (4.25); the use of lists of vices (4.31; 5.4f.) and virtues (4.32; 5.9); the echoes of Old Testament scripture (4.25; 5.18) and general moral maxims (4.28f.); and most distinctively of all, the ethic of response to grace, the imitation of divine forgiveness in the cross of Christ (4.32 – 5.2), the deliberate correlation of the theological indicative with the moral imperative (5.8) and the appeal to future judgement (5.5).

The actual content of the ethic, however, is unremarkable: it denounces sexual licence, falsehood, anger, theft, bad language and drunkenness in ways that are easily paralleled from contemporary Jewish and Hellenistic moral instruction on the behaviour of the individual. The modern reader is likely to notice the absence of any sensitivity to the wider framework of ethics and the political and economic factors that lie behind socially destructive behaviour. The ethic is, however, more remarkable in the way it employs religious motivations and sanctions in support of this conventional morality, and the way it uses conduct both as a criterion for right belief and as a means of strengthening unity within the Church.

A   Old and new humanity (4.17–24)

(17) So this is my instruction, as I bear witness in the Lord, that you are no longer to behave as the Gentiles do, in the futility of their minds, (18) darkened in their understanding, alienated from the life of God through their inherent ignorance with their hearts hardened, (19) who in their insensitivity have abandoned themselves to depravity, producing all sorts of uncleanness, with covetousness. (20) You did not so learn Christ, (21) assuming that you have heard of him, and were taught in him

– as the truth is in Jesus! (22) Put away the old humanity with its former behaviour, which is being destroyed through deceitful desires, (23) and be renewed in the spirit of your mind and (24) put on the new humanity which has been created by God in true righteousness and holiness.

This paragraph (4.17–24) has three parts: the rejection of pagan conduct (vv. 17–19), the appeal to Christian tradition (vv. 20–1) and the command to put away the old humanity and put on the new (vv. 22–4). The first two themes have especially close affinities with Rom. 1.21–4 and 1 Thess. 4.1–6. The last draws on the motif of the old and new and the metaphor of putting on clothes, both of which are frequent in Paul's letters (Rom. 6.6; 2 Cor. 5.17; Rom. 12.2; Gal. 3.17; Rom. 13.14 (cf. 1 Thess. 5.8 and Rom. 13.12); 1 Cor. 15.53f.; and of course Col. 3.5–10). If Ephesians is represented as simply dependent on the Pauline writings, source analysis in this section produces an embarrassment of riches. Nearly every idea in the first and third parts of it can be accounted for, although the second part is more distinctive. But the plausibility of such an analysis decreases as the possible sources are multiplied, until at last unitary composition by Paul himself becomes preferable as a more economical solution.

For some commentators, it seems, the sheer plethora and combination of Pauline parallels arouses their suspicion against this entirely typical piece of moral exhortation, as though it is too Pauline to be by Paul. But at the same time, they point out that the words for 'darkened', 'ignorance', 'insensitivity', 'being destroyed', 'renewed' and 'holiness' are *hapax legomena* in the Pauline corpus, and argue against Pauline authorship on linguistic grounds; the passage is not Pauline enough to be by Paul. But these arguments cancel each other out. One might reasonably hesitate at certain points. For example, at verse 18 it is Gentiles who are said to have 'hardened hearts', whereas Paul more normally uses the phrase of non-Christian Jews, and at verse 19 the really unusual verb, 'having become insensitive', occurs; but again this argument is inconclusive – Paul may be employing a stock phrase in order to explain a term he is going to use for the first and, as it happens, only time.

The existence of two separate treatments of the subject of pagan immorality in the same letter (here and at Eph. 2.11–12) which share the key terms 'alienated' and 'godless' or 'alienated from the life of God' yet use them with different nuances, raises the issue of their relation to each other. This passage is the closer of the two to what Paul says elsewhere and may be what he originally wrote to his correspondents. If so, the other passage (see on 2.11–13) may be explained as an editorial duplicate and revision.

17 The first person pronoun (see on 4.1) reappears: **so this is my instruction** (lit. 'what I am declaring'). **As I bear witness in the Lord** implies that Paul is a witness in a court case speaking on oath and recalls his use of this metaphor for moral exhortation at 1 Thess. 2.11: 'we exhorted and encouraged and *bore testimony* to you' (cf. 1 Thess. 4.6). On the phrase **that you are no longer to behave** (lit. 'walk'), in reference to moral conduct, see on 2.2, 2.10 and 4.1. The original addressees, being largely non-Jews, would have understood the instruction not to behave **as the Gentiles do** to mean 'as *other* Gentiles do' (and some MSS actually include this missing word, $\aleph^c$ D^c). But for the writer of Ephesians 'Gentile' has begun to denote non-Christian rather than non-Jew; see on 2.11 (and cf. Matt. 5.47; 6.7, 32; 18.17). That earlier passage in Ephesians was written from a determinedly Jewish Christian perspective ('alienated from the polity of Israel' and 'strangers to the covenants of promise', 2.12), apparently addressed to those who were 'formerly Gentiles in the flesh' but who as Christians no longer answer to that description. Here, more in keeping with Paul's own perspective, the alienation is from God, an estrangement and hostility which involves all humanity, whether Jewish or Gentile (see Rom. 5.10), and is developed in moral categories that have universal application.

There is no explicit parallel in Colossians to this warning about pagan immorality (but cf. Col. 3.7), perhaps because the focus of that letter is the threat from a 'judaizing' mission. But the idea and the wording are Pauline – see 1 Thess. 4.5, where Christian marriage is not to be 'in the passion of lusts *like the Gentiles* who know not God'.

The similarities between Eph. 4.17–19 and Rom. 1.21–4 are often noted: the use of the words 'futility', 'darkened', 'abandoned' and 'uncleanness' – in all, a remarkable coincidence. The Romans passage is a set-piece onslaught against the idolatry, perversion and immorality of Hellenistic society, as a foil to Paul's real target – the self-satisfied superiority of the Pharisaic Jew (see Rom. 2.1, 17). Here the stereotyped criticism is rehearsed but without the anti-Jewish spin.

The only contact between Eph. 4.17–19 and Col. 3.5 consists in the linking together of uncleanness and covetousness, but those two words are almost adjacent in Romans too (1.24 and 1.29). This pairing is repeated twice more in Ephesians (at 5.3 and 5.5) and these duplicates diminish the force of the argument that Colossians is the source. Furthermore, while Col. 3.5 includes these vices in a much longer list of 'what is earthly in you', in Ephesians they are typical of other people, unbelieving Gentiles, and have no place in the Church. Both views could be Pauline, but neither is obviously derived from the other.

The phrase **in the futility of their minds** should be compared with 'renewed in the spirit of your mind' at verse 23. Rom. 8.5f. (cf. 8.20) explains the contrast: 'the mind that is set on the flesh' ends in the futility of death, while 'the mind that is set on the spirit is life and peace'. 'Minds' is synonymous with 'understanding' and 'hearts' in the next verse. Whereas in Eph. 2.12–18 the states of alienation and salvation could be said to be 'objectified' (in terms of distance or nearness to the historic covenant of God with Israel; so Gese 1997: 125–45), here, in a manner more typical of Paul, objectivity is balanced with a concern for the inward, subjective experience of alienation from God (cf. Rom. 7.23; 1 Cor. 2.14). Futility (or vanity) is a term frequently used in Ecclesiastes and the Psalms. The most basic futility is to deny human dependence on God the Creator (Rom. 1.21; cf. Ps. 14.1).

18 The condition of former Gentiles is further elaborated as **darkened in their understanding**. This is identical in substance to Rom. 1.21 ('their senseless heart was darkened') but the verbs used are actually different in the Greek. A pseudepigrapher may have misremembered Romans, substituting slightly different words, or Paul himself may be ringing the changes on the way he expresses the same idea in two of his letters. The opposite of 'darkened in their understanding' has occurred earlier: 'with the eyes of your heart enlightened' (Eph. 1.18), so as to know God (1.17) and the power of God (1.19, cf. Rom. 1.20).

The deeper significance of human blindness is underlined with **alienated from the life of God**. On the verb, see on 2.12. It is used here in a different sense, referring not to Gentiles alienated from Israel, but to all humanity alienated from God, and it is closer therefore to Col. 1.21. The 'life of God' is a striking phrase not found anywhere else in Paul or the New Testament; it means the life that God authors and bestows, not the inner life of the deity.

The following phrase, **through their inherent ignorance** (lit. 'the ignorance that is in them'), offers a measure of excuse for pagan darkness. The noun occurs only here in the Pauline corpus (cf. 'your former ignorance' at 1 Pet. 1.14 in a similar context), although the related verb is common in Paul's formula, 'I would not have you ignorant, brethren' (e.g. 1 Thess. 4.13). The phrase could equally well be translated 'the ignorance that is prevailing *among* them' (Caird 79), which might then be an allusion to the notable failure of Greco-Roman culture to bring the best insights of its philosophers to bear on its crudely polytheistic religious practice. But the surrounding references to 'their minds' and 'hearts' make our translation more likely. Comparison with Acts 17.30, 'God has overlooked times of ignorance', would indicate that there is some element of mitigation implied in the phrase (*contra* Lincoln 278), though admittedly not much.

This ignorance is spelt out in what follows, **with their hearts hardened** (lit. 'through the hardening', *pórósis*). In an erudite note,

Robinson (264–74) argued that *pórósis* should be translated 'blindness'. In Greek medical writers, the word refers not only to the hardening of skin over surface wounds, or of the bones after a fracture, but also to the lack of feeling in the body caused by an excessive layer of fat. (Compare John 12.40, 'he hardened their heart', with its source, Isa. 6.10, 'Make the heart of this people fat' KJV/AV.) Accordingly, when used with reference to the eyes, it denotes the blindness caused by cataracts. In a metaphorical sense as here, the two ideas of hardening and blindness merge into each other, though it is perhaps worth pointing out that the word implies not the complete petrifaction of all moral sense, but its covering with an outer layer of insensitivity. There may be some hope of remedy for such a condition!

The classic Old Testament instance of the hardening of the heart was Pharaoh (e.g. Exod. 4.21) and it was God himself who hardened his heart, creating in him an irrational obstinacy that led to the greater glory of the Exodus, the signs and wonders in Egypt culminating in the Passover itself. In the Gospels, both Jesus' murderous opponents (Mark 3.5f.) and his own bewildered disciples (Mark 6.52) are said to have 'hardened hearts'. In the first example the phrase indicates implacable opposition, but in the second temporary failure to appreciate the scope of Jesus' mission. These two senses seem to be reflected also in Paul: the first at 2 Cor. 3.14 and the second at Rom. 11.7, 25. While most of the New Testament references are to *Jewish* stubbornness, the case of Pharaoh should remind us that the concept is equally applicable to the non-Jew. In this passage, it is unclear whether the Gentiles have hardened themselves against the truth, or whether God has done it for them by allowing them to sink into their own depravity. In either case, a redemptive possibility is left open: corruption will lead to revulsion and so ultimately to acceptance of the purifying word of the gospel.

19 Who in their insensitivity (lit. 'having ceased to feel pain', *apalgein*). This rare verb occurs nowhere else in the New Testament. It underlines the sense in which Gentiles have 'hardened hearts'. But there is a certain irony in its use in the present context: the sexual licence about to be described is not, whatever its participants may think, genuine indulgence in pleasure but a desensitizing to pain. In a religious ethic, goodness is the only true delight; pleasurable evil is a contradiction in terms.

The Gentiles **have abandoned themselves** (lit. 'handed themselves over'). In Romans 1 it is God, emphatically (three times: vv. 24, 26 and 28), who hands them over to impurity, dishonourable passions and a base mind. With God as its subject the verb means 'delivered to the consequences of their actions' (see Rom. 1.27). But with a reflexive pronoun the verb means that the Gentiles have voluntarily surrendered themselves to the powers that dominate human beings through the desires of the flesh (cf. Rom. 6.12f.). There is no theological discrepancy between the two statements and Paul could have written both. If Paul originally wrote to the Laodiceans from Ephesus, then assuming that this is part of his original letter, we ought finally to notice that what he says here preceded what he later wrote to the Romans.

To depravity, producing all sorts of uncleanness, with covetousness. There follows a short list of three vices to which Gentiles are prone. The first and the last also appear in the list of 'things that defile' issuing from the human heart in Jesus' saying at Mark 7.21f. All three terms seem to refer to illicit sexual activity. **Depravity** (*aselgeia*) is paired at Rom. 13.13 with the word *koitai* (lit. 'beds', i.e. going to bed with someone; cf. KJV/AV, 'chambering and wantonness'). Depravity and uncleanness are linked together at 2 Cor. 12.21 and Gal. 5.19, in both places accompanied by 'fornication', a combination also found later in Ephesians (5.3). **Uncleanness** (*akatharsia*) is extended to cover 'all sorts', perhaps to indicate homosexual (1 Cor. 6.9) and heterosexual (1 Cor. 6.15) prostitution. **Covetousness** or greed (*pleonexia*) is associated with fornication at 1 Cor. 5.11 and in context means insatiable sexual desire.

The sexual mores of the upper classes in Hellenistic society were an easy target for this kind of tirade (cf. Rom. 1.18ff.) and many Gentiles as well as Jews would have applauded it. After a very long discussion, Best (421–5) asks the questions:

> What did [the author of Ephesians'] converts from the pagan world think of his description of it? Did they nod their heads in agreement, or did they mutter 'He's got it all wrong'? And if the latter, did it shake their confidence in the other things he wrote?

Perhaps the answer to these questions is that Paul certainly expected his original Gentile readers to give their assent, since they had probably been drawn into the Church from already disaffected sections of Hellenistic society that had no vested interest in defending it against such exaggerated criticism. The author of Ephesians, on the other hand, may have included this material not only because it helped to mark out the Church more sharply from its pagan environment, but also because, as a Jewish Christian, he expected fellow Jews in his audience to receive this denunciation with enthusiasm.

20–21 You did not so learn Christ, assuming that you have heard of him, and were taught in him – as the truth is in Jesus! These two verses are an example of something in Ephesians that is unparalleled in Colossians, but is nevertheless so unexpected, original and ironic that it almost has to be by Paul. It appears in a section whose preceding and following parts, as we have seen, possess ample parallels in the Pauline corpus. But this sentence is unique. One of the difficulties in deciding whether a sentence is genuinely Pauline is that Paul can often be quite unpredictable. The liveliness of his language defies conventional usage. In straightforward Greek one might say 'to learn about Christ' or 'to accept Christ as Lord' (Col. 2.6). However, 'to learn' with 'Christ' as its direct object is a peculiar idiom, comparable with 'to proclaim Christ' (Gal. 1.16; Phil. 1.17), 'to preach Christ' (1 Cor. 1.23; 15.12), 'to gain Christ and to be found in him' (Phil. 3.8). Would an imitator have been able to coin an expression with such an authentic ring to it?

'Assuming that' (lit. 'if at least', *ei ge*) is teasing irony. Lincoln (280) denies this, claiming that the wording implies confident assumption that something is the case, but the use of any conditional with the minimizing particle 'at least' must imply something less than a statement of assured fact. It is often pointed out that among the stylistic differences between Ephesians and the undisputed Paulines is the absence of rhetorical questions in the former (with one exception perhaps, but see on 4.9). But rhetorical questions are unevenly distributed through Paul's letters in any case; and what is more constant is the tongue-in-cheek attitude which gives rise to them. The tone of this passage deserves to be compared to Paul at his most ironic in Gal. 3.2f., 'Let me ask you one question. Did you receive the spirit by means of the law or by hearing with faith? Did you experience so many things in vain – *if it really is* (the same expression as here) in vain?'

Again, surely no imitator of Colossians or Paul would have come up with the concluding phrase of this sentence, 'as the truth is in Jesus'. 'The truth' lacks the article but it is presumably implied, and Paul often does omit it with abstract nouns (BDF s. 258). The disarming use of the unembellished name 'Jesus' without Lord or Christ is unparalleled elsewhere in Ephesians (or Colossians), but is to be found in the undisputed letters. Other writers may have felt the need to observe conventional reverences with regard to the name of the Saviour, but Paul himself was daring enough to employ understatement even on this matter, when a suitable occasion invited (cf. e.g. 2 Cor. 4.10f.; Gal. 6.17).

You did not so learn Christ. More soberly put, but conveying the same sense, is 1 Thess. 4.2: 'For you know what instructions we gave you through the Lord Jesus.' In that passage also, Paul's chief concern was with pagan laxity on matters of sex (1 Thess. 4.3f.) and two of the terms discussed above ('uncleanness' and 'covetousness') also occur there (1 Thess. 4.6f.). **Assuming that you have heard of him, and were taught in him**: in the Greek the ironic tone is even more pronounced than in our translation, since 'of him' is actually an accusative object. The Greek verb 'to hear' takes the genitive of the person heard and the accusative of the thing heard. So, literally, it could mean 'assuming you have heard *it*' (i.e. the word 'Christ'). The phrase 'were taught in him' most likely refers to the substantial body of moral instruction that Paul customarily delivered to his converts when he set up a new community (see again 1 Thess. 4.2; also 2 Thess. 3.6; 1 Cor. 11.2; Rom. 6.17). In the case of the Laodiceans he had entrusted this task to Epaphras (Col. 4.12f.), which may be why, just to make doubly certain, he does not merely allude to that moral teaching here but repeats substantial blocks of it in subsequent paragraphs.

As the truth is in Jesus! Since 'the truth' lacks the definite article in the original Greek (see above), 'as there is truth in Jesus' is a possible alternative translation, though rather lame. 'As he (Christ) is truth in Jesus' is, however, surely impossible (*pace* de la Potterie 1977; see Lincoln 281). 'Truth' refers not just to the reliability of the gospel message but also to the moral integrity that lives it out authentically (cf. on 5.9).

22–23 Put away the old humanity with its former behaviour, which is being destroyed through deceitful desires, and be renewed in the spirit of your mind. Since this whole section consists of moral exhortation, verses 22–4 must have imperatival force, as reflected in the translation above (so also RSV; contrast NRSV), even though the Greek uses infinitives. If the infinitives were intended to specify the content of the teaching in verse 21 (as Houlden 318 and Lincoln 284 claim), it ought strictly to be translated: 'You were taught that you *have* put away, *are being* renewed, and *have* put on'. It would then be an allusion to *earlier* instruction about the once for all change in the converts' lives, in preparation for baptism perhaps, and the need for the catechism to be continually recalled. This is possible, but the context seems to imply more immediacy.

The infinitive can be used in place of the imperative in Greek (as it is at Rom. 12.15 and Phil. 3.16) and may be so here. If the presence of the personal pronoun in the accusative is felt to preclude that option (as BDF s. 389), then it would be possible to link this verse grammatically to the solemn opening: 'This is what I tell you, to behave (v. 17) . . . to put away (v. 22) . . . and to put on (v. 24)'.[7]

The relation between Eph. 4.22–4 and Col. 3.8–10 is a highly controversial issue that requires a little patience to unravel. The latter reads:

> But now put away everything, anger, rage, malice, slander and filthy talk from your mouth. Do not lie to one another, seeing that

---

[7] For this kind of delayed construction of accusatives and infinitives after verbs of telling or exhorting, compare Titus 2.2–5 (cf. 2.1) and Titus 2.7–10 (cf. 2.6).

you have completely taken off the old humanity with its deeds and put on the new humanity which is being renewed in knowledge according to the image of its creator.

If Ephesians is dependent, we have to suppose the following changes: (1) 'Put away' (from Col. 3.8) has been used instead of 'take off' (Col. 3.9) in regard to the old humanity. (2) The vice list has been delayed and divided between Eph. 4.29, 4.31 and 5.4. (3) 'Do not lie' has again been delayed until Eph. 4.25 and become 'put away lying'. (4) The adjective 'new' and the verb 'renew' (different roots in Greek) have been swapped around. (5) The participle 'renewed' has become a separate injunction and been placed earlier, before the reference to putting on the new. (6) God as Creator is common to both passages, but the words 'knowledge' and 'image' in Colossians have been dropped and ethical emphases added. These differences will be considered as and when they appear in the text of Ephesians below, but it is quite illuminating to survey them all together in this way, for almost every word of Col. 3.8–10 finds a parallel somewhere in Ephesians, which implies deliberate and conscious reuse by its author. Yet the changes are so inconsequential as to be inexplicable except on the hypothesis of some vague misremembering. It is more likely, then, that what we are dealing with here is two versions of a cluster of ideas from the pen of the same writer.

For the moment, let us look at just the first of the six points listed above. Lincoln (285) may be right to claim that the two motifs, the contrast between old and new and the idea of being clothed with Christ, usually functioned for Paul quite independently, and were combined for the first time in Col. 3.9f. If so, Ephesians is closer to Paul than is Colossians, for the images are not as neatly combined. **The old humanity** (lit. 'the old person', *ho palaios anthrôpos*) is to be **put away** (*apotithenai*) or 'laid aside' (cf. Rom. 6.6, where the old humanity was 'crucified' with Christ); it is only at verse 24 that the new humanity is 'put on' like a garment. The sequence in Rom. 13.12 is similar: 'Let us *put away* the works of darkness and *put on* the armour of light.'

The factors that inhibited the co-ordination of put-off/put-on terminology (except at Col. 3.9f.) may have been partly liturgical, partly theological. If the clothing metaphor is baptismal in origin, then it is likely that the candidate did not disrobe completely (for decency's sake) and, as he or she emerged from the water, was further clothed (cf. Gal. 3.27), perhaps in a special white robe symbolizing Christ. A more theological reason for this lack of exact co-ordination of the two images is that it is not possible yet for Christians to disrobe themselves entirely of their old nature inherited from Adam, for they are still inevitably subject to mortality (1 Cor. 15.22; Rom. 5.12); but they can consciously resolve to 'lay it on one side' (cf. again Rom 13.12 and 14) and reject the influence that it has over their behaviour and values.

While this verse speaks of the old and new *person*, the language should be taken corporately. It is not that each individual has an 'old person' inside them which is to be replaced by his or her new character as a Christian, but that the old shared human nature, the old Adam which Paul, originally writing to Gentiles, has just described in terms of its futility, darkness, alienation and insensitivity exemplified in sexual licence, is to be laid aside in favour of the corporate new humanity, Christ.

It is difficult to be sure whether the phrase **with its former behaviour** (cf. Col. 3.9, 'with its deeds') is meant to be taken, as in our translation, with the 'old person', emphasizing that a change in the whole way of life is required, or with the participle 'being destroyed', implying that wrong behaviour is the reason for humanity's subjection to decay. The former is more likely, since the participle already has a qualifying clause of its own ('through deceitful desires', see below). The noun **behaviour** (*anastrophē*) occurs elsewhere in Paul at Gal. 1.6, where he is referring to his former way of life as a Jew and persecutor of the Church, behaviour which he repudiated when he became the Apostle to the Gentiles. That reference does not prevent him from using it with a different application, here suited to a new context. The cognate verb was used at 2.3 above, where it referred to Jewish as well as pagan misconduct. **The old humanity ... is being destroyed**: the present tense is important, signifying a gradual process of decay and destruction. For most human beings, life involves an inexorable physical decline towards old age and death, and often, except for God's grace, a corresponding moral decline. What is true of the individual is also, more importantly, true of humanity as a whole: our race collectively is subject to decay and degeneration. While the verb (*phtheirein*) occurs only here in Paul, the related noun appears in similar contexts at Rom. 8.21 and 1 Cor. 15.42 (cf. v. 54), and a compound form of the verb at 2 Cor. 4.16 (quoted below).

The corruption of humanity occurs **through deceitful desires** (lit. 'according to the desires of deceit'). The negative sense of 'desire' predominates in Pauline usage (Rom. 1.24; 6.12; Gal. 5.16; 1 Thess. 4.5). This phrase may possibly be intended to evoke the Genesis myth (cf. Rom. 7.7f.) of Adam's *desire* for god-like self-determination, by which the Serpent *deceived* him (Rom. 7.11; cf. 2 Cor. 11.3). Admittedly there is no obvious Adamic allusion present in the other uses of the noun 'deceit' in the Pauline corpus (2 Thess. 2.10 and Col. 2.8), but it would nevertheless be quite in line with Paul's theology and would fit nicely here in proximity to a reference to 'the old humanity'. However, the Semitic construction (the genitive noun in place of an adjective) and the distinction the wording may imply between 'deceitful' and non-deceitful desire (Paul invariably using 'desire' in an emphatic negative sense requiring no further qualification, see above) may point to an addition by the editor.

The opposite of to be destroyed is not here (as it is at Eph. 2.6) to be resurrected, but to **be renewed**, which retains the typically Pauline 'eschatological reserve' (i.e. that certain aspects of eschatological hope are reserved for future fulfilment, cf. Rom. 6.4). But although the thought is Pauline, the wording is somewhat unusual, for elsewhere Paul uses a different verb for renew (*anakainousthai*) (see Rom. 12.2; 2 Cor. 4.16; Col. 3.10). Here, however, we find the near synonym (*ananeousthai*). The slight difference between the two verbs can be appreciated by looking at the way their root adjectives are used at Mark 2.22: 'New wine (*neos*, young, immature) for new wineskins (*kainos*, fresh, unused).' If the distinction were to be pressed, the connotation would be 'renewed' in the sense of 'rejuvenated'. Compare the removal of every 'wrinkle' from the Church as bride of Christ at Eph. 5.27. This would chime in with the images of turning again to become as a child (Matt. 18.3) or of rebirth from above (John 3.5–7). If Ephesians has derived this material from Col. 3.10, then the verb for 'renew' and adjective for 'new' have merely been changed around through some peculiar misremembering (see Schnackenburg 200).

Unlike most of the other references to the Spirit in Ephesians, **in the spirit of your mind** clearly means the human spirit. The phrase then is almost a tautology. But as such it is not un-Pauline. For this idea, compare 1 Cor. 1.12: 'For who knows a person's thought except the spirit of the person that is in them?' At Rom. 12.2 Paul also refers to 'the renewal (*anakainôsis*) of your mind'. The decisive break with the past implied by the old/new person distinction is here modified by a more gradualist transformation that reflects Paul's other, outer/inner person distinction (see 2 Cor. 4.16: 'Though our outer person is wasting away, our inner person is being renewed day by day'; and cf. Rom. 7.22 and Eph. 3.16 with the comment there).

24 The clothing metaphor at last appears explicitly with **put on the new humanity** (*kainos anthrôpos*). On the new humanity, see above on Eph. 2.15, where the phrase was used in the context of the reconciliation of Jews and Gentiles in Christ (cf. also Gal. 6.15). Here it is the moral rather than the ethnic issue that is in view. Is there also an implication that Christ is the 'new person', whom believers are to 'put on' (as at Gal. 3.27) and grow up into (Eph. 4.13)? The reluctance of some commentators to see a christological reference in this verse may be due to the following participle, 'created'. Paul, however, did not share the later Patristic aversion to this way of speaking: 'the first born of all creation' (Col. 1.15; cf. Rev. 3.11, 'the beginning of God's creation'), for it denoted for him the idea of Christ's utter dependence on God, without any implication of temporality or change. It is sufficient to claim that 'The Word was *in the beginning*' (John 1.1); nothing would be added, for basically Jewish thinkers like Paul or John (or the writer of Ephesians), by saying that the Word was *before* the beginning.

The new humanity **has been created by God** (lit. 'created according to God'). The precise sense of the adverbial phrase is unclear: is it created 'in the way God creates' or 'according to God's will', or as a kind of shorthand for 'after God's image and likeness' (from Gen. 1.26, as explicitly RSV; see Col. 3.10, which is much clearer, and cf. Col. 1.15)? Or again, the phrase could point to the christological interpretation of the 'new humanity', i.e. Christ himself was created 'according to God' (as his first image), and humanity in the beginning and even now is created 'after the image of the image of God'.

At 2.10 believers were also said to be 'God's handiwork, created in Christ Jesus for good works'. Apart from these two places, elsewhere in Paul the verb 'create' (*ktizein*) refers to the physical creation of the world (Rom. 1.25: 1 Cor. 11.9); but the noun (*ktisis*) is more frequent (nine times) and can sometimes refer explicitly to 'the new creation' (cf. 2 Cor. 5.17; Gal. 6.15).

When the metaphor of clothing ('putting on Christ') is combined with that of the new human person, the christological reference of the former (as at Gal. 3.27) is to some extent carried over to the latter (see also on the 'perfect Man' at Eph. 4.13). The risen Christ is not just the agent of the new creation, he is also the first example of it. Already at 1 Cor. 15.45 Paul had put these two thoughts together: 'the last Adam became life-giving Spirit'.

The new creation is created **in true righteousness and holiness** (lit. 'in the righteousness and holiness of truth'). The expression is parallel to 'being destroyed by deceitful desires' in verse 22. For this reason we have preferred to take 'of truth' as a Semitic adjectival idiom (as RSV). But it might carry more emphasis than this (as Lincoln 270 argues, translating 'in the righteousness and holiness that comes from the truth'). Truth is linked with goodness and righteousness as the harvest of light at Eph. 5.9.

Righteousness (*dikaiosunē*) seems not to be used in the specialized sense of God's gift and power of salvation in Christ which it has in Romans and Galatians, where Paul polemicizes against the works of the Law, but in the more straightforward ethical sense (as also at Eph. 5.9 and 6.14) which can also be found in Paul (cf. Phil. 1.11, 'the fruits of righteousness').

Holiness (*hosiotēs*) occurs elsewhere in the New Testament only at Luke 1.75, where it is similarly paired with righteousness to describe the manner of life of the redeemed. This is probably the sense here also: believers have been re-created so as to produce these qualities.

Paul normally prefers words from a different root (*hagios*) with similar sense, notably 'sanctification' (*hagiasmos*, Rom. 6.19; 1 Thess. 4.4, 7), though he can also use the abstract noun (*hagiosuné*, 1 Thess. 3.13) and may just once have used a form close to the one here, *hagiotés* (2 Cor. 1.12). One should not therefore jump to the conclusion that this *hapax legomenon* is un-Pauline. Indeed, Paul uses yet another near synonym for holiness, 'purity' (*hagnotés*), again only once for certain, at 2 Cor. 6.6.

The preceding comments assume that 'righteousness and holiness' are the moral qualities which Christians have been created and re-created to achieve. That is probably correct at the surface level of Ephesians as we now have it (see Eph. 2.10; 5.9). But it is not impossible that, below the surface, there is another idea, that these are the characteristics of the Creator (cf. e.g. Deut. 32.4; Rev. 16.5) who re-creates believers through Christ, who is 'our righteousness and sanctification' (1 Cor. 1.30).

B   Rules for community   (4.25 – 5.5)

(25) Have done with lying, then, and 'tell the truth each one with his neighbour', because we are members one of another. (26) 'Be angry and sin not.' Do not let the sun set on your angry outburst; (27) do not give the devil any room. (28) The thief should not steal any longer, but be employed doing honest work with his own hands, in order to have something to share with the one in need. (29) Let no foul language come out of your mouth, but only what is good for edification as the occasion requires, in order that it may bestow grace on those who are listening. (30) Do not grieve the Holy Spirit of God, by whom you were sealed for the day of redemption. (31) Let all bitterness, rage, anger, shouting and slander be removed from you, along with all wickedness. (32) Instead, be kind to one another and compassionate, forgiving one another as God in Christ has forgiven you. (5.1) So, be imitators of God like beloved children (2) and walk in the way of love, just as Christ also loved us and gave himself on our behalf as an offering and a sweet-smelling sacrifice to God. (3) But let fornication and all uncleanness or covetousness not even be named among you, as is fitting with saints, (4) and obscenity, frivolity and facetious- ness which are hardly appropriate, but rather thanksgiving. (5) For you should know this, that no fornicator, unclean or covetous person, idolaters in other words, has any inheritance in the kingdom of Christ and of God.

After the general exhortation to put away the old humanity and put on the new comes more specific advice on avoiding the sins of speech (v. 28

is an odd exception, see below): namely lying (v. 25); anger (vv. 26f.), and foul language (v. 29). The last is then spelt out in more detail in two lists of types of violent language (4.31) and types of smutty and frivolous talk (5.3f.). The passage ends with a shift from warnings against the sins of speech to the perpetrators of sinful deeds, who have no place in the community at all (cf. 5.5). Interspersed in this sequence are more positive references to theological motivation arising from the Church as body (4.25), from resistance to the devil (4.27), from the sealing of the Spirit (4.30), and from the sacrifice of Christ (4.32 – 5.2). The opposites of the sins are also mentioned: edifying and gracious speech (4.29), forgiveness (4.32), and thanksgiving (5.4). The main point of the section is to warn against the sins of speech that disrupt community life; other sins may be more serious but less likely to cause disunity.

The form of this material is basically a list of vices (see Kamlah 1964) expanded at certain points into moral sentences. Such lists are common in Hellenistic ethical discourse and were taken over into Greek-speaking Judaism and early Christianity: Rom. 1.29–32 and Gal. 5.19–21 are notable examples. One important function of this type of teaching in Pauline churches would be catechetical, to prepare Gentile converts for initiation into the community and remind them thereafter of the implications of their new faith. At 1 Thess. 4.2 Paul alludes to a much larger body of moral instruction than the one point he goes on to mention (1 Thess. 4.4f.). In Ephesians (and Colossians) there are more extensive presentations than we find in the letters to churches he knew personally (cf. also Rom. 12–15), presumably because their original addressees had not had the benefit of teaching from Paul himself when they were converted.

The similarities between this passage and Col. 3.5–14 are often noted by commentators: 4.25, cf. Col. 3.9; 4.26, 29, 31, cf. Col. 3.8; 4.32, cf. Col. 3.12–14; 5.3, cf. Col. 3.5; 5.4, cf. Col. 3.8. But the differences should also be noted. The undressing/dressing metaphor which provides the Colossians passage with a clear structure, and has already been used at Eph. 4.24, is not carried through into this section. The Colossians material is not reproduced in sequence; and some parallels to it in Ephesians appear in other places (e.g. Col. 3.6, cf. Eph. 5.6; Col. 3.14, cf. Eph. 4.3). One memorable verse of Colossians is not reproduced at all in Ephesians (Col. 3.11) and several verses of Ephesians have no parallel at all in Colossians (4.28; 4.30; 5.1–2; 5.5). It is this last point that makes the dependence of Ephesians on Colossians so improbable, especially since there are indicators in this extra material of Paul's own particular outlook and style (see on 4.28 and 5.5).

There is a clear start at 4.25, but where does the paragraph end? The standard modern edition of the Greek New Testament (NA[27]) marks a break after 5.5 and this is probably correct. However, the RSV also breaks after 5.2; JB breaks after 4.32, but at neither of the later points; REB breaks at the earlier points but not at 5.5. There are particles at 5.1 and 5.3 ('so' and 'but') but none at 5.6, which seems to begin a new and different topic. The theme of various kinds of bad language at 4.29 is continued with warnings about angry words (v. 31) and resumed after the interruption of 5.1–2 with warnings against sexually improper talk (5.3, 4). It is true that 5.1–2 might be seen as a 'concluding rhetorical flourish' (Lincoln 312), but it could also be an expansion of the thought of 4.32; if omitted, the triplet 'kindness, compassion and forgiveness' (4.32) would be more clearly answered by the other triplet, 'fornication, uncleanness and covetousness' (5.3).

Two other factors influence a decision on this issue. First, the similar material in Colossians (3.5–11) does not separate sex (v. 5) from lying (v. 9) and violence (v. 8) but runs them together. This supports the view that Eph. 4.25 – 5.5 should also be treated as a unit. Lincoln's argument (297) that the writer of Ephesians, having used parts of Col. 3.5–15 earlier at 4.2–4 and 4.17–24, 'returns to other elements in these sections, Col. 3.8, 9a, 12–14a, as the main source of his paraenesis' reveals how artificial the theory of literary dependence on Colossians can sometimes become. One cannot reasonably claim both that the author of Ephesians conflates and vaguely misremembers fragments of Colossians, and also that he pores over the same paragraph and separates out elements of it for three new ones of his own, carefully avoiding any duplication. Secondly, if 5.3–5 is linked closely with the warning about those 'who deceive with empty words' at 5.6, then the content of that threat becomes the deceptive advocates of licentious non-Christian behaviour, rather than deviant (if unspecified) opinion within the Church. This difficult issue is discussed further on 5.6–14 below.

25 Have done with lying, then, and 'tell the truth each one with his neighbour', because we are members one of another. The passage starts by echoing the preceding paragraph. The same verb used for 'to put away' the old humanity at 4.22 is used here for **have done with** lying. Truth was the last word in the Greek of 4.24 (see above) and it leads into the contrast with telling lies. Our translation takes the opening participle as an imperative (see on 5.21), and so equivalent to Col. 3.9, 'Do not lie to each other', and the following Old Testament allusion supports this view, i.e. it is added to expound more positively the sense of the opening injunction. If, alternatively, it is taken to be a genuine past participle, the sense would be rather different: 'Having put away the (great) lie' of a life alienated from God (cf. 4.18) you are now to 'tell the truth, each one with his neighbour'.

The allusion is probably to Zech. 8.16 (LXX), 'Speak the truth towards the neighbour', which in turn echoes the commandment, 'You shall not bear false witness against your neighbour' (Exod. 20.16). Houlden (321) detects other echoes of a Christian version of the Decalogue in this section (see v. 26; cf. Matt. 5.21f. and Exod. 20.13: anger/murder; v. 28, cf. Exod. 20.15: stealing). The **neighbour** in the Old Testament texts quoted above was, of course, the fellow Jew, and, unlike the wider reference of the term at Luke 10.36f., it seems to have the narrower sense here also of 'fellow Christian'. By this added scriptural allusion, the horizon of moral obligation seems to be drawn in to a narrower circle, as it is in the Fourth Gospel (cf. John 13.34).

The motivation for truthfulness is **because we are members one of another**. Ephesians has added references to Paul's image of the Church as body at 1.23, 4.4 and 4.16, and will develop the idea further in the nuptial analogy at 5.23–32. In that light, one would have expected the author to say here 'because we are members of Christ' or 'of the Body of Christ'. Understatement of the doctrine in passing in an ethical context is more typical of Paul himself, as at Rom. 12.5, which uses the same phrase, 'members of each other'.

For the stress on truth-telling as a vital constituent of community life, see also on Eph. 4.15 and 5.9 (and cf. Gal. 4.16).

26 'Be angry and sin not.' The Hebrew parataxis identifies the maxim as a probable allusion to Ps. 4.4. Clearly, it does not instruct people to be angry, but means 'When and if you get angry, do not sin' as the following clause explains, **Do not let the sun set on your angry outburst**. A fit of (righteous) anger is not necessarily sinful; it is the nursing of angry resentment that is condemned. The thought in this moral sentence is thus slightly different from, and not inconsistent with, the straightforward rejection of 'bitterness, wrath and anger' in the list of vices at 4.31. Anger is included with other vices at Gal. 5.20 and warnings against it are a standard feature of Old Testament wisdom (Prov. 15.1; Eccles. 7.9), taken over into Jewish Christian paraenesis (Jas 1.19f.; Matt. 5.22).

The word used for an **angry outburst** or 'fit of temper' is not found elsewhere in the New Testament. The Greek (*parorgismos*) usually means 'something that provokes to anger' rather than, as here (and Jer. 21.5 LXX), the emotion itself. Sunset of the same day is specified as the time-limit for righteous anger. A similar time-limit for the restoration of communal harmony is referred to at Deut. 24.15 (regarding the payment of a poor man's wages). And it is specifically applied to reconciliation after the legitimate rebuke of a fellow member of the Essene community at CD 7.2f.: 'They shall rebuke each man his brother according to the commandment, and shall bear no rancour from one day to the next.'

27 Do not give the devil any room. Presumably this is not a separate new injunction but refers back to anger as creating opportunities for

225

temptation by the devil. Similarly at 2 Cor. 2.11 the failure to forgive would allow 'Satan to gain an advantage over us'. Pointless controversies and quarrels are the devil's 'snare' at 2 Tim. 2.26 (contrast 1 Tim. 3.6f., where it is conceit and dubious reputation in a candidate for bishop that may let the devil in).

Ephesians uses the ordinary word for the devil (*diabolos*) here and at 6.11 (see also the comment there). Paul never uses it elsewhere: 'Satan' or some other designation does duty for it. Some commentators hold this to be a significant argument against Pauline authorship. But Paul must have known the word, since it is so common (it occurs 22 times in the LXX, for instance); and he would surely have recognized its derivation from the verb to 'accuse' or 'slander' (*diaballein*). The function of the devil as the great Accuser is particularly appropriate in this context. Anger at an offence, which then turns to resentment, gives the prosecuting *diabolos* the opportunity to frame a counter-charge against the otherwise innocent offended party.

28 The thief should not steal any longer. It is not surprising, given the commandment in the Decalogue, that theft is frequently condemned in Christian moral discourse (cf. Mark 10.19; Rom. 13.9; Rom. 2.21; 1 Cor. 6.10). What is more surprising is the sudden interruption of this topic after the reference to fits of anger, and the possible implication of this wording that there were thieves in the early Church (see Best 1997b: 179–88) who were being told to desist and earn an honest living.

To take the last point first: one solution might be that this is directed against some kind of activity that was not self-evidently stealing or burglary. This is rather too hastily rejected by Best (1997b: 182). Slaves, for example, would have regular and ample opportunity to 'steal' their owner's time and pilfer extra food and goods (Gnilka 271; Caird 82) and might not have thought of this as theft at all.

There are two immediate difficulties with this otherwise attractive explanation: first, that the denunciation of theft is insufficiently nuanced to capture minor forms of dishonesty; and secondly, a slave would hardly have had enough income, if any, to share with the poor. These difficulties make most commentators conclude that the verse is no more than a flag-waving moral platitude.

Although this may well be the true for the use of the maxim in its present context, it is inadequate as an explanation of its origin, for it fails to account for the peculiar logic. The thief who has no surplus to give to the poor has presumably been driven to crime by unemployment; it is cold comfort to tell him to get a job! On the other hand, a Robin Hood type of thief (who stole only from the pagan rich) would have even more goods than an honest man to share with the Christian poor. Let us therefore explore an alternative explanation, namely that this injunction was originally an oblique reference, surviving from Paul's original Laodiceans, to the notorious contemporary case of Philemon's runaway slave.

Philemon probably lived in Colossae; as a wealthy man he may have had business dealings also in nearby Laodicea, the more important commercial centre. That would explain why both of Paul's public letters, written at the same time as the private note to Philemon, contain references to wrongdoing (Col. 3.25 and here) and to the slave's duty of obedience (Col. 3.22–4 and Eph. 6.5–9). After perhaps stealing from his master and running away to Ephesus, Onesimus became a Christian through acquaintance with Paul and worked to support the Apostle in prison. In his letter to Philemon, Paul delicately requests that the master should forgive the slave's offence (Phlm. 18) and even release him (Phlm. 14) into Paul's service. (For a different account of the Onesimus affair, see Introduction, p. 26.)

If we return to the present text, this background accounts for the otherwise strange and abrupt intrusion of a warning against theft immediately after the preceding reference to a 'fit of righteous anger' (v. 26), for Philemon would have had good cause to feel aggrieved! It also explains, in the special circumstances of this case, the reference to working 'to support someone in need' (see below). All this is, of course, rather speculative, though it may gain some support from the later section on slavery (see the commentary on Eph. 6.5–9). As far as the readers of the present letter are concerned, the consensus view remains correct, i.e. this verse is a general moral dictum.

The former thief should now **be employed doing honest work with his own hands** (lit. 'let him toil, producing with his own hands the good'). The Greek text at this point is uncertain. Different MSS omit 'his own' (or even the whole phrase 'with his own hands') and 'the good', or have the different elements of the clause in another word order. The disruption of the text may have been caused by the removal of the unnecessary adjective 'his own', over-used in koine Greek, and by various attempts to move its object 'the good' closer to a verb which does not lead one naturally to expect an object at all. At 1 Cor. 4.11 Paul, speaking of himself and Apollos, says: 'We toil, working with our own hands'; at 1 Thess. 4.11, he exhorts believers to 'work with your own hands ... and have no need of anybody [i.e. to support you]'. In neither place does the verb 'to work' (*ergazesthai*) have or need a stated object, for it means 'to go to work' or 'to be gainfully employed'. On the other hand, Gal. 6.10 reads literally, 'Let us work the good thing to all, especially to those of the household of faith' in a context that concerns acts of charity, not paid employment. That a pseudepigrapher combined two phrases from Paul, 'to work with one's own hands' and 'to work the good', with different meanings but which both just happen to use the same verb seems most unlikely. If the original allusion was to the Onesimus affair, this particular form of words becomes more explicable: the thieving slave is now to work with his own hands for the 'good thing', i.e. the progress of the gospel. (Notice that Paul uses the same phrase, 'the good thing', at Phlm. 14, to allude to Onesimus' release from slavery as something which he wants Philemon to perform voluntarily.) Working for a living, he will then **have something to share with the one in need** – and the singular '*the one* in need' becomes pertinent, for it is one particular person who will be assisted, namely Paul himself in prison.

29 Let no foul language come out of your mouth. Foul (*sapros*) has the meaning 'rotten' or 'decaying' in the gospel parables about rotten fish (Matt. 13.48), trees or fruit (Matt. 7.17). But this is its only occurrence in a metaphorical sense. It presumably has the same sexual connotation as 'repulsive talk' (*aischrologia*) at Col. 3.8. In both places the sentence continues with a Semitic idiom, 'let it not come out of your mouth' (cf. e.g. Deut. 8.3; cf. Luke 4.22). Foul language is contrasted with words which 'bestow grace on those who are listening'. And again this is partly parallel to Col. 4.6, 'gracious speech seasoned with salt'. But the two Colossians verses are widely separated from each other. In order to explain how Ephesians might have brought them together, Lincoln (305) toys with the suggestion that 'the force of the salt imagery . . . in Col. 4.6 is as a preservative, and the writer has that text in mind' when he refers to rotten language. But this is a desperate attempt to make Ephesians dependent on Colossians at a point of blatant contradiction between the two (see further on 5.4, below).

The opposite of foul language is that which builds up community life: **what is good for edification as the occasion requires**. This is an echo of two words used in the preceding sentence, 'good' and 'need', which may be pure coincidence, or it may be that such superficial similarities ('link-word' is the form-critical term) assist in making sequences of disparate rules for community life (cf. Mark 9.42–50) easier to memorize. **Edification**, the work of building up the community, has been mentioned before at 4.12 and 16, where the role of leaders in the process was stressed. That may be in mind here too, though the actual instruction has a more general application (cf. Rom. 14.19).

The literal rendering of the phrase, 'towards the building up of need', is open to misunderstanding, as though 'need' were the object of the verb, i.e. was itself to be increased. So it invited correction in the scribal tradition (D* F G read 'for the building up of faith'). But the dependent genitive is a Semitism representing an adjective, viz. 'necessary upbuilding'.

The communal setting of good, edifying speech is implied in the following purpose clause, **in order that it may bestow grace on those**

who are listening. The occasion of worship may be chiefly in mind, see on 5.19f., in which the words of those who speak are designed to 'minister grace' to the assembled congregation who 'listen'. For edification in worship, see 1 Cor. 14.26 and Col. 3.16, 'singing in grace'. Although the wording is similar to the 'gracious speech' of Col. 4.6, the context there is rather different, not so much worship within the community as conversation with those outside it.

30 Do not grieve the Holy Spirit of God, by whom you were sealed for the day of redemption. The change in style and content from verse 30 is noteworthy. The purpose of this sentence is not to warn against any specific sins (either those mentioned before, v. 29, or after, v. 31) but to direct all morality towards its end in pleasing God (cf. 5.10) in response to the gift and promise of salvation. The author has made a comparable addition at 1.13f. and may have done the same here both to relieve the monotony of the paraenesis and to heighten its tone. For a discussion of sealing with the Spirit, see above on 1.13. For redemption, compare 1.7, where it is a past event, with 1.14, where it is a future hope, as here.

The idea of grieving the Holy Spirit may be derived from the Hebrew text of Isa. 63.10 ('they grieved his Holy Spirit': the LXX has 'they provoked'). As Houlden (322) observes, the concept of the Spirit here is 'more personified than elsewhere in this writing'. Personal and impersonal references to the Spirit are found in Paul too, but only the Johannine literature in the New Testament speaks in quite such a personal way of the Holy Spirit (see e.g. John 14.26; Rev. 2.7; 22.17).

31 Let all bitterness, rage, anger, shouting and slander be removed from you, along with all wickedness. The paraenesis continues with a list of six vices that spell out the types of the foul language denounced at verse 29. It should be compared with the list in Col. 3.8, with which it has four items in common, though in a different order. Some of the shared elements are found in similar lists in Paul (e.g. 2 Cor. 12.20; Gal. 5.20). At Rom. 2.8 'rage' and 'anger' are linked, though not as human sins but as God's righteous response to them. The two sins that are not mentioned in Colossians are 'bitterness' and 'shouting'. **Bitterness** (*pikria*) comes in a quotation from Ps. 10.7 at Rom. 3.14, where Paul utters a tirade against sins of speech. **Shouting** (*kraugê*; cf. Acts 23.9) occurs only here in the Pauline corpus and means angry, not just loud, speech. These two items add an extra vividness to the list: the Christian is to avoid nagging and slanging matches.

32 Instead, be kind to one another and compassionate, forgiving one another. If Ephesians in the previous verse is dependent on Col.

3.8, it must have lengthened the standard list of vices with a couple of rarer items to enliven it. If it is dependent on Col. 3.12 at this point, it has, on the contrary, shortened the list of virtues, selecting just three of the seven and omitting the others ('humility, gentleness and patience, tolerance') because they have already been used at 4.2. Thus the content of Col. 3.12 is precisely cut into two, with no omission and no overlap, and divided between Eph. 4.2 and Eph 4.32. Such exactitude in reusing Colossians is very rare. The alternative view is that Paul, well remembering what he wrote in Col. 3.12, has divided his own material. (See further the introductory remarks on Eph. 4.1–16.)

To **be kind** is a characteristic of God at 2.7 (cf. Rom. 2.4; 11.22). At Rom. 3.12 (from Ps. 13.3), 2 Cor. 6.6 and Gal. 5.22, it refers to a human virtue; in the last two references it appears in similar lists of virtues. Berger (*EDNT* 3.457) argues that the final phrase in the Ephesians list should not be translated **forgiving one another** but 'being gracious to one another'; when the verb (*charizesthai*) is used in this sense (cf. e.g. 2 Cor. 2.7) it normally takes an accusative object, not a dative as here. This is possible; or it may be that both in this clause and the next the unstated direct object 'offences' is to be understood.

The motive for mutual forgiveness is that **God in Christ has forgiven you** (cf. also 1 John 4.11). The same thought is present at Col. 3.13, where, however, it is Christ himself ('the Lord', see the variant readings) who has forgiven. Differences of this sort are often explained by appeal to the more theocentric standpoint of the writer of Ephesians, but implausibly, for almost immediately he will go on to speak of Christ's own love and self-offering for us (5.2b). This is rather more like Paul's own regular emphasis on the divine initiative, the christocentrism of Colossians being provoked by the special circumstances of that letter.

Some MSS have 'us' here instead of 'you'. Their similar pronunciation in koine often causes confusion, since MSS were regularly copied from dictation. The textual support is evenly balanced and there are two similar variants in the pronouns at 5.2. If 5.1–2 are an addition (see comments below), partly phrased in the first person plural (5.2b), this might have caused the change from 'you' to 'us' here in the textual tradition.

5.1 So, be imitators of God like beloved children. This sentence expands the thought of the preceding one. While Paul often instructs his readers to imitate him (1 Thess. 1.6; 2 Thess. 3.6ff.; 1 Cor. 4.16; Phil. 3.17), as he himself imitates Christ (1 Cor. 11.1), the unmediated imitation of God (*imitatio Dei*) is confined in the New Testament to this verse. It is taken up enthusiastically, probably from here, by Ignatius of Antioch in his letter to the Ephesians (1.1).

The thought is similar to the antithesis on love of enemies in the Sermon on the Mount. 'In order to become children of your Father in heaven' (Matt. 5.44f.), Christians must imitate God's indiscriminate beneficence in rain and sunshine towards the just and the unjust alike, and 'be perfect even as your Father in heaven is perfect' (Matt. 5.48). It also bears comparison with the Johannine understanding of salvation as the replication of the union of the Father and the Son in the relationship of believers with Christ (e.g. John 14.20; cf. 1 John 5.1). The imitation of the love of God is particularly implied by the following phrase, **like beloved children**. 'Children' and 'beloved' are the favourite forms of address in 1 John (see 2.1; 2.7 etc.), and 1 John 4.11 sheds particular light on Ephesians here: 'Beloved, if God so loved us, we also ought to love one another.' If the Johannine author refrains from actually using the word 'imitate' with its visual connotation of 'copy', it is because, as he goes on to say (v. 12f.), 'No one has ever *seen* God, but if we love one another God abides in us ... as we abide in him.'

2 There have been several references in Ephesians so far to the love of God (1.4) and of Christ (3.19) and the theme will come to a head in the nuptial imagery of 5.21–33 (see esp. vv. 25 and 29). Here it is applied to conduct: **and walk in the way of love** (cf. Rom. 14.15).

    Christ also loved us and gave himself on our behalf is an echo of Gal. 2.20, which had perhaps become a standard phrase in Pauline circles. On the christocentric emphasis see on 4.32 above. **Gave himself** is literally 'handed himself over'. The verb (*paradidomai*) is used of Jesus' being handed over (i.e. betrayed) by Judas to his enemies (Mark 14.21; 1 Cor. 11.23) and also of his being handed over to death according to the divine plan (Mark 9.31; Rom. 4.25). Here he surrenders himself for our sake. Explicitly sacrificial language such as this, **an offering and a sweet smelling sacrifice to God**, is not particularly common in Paul to describe the death of Christ, apart from Rom. 3.25 (and that may be a quotation from a Jewish Christian credal statement; see above on Eph. 1.7). But Paul does use the term 'offering' of his own missionary work (Rom. 15.16) and calls the Philippians' financial assistance to himself in prison a 'sweet-smelling sacrifice' (Phil. 4.18). The terms are found together at Heb. 10.5 (citing Ps. 39.7; cf. Heb. 10.10) in a treatment of the death of Christ as superseding Old Testament sacrifices; and the voluntary nature of his self-offering is emphasized at Heb. 9.14. In the New Testament, apart from Hebrews, it is perhaps the Johannine Epistles that contain the clearest affirmation of the death of Christ as an expiatory sacrifice (1 John 2.2; 4.10).

3 But let fornication and all uncleanness or covetousness not even be named among you. Lists of sins continue in the same vein as before in this verse and the following two, though we move from a focus on anger to talk about sex. This corresponds to 4.19 earlier and to the probable meaning of 'foul language' at 4.29 (see above). It is not so much the commission of these sins which is prohibited as the very mention of them; those who actually commit them are beyond the pale altogether (see 5.5). The same three terms appear in a longer list at Col. 3.5 that includes also 'passion' and 'evil desire' and links sexual sin with idolatry (as at Eph. 5.5). But there is a difference that should also be noted: in Colossians these sins themselves and not just talk about them are still latent in believers ('your earthly parts', Col. 3.5), whereas here they are completely excluded. The list should also be compared with the works of the flesh at Gal. 5.19, which start with fornication, uncleanness, depravity (as Eph. 4.19) and idolatry, before moving on to various kinds of anger (as Eph. 4.31) and end with drunkenness and revelling (as Eph. 5.18). It is a pretty standard collection (cf. also 1 Cor. 5.9; 6.9f.).

The notion of what is **fitting** (*prepei*) recalls the Stoic idea of conformity to nature (cf. 1 Cor. 11.13). However, here it is not Stoic natural law but the character of the Christian community as **saints** (lit. 'holy ones'; see on 1.4) that provides the norm for conduct. For a similar adaptation of Stoic ethical vocabulary, see the next verse.

4 The ways in which the three sexual sins of verse 3 can be named or talked about are now specified in another triplet: **obscenity, frivolity and facetiousness**. If they correspond precisely, they would seem to be in decreasing order of seriousness. Thus, 'obscenity' (*aischrotēs*) would be the verbal equivalent of fornication, the shamelessness that treats sexual licence as normal behaviour. (If Ephesians were dependent on Col. 3.8, the latter's more precise term 'shameless speech' (*aischrologia*) might have been preferable.) 'Frivolity' (lit. 'foolish talk', *mōrologia*) in this context would be prurient gossip about the 'uncleanness' and misdemeanours of others. 'Facetiousness' is our attempt to translate a word (*eutrapelia*) which Greek moralists like Aristotle viewed not as a vice but as a virtue, i.e. 'wittiness', the golden mean between pedantry and stupidity. So its presence here in a negative sense is very surprising, as it also is for another reason. At Col. 4.6 speech towards outsiders that is gracious and 'seasoned with salt' (the regular Greek metaphor for 'wit') is positively commended. Ephesians is unlikely to be deliberately contradicting Colossians on such a minor point, and a fine line could perhaps be drawn between the wit that is intended to humiliate and the sort of wit that is amusing courtesy aimed at putting others at their ease. But no fine lines are drawn here. *Eutrapelia* is simply rejected. The negative connotations of the word come from the context rather than the term itself. To make jokes, even disparaging jokes, about 'covetousness' ('who fancies whom') is **hardly appropriate**. This verb (*anēken*; cf. Col. 3.18), like 'it is fitting' (see on v. 3), employs Stoic moral vocabulary in a non-Stoic way to refer to the norms of Christian morality.

Instead of smutty talk of any of these three kinds, there should rather be **thanksgiving** (*eucharistia*). It is not perhaps the most obvious contrast to draw. And some Patristic commentators knew a variant version that substituted the very similar sounding 'graciousness' (*eucharitia*) and presumed it to be a coinage from *euchareia*, 'urbanity'. But this makes the sense in which *eutrapelia* can be called a sin even more obscure and, in any case, no surviving MS has that reading.

'Thanksgiving' highlights the positive aspects of other people's behaviour, unlike the other kinds of speech mentioned, and directs attention away from the absurdities of the human theatre to the economy of divine grace. Thanksgiving as the central theme of Christian worship is mentioned in Col. 3.16 and in the parallel at Eph. 5.20 (cf. 1 Thess. 3.9; 1 Cor. 14.16; 2 Cor. 4.15). It is not impossible that the technical sense of the word in relation to the Eucharist (Ign. *Eph.* 13.1; cf. *Did.* 14.1) is already implied here. Foul language would be particularly offensive and utterly inappropriate in such a sacred context and should also be shunned on other occasions.

5 The passage ends with a traditional Pauline formula of exclusion (cf. 1 Cor. 6.9f.): **For you should know this, that no fornicator, unclean or covetous person, idolaters in other words, has any inheritance in the kingdom of Christ and of God**. The wording should also be compared to that of Gal. 5.21: 'those who commit [fornication and uncleanness etc.] will not inherit the Kingdom of God'. The link between idolatry and sexual depravity is explained in Rom. 1.18–23. It is likely that all the preceding offenders are described as idolaters – there would be no obvious reason to differentiate. Literally, the Greek means 'that is an idolater', though some MSS have 'who is . . .' (cf. Col. 3.5) narrowing the referent to the covetous person alone. The relatively unusual statement that the kingdom is 'of Christ' as well as 'of God' is not impossible for Paul (see 1 Cor. 15.24–8) but the idea is more emphatically asserted in post-Pauline literature (Rev. 11.15; 2 Tim. 4.1, 18; 2 Pet. 1.11; and the Gospels, Matt. 20.21; Luke 23.42; John 18.16) and may be due to the editor.

C   Light in a dark world   (5.6–14)

(6) Let no one deceive you with vain talk, for this is the reason that God's wrath is coming on the sons of disobedience. (7) So do not have anything to do with them. (8) For you were once darkness but now you are light in the Lord. Behave as children of the light – (9) for the light produces a harvest of pure goodness, righteousness and truth (10) – approving what is well-pleasing to the Lord. (11) Take no part in the sterile works of darkness, but

rather expose them. (12) For what is done in secret by them it is shameful even to mention. (13) But all things that are being exposed by light are becoming clear. For everything that is being made clear is light. (14) Thus the saying goes:

Wake, sleeper
And rise from the dead:
And Christ will shine upon you.

The Epistle to the Ephesians in its present form is notably different from Paul's genuine letters in one major respect. In all his letters to churches, at certain points, and in some (Galatians for instance) continually, Paul was engaged in controversy with various opponents and detractors, some of whom were well known and plain to him, while others had perhaps been coloured in by fears and suspicions on his part. Ephesians by contrast is wonderfully calm. Its opening blessing sets a tone of cosmic serenity. It goes on to speak of Christians as enthroned in heaven, already saved by grace, united in Christ and filled with all the fullness of God. These great assurances of the first half of the letter are echoed in the second, especially at the points where we have grounds for suspecting expansions by the editor. The final battle-cry of 6.10–17 is no exception, for the antagonists of the Christian foot-soldier, who is dressed in God's own armour and certain thereby of victory, are not 'flesh and blood' people at all (6.12). Since the writer of Ephesians knew other letters of Paul, he must have consciously decided, like Paul's biographer in Acts, to play down this element of controversy. So to look for subtle and hidden allusions to 'flesh and blood' opponents in Ephesians is probably to misunderstand its basic motivation.

Nevertheless, at two points earlier in the letter, there have been passing references to possible threats to peace and harmony in the Church. At 2.2 the devil was said to be at work among 'the sons of disobedience', whoever exactly they might be; and various winds of doctrine 'promoted by human vagary and cunning' were mentioned at 4.14. In this passage human opponents come back into view briefly. They are 'sons of disobedience' again, who seek to deceive with empty words (v. 6); they are to be shunned and their secret deeds exposed (v. 11). But we are none the wiser as to their identity: are they pagans, or Jews, or deviant Christians? Are they libertines or rigorists? And what do they do in secret which it would be shameful even to speak about but which yet needs to be exposed (v. 12)? The writer is content to leave these questions unanswered and unanswerable, because his point is not to refute particular errors but to keep his readers always vigilant, united in the Church and loyal and obedient under the guidance of its leaders.

If Paul wrote at least some of this material – the Paul who did not shrink from a fight – he would have had a specific target in mind. If, furthermore, we can assume that he was writing to a community near Colossae at about the same time and knew that they would soon be able to read what he had written to the Colossians, then some of the vagueness might belong to the original letter. His correspondents were about to receive a fuller statement of the problems facing their neighbours and would be forewarned if the infection began to spread. If the unidentified opponents are those attacked in Colossians, they are probably Jewish Christian mystics promoting visions of angels through ascetic rules and practices (see Francis & Meeks 1975).

The author of Ephesians, however, is himself a Jewish Christian with mystical and ascetical leanings. There is his problem! No doubt he accepted that Paul in his day had good reason for the stand he took in Colossae, but unity and peace in the Church are not served by continuing old controversies and tarring all Christian Jews with the brush of 'heresy'. The effect of his expansion and redirection to Ephesus of Paul's original letter is to detach its interpretation from Colossians and make it stand on its own. And here he edits Paul's warnings against deviant opinion within the Church, so that they can be read instead as an attack on the licentiousness of the pagan world outside. In so doing he creates the sharp turns and flat contradictions in this passage, like the exposure of secret things without even mentioning them. Is it any wonder that commentators find it hard to decide what it is all about?

6 A new paragraph and topic begins here: **Let no one deceive you with vain talk**. If this were merely a continuation of the previous moral warnings, one would expect a direct address to the reader, like Gal. 6.7, 'Do not be deceived'. This, on the other hand, sounds more like a warning against false teachers. Moreover, the combination of the words 'vain' and 'deceive' is reminiscent of the description of the Colossian error as 'vain deceit' (2.8) and the caution delivered at Col. 2.4: 'I am saying this so that no-one may deceive you with plausible arguments.' Lincoln (335), in order to make the thought more homogeneous and consistent, resists these parallels and this conclusion and argues instead that this is a warning against unbelieving Gentiles 'who attempted to justify their vices as matters of indifference'. But we may reasonably ask why outsiders would feel under any obligation to justify themselves to Christians in this way. The references to deceptive and specious arguments point, rather, towards a deviant group within or on the fringe of the Christian community (so Best 484 and many other commentators), but then it would have to be the opposite problem to that in Colossians, i.e. some kind of Christian libertinism. Both views may be partly correct if the underlying source is warning in a general way against the enemy within while the editor, by context and by an added explanatory clause that evokes an earlier comment at 2.2, is directing his readers' attention towards the enemy without.

Part of the problem here arises from the historical and rhetorical situation of a pseudepigraphcal letter: the author is unable to be too specific about features of his own contemporary setting. To gain some insight into the latter, it is interesting to compare the deviants attacked in the letters to the churches in Revelation 2–3. The problem of the exact relation between the heresy of the 'Nicolaitans' at Ephesus (2.6) and Pergamum (3.15) to the synagogue of Satan (2.9) or the teaching of Balaam (2.14) or Jezebel (2.20) is a nightmare for commentators on the Apocalypse of John. But one thing at least is clear from this evidence: false teaching of various kinds was blowing in the wind in Asia Minor towards the end of the first century. The author of Ephesians wants to promote unity and sound doctrine in this situation, not by direct confrontation but by an inspiring vision of the ideal Church.

He attaches his next comment with the connective **for this is the reason** (lit. 'because of these things'). It is natural to take 'these things' to refer to the deception with empty words just mentioned, especially if a paragraph break is made at the beginning of verse 6 (see above). Without such a break, 'these things' might also refer to the types of sinners listed in verse 5. There they had been excluded from the kingdom, and here they would be threatened with an even worse punishment. However, if 'these things' is a reference backwards not just to the deception with empty words of verse 6 but to the people mentioned in verse 5, then it is difficult to stop there and not also include the lists of unfitting or inappropriate talk in verses 3–4. But then the punishment starts to look excessive for the crime. The solution to this problem may be to recognize a loosely connected addition by the editor in the second half of verse 6.

This Semitic idiom, 'sons of disobedience', has already been used at 2.2 to refer to those among whom 'the prince of the power of the air' is at work. The reference was not exclusively to Gentile unbelievers even there (see 2.3, 'among whom *we all* once lived'), nor is it here. Pagans, non-Christian Jews and deviant Christians are all being lumped together, as they regularly are in post-apostolic literature (see e.g. 2 Pet. 2.1). Any kind of disobedience to God (or the teaching of his Church) will be punished at the last judgement.

The statement that **God's wrath is coming** is in the present tense, probably with a future sense though not excluding possible present anticipations of the Last Judgement. In Paul, similarly, wrath (Rom. 2.5; 1 Thess. 1.9; 5.9) is mainly associated with future punishment, but it is already working itself out amid the moral chaos of the pagan world which has turned its back on God (Rom. 1.18ff.) and among Jewish opponents of the gospel (1 Thess. 2.16).

7 If Paul wrote the words **so do not have anything to do with them** (lit. 'so do not become co-partners with them'), he could not have been advocating a policy of complete separation from the godless world. He had explicitly rejected that as an option at 1 Cor. 5.9: 'to have nothing to do with the immoral you would have to leave the world altogether.' Verse 7 looks much more like a statement of the policy of ostracizing deviant members of the Christian community (see also 1 Cor. 5.11: 'Do not even eat with them'). 'Co-partners' (*summetochoi*) appears in the New Testament only here and at Eph. 3.6 (see comment there). Without its emphasizing prefix, the noun is also used at Luke 5.7 of James and John who share a fishing business with Peter and Andrew. The rejection of 'partnership' thus probably includes every kind of social or commercial dealings with those put under the ban; it is not merely prohibiting assent to their views or intimate involvement with them (*pace* Lincoln 326).

8 For you were once darkness but now you are light in the Lord. Behave as children of the light. The deliberate correlation of a theological indicative ('you are light') with a moral imperative (lit. 'walk as children of light') is thoroughly characteristic of Paul (cf. e.g. Gal. 5.25). Similar imagery is used at 1 Thess. 5.5: 'You are all sons of the light and sons of day: we are not of the night or of darkness (cf. also 2 Cor. 6.14). So then let us not sleep as others do.' The parallel at Col. 1.13 is less relevant, for its context is not one of moral exhortation.

There are, however, grounds for suspecting a degree of rewording by the editor here. The strong identification of the audience with 'light' creates a certain tension with the weaker description of them as 'children of light'; it also makes it difficult to follow the sequence of thought from the preceding two sentences. If verses 7f. were originally concerned with false teaching or immoral behaviour in the Church (see above), then perhaps this addition is designed to shift attention elsewhere. The 'darkness' that the readers once were becomes pagan ignorance, along the same lines as 2.11–12 and 4.17–19, and cannot be understood to refer to those who have seen the light and chosen darkness instead (whether Christian Jews who have lapsed back to Judaism or deviant Christians who have moved into heresy and schism). It is not that the author is ignoring or underestimating the danger of internal division in the Church. Far from it! But his rhetorical strategy is to secure unity by emphasizing that the community is pure 'light'.

The dark–light contrast is new here; only the then–now pattern was used in the earlier passages. 'You are light' might be compared to the saying at Matt. 5.14: 'You are the light of the world', but the difference should also be noted. In the Gospel, the role of the disciples is to illuminate the world (cf. 'You are the salt of the earth'): here it is rather to deepen its darkness by contrast. The actual thought is closer to that of the Johannine literature, where a light–darkness dualism similar to that in the DSS is constantly used in relation to outsiders, whether the pagan world, non-Christian Jews or schismatic Christians (see John 1.3f.; 7ff.; 3.19ff.; 8.12; 9.5; 11.9f.; 12.35ff.; 1 John 1.5, 7; 2.8f.; Rev. 22.5). Of this evidence the most relevant for our present purposes is John 3.20f (on the words in italics, see below):

> For every one who does evil hates the light, and does not come to the light, lest his deeds should be *exposed*. But he who does the truth comes to the light, that it may be *made clear* that his deeds have been wrought in God.

It is useful also to quote John 12.35f.:

> The light is with you for a little longer. Walk while you have the light, so that the darkness may not overtake you; if you walk in the darkness you do not know where you are going. While you have the light, believe in the light, so that you may become *children of light*.

These Johannine references are clearly christological, for Christ himself is the light (John 1.9). This may also be implied here already, and it will become explicit at verse 14.

9 For the light produces a harvest of pure goodness, righteousness and truth. This is a loosely connected parenthetical statement emphasizing the moral qualities that are the harvest or fruit of the light. Paul had spoken about the harvest of the Spirit at Gal. 5.22, and P[46] and a number of other MSS harmonize to this parallel by reading 'spirit' instead of 'light' here. **Righteousness and truth** (or 'true righteousness') were said at 4.24 to be characteristic, along with holiness, of the new creation; and Christians 'were created for good works' at 2.10. 'Truth' here is not so much truthfulness (in contrast to lying or deceit; cf. 4.14f.; 4.22, 24) but has the larger sense that it often has in Jewish ethical tradition, of loyalty and faithfulness (compare 'doing the truth' in John 3.21 quoted above). Moral fruits, it is implied, are the criteria for right belief (cf. Matt. 7.16, 20). The **light** may perhaps deserve an initial capital in English. It could merely mean Christian character that produces virtues, but it might also have the christological sense of Christ as the one true Light, the distinctively Johannine idiom.

10 After the parenthesis the phrase **approving what is well-pleasing to the Lord** continues the statement of verse 8, 'behave as children of the light'; in its present context it seems to be unnecessary and an anti-climax after verse 9. The language is Pauline and Rom. 12.2 is particularly close: 'approving the will of God, what is good, well-pleasing and perfect'. The basic meaning of the verb (*dokimazein*) is 'to test' or 'prove'; it can be used of the act of moral discernment and also of the 'tried and tested' character of the moral agent. In Paul's ethic, the will of God is revealed chiefly not in Torah but in the pattern of the Christ-event as it is lived out by the Spirit-filled community. And in cases of conflict between them, e.g. over circumcision, Sabbath and food laws (cf. Col. 2.11,16), Torah is superseded. Some of the language in this section may bear the marks of that earlier struggle, but now all the tension has gone. In the terms used in Rom. 2.18 (but without its polemical edge), 'to approve what is excellent' is, according to the author of Ephesians, 'to be instructed by Torah' and 'to be a light to those in darkness'.

11 Take no part in the sterile works of darkness. Sterile or 'fruitless' picks up 'fruit/harvest' at verse 9, but a different point is being made. It is not that the darkness produces works, whereas the light produces fruit (as Paul says in Gal. 5.19, contrasting works of the flesh with fruit of the Spirit). It is rather that deeds of darkness, like drunkenness (5.18) and worse (5.12), are entirely barren and unproductive. Compare the description of heretics as 'fruitless trees' at Jude 12, and the branches cut off from Christ who bear no fruit at John 15.2, 5f. It is difficult yet again to decide whether the author means general moral turpitude or dark deeds of a more devilish hue (cf. 6.12). **Take no part in** (lit. 'Do not have anything in common with'): this verb (*sugkoinein*) is used positively of the Philippians' support for Paul in prison (Phil. 4.14); and the related noun occurs similarly at Rom. 11.7; Phil. 1.7; 1 Cor. 9.23. With a negative as here, it means more than just 'Do not take part in' but rather 'Have no truck with' (cf. on v. 7).

   But rather expose them. The verb translated 'expose' (*elegchein*) has a wide field of meaning, including also to blame, rebuke, punish, convince and convict. If an impersonal object (works) is understood (no pronoun is expressed in the Greek), the possibilities are narrowed somewhat but there is still room for ambiguity. Are the deeds of darkness to be reproved (whether verbally or by actions that 'show them up') or are the deeds to be punished (by disciplining or expelling those who commit them)? But the unstated object may be personal, and this is the more common usage. Herod, for instance, is 'rebuked' by John the Baptist at Luke 3.19; and a child 'disciplined' by his father at Heb. 12.5; fellow Christians are 'corrected' at Matt. 18.15–17; 1 Tim. 5.20; 2 Tim. 4.2; Titus 1.9, 13; an outsider at a meeting in 1 Cor. 14.24 is 'convicted' of his secret sins and promptly converted. The fact that the participle 'exposed' in verse 13 is used in the neuter would not necessarily preclude this possibility, for the neuter can be used in a generalizing personal way (BDF s.138).

The tension we have traced throughout this section between the inner-ecclesial and extra-ecclesial interpretations remains unresolved. It has been caused by the writer's strategy to move the focus from the former to the latter.

12 For what is done in secret by them, it is shameful even to mention. 'By them' presumably refers right back to 'the sons of disobedience' at verse 6, no other group having been mentioned in the meantime. Several interpretations of this dark allusion are possible: the private sexual practices of pagan outsiders (Lincoln 330) or deviant believers (Best 495), the secret goings-on of a schismatic group (Col. 2.8ff.; W. L. Knox 1939: 199), or the rituals of a mystery cult (Schlier 239). Kreitzer (1998), in support of his view that this letter was directed at the congregation at Hierapolis as a warning against the cult of Demeter/Cybele connected with its famous Plutonium (or cavern entrance to the underworld, see on 4.9 above), links verse 12 to the 'crude language' of 4.29 and translates 'shameful things done in secret'. But strictly speaking, it is not the shamefulness of the secret deeds that Ephesians emphasizes but the shamefulness of Christians talking about them. Further, it is worth noting that 'shameful' in the New Testament does not inevitably have a sexual connotation. At 1 Cor. 11.6 it is the 'shame' of a woman having shorn hair (not any earlier impropriety that might have led to it); at 1 Cor. 14.35 it is a woman speaking in church; at Titus 1.11 it has to do with greed for money, which is also the association of the word in compound phrases at 1 Tim. 3.8; Titus 1.7; 1 Tim. 3.3; 1 Pet. 5.2. Finally, and most importantly, the really offensive aspect of the Demeter/Cybele cult, both to contemporary pagan moralists and to the much later Christian detractors whom Kreitzer cites at length, was precisely that it was not conducted in secret but was a lewd *public* display.

At 5.3 fornication, uncleanness and covetousness should not even be named (which is obviously hyperbole, since they just have been). Unfortunately, the author here follows his own injunction too strictly and leaves the allusion entirely obscure. But if the deeds are done in secret, how does he know about them? And if he is too ashamed to mention them, how can he expose them?

Lincoln answers these questions with his theory that simply by exhibiting a different quality of life, Christians will 'cast their illuminating beam into the dark recesses of the surrounding society and will show up its immoral practices for what they are' (330). Best's answer, on the other hand, is to surmise that some Christians have engaged in illicit sexual activities which, though covert, would quickly become common knowledge in a small religious group, and that, although it will be shaming to have to admit the existence of such faults within the Church, it would be even more shameful not to bring them into the open (494f.). Despite the subtlety of these interpretations, difficulties remain. Those who have taken the precaution of cloaking their secret sins from the public censure of pagan society would surely be the least likely to feel rebuked by some kind (what kind?) of display of sexual purity on the part of Christians. And backsliding Christians whose surreptitious liaisons are to be censured in the assembly can hardly be identified with the sons of disobedience on whom the wrath of God is coming, since presumably the whole procedure of exposure and discipline would be intended to bring them to repentance and restoration. The underlying sequence of thought, which the additions of the editor have obscured, is the normal reaction to doctrinal dissent in the early Church, namely:

Do not be deceived by the arguments of 'heretics',
ostracize them completely,
for what they say is merely a smokescreen for immorality.

(Compare the sequence of thought in Col. 2.8, 16 and 23.)

13 But all things that are being exposed by light are becoming clear. This sentence, apparently ignoring verse 12 altogether (indeed, virtually contradicting it), continues the theme of verse 11 in a more positive manner. The tenses are present, as the above translation emphasizes. Exposure to the light clarifies through a gradual process, not a sudden moment of reproof or conviction of sin. The writer's thought seems to be turning towards that process of Christian growth towards maturity and illumination which he emphasized in the earlier passage on the threat of false teaching (4.14; cf. 4.13, 15), and the essential role in that process of the correction and pastoral oversight of the Church's leaders.

14 A new verse begins at this point in the traditional divisions of the text of the New Testament, but modern editions (including NA^{27}) start verse 14 slightly later, with the quotation. This is symptomatic of a more significant exegetical indecision. Are we to take the sentence **For everything that is being made clear is light** as a final comment on the idea of the exposure of the works of darkness, or as the introduction to the idea that Christ is the true light? If 'to make clear' is an explanation of one of the senses of 'expose' (*elegchein*, see above on v. 11), then the meaning might be that exposure of sins is the 'necessary first step towards transformation into light' (as Caird 86). But it can only be the first step and on this understanding the statement would be highly optimistic. Corrupt pagans, non-Christian Jews or deviant Christians might well react in a very different way to the exposure and making clear of their secret sins!

The participle translated 'being made clear' could be middle rather than passive (see KJV/AV: 'Whatsoever doth make manifest is light'). Since the same verb has just been used in the passive, for this rendering to be possible at all it would be necessary to suppose a rather sharp break with the preceding sentence. The meaning would then become either a platitude ('Light helps you to see things'), or a metaphor anticipating the following hymnic citation ('Everything that illuminates is the Light (i.e. Christ)'). On balance, however, the passive seems preferable.

As we have suggested above on verse 13, the train of thought has moved on to the process of Christian nurture. What is made clear, i.e. in education and growth in holiness, conforms the Christian to the Light. This is similar to 2 Cor. 3.18, 'All of us, with unveiled faces, gaze into the glory of the Lord as into a mirror and are transformed into his likeness, from one degree of glory to another.' The theme of the exposure of false teaching or pagan vice (or both) has finally been eclipsed by the idea that Christians themselves are beneficially exposed to the light of the risen Christ.

Thus the saying goes. The same words were used to introduce a modified quotation from Psalm 68 at Eph. 4.8, which was also perhaps mediated through the hymnody of the community (see the commentary there).

> **Wake, sleeper**
> **And rise from the dead:**
> **And Christ will shine upon you.**

What is quoted here, however, is not identifiable as any part of extant Jewish scripture. Echoes have been detected of Isa. 26.19 combined with Isa. 60.1f. (see Moritz 1996: 97ff.), or even more tenuously Jon. 1.5f. (see A. T. Hanson 1980: 142). But neither suggestion is very likely. Quotation from a lost apocryphal work is a possibility. Clement of Alexandria (*Protr.* 9.84.2) stated that it came from an apocryphal saying of the Lord and went so far as to quote its second verse: 'The sun of resurrection, begotten before the day star, who has given life with his own beams'; what his evidence was for this statement, we cannot tell. Epiphanius (*Haer.* 42.12.3) claims that the saying comes from the *Apocalypse of Elijah*; if so, it must be from a different version of that work than the one we know (or from a missing portion of it) (see Charlesworth 1983: 2. 721–53). Nevertheless, origin from a Christianized version of some Jewish apocalypse is not as implausible as recent commentators seem to feel (e.g. Schnackenburg and Lincoln; contrast Noack 1952). One can imagine a situation in which a seer, anticipating in some visionary experience the End of the ages, is addressed by an accompanying angel with such words as these (cf. Rev. 1.17, where it is Christ himself who 'raises' the seer from a death-like trance). That the imperatives are in the singular is, therefore, not a conclusive argument (*pace* Best 499) against such an original eschatological setting for the text (cf. Matt. 25.23, which has a similar eschatological imperative, also phrased in the singular: 'Enter into your master's joy').

However, the majority view among commentators is that the material is drawn from an early Christian hymn, probably composed to accompany the rite of baptism (Lincoln 319). The pre-Christian life is characterized by the metaphors of sleep and death and contrasted with being awake and fully alive in the light of Christ (cf. Heb. 6.4). If this is correct, it should be noted that the implied understanding of baptism would involve a more realized eschatology, the 'resurrection of the believer', than is found in most other New Testament texts; but Col. 3.1 and Eph. 1.20 show that it is possible. Death, in the second line, is used metaphorically of the domain of sin from which believers have been delivered by dying, and being buried, with Christ in baptism (Rom. 6.4; cf. Eph. 2.1). It is less easy to demonstrate that sleep was used as a metaphor for the pre-baptismal state, though it is regularly used as a metaphor for those awaiting resurrection (1 Thess. 4.15; 1 Cor. 15.51) and for moral torpor in this life (Rom. 13.11; 1 Thess. 5.6).

To awake from the sleep of sin and death is to emerge into the light of Christ. The verb 'shine upon' (*epiphauskein*) only appears here in the New Testament. A similarly constructed verb, *epiphōskein*, meaning 'to dawn', occurs at Luke 23.54 and Matt. 28.1. Furthermore, Rev. 22.16 refers to the light of Christ as 'the bright morning star' (cf. also Luke 1.78). The imagery of this verse may be the same, i.e. not Christ as the full light of the sun at noon, but Christ as the dawn of a new and eternal day. If so, that would introduce into the image a possible hint of still future development.

Whether this spiritual song had its origin in baptismal liturgy or in an apocalyptic vision of future resurrection, in its present context its meaning is ethical. Its terms denote moral categories: the sleeper is one who lacks moral vigilance; the dead are those sunk in sin; and the light is what both exposes immorality and also produces the fruit of good works.

D   The wisdom of praise   (5.15–20)

(15) Therefore watch out that you behave strictly, not as fools but as wise, (16) making every moment count, because these are evil times. (17) Therefore do not be mindless, but understand what the Lord's will is; (18) and do not get drunk with wine – that way ruin lies – but be filled with the Spirit, (19) speaking to each other in psalms and hymns and spiritual songs, singing and chanting in

your hearts to the Lord, (20) always giving thanks for everything in the name of our Lord Jesus Christ to him who is God and Father.

After the warning against surrounding or invading darkness (5.6–14), which the enlightened Christian is to shun, the theme of moral conduct is resumed with a contrast between foolishness and wisdom, illustrated respectively by drunkenness and being filled with the Spirit (sober intoxication!). And the rules for conduct turn finally to their basis and motivation in worship.

The material in Colossians with which this section has most affinity comes in two separate passages, before and after the household code (Col. 3.16 and 4.5). The former contains the sequence 'psalms, hymns and spiritual songs' and the latter the phrase 'redeeming the time'. But these striking similarities between Colossians and Ephesians are found in two different contexts amid variations which are difficult to explain: 'teaching and admonishing each other' is plainer in Ephesians ('speaking to each other'), but 'singing to God' is fuller ('singing and chanting to the Lord'). The Colossians phrase 'doing everything in the name of the Lord Jesus and giving thanks to the Father through him' (3.17) is differently worded in Ephesians: 'giving thanks for everything in the name of our Lord Jesus to him who is God and Father'. At Col. 4.5, 'redeeming the time' is found in an injunction about conduct towards outsiders that goes on to commend gracious speech towards them, 'seasoned with salt' (4.6). This context is entirely missing from Ephesians, and witty speech has earlier been condemned (see on 5.4). Instead, Ephesians explains the phrase 'redeeming the time' with 'because the days are evil', which turns our attention to a topic somewhat muted elsewhere in the epistle, though prominent in Paul's own writings, namely the wickedness of this passing age which will soon be ended by the parousia and which imposes urgency on believers' use of time. Finally, the wise–foolish distinction in Ephesians and the attack on drunkenness are missing from Colossians.

Thus, the differences from Colossians are far more numerous than the points of similarity. So either the author, having read Colossians, has recalled just two phrases and worked them into a new composition of his own, or Paul, having just used these phrases in his letter to the Colossians, liked them enough to reuse them in his companion piece to the Laodiceans. We prefer the latter hypothesis, because the eschatological explanation of 'redeeming the time' is demonstrably closer to Paul's view than to that of the editor, and because the contrast between drunkenness and Spirit-filled praise makes a lively and original point (see below). If the editor's hand can be detected in this passage, it is at the beginning, which provides a transition from the previous section with elements more characteristic of traditional Jewish than Pauline moral discourse, especially the use of 'strictly' (v. 15) in reference to behaviour (see below).

15 Despite the opening **therefore**, the connection with the preceding section is not particularly close and no deduction is being drawn from the hymn just quoted. This verse would follow on better if verses 13–14 (along with the other additions that prepare for them, see commentary above) were omitted. **Watch out** (*blepete*) would then be a natural word to use after describing the danger of false teaching (cf. Phil. 3.2; Col. 2.4; cf. Mark 13.5).

The translation above, following the majority of MSS, takes **strictly** (or 'accurately', *akribôs*) with 'behave', i.e. 'watch out that you behave (walk) in strict conformity with ethical standards' (cf. KJV/AV, 'See that you walk circumspectly'). (Gal. 2.14 uses a not dissimilar expression for 'walking straight (*orthopodein*) in accordance with the gospel', in an accusation against Peter and Barnabas who have suddenly decided to 'walk straight' in accordance with the Jewish food laws.) In Jewish contexts, and probably also conservative Jewish Christian ones, 'strictly' would imply conformity to the Law; that is the meaning of similar usages at Acts 18.25; 22.3; and 26.5. Its equivalent in 1 Tim. 1.8 is 'legally' or 'correctly' (*nomimôs*). The word is not, however, used in this moral sense by Paul anywhere else; its only other occurrence is at 1 Thess. 5.2, where it refers to something that is 'plainly known'. So it may be an addition by the editor.

A few MSS, including P⁴⁶ ℵ B (and the printed text of N-A²⁷), connect the adverb with the opening imperative, i.e. 'Watch out strictly' – a virtual tautology; but no other use of 'Watch out' in the metaphorical sense in the New Testament is felt to need such adverbial reinforcement. The origin of this minority reading is easier to explain as a textual corruption than the other way round; a scribe who did not recognize the moral connotation of the adverb in reference to strict behaviour associated it instead with accurate seeing.

The contrast **not as fools but as wise** is a feature of Jewish ethical instruction (Prov. 4.10–19) reflected both in the DSS and the New Testament (Matt. 7.24–7; 25.1–13; 1 Cor. 1.18 – 3.23). It is worked up into the standard topic of 'the two ways' (Matt. 7.13f.; cf. *Did.* 1.1f.). Col. 4.5 recommends 'wise' conduct towards outsiders and implies thereby a certain degree of tolerance and accommodation to the world which is missing, by and large, in Ephesians. In this respect, our author is moving in the direction of the stark either/or of post-apostolic, and especially Johannine, moral teaching (compare above on the light/darkness imagery, 5.8).

16 The Greek for **making every moment count** means literally 'redeeming [or buying out] the time' (*exagorazomenoi ton kairon*). The expression can be negative (as at Dan. 2.8 LXX) and mean 'buy time', i.e. 'prevaricate'. Paul uses the verb in its positive soteriological sense at Gal. 3.13 with a personal object, 'Christ has redeemed us', though it can hardly have that sense here, for it is people who are redeemed in the soteriological sense, not time. In this ethical context it must mean 'buying up' or 'cornering the market in time' or 'making the most of every opportunity'. The reason given for not wasting time – that precious commodity – is **because these are evil times**.

A more natural reason for such an injunction would be that human life is short; what we have here is something more eschatological. Taking note of the frequent allusions so far to the wickedness of the contemporary pagan world (2.2, 12; 4.17f.; 5.3), Lincoln (342) gives the following explanation of the logic: the opportunities for wise and good deeds in relation to the outside world will be few and far between, so each must be seized. But if that were what was meant, the omission of any reference to behaviour towards outsiders (in contrast to Col. 4.5) becomes doubly surprising. The logic is easier to follow if the verse is an appeal to the doctrine of Jewish apocalyptic (cf. 1.21): the end days are evil, and *precisely because they are evil*, they are short (see Mark 13.20: 'If the Lord had not shortened the days') and therefore one must make the most of the time available. Of course, this is not a line of thought which the editor himself could have constructed out of a phrase lifted from Colossians. But it is entirely typical of Paul (cf. Rom. 13.11–14; 1 Thess. 5.8–9).

Sleep and drunkenness are good examples of wasting one's time and missing opportunities for good works; and in the two Pauline passages just referred to they are also mentioned. This might have been a suitable place to include a reference to the sobriety of the soldier of Christ, as indeed Paul does in his use of the military metaphor in the same two passages. But in Ephesians that has been delayed until 6.10–17 and expanded to form an impressive finale.

17 Therefore [i.e. because of these evil times] **do not be mindless** (*aphrōn*). In Jewish tradition (Ps. 39.8; 49.10–12; Sir. 11.18f.; 14.4, 5) 'mindless' or 'foolish' (cf. v. 15) is a strong word often referring to that extremity of folly that consists in throwing away the chance of salvation. This is the context for the use of this term or of closely related ones in the Gospels (Luke 12.20; Matt. 3.26; Mark 7.21f.; Matt. 25.8). Paul also conceives of folly in this dramatic sense (Rom. 1.22), but in addition he can use the term 'mindless' in its softer Greek meaning of stupid or unphilosophical (see 1 Cor. 15.36) and he plays on the wise/foolish contrast in his apologetic for the gospel of the cross (1 Cor. 1.18–31) and for his own apostolic ministry (2 Cor. 11–12, where this adjective or its abstract noun occurs a full eight times). No irony, however, is intended here: Christians are to avoid the mindlessness of pagan unbelief in these evil days and resolve instead to **understand what the Lord's will is**. The wording here is a variation on 'approve what is well-pleasing to the Lord' at 5.10 (cf. Rom. 12.2). In Ephesians, Christ is usually meant by the title 'the Lord', but not always: here and possibly at 5.10, the traditions used are more naturally understood to be referring to God.

18 Do not get drunk with wine may be a scriptural allusion (if so, it is probably to Prov. 23.31), though it could simply be a commonplace of moral instruction. But a more precise reason for what, in the present arrangement of the text at least, seems a sudden introduction of this topic has been felt to be necessary by many commentators. Some (Best 507, following Barth and Mitton) see drunkenness as an anaesthetizing reaction to the evil days of the End time (cf. v. 16). Equally, though, the *delay* of the End time could lead to drunkenness as an indulgence born of complacency (see Matt. 24.49). Others (e.g. Lincoln 344) see this as simply derived in a literary way from statements in 1 Thess. 5.6–8 and Rom. 13.12; but on that hypothesis it is difficult to explain why the light–darkness motif in both passages is absent here, though it was, of course, strongly present in the preceding paragraph. Others see an implied warning against participation in drunken rituals connected with pagan religion, especially the cult of Dionysus (Hengel 1983: 188 n. 7): but verse 18 is now rather distant from verse 12. Yet others, taking the view that the problem is internal to the Church rather than external, have seen here a reference to drunken disorder at the Eucharist (cf. 1 Cor. 11.21; so e.g. Houlden 328). The strength of the latter view is that it helps to explain how the contrast between drunkenness and Spirit-filledness (cf. Acts 2.13) leads without interruption into a description of Christian worship (vv. 19f.; cf. Acts 2.46–47a).

In the Pastoral Epistles moderate consumption of wine is recommended on health grounds (1 Tim. 5.23), but excessive use is a disqualification for holding church office (1 Tim 3.8; Titus 1.7). These rules may not be irrelevant to the interpretation of this verse. Since the rhetorical situation of a pseudepigraphon is multiple and varied, the author may have one eye on potential readership among church leaders.

Drunkenness is the road to **ruin** (*asōtia*) – a word used elsewhere in the New Testament at Titus 1.6 and 1 Pet. 4.4 (cf. Luke 15.13). It has the same root as the word for salvation (*sōtēria*, see on Eph. 6.17) and means 'unhealthiness' or 'dissipation'. The opposite of a drunken, dissolute life is to **be filled with the Spirit**. The idea of fullness (frequently encountered already, see 1.23; 3.19; 4.13) is especially appropriate in contrast to excessive drinking, and the liquid metaphor in regard to the Spirit is reminiscent of similar ones elsewhere: 'made to drink of the one Spirit' (1 Cor. 12.13), 'poured out' (Acts 2.33; cf. Rom. 5.5) and 'streams of living water' (John 7.38f.). The present tense of the imperative does not imply that believers are gradually to be filled, but that they should continually be full. **With the Spirit** is ambiguous in Greek; it could be translated 'in the spirit'. If so, it would refer to the human spirit as the place where the divine fullness is experienced, rather than to the divine Spirit as the content of the human fullness (see on 1.23). Both make sense, and the writer of these words, not least if he was Paul, may not have wanted to distinguish between them in this sort of context.

19 Speaking to each other in psalms and hymns and spiritual songs, singing and chanting in your hearts to the Lord. The similarities and contextual differences between this verse and Col. 3.16 have been commented on in the introduction to this section. The Greek reflexive pronoun is used here, presumably doing duty for the reciprocal pronoun, **to each other**, as earlier at 4.32. If pressed, a true reflexive would mean 'speaking to yourselves' and the maxim would then be recommending inward praise during the daily life of believers (as, probably, 1 Thess. 5.16f. and Phil. 4.4–6). But the larger context implies corporate worship and interaction with other Christians (and this must be the sense at Col. 3.16, with its 'teaching and admonishing each other'). Whether the reciprocity is precise and refers to antiphonal recitation and singing is unclear, though the practice is known from the liturgy of the Jerusalem Temple (Ezra 3.11) and from Pliny's report of early Christian worship (*Ep.* 10.96).

The similarity with Col. 3.16 seems to have led to some further harmonization in the textual tradition: ℵ A D etc. omit the preposition before the list: A also adds 'by grace'. More significantly, P^{46} and B omit the adjective 'spiritual' before the last item, which if correct means that most other MSS have harmonized to Colossians at this point. However, other factors support the longer reading; see below.

Psalms, hymns and spiritual songs could be three words for the same thing or for three different kinds of thing. **Psalms** might be the Psalms of David (cf. Luke 20.42) if they were already used in Christian worship (cf. 1 Cor. 14.26) or later compositions, of which there were many, some Jewish (*The Psalms of Solomon*; the Qumran Hodayoth), some Christian (see Luke 1.46–55, 68–75; 2.29–32 and see on Eph. 4.8 above). The noun 'psalm' is underlined by the following participle translated 'chanting' (the two words being from the same root); it refers strictly to a song accompanied by a stringed instrument. **Hymns** may just be a synonym for psalms: at the Last Supper the disciples 'sang a hymn', presumably a Passover psalm, Mark 14.26. If a difference is intended, then a song about salvation in Christ, such as the blessing of Eph. 1.3–10, or the hymn to Christ our Peace at 2.14–16, 18 (cf. Col. 1.15–20 and Phil. 2.6–11), may be meant. These hymns are not composed in the Hebrew poetic form of parallel couplets, the distinctive feature of Jewish psalmody. **Songs** (or odes) is the term used in Revelation (5.9; 14.3; 15.3) to describe the praises in the heavenly liturgy. Some are short choruses, others have more substance to them. They presumably reflect the kind of earthly worship known in the churches of Asia to which that book, as well as this, are addressed. The songs are described as **spiritual** not because songs is a more secular or general term than the preceding ones, nor probably because songs are understood as spontaneous or charismatic, but most likely because the list needs to finish with a flourish.

Singing was an important part of worship in the Jerusalem Temple, and communities like the early Christians (Eph. 2.21 and see note there) or the Essenes (Philo *Vita Cont.* 84), who understood themselves as a new temple (see Gärtner 1965), carried on the practice. There is little or no evidence for the way music may have been used, if at all, in the contemporary Jewish synagogue. If Diaspora Jews were trying to distinguish themselves from the practices of Hellenistic pagan religion by doing without music in their worship, then the Church took a different line and 'baptized' music into the service of Christ (similarly, the practice of speaking in tongues, 1 Cor. 12; see esp. v. 2). In the discussion of worship in 1 Corinthians, Paul goes on to refer to musical instruments at 13.2 and 14.7f. and can speak both of 'singing with the Spirit' (i.e. in tongues) and also of 'singing with the mind' (i.e. in prophecies), which were rational and sometimes (cf. 1 Corinthians 13) highly theological hymns of praise.

20 The two participles 'singing and chanting' continue into this verse with a third, **always giving thanks** (*eucharistountes*) **for everything** (or possibly 'for everybody', the Greek is ambiguous). Constant and comprehensive thanksgiving is the hallmark of Paul's spirituality (Rom. 1.9; 1 Cor. 1.4; Phil. 1.4; 4.4 etc.) and it was a regular part of worship in his churches (1 Thess. 5.18). By the time of Ephesians, this term may have collected the more technical sense of that great Thanksgiving, the Eucharist (see on 5.4). **In the name of our Lord Jesus Christ** implies an official gathering of the Church in the name of Christ for worship and deliberation (1 Cor. 5.4; cf. Matt. 18.20), and whatever may have been the case earlier, by the end of the first century (Ignatius; *Didache*) such meetings normally included the Eucharist. Thanksgiving 'in the name' is addressed **to him who is God and Father**.

The formulation in Col. 3.17, which connects 'in the name' to 'whatever you do in word or deed', ends with (literally) 'giving thanks to the God, Father, through him'. It is difficult to argue (with Mitton 1951: 253) that Colossians is more fluent (or Pauline) than Ephesians here. Both epistles are saying similar things and using many of the same words to do so. But what is more significant is the presence in this passage of typically Pauline eschatology, asceticism and pneumatology, all of which are missing from the Colossians parallel.

This section ends here; to continue with verse 21 (see below) would be an appalling anti-climax. Moral instruction has dominated the epistle since 4.17, and has here and there perhaps lapsed into moralizing. But the deeper source of Christian conduct in the worship and praise of God through Christ is given its proper emphasis in this conclusion.

VI Christian obedience (5.21 – 6.9)

In contrast to the preceding section, in which various maxims for community life were laid down in no obvious order, a clearer structure emerges now around the theme of Christian obedience sustained over three distinct paragraphs (5.21–33; 6.1–4; 6.5–9). The structure has been taken over by the writer of Ephesians from his source and expanded to serve his purpose of spelling out the moral consequences of the unity which Christians have in Christ, illustrated by the analogy of basic relationships within a household.

A note on the household code

The section is usually called the household code (or in German, *Haustafel*), though that formal classification should not be allowed to predetermine the question of its present literary function within the letter. As we shall see, even in the Pauline original the purpose of using this form was not to offer general advice on the conduct of family life for its own sake, but something much more specific; and in Ephesians, the use of the code must be seen in the light of the rhetorical situation implied by the pseudepigraphy (see Introduction, pp. 44–7).

Martin Dibelius in his commentary on Colossians (1912) pioneered the form-critical analysis of household codes, drawing attention to examples in Greco-Roman literature, especially in the writings of Aristotle, Plutarch and Seneca, which give conventional advice to the heads of households on the way they should treat their wives, children and slaves. This Hellenistic form influenced Greek-speaking Jewish writers, among them the authors of the New Testament epistles, and it appears in full or in part in several early Christian writings: above all Col. 3.18 – 4.1, but see also 1 Pet. 2.18 – 3.7; 1 Tim. 6.1–2; Titus 2.1–10; *Did.* 4.9–11; *1 Clem.* 21.6–9; Ign. *Pol.* 4.1 – 6.1. The differences should also be noted. The Christian examples often directly address the subordinate parties and not just the heads of families, and they often add extra motivation clauses of a religious kind.

The origin and purpose of the household code in early Christianity have attracted much scholarly attention: the works of Crouch (1972) on Colossians, and Balch (1981) on 1 Peter provide detailed discussions of the evidence and reach rather different, though not necessarily mutually exclusive, conclusions. On the one hand, with Crouch, it is possible to see the code form, which early Christianity borrowed from Greek ethics via the Diaspora synagogue, as a means of mapping orderly relations within local congregations and establishing standards of decent behaviour against those who deduced a more radical egalitarianism from Paul's teaching (see Gal. 3.28). In regard to Colossians, Lincoln (364) goes further along the same lines and suggests that the code is used to combat an otherworldly asceticism which would reject domestic entanglements altogether. But it should be noted that the error which the letter attacks (Col. 2.8–23) does not include explicit opposition to marriage and the family (contrast 1 Tim. 4.3).

It is possible, on the other hand, to emphasize, with Balch, the function of the code in regard to the community's external relations with contemporary society, since the proper management of the household, the basic unit of society, was treated as a matter of public and political concern. Religious sects, among them certain mystery cults, Judaism and, of course, early Christianity, that appeared to encourage insubordinate aspirations in women and slaves would soon come under suspicion; and the adoption of the household code could be seen as an apologetic move to deflect such criticism.

For those who take all the writings in which the code form appears to be post-apostolic, yet another motive suggests itself (MacDonald 1988: 102–22). Awareness of the delay of the parousia would, so they claim, have led to a more positive estimate of the structures of family life, and they go on to link this with other evidence of institutionalization in the sub-apostolic period, such as regulations for the appointment of particular orders of ministry and the development of the concept of doctrinal orthodoxy – features which are prominent in the Pastoral Epistles, though less so in Colossians or Ephesians. There are, however, some difficulties with this theory. It is not in fact so evident that early eschatological enthusiasm downgraded the significance of marriage; the Jesus tradition is ambiguous on this point. On one side, disciples were called away from family ties to a life of itinerant ministry; but on the other, Jesus' rejection of divorce, which Paul himself knew (1 Cor. 7.10), reinforced the institution of marriage. Although for Paul 'the form of this present world is passing away' (1 Cor. 7.31), he did not deduce from this that celibacy was a universal obligation; he saw it as a special gift granted to a select few like himself (1 Cor. 7.7). Opposition to marriage does arise in second-century gnosticizing circles but their disdain for the flesh stems from an atemporal dualism, resulting precisely from the waning of eschatological hope. Paul would not have objected to the idea that wives ought to obey their husbands, children their parents, or slaves their masters, nor that men should respond to the obedience of their subordinates with love, patience and fair-mindedness. So the household code as such does not imply any loss of eschatological consciousness. As can be seen from 1 Thess. 4.11f. (cf. 1 Thess. 5.4ff.), Paul's normal advice was that Christians should continue faithfully with their daily responsibilities in the time that remained before the return of Christ.

Supposing that Col. 3.18 – 4.1 is an original part of the letter Paul wrote to the Colossians, we may be able to offer a rather simpler explanation of the code form's inclusion than those mentioned above, without denying its wider implications. It is remarkable that the injunctions to wives/husbands and children/parents are expressed very briefly (42 words in Greek) with a minimum of Christian adaptation ('in the Lord' at 3.18 and 20), whereas the slave/master section is almost twice as long as the first two put together (74 words in Greek) and has been much more thoroughly Christianized. If we also suppose that the Epistle to Philemon was sent at the same time as the original Colossians (the similar lists of names in Philemon and Colossians effectively demand that supposition) then the notorious case of Philemon's disobedient but now converted slave, Onesimus, would have been in the forefront of Paul's mind (Caird 208; cf. Introduction, pp. 25f). As Houlden comments (210, following the suggestion of J. Knox 1935):

> We are inclined to think that it was the specific case of Onesimus which led Paul to introduce the material about slaves and masters in a context which gave him barely sufficient justification and that he added the whole formula of instruction which usually went with it partly in order to disguise it – thinly.

On this view we do not have to ask how Paul's lofty ethic of the transformed moral agent in Col. 3.1–17 could have collapsed so suddenly into the commonplace aphorisms of a household code; his purpose was not to inculcate conventional morality but to allude in a diplomatic, 'thinly disguised' manner to a specific problem. If Onesimus not only delivered the letter to the congregation at Colossae (Col. 4.9) but was also invited, as he might have been, to read it aloud to them, this passage would take on added poignancy as an act of public contrition on his part for the wrongs he had done his master (see Col. 3.25; Phlm.18; cf. above on 4.28). A similar explanation may also account for the disproportionate emphasis on slaves in the original code that has been adopted by the writer of Ephesians.

We may compare the slavery material (6.5–9) with the two other topics. The detailed comments below will offer reasons for believing that the wives/husbands section has been extensively expanded with other traditions; similarly, though to a lesser extent, the section on children/ parents. The original text might have been as meagre as the following:

> 'Wives, submit in the Lord to your husbands.
> Husbands, love your wives.
> Children, obey in the Lord your parents.
> Fathers, do not provoke them.'

However, the third section on slaves/masters cannot be reduced to a basic injunction in the same way by removing elements that reflect the editor's interests. It is, like the Colossians parallel, more wordy and belaboured, using some of the same vocabulary but in new configurations and displaying a more, not less, distinctively Pauline style when it diverges from Colossians.

We know that the Laodicean letter was also to be read out to the Colossians. And Paul, who had visited neither congregation in person, was clearly concerned to treat both of them even-handedly (see Col. 2.1). Both of these neighbouring churches would have heard the apostle's use of the household code, with particular emphasis on the slave–master section, as a reassurance in the aftermath of the Onesimus affair. They would have concluded that no general demand to release slaves was to be imposed, and that the appeal to Philemon was to be understood as an exceptional case. The pointed allusion to wrongdoing in Col. 3.25 is here replaced (but cf. Eph. 4.28) with a more general promise of reward for doing good directed towards all, whether slave or free (Eph. 6.8). Similarly the topic of partiality, raised rather sharply by Paul's offer to pay damages for Onesimus' misdemeanours, is here treated more generally, as it is elsewhere in Paul (see Rom. 2.11), in connection with the impartiality of the heavenly judge (see further below on 6.5–9).

The first conclusion to which this argument points is that the slave section of the household code, both in Ephesians and Colossians, was originally the chief reason for including it. It seems that Paul was less concerned with giving guidance on relations within the community, or between the community and the outside world, than he was with his own relations with the churches of the Lycus valley. With the same delicacy and obliqueness that characterize the letter to Philemon as a whole, he attempts to restore order and friendship. Slaves in other Christian households, lacking Onesimus' fervour and useful talents, are to be discouraged from appealing to his case as a precedent for their own manumission; they are to remain as they are (cf. 1 Cor. 7.21ff. and see Bartchy 1973), since, according to Paul, all, whatever their social status, are slaves of Christ and free in the Spirit. In any case, to be released from slavery without the means to provide a home and livelihood for oneself would be a worse fate than to remain under the benign protection of a Christian master.

The second conclusion is that the editor of Ephesians has expanded the two other sections with new christological and scriptural elements and created from them something more worthwhile for later, differently situated readers; he has developed them to serve his overriding message of the unity of the Church. Marriage and the family are of interest to him only because they illustrate the call to Christian obedience in the Church. Far from intending to reinforce social structures of subordination with theological sanctions, the editor has relativized earthly ties by pointing to a higher, heavenly analogue. It is the divine Father, after whom every family on earth and in heaven is named (3.15), to whom Christians within God's household (2.19) owe their first allegiance. The eschatological wedding feast of Christ and his bride the Church, and the imitation of God that makes us children of the heavenly Father (5.1) – these are to him much more important topics than mundane domestic relationships.

In assessing the impact of the code on the readers of Ephesians, it is important to remind ourselves of the rhetorical situation of a post-Pauline audience 'overhearing' what Paul had said to an earlier generation. They would not necessarily have felt themselves to be directly addressed, and they would not expect Paul to have had detailed prescient knowledge of their own later circumstances. It is unhelpful, therefore, to speculate, on the slim basis of this text, about the contemporary social structure of the epistle's potential audiences. Their attention might well have been focused more on the implied attitudes of Paul himself than on any specific response that they might be expected to make to his advice.

We have argued a similar case above in relation to the doublet of passages (2.11–13 and 4.17–24) which contrasts the former pagan darkness of Paul's Gentile converts with their new life in Christ. It should not be assumed from this that the intended readership of the letter was mainly Gentile; on the contrary, it was precisely to reassure later Jewish Christians of Paul's staunch opposition to corrupt pagan practices (against any slanderous rumours to the contrary, see Rom. 3.8 and cf. Jas 2.18–26) that this theme was given such repeated emphasis. In the same way, Jewish Christians in and around Ephesus, who had remained in the synagogue until they were expelled, and whose experience is reflected in the Fourth Gospel (see Introduction, pp. 36–39), would have developed structures of church leadership modelled on Jewish ones and different in some ways from those in Paul's Gentile congregations. In these, naturally, women would have played a less prominent role and seniority *per se* would have been afforded greater respect. The first two sections of the code should be seen in this light. Readers would conclude that the historical Paul had endorsed their own understanding of the respect due to male gender and to age in the structures of leadership in the Church, as well as in the home. They would have been pleased to hear that Paul had not been a dangerous radical attempting to overthrow the religious and ethical legacy of Judaism which had now been inherited by the Church, the true Israel.

That marriages will normally be contracted within the Christian community and that children and any domestic slaves in the household will be required to adopt the family religion is the standard post-apostolic assumption made by the writer of Ephesians. Things were very different in the nascent communities of Paul's own day. Onesimus did not automatically become a Christian when his master was converted; Paul refers to the problem of living with a pagan husband, and even of wives refusing to accept their husbands' new faith (1 Cor. 7.12f.). The evidence of 2 Cor. 6.14 – 7.1, where mixed marriages with unbelievers are forbidden, does not necessarily count against this view since there are many other indications that this passage is a later, post-Pauline interpolation (see Fitzmyer 1971: 205–17; Furnish 1984).

The assumption that the whole household will be Christian helps to mitigate some of the hermeneutical problems associated with the appeal for obedience in this section. It can be taken for granted, for instance, that no service will be demanded that is immoral or against the conscience of the subordinate party, and that the virtues of humility and self-sacrifice are equally enjoined on heads of households. But mitigated as they may be, problems remain for modern readers who treat Ephesians as Scripture. We have to ask ourselves whether a wife, employee or adult still living with his or her parents, who possesses more competence in any particular matter or wants to be more independent, will not be inhibited by this imposition of a duty to obey; and whether the factors of sex, age and social status are being sanctioned with a theological rationale that gives the boss, however benevolent in practice, an exaggerated sense of his own importance.

On the other hand, if the main thrust of this section is, as we have suggested above, to place lesser earthly obligations within the framework of the higher duty of obedience to Christ, then it has the effect of *relativizing* them. And obedience to God through Christ is qualitatively different from obedience to any human authority, for it is essentially liberating, not alienating: 'his service is perfect freedom'. (For more detailed treatments of this issue, see Kittredge 1998: 111–74 and Keener 1992: 139–83.)

It should be noted, finally, that although arguments will be offered for holding that Colossians is *not* the precise source for the household code section in Ephesians, something very like Colossians is, and most of the observations below on the editor's expansions of his source would remain valid even if it were.

A   Husband and wives, Christ and the Church   (5.21–33)

(21) Submit to each other out of reverence for Christ: (22) wives, to your own husbands as to the Lord, (23) because Man is the head of Woman as also Christ is the head of the Church, being himself the saviour of the Body. (24) But as the Church is submissive to Christ, so also wives are to be to their husbands in everything. (25) And husbands, love your wives, just as Christ loved the Church, and surrendered himself for her, (26) in order that he might purify her through the cleansing bath of water, with the word, (27) and that he might present the Church to himself in all her glory, without spot or wrinkle or anything of that kind, but as pure and faultless. (28) Similarly, husbands also must love their own wives like their own bodies. (29) For no one ever hates his own flesh but feeds and looks after it, just as Christ does for the Church. (30) For we are members of his body, part of his flesh and bone. (31) 'And for this reason a person will leave father and mother and be joined to his wife, and the two of them will become one flesh.' (32) This is a great mystery, and I take it to refer to Christ and the Church. (33) However, let each of you love your own wife as himself and let the wife respect her husband.

The writer has expanded an original brief injunction to husbands and wives with other traditions relevant to his exalted understanding of the Church, which is already the body that is growing up into Christ its head, and which is destined to be the virgin bride of Christ when her eschatological wedding–day dawns. These themes are much more important to the author than that of marital relations, as can be seen from the fact that at certain points they rupture the underlying analogy.

21 Submit to each other. The verb is a participle (lit. 'submitting') used in place of an imperative, a not uncommon idiom in a series of ethical exhortations (see Rom. 12.9–13; 1 Pet. 3.1, cf. 1 Pet. 2.18). It is grammatically possible, in the absence of any particle indicating the beginning of a new sentence, to see this verse as the completion of the series of participles in the preceding sentence: 'speaking, singing, chanting and giving thanks'. However, the doxological phrase at the end of verse 20 makes a satisfactory closure and would surely force the reader to draw breath for a new paragraph. And in terms of content, 5.21 changes the subject and forms an introduction to the section that follows.

'Submit to each other' is a paradox that is perfectly intelligible when applied to the relations between members of the Church, but is inappropriate as a summary of the unequal relationships described in the code (Sampley 1971: 116f.). It reveals where the writer's real interest lies. The idea of mutual subordination echoes the reference to mutual forbearance in the Church at 4.2 and reflects Paul's own teaching on relations in the Christian community: see Phil. 2.3, 'in humility count others better than yourselves' and Rom. 12.10, 'outdo one another in showing honour'.

In contrast to the one-sided demand for obedience in the code, Paul himself acknowledged that a certain degree of *mutual* submission was appropriate between husband and wife (1 Cor. 7.4): 'The wife does not have authority over her own body, but the husband does; likewise the husband does not have authority over his own body, but the wife does.' But Paul also argued later in the same chapter against getting married at all, on the grounds that it might distract the believer from undivided devotion to the Lord through too much mutuality between husband and wife (see 1 Cor. 7.32ff.). So the editor seems to have created verse 21 himself, as a new introduction to the code, guided both by Paul's teaching on the mutual interdependence of church members to one another (cf. 1 Cor. 12.25) and perhaps also by Paul's own reservations about marriage as the source of possible conflict with the Christian's allegiance to the one Lord. His introduction indicates how what follows is to be taken, not so much as an ecclesiological insight into the dignity of marriage but as a marital illustration of the dignity of church member-ship.

Out of reverence for Christ. The fear of the Lord, a frequent motif in the Hebrew Bible, is often echoed by Paul (see e.g. 2 Cor. 5.11; 7.1; Phil. 2.12). Here the editor has made the christological transfer of the phrase explicit. In such contexts 'fear' does not mean terror, but neither is it merely respect, which would draw attention too much to the subjective attitude of believers rather than the objective majesty of their Lord: 'reverence' perhaps better conveys the sense. The cognate verb appears in the added summarizing statement at the end of the paragraph (v. 33), forming a verbal *inclusio*; there, however, it refers to the wife's attitude towards her husband, so 'respect' might be the more suitable translation.

22 There is no verb present in P[46] or B but the majority of other MSS have supplied the obvious one, 'submit', placing it either before or after the reference to husbands and in either the second ('wives, submit') or third person imperative ('let wives submit'). The shorter text should probably be preferred, and then this verse will depend grammatically on verse 21: 'Submit to one another ... wives to husbands'. One then expects the sentence to conclude 'and husbands to wives'. The motive behind the longer readings is precisely to avoid creating that unfulfilled expectation. The grammatical awkwardness of verse 22 has resulted from the editor borrowing its verb for his formulation of verse 21. He will remind us again of this opening injunction of the code later at verses 24 and 33.

The general injunction to submit becomes specific: **wives, to your own husbands**. The adjective 'your own' (*idiois*) is weaker in Greek than in English, but emphasis on the exclusivity of the marriage relationship reappears later with regard to the love of husbands 'each for his own wife' at verse 33; cf. also verse 28. This suggests that there is also some reason behind the added emphasis here. The Greek words rendered 'wives' and 'husbands' are simply those for 'women' and 'men'– their married relationship has to be deduced from the nature of the instructions involved. Submission on the woman's part (and love on the man's) will be appropriate only if the two are married. The original tradition (like Col. 3.18) did not need to specify this obvious fact. But since the editor's attention is focused more on the Church, he may have added the qualifier ('own') to avoid any doubt in a wider context. The allegiance that all Christians together owe to Christ their only Lord is analogously exclusive.

Comparison should be made with 1 Cor. 14.34–5, which reads:

> Let women be silent in the congregations, for it is not permitted for them to speak, but let them submit, just as the Law also says; and if they want to know anything let them ask their *own men* [i.e. husbands] at home. For it is shameful for women to speak in the congregation.

This general instruction about female behaviour in Christian meetings requires the clarifying adjective ('their own') because it continues with a particular concession applicable only to married women (i.e. that they are permitted to interrogate their husbands later at home). The problems of this passage (its conflict with 1 Cor. 11.4, where Paul permits women to participate vocally in public worship; the variation of its position in the MSS (some include it after v. 40); and the unqualified appeal to the authority of law in v. 34), have led several recent commentators on 1 Corinthians (e.g. Fee 1987: 705) to suspect a later marginal gloss. If this is correct, the author of Ephesians has taken the same Jewish Christian view as the glossator of 1 Corinthians 14.

At 6.5 slaves will be told to obey their masters 'as to Christ' and the parallel here, **as to the Lord**, suggests that 'Lord' is meant as a christological title (as also at e.g. 2.21 and 5.19), preparing the way for the next verse. At 1 Pet. 3.6, Sarah, the model wife, is praised for calling Abraham her 'lord', and it has been claimed (Mussner 156) that here also it is the husband who is being referred to, with the singular used collectively, i.e. '(each) to her lord'. But the similar instruction to children at 6.1 to 'obey their parents in the Lord' tells against this suggestion. The husband is not to be respected because he directly mediates the authority of Christ to the wife, for she, like any other member of the Church, benefits from the ministry of those authorized to perform that function (see 4.11). Rather, her Christian discipleship provides an additional distinctive rationale for observing her duty as a wife.

23 Because Man is the head of Woman. The conjunction 'because' (*hoti*) implies that this clause is meant to provide another motive for obedience on top of the one already given. But it fails to do so unless some further idea is implied, e.g. that male headship is part of the created order, or that the superiority of the man is a deduction from the maleness of the divine image in Christ. However, instead of making explicit either of these points (which have, regrettably, been read into the text by later interpreters), the author moves on immediately to a comparison with Christ's headship over the Church. The following clause begins 'as also' (*hos kai*), as though this one had been a new independent statement and not a dependent causal clause. A possible solution to this problem is that the author is here beginning to incorporate an independent tradition that read:

> *Just as* Man is the head of Woman,
> *so also* Christ is the head of the Church
> and himself the saviour of the Body.

He will have changed 'just as' into 'because' in order to tie it into what has gone before. Further support for this suggestion may be derived from the following observations.

The original purpose of such a tradition will have been to illuminate the relationship of Christ to the Church from that between Man and Woman (and not the reverse). The Man and the Woman to which the tradition referred were Adam and Eve, following the classic myth of creation. Pauline Christianity was particularly interested in the early chapters of Genesis: the eschatological kerygma of salvation through Christ was reinforced by co-ordinating it with that 'protological' account of the human situation, and the parallel between the first and the last Adam allowed the division of humanity into Jews and Gentiles to be transcended. The feature of the Genesis story which this tradition picks up is that of Adam as the 'head' of Eve in both metaphorical senses of the word, i.e. as ruler and source; see Gen. 3.16, 'He will be your master' and Gen. 2.23, 'She shall be called woman for she was taken out of man'. This Jewish myth is then applied to Christ as the last Adam (cf. 1 Cor. 15.45) and to the Church as the type of Eve. See further Scroggs 1966 and Meeks 1974.

Paul thought of the Church in the imagery of Scripture, as the virgin daughter of Zion, the Jerusalem above and the free mother of us all (Gal. 4.26). But he admitted that the Church also retained some of the characteristics of the fallen Eve (see 2 Cor. 11.3). We should, however, notice that Paul by no means exclusively associated disobedience with the female figure in the Jewish myth of creation. In 1 Cor. 15.22 Adam is the first human being (*anthrōpos*), symbolizing universal human mortality in contrast to the immortality of the risen Christ, the last Adam; and in Rom. 5.14, Adam is the type of disobedient humanity as a whole, men and women alike.

It is against this background that we should understand Paul's teaching at 1 Cor. 11.3: 'Christ is the head of every Man, and the Man is the head of the Woman, and God is the head of Christ'. In context, he reminds the Corinthians of 'traditions' (v. 2) which he had passed on to them, and he deduces from these traditions, with several other intricate arguments, a practical conclusion about women keeping their heads covered in worship. It is unlikely that the traditions to which he alludes dealt with that practical issue at all, or that Paul is simply reproducing them in the whole of this passage, since the Corinthians are first praised for their loyalty to them but later warned not to dissent from the advice (11.16). In other words, the traditions must have dealt not with the mundane question of headgear but with fundamental tenets of faith. They would have offered an interpretation of the Genesis motif of Adam as the head of Eve (see 11.8) in terms of Christ as head of the new humanity. The use of the word 'head' in 1 Corinthians 11 seems to play on the two metaphorical senses of ruler and source (see Hooker 1964; Grudem 1985; Kroeger 1987). This supports the suggestion made above that the editor of Ephesians has incorporated a similar tradition here (cf. Gielen 1990: 251–60).

Earlier separate references in Ephesians reflect the two different connotations of headship (see 1.22 and 4.15f.) and they are combined in this passage. The present context, a call to submission, requires the idea of rule to be uppermost, but the phrase 'Christ the saviour of the Body' could already be an allusion to the idea of source and goal (see below). Commentators who take a unitary view of the composition of Ephesians, making context the determinative factor for interpretation (e.g. Lincoln 369), are unwilling to admit an Adamic allusion already in this verse; but critics who recognize the composite character of this passage (e.g. Militic 1988; Sampley 1971) argue plausibly that verse 23 introduces the two themes that are to be developed later: Christ as head (ruler) of the Church his bride; and Christ as head (source) of the life of the Church his body.

The quotation from Gen. 2.24, which will form the climax of the argument, supports this, for it understands marital love as arising from the physical derivation of Eve from Adam's body (see on v. 31 below).

There is a complicated web of ideas derived from the starting point that Man is the head of Woman. It may be represented in this way:

Just as	**So also**
Man is	Christ is
A.1 the head (= ruler)	A.2 the head (ruler) and A.3 present saviour
B.1 and the head (= source)	B.2 and the head (source) and B.3 future saviour
C.1 of Woman (his own flesh)	C.2 of the Church, his bride and C.3 his body.

These ideas are then expounded in the following verses:

(24) Wives submit to the headship/rule of husbands A.1
(25) because husbands imitate the headship/rule of Christ A.2
          whose atoning death already saves A.3
(26) Christ is the source of the Church's life B.2
(27) and will be united with her at the end as her future saviour B.3
(28) Similarly husbands are to love their wives as their own bodies B.1
(29) and the love and care for the body in the marital relationship C.1
(30) points to Christ's love for the Church his bride C.2 and his body C.3.

Christ is the head of the Church. Christ as the head of creation and head of the Church are already well established themes in Ephesians: Christ is the one in whom all things are summed up (see on 1.10), in whom the elect are chosen from the creation of the world (1.4); and in the present form of 1.22–3, Christ is said to be the 'head over all things for the Church, his body', again combining in a complex way the themes of creation and ecclesiology. This is apparent also at 2.10; 3.10; 4.13; 4.24 and 5.8 (see commentary on these passages).

The most obvious parallel in Colossians is the hymnic passage 1.15–20, probably based on Gen. 1.1 and 1.27, in which Christ is described as 'the image of the invisible God, the first-begotten of all creation'. If our author were dependent on the text of Colossians as we know it, it would be difficult to excuse his neglect of those powerful statements, which chime in so well with his own views. But he is evidently not dependent here. He is using a different but not dissimilar tradition, a Christian meditation and exegesis on Gen. 2.24; but in order to fit the material into the household code which he is expanding, he has to keep pulling it back with repetitions and strong adversatives; see comments on verse 24, 'but', and verse 33, 'nevertheless', below.

Himself the saviour of the Body. Some commentators (e.g. Bruce 385) have suggested that the analogy between the husband as head of the wife and Christ as head of the Church continues here, so that the husband is in a sense also 'saviour' of the wife. Indeed, if the statement about Christ's headship of the Church were taken in parenthesis, the husband ('himself') could even be the sole referent of the phrase, in effect 'saviour of his wife as of his own body' (anticipating 5.29, see below). Support for this interpretation might be drawn from 1 Cor. 7.16, where Paul says that the Christian husband, by staying in a mixed marriage, may hope to 'save' his wife by bringing her to faith. Furthermore, the word 'save' can have a material connotation of protection and welfare appropriate to a husband's care for his wife, as it does at Tobit 6.18, where Tobias will 'save' Sara, that is, deliver her from her illness. There are, of course, several objections to this interpretation: the daring comparison between a man's body and his wife is not actually made until later; the nearest antecedent for 'himself' is Christ, not the husband; 'saviour' had, by the time of the writer, entered the standard vocabulary of Christology; and the next sentence begins with 'but', indicating that only then will we return to the marriage analogy. But, although unlikely, this suggestion does well illustrate the tension, which runs through the passage as a whole, between the ethical context and the theological content of the added traditions. Are the christological statements to be put in brackets, in order to make the focus on ethics clearer, or is it the ethical statements that are effectively bracketed by the christological insertions?

Saviour as a christological title is rare in Paul, occurring only at Phil. 3.20; but it becomes more frequent in the deutero-Pauline letters (2 Tim. 1.10; Titus 1.4; 2.13; 3.6) and in post-Pauline literature from Asia Minor (2 Pet. 1.1 etc.; John 4.42; 1 John 4.14). It is a regular designation for Yahweh in the LXX (cf. Isa. 45.15). The initial reluctance on the part of early Christian writers to use it of Christ is surprising; it may have been caused by the associations of the title with the cult of the Roman Emperor, as *salvator mundi*. However, as the conflict between the Church and the Roman state intensified towards the end of the first century and became more official, Christians more and more claimed the title, polemically, for Christ rather than Caesar as the real saviour of the world. The older view that the phrase 'saviour of the body' reflects gnostic speculations about the redeemer who saves fallen Sophia (see Schlier 266–76) has seemed less plausible to recent commentators, both because of the chronology of the surviving identifiably gnostic evidence, and also because of the likelihood that such speculations were themselves dependent on a particular misreading of texts in the Pauline letters such as this.

The editor has identified the Church as the body of Christ so often before that he can assume that identification here, especially since Christ's headship of the Church has just been mentioned. What is less clear is whether Christ is thought to have saved the Church already (see the emphatic perfect tenses at 2.5 and 8) or whether that is still in the future (as at 1.13f. and commonly in Paul, see e.g. Rom. 5.9). The image of the wedding ceremonial that follows in verses 26–7 can be taken either way (see below). Paul's own allusions to the motif of the Church as the bride of Christ, on the analogy of Eve and Sarah (see 2 Cor. 11.2

and Gal. 4.26f. respectively) include both present and future references. And the same duality is found in the nuptial imagery for the Kingdom of God in the Jesus tradition (see Mark 2.19 and compare Matt. 25.11–13). Probably, therefore, both senses are meant: Christ saved the Church when he sacrificially offered himself for her and he will save her finally when the fruit of his work appears, holy and blameless, at the last judgement.

24 But as the Church is submissive to Christ, so also wives are to be to their husbands in everything. This sentence does nothing to advance the argument so far. It simply repeats the substance of verse 22 in reverse order, so as to introduce the injunction to husbands in verse 25, which has been delayed because of the insertion of the tradition quoted in verse 23. It begins with the adversative conjunction 'but' (*alla*); and an even stronger adversative (*plēn*) appears at verse 33, when the editor descends from the heights of theology to offer a final ethical summary. So the same reasoning probably lies behind this wording, viz. 'I want to say more on the relationship of the Church to Christ in a moment; however, if you wish to stay at the more mundane level, wives should submit to their husbands.'

The attempt to find more significance in this verse with reference to some particular quality in the Church's obedience to Christ that ought to inform the submissiveness of wives is, therefore, mistaken. Lincoln, for example (372), suggests that the point is that it should be freely and willingly given. But in the days of arranged marriages, and when brides had often scarcely reached puberty, that implication would probably be lost on the readers.

In the sections of the Colossians code on children (3.20) and slaves (3.22), obedience 'in everything' is demanded, but not, it should be noted, in the section on wives (3.19). The opposite is the case in Ephesians; the requirement of total submission **in everything** is absent from the sections on children and slaves but included, less appropriately, here. The editor seems to have allowed this idea to spill over from the Church's obedience to Christ, where it is highly appropriate, to that of wives towards husbands, which would rarely have been total in practice. If this is correct, then it would be a further indication that he is thinking first and foremost about ecclesiology rather than marriage, and that it is this that has resulted in the redundant repetitions in this section.

25 Husbands, love your wives. The corollary of the wife's duty of submission is the husband's general duty to love his wife. At Col. 3.19 this is spelled out in a specific way: 'Do not be resentful', and a similar prohibition is found in Ephesians in the sections on children: 'Do not provoke them to anger' (6.4), and slaves: 'Avoid threats' (6.9). So one would also expect some more practical expression of marital love to be specified here, if the editor's interest was in regulating family life. But it is rather love as the general hallmark of life in Christ which the editor is emphasizing, as he has so often before (see 1.4; 3.17; 4.2, 15, 16). The children of God as a whole, and not just those who happen to be husbands, are called on to imitate Christ's sacrificial love (see 5.1f.). To reduce such a lofty vocation to specifics would risk its trivialization.

We again rise above the marriage analogy in verse 25b and stay at the more sublime level for the next two verses: **just as Christ loved the Church, and surrendered himself for her**. For the meaning of this phrase and its Pauline origins, see on 5.2 above. The theme of sacrifice, not only Christ's for the Church but also that of the Church as a living sacrifice in response to him (cf. Rom. 12.1) runs through the following verses.

It is grammatically possible to start a new sentence with verse 25b, 'Just as . . .', which would then be completed by 'so also . . .' at verse 28. But this arrangement would leave the command to husbands in verse 25a very bald and would subordinate verses 25b–27 to the moral injunction at verse 28, a verse which fails to pick up any of their details and continues instead with the idea, to which they have not referred, of love of wife as love of one's own body (see further below on verse 28).

26 The purpose of Christ's self-offering for the Church is **in order that he might purify her**, a Jewish cultic metaphor that is frequent in this epistle (see 1.4 and the comments there), as it is in Paul (e.g. Phil. 1.9f.; 1 Thess. 3.12f.), and in John (17.17, 19). To purify or sanctify is to set apart for religious use and it often refers in the Old Testament to the setting apart for sacrifice of an unblemished animal whose blood in turn sanctifies the worshippers (see Heb. 9.13 for the Christian application of this theme). The imagery of a wedding begins here to be blended with the imagery of sacrifice in relation not only to the death of Christ but also to the preparation of the Church, in a way strongly reminiscent of the wedding between the Church and 'the Lamb slain before the foundation of the world' in the Apocalypse of John: 'Let us rejoice and exult and give him the glory, for the marriage of the Lamb has come, and his Bride has made herself ready' (Rev. 19.7f.).

The phrase **with the word** could be taken either with 'purify' or with the participial phrase, 'having cleansed by the bath of water' (see below). Ephesians is quite fond of such limping additional phrases delayed until the end of a clause but connecting grammatically with an earlier part (see e.g. 6.24). When the passage was read aloud, this ambiguity would have to be resolved, one way or the other, by phrasing and intonation. It is likely that 'purify' and 'with the word', if taken together, refer to the sanctifying effect of Christ's word, i.e. to the process of Christian nurture through preaching and teaching. A similar idea is present in the Fourth Gospel: 'Sanctify them in the truth. Your word is truth' (17.17 and cf. 15.3).

Through the cleansing bath of water (lit. 'having cleansed by the bath of water'). The aorist participle can indicate an action prior to that of the main verb 'purify' or coincident with it. In favour of the latter, Paul refers to Christians as already washed and already sanctified at 1 Cor. 6.11, implying that these are simultaneous past events. But it is also possible, both at the level of symbolism and at the level of the thing symbolized, that the 'cleansing' is an action prior to that of sanctification. If there is an allusion here to the bride's prenuptial bath, then that definitely precedes the wedding ceremony (Lincoln 375, who sees a parallel with Ezek. 16.8–14; though it is should be noted that Ezek. 16.9 refers not to the bridal bath but to the washing of a new-born child, see 16.4, 6). But the allusion is more likely to be to the cultic ablutions that precede the offering of sacrifice. What is referred to symbolically is taken by the majority of commentators to be the sacrament of baptism (on which see 4.5). One might hesitate a little in view of the choice of the word for 'bath' (*loutron*) instead of the usual term (*baptisma*). However, Titus 3.5, the only other place in the New Testament where the word occurs, clearly means baptism when it speaks of the 'bath of regeneration' and the choice of vocabulary here is probably due to the desire to accommodate the additional allusions to bridal and/or cultic washings mentioned above. An oblique reference to baptism is therefore likely, though it is not sufficiently emphatic to support the weight that is placed upon it by some interpreters (*contra* Kirby 1968). And again, this supports the view that the cleansing bath *precedes* and symbolizes ultimate sanctification (see Rom. 6.22; cf. 6.3; 1 Thess. 4.3).

Commentators who link the water-bath with 'the word' are required to discuss whether this word is the baptismal confession pronounced by the candidate (Rom. 10.9), the threefold name pronounced by the baptizer (Matt. 28.19), or more generally the preaching of the gospel that first evoked faith. But we have preferred the view above that sanctification by the word is that process of Christian edification which is *subsequent* to the initial act of commitment in baptism (see John 3.3, and compare John 13.10 with 15.3) and is completed only at the final consummation.

27 And that he might present the Church to himself in all her glory. At 2 Cor. 11.2 Paul had claimed that he himself 'presented' the (Corinthian) church to Christ as a pure virgin, assuming the role of the bride's father or the marriage broker. But the verb 'present' does not need to carry that technical sense; it is, for instance, not required at Col. 1.22 and no correction of what Paul had claimed there is intended (*pace*

Lincoln 376). The Church is to be presented 'in all her glory' (*endoxon*). The word is used of fine clothing at Luke 7.25 and could be an allusion to the splendid attire of a bride on her wedding day (cf. Ezek. 16.14; Ps. 45.13; Rev. 21.2; and especially in the passage from the Apocalypse quoted above (Rev. 19.8): 'it was granted her to be clothed with fine linen, bright and pure – for the fine linen is the righteous deeds of the saints'). But, rather surprisingly, apart perhaps from the use of this word, nothing is said about the beauty of the bridal gown; it is only the bride's lack of physical defect that figures in the following explanation of the adjective. The only other use of *endoxos* in Paul is at 1 Cor. 4.10 where it has the quite different sense, frequent in the LXX, of 'renowned'.

Without spot or wrinkle or anything of that kind. The glory of the Church is explained as the absence of any disfiguring skin blemish (*spilos*; cf. 2 Pet. 2.13) or sign of ageing (*rutis*, wrinkle, only here in the Bible), understood metaphorically as the absence of any moral fault. The absence of wrinkle in the eschatological bride could be understood as an allusion to the idea that, although predestined before the foundation of the world (see 1.4), the Church is rejuvenated and youthful at the end (compare the images of the old and young woman in *Hermas* 9.6.4; 9.8.7; 9.26.2). But, more importantly, there has been another slide in the thought from nuptial to sacrificial imagery. The criteria for the selection of an animal for sacrifice is that it should be without blemish or wrinkle, i.e. a young and perfect specimen. The author, then, is not as much of a male chauvinist as he may at first sound to a modern reader; he is not assuming that what a woman brings to a marriage is merely her youth and beauty. What he has in mind is the ultimate sanctity and *sacrificial* devotion of the Church.

For the formula **pure and faultless**, see the comments on 1.4. What is meant must be the end result of the process of sanctification, rather than the present perfection of the Church. If the sacrificial metaphor had not intervened, the moral purity of the bride would more naturally have been represented by bright, clean linen clothing (see Rev. 19.8 above, and cf. Rom. 13.14 and Col. 3.12).

28 Similarly, husbands also must love their own wives like their own bodies. One would expect 'similarly ... also' (or 'so also') to refer to what has just been said about the perfection of the Church, but that would hardly explain the deduction about the husband's love of his own body. 'Similarly' might refer right back to 'just as' at 25b and complete the sentence begun there (but see the arguments above against that view). Another alternative would be to make a completely new start with this verse and take the adverb with what follows, thus: 'Husbands also ought to love their own wives *in the same way* as they love their own bodies' (so Schnackenburg 252). This would be easier in Greek if the 'also' were omitted (with ℵ *et al.*) and the verb delayed (with A *et al.*). But even so the break in the train of thought would be very sharp; and these variant readings are secondary, caused precisely by attempts to clarify the original ambiguity.

We suggest that the awkwardness in the expression has arisen from the editor's need to stitch the tradition he is using on to the underlying code material. 'Similarly' then has no precise grammatical function, but refers to everything that has been said since he last quoted the injunction to husbands to love their wives. It is noteworthy that in this resumptive repetition, the second person direct address is changed into a third person statement, implying that it is not part of the underlying material.

The author might have written, instead of **like their own bodies**, simply 'as themselves', see verse 33, with an obvious echo then of Lev. 19.18: 'Love thy neighbour as thyself'; that would surely have supplied sufficient practical grounds on which to base the command to marital love: to treat the other with the same love and care as one treats oneself and expects to be treated. The following gnomic summary, **He who loves his own wife loves himself**, despite its unfortunate and unintended connotations of possessiveness and narcissism to the modern ear, should be seen in the light of this practical universalizing moral principle. However, the reference to loving one's own body prepares for a unique kind of bodily union and identification, that of Christ with the Church, and this wording has been chosen in anticipation of that mystery.

29 No one ever hates his own flesh. The writer takes a world-affirming view of material existence, despite his personal asceticism. He is clearly not dependent on Colossians, for his assumption of the simple truth of this statement indicates that he is not trying to refute some species of 'flesh-haters'. If he had been, he could hardly have made such a statement without qualification (contrast Col. 2.18, 23). He may well be aware of the perfectionist error combated in both Colossians and the Johannine Epistles, but his tactic for dealing with it (cf. 4.14) is not to argue with the schismatics theologically but simply to ignore them and celebrate the Church's unity.

But feeds and looks after it. The word 'feed' (*ektrephein*) reappears at 6.4, where fathers are to nourish children with a Christian education; here the more literal sense of feeding applies. 'Looks after' (*thalpein*) or 'nurses' (see 1 Thess. 2.7, where Paul calls himself a 'nursemaid' to the Thessalonians) is the more general term covering everything beyond basic sustenance, such as shelter, heating and clothing. The primary meaning is a person's attending to his own necessities of life, but some commentators discuss whether a further allusion may not also be implied, for instance to a bridegroom's promise to care for his wife, or to both parents' duty towards their children. Gnilka (285) quotes a marriage contract, surviving in a Greek papyrus, that specifies the husband's promise to 'cherish, feed and clothe' his spouse. Best detected here a shift from the image of the Church as bride to that of Christians as children of the marriage (1955: 178n; a suggestion retracted in his commentary 550).

Just as Christ does for the Church. Christ therefore feeds and cares for the Church. There may be an oblique allusion here to Christ's feeding the Church in the Eucharist – an interpretation that is already found in Irenaeus (*Haer.* 5.2.2f.). Such an allusion would, for instance, explain why 'feed' takes precedence over the more inclusive term 'look after' (cf. also perhaps John 21.17); it would also form a neat parallel with the reference to baptism in verse 26. Furthermore, the growth of the Christian body up into Christ has been a major theme earlier in the letter (see 4.16), and the Eucharist is an important way of furthering that growth, other ways such as worship, preaching and fellowship notwithstanding. It would, finally, be rather surprising if there were no allusion anywhere in Ephesians to the Eucharist as the means of union with Christ and unity in the Church, given Paul's understanding of it in that way (1 Cor. 10.14–17); and the Johannine community particularly emphasized that Christians were fed and nourished by Christ's own flesh in the Eucharist (John 6.51). (See also the comments on 'thanksgiving' (Eph. 5.4) and 'giving thanks' (Eph. 5.20) above.)

30 For we are members of his body. This credal affirmation in the first person plural (cf. Rom. 12.4f.) summarizes a theme that runs through the whole letter (1.23; 3.6; 4.16). It is used here not to emphasize the 'horizontal' dimension of church membership (cf. 4.25) but to refer to the material and fleshly character of the 'vertical' union with Christ, in the sense about to be explained.

There is a major textual problem in this verse. A large number of MSS (including ℵ^c D P G, as well as Irenaeus, the old Latin and the Syriac peshitta) add after 'his body' **part of his flesh and bone**. The phrase in the Greek is literally 'out of his flesh and of his bones' which is a partitive genitive (i.e. *some of* his flesh and bone') and not (*pace* Lincoln 351n.) a dependent genitive. It is not difficult to see why the words, if originally present in the text, would be omitted: that Christians are the Body of Christ is standard doctrine; but the extension 'part of his flesh and bone' would seem very strange to a later scribe who had failed to pick up the allusion to Gen. 2.23, where Adam says of Eve, 'This at last is bone of my bone and flesh of my flesh.' Accidental omission is also a possibility. The shorter text, though it has early MS support (P⁴⁶ ℵ* A B), is the easier reading and is probably secondary.

31 'And for this reason a person will leave father and mother and be joined to his wife, and the two of them will become one flesh.'
The quotation from Gen. 2.24, for which the previous verse has paved the way, forms the climax of the section. The wording is almost identical to the LXX (and to the citation at Mark 10.7), the only differences being in the preposition used in the phrase 'for this reason' (*anti* instead of *heneken*) and the omission of the personal pronoun 'his' from 'father and mother'. Some MSS, including P[46], omit 'and be joined to his wife', the motive probably being squeamishness about referring to sexual intercourse. But the text is secure, which is more than can be said of the interpretation.

Some commentators take it to refer exclusively to the husband–wife relation, providing scriptural support to the injunctions of submission and love. The reference in the next verse to the 'great mystery' will then be not to the text of Gen. 2.24 itself but to the preceding argument from analogy to the union of Christ and the Church. Others take only that part of the quotation which speaks of the two becoming one flesh as allegorical and discount the rest. A third possibility is to see the whole citation as an allegory.

If the tradition which the editor has incorporated in his expansion of the household code is, as we have argued, focused principally on the headship of Christ over his body the Church, then the thoroughgoing allegorical view, favoured by the early Church Fathers, deserves to be taken seriously. At the literal level, Gen. 2.24 is very problematic: while every other man may have to leave his parents in order to marry, this was singularly not the case with Adam, for he had no father or mother to leave! And while every other legitimate marriage is exogamous, Adam in a sense married his 'own flesh and blood'. Obviously the text of Genesis must be jumping ahead of itself at this point to refer to common human experience later, and one could simply ignore the difficulty, were it not for the fact that this general rule is tied in emphatically with the previous verse in Genesis ('And for this reason') about Eve's unique origin from the body of Adam. There is then something deeply puzzling about the text of Gen 2.24 when taken in its context (see above on v. 30), which positively invites allegorical exegesis. (A comparable and not unrelated example of allegory in an undisputed Pauline letter is the treatment of the two wives of Abraham in Gal. 4.24ff., where the free woman 'corresponds to the Jerusalem above . . . and she is our mother'.)

The writer will go on to claim in the next verse that the hidden meaning in this text is a great mystery; that would hardly be the case if the bodily union between Christ and the Church were merely illustrated analogously by the second half of the citation. How would a late first-century Jewish Christian in Asia, who treasured the Pauline tradition and was concerned for the Church's unity, have expounded this text? The allegory of the Church as the bride of Christ, as the New Jerusalem (Rev. 21.2), and as the mother of the messianic community (Rev. 12.17) in the Apocalypse of John provides a relevant contemporary guide to how the text might be interpreted, perhaps in something like the following way: since the first Adam did not leave father and mother to be joined to his wife, the Genesis text must be referring to the last Adam who indeed abandoned family ties in order to devote himself to the Kingdom of God. And just as the body of the first Adam was the source of Eve at creation, so also the last Adam was the source of the Church at the moment of his self-sacrifice for her on the cross, and he will be united with her on the eschatological wedding day.

The crucifixion scene in the Fourth Gospel (John 19.26–37) offers some interesting parallels to this allegorical interpretation of Gen 2.24 (see Brown 1966, 1970: 925–6 and 949). Jesus is portrayed as entrusting his mother to the beloved disciple and him to her, replacing earthly relationships with a symbol of the Church; and at his death, water and blood, symbolizing the sacraments, flow from the wound in his rib (*pleura*) – the same word that is used of Adam's rib at Gen. 2.21 LXX. If it is objected that the mother symbol and the bride symbol for the Church are incompatible, we should compare again Gal. 4.24, 26 and 2 Cor. 11.2. One cannot be sure exactly how the author of Ephesians would have developed the great mystery of Christ and the Church on the basis of Gen. 2.24. The constraints of editing an existing text left him all too little room for manoeuvre (cf. also on 4.9), as the tone of his next comment implies.

32 This is a great mystery, and I take it to refer to Christ and the Church. The editor clarifies his understanding of the text just quoted, that it is an allegory of Christ and the Church and not a statement about ordinary marriages. The 'I' (*ego*) is emphatic in contrast to 'however, let each of you . . . ' in the next verse: with the implication 'That is the way I see it personally, but if you nevertheless prefer to take it literally – then, husbands, love your wives . . . '

On the meaning of 'mystery' in Ephesians and comparison with Paul, see on 1.9 and 3.3–5, 9. This usage stands slightly apart from the 'mystery' as God's hidden plan of salvation revealed in Christ to incorporate all humanity, Jews and Gentiles, into the Church. Here, it seems to refer to the deeper meaning in a puzzling text of Scripture (so Bornkamm, *TDNT* 4. 823; Bruce 393f.; Bockmuehl 1990: 204); since this verse is editorial, the change in usage is perfectly understandable, and in any case the mystery of the text is closely connected with the mystery of salvation, that Christ and the Church are one (cf. Dawes 1998: 181). It is unlikely that the marriage relationship itself is being referred to as a mystery, for it is spoken of in a rather mundane way in the ethical injunctions of this passage.

However, in the history of interpretation (see Fleckenstein 1994: 25–92), this text became the basis for the theory of Christian marriage as a divine 'mystery' (translated into Latin as *sacramentum*) and of the indissoluble bond created by the sacrament of holy matrimony. For later theologians and canon lawyers, it was just as unthinkable to separate a man and a woman united as one flesh in marriage as to separate Christ and the Church. But this line of interpretation is a prime example of reading a biblical text in the wrong direction. The author's interest is in the indissoluble eschatological union of Christ and the Church, into which human marriages may provide some kind of earthly insight – at their best, we might want to add, i.e. when they combine love and respect in equal measure on both sides. But when marriage is treated as a sacrament in the legal sense, the inspiring ideal of indissolubility risks degeneration into a cruel and rigid dogma and begins to serve political ends. By keeping marriages under the control of the ecclesiastical rather than the civil courts, this development was to have enormous consequences in bolstering the temporal power of the Church.

33 However, let each of you love your own wife as himself and let the wife respect her husband. The final comment of the editor is yet another repetition of the injunctions of the code (see above on 22, 24, 25, 28). It is introduced by a strong adversative, 'however' or 'nevertheless' (*plén*), which is found occasionally in Paul (e.g. 1 Cor. 11.11). It signals a descent from the heights of theology to the practicalities of daily living. The husband is to love his wife as himself, apparently echoing the 'love of neighbour' commandment (see above on v. 28). That being so, we should notice that this puts the husband's love, goodwill and solicitude towards his wife on the same level as his obligations to anyone else. Wives are, in return, to show a healthy respect (lit. 'fear') towards their husbands.

B   Parents and children   *(6.1–4)*

(1) Children, obey your parents [in the Lord] for this is just. (2) 'Honour thy father and thy mother' which is the commandment foremost as to promise: (3) 'in order that it may go well with thee and thy days be prolonged on the earth'. (4) Fathers, do not enrage your children, but nurture them in the schooling and instruction of the Lord.

The second section of a household code naturally deals with relations between parents and dependent children. The author of Ephesians seems to have expanded a brief original statement, similar to, but not identical with, that in Col. 3.20, with a supporting quotation from the Old

Testament, as he has in the preceding section. The intention of this expansion is partly to underpin conventional Hellenistic morality with the authority of Jewish scripture. But the addition also has the effect of extending the range of the child–parent model by including the idea of a life-long obligation, for the word 'children' does not denote dependent minors only; adult offspring can also be so addressed (see Luke 15.31), especially in the Jewish tradition, as the citation from the Decalogue makes clear.

The reasons for doubting that this passage can be derived from Colossians have to do with both wording and content (see Schlier 280, *contra* Lincoln 396). Col. 3.20 reads: 'Children, obey your parents in all things for this is well pleasing to [or 'in'] the Lord.' If Ephesians were dependent on this, we would have to suppose that the reference to 'the Lord' (assuming it is the original reading, see on 6.1 below) has been transposed to an earlier position in the sentence, leaving a rather lame ending: 'for this is just'. Furthermore, the omission of 'in all things' tones down the demand, unlikely as a conscious alteration of Colossians on the part of an author who favours hyperbole (using the adjective 'all' 52 times). If we leave aside Eph. 6.2–3, which is an addition without parallel in Colossians, the injunction to fathers is equally difficult to derive from Colossians. Col. 3.21 reads: 'Fathers, do not provoke your children, lest they become discouraged.' The verb translated 'provoke' (*erethizein*, embitter, irritate) is used once elsewhere in the Pauline corpus, at 2 Cor. 9.2, but in the positive sense of 'stir up' (RSV) or 'spur on', which is almost impossible at Col. 3.21. ('Do not encourage your children, lest they become discouraged' (!) could, just possibly perhaps, be an ironic insight into the counter-suggestiveness of children, but something more straightforward is required, surely, in a one-line summary of paternal duty.) Presumably what the author of Colossians was trying to say was 'Do not pull your children to pieces, or find excessive fault with them.' If so, he did not quite find the word he needed and his inexactitude would invite improvement. That said, Ephesians still has not hit on the *mot juste*, for 'enrage' (*parorgizein*) directs attention to the fault of a child given to tantrums when what the context requires is some admission of the possibility of fault on the part of the parent. Thus the variation in the choice of verbs, 'provoke' and 'enrage', is best explained as free composition within the stereotypes of a household code, rather than literary reworking of one text by the improving author of another. Both phrases may have come from the hand of someone who found it hard to put his finger on any faults in fathers which might provide the balancing idea to disobedience as the besetting sin of children. Paul's dealings with his recalcitrant 'children' in Corinth and his claim to be their father (1 Cor. 4.15), to be imitated and obeyed, support the possibility that Paul himself is the source of the appeal to filial duty in the household codes of

Colossians and Ephesians. The two versions are therefore genuinely parallel; neither is derived from the other. In any case, the wording of the two passages is quite dissimilar, apart from the words 'fathers' and 'your children' demanded by the context.

1 Children, obey your parents. As in the Colossians parallel (3.20), obedience to parents of both sexes is required; this is reinforced in Ephesians as the ensuing quotation from the Decalogue makes clear, but it is noticeable that only fathers are addressed in the second limb of the exhortation, for they, rather than mothers, would have had charge of the male child's formal education.

Some MSS, including B D* G, omit the phrase **in the Lord** and it could be a later scribal addition, attempting to provide a distinctively religious rather than merely conventional motivation for obedience. But if so, this would create an even greater difficulty, namely to explain why it is only the injunction to children that lacks a distinguishing Christian element. The longer text should therefore be preferred (Metzger 1994). The ambiguity of the position of 'in the Lord' may have led to its omission, for the phrase could be taken either with the verb or with the noun, i.e. 'Obey in the Lord your parents' or 'Obey your parents-in-the-Lord'. The underlying code tradition presumably intended the former; but the author of Ephesians may have intended the latter, for it allows of a broadening of the sense: 'parents-in-the-Lord' are not simply earthly parents but all those who have a parenting role in the Christian community, like those described as 'shepherds and teachers' at 4.11. The editor is more interested in relations between members of the Church than between family members. Just as the husband–wife relationship in the preceding section was eclipsed by that between Christ and the Church, so here also 'children' and 'fathers' are terms that are redirected to the relations between leaders and members within the Church.

The motivating clause **for this is just** (or 'righteous) may originally have been an appeal to the natural order of justice, in a manner characteristic of Stoic thought. Paul reflects such ideas occasionally, especially in Philippians (cf. Phil. 4.8). But the editor takes it as an invitation to add a proof text from what is for him the textbook of divine righteousness, the Old Testament Law. At Eph. 5.9 righteousness has been listed with goodness and truth as the marks of those who are 'children of the light'. In 2.1–10 the author deliberately avoided the peculiarly Pauline usage of righteousness to describe God's saving act and gift in the death and resurrection of Jesus, preferring to use instead the language of salvation, which was not so liable to misunderstanding. The same Jewish Christian reservation is apparent at Jas 2.24, and in 1 John 3, a passage that is in several respects similar to this; see especially verse 7,

'Children, let no one mislead you, he who does what is right is righteous', and verse 10, 'This is what reveals the difference between the children of God and the children of the devil; anyone who does not do what is right and love his fellow Christian is not of God.'

2–3 'Honour thy father and thy mother'. Obedience to elders is reinforced by the citation of the Decalogue. It may at first seem the obvious choice of a scriptural proof-text, but in fact it is not a commandment particularly directed to children of minority age. It is honour towards aged parents by *adult* children that explains the accompanying promise of longevity, for general observance of this law will ensure that they in turn will not be neglected in their own old age (see Sir. 3.1–16 for an exposition of this theme). And this is the context in which the Decalogue is quoted in the Jesus tradition, see Mark 7.9–13 and 10.19; in both cases it is the attitude of adults towards their parents that is at issue.

The citation is from Exod. 20.12 and/or Deut. 5.16. In the Hebrew of Exodus the promise of long life is missing, but the LXX adds it from the parallel in Deuteronomy. There are a few other, very minor, alterations and omissions which make it difficult to determine the precise source. But if, as is likely, the Decalogue retained living authority for the author, then he would naturally quote from the conflated version of his Jewish Christian tradition rather than directly from either of the two forms of it found in the text of the Old Testament (*contra* Lincoln 1982: 37–40). The description of the land as that 'which the Lord your God gives you' has been omitted, since possession of the land of Israel is no longer of any relevance to the author. Without that extra phrase, the 'land' changes its meaning and refers to the whole earth: the Greek word (*gê*) has both senses.

The logic of the promise attached to the commandment was, of course, enlightened self-interest: 'If you recognize the obligation to care for your parents, you will live long in the land, because your own children will equally be obliged to take care of you.' The promise of earthly prosperity and longevity as a reward for obedience has often been seen as an indication of loss of End expectation in the post-Pauline period, but this can hardly be the dominant motive for the author's amplification of the original code, because it would be open to the challenge of the counter-example of Christians whose exemplary obedience was nevertheless rewarded by poverty and premature death, starting with Paul himself. Philo (*Spec. Leg.* 2.262) spiritualizes the scriptural promise of reward, seeing it in terms of virtue and immortality; and the author of Ephesians probably does the same, interpreting it in a less self-interested way, i.e. obedience will receive divine favour. Much more important as the reason for the added promise is the parallel (on one view of v. 1, see above) between obedience to parents in a well-run household and obedience to presbyteral leadership in the Church which is given express warrant from the scriptural tradition.

The commandment is said to be **foremost as to promise**. The adjective translated 'foremost' (*prôtē*) is usually temporal in meaning ('first') and the simplest interpretation is that this is the first commandment in the biblical order that has a promise attached to it. (But this would be a strange claim to make, for the commandment against graven images (Exod. 20.4–6) already carries a promise (as well as a spine-chilling threat!), and no later commandment carries any promise at all.) Ancient and modern commentators have attempted to explain the oddity. Origen, for example, claimed that 'first' referred to the whole Decalogue as the primal law and not to any one part of it, while Ambrosiaster suggested that Paul numbered this as the first commandment of the so-called second table of the law. But as far as we can tell from Rom. 13.9, where unfortunately the text is uncertain, the commandment to honour one's parents was probably counted by first-century Jews like Paul as the last of the first table, not the first of the second (see further Best 566). Modern suggestions to escape from this difficulty include those of Abbott (1924: 176), that this commandment is 'first' in the sense that it is the first that a child learns, which may be true in terms of practical behaviour but surely not in terms of explicit instruction.

In view of these difficulties, Schlier (281), followed by many others, took 'first' in the sense of 'foremost' (as in the above translation), and explained it as the commandment that is the most difficult to obey since it is a duty that arises every day. (The Midrash on Deuteronomy, *Deut. R. 6*, also describes this as the hardest commandment to obey and compares it with the easiest, the prohibition against bird-nesting, Deut. 22.7, both of which carry the same promised reward of long life.) To claim that the fifth commandment is 'foremost as to promise' is a fair point since none of the other Ten Commandments offers such a reward for obedience. The emphasis on promise could also be seen as an answer to any objection, taken to have been inspired by Paul, that Christ has nullified 'the law of commandments in decrees' (see on 2.15 above). Honour to parents is not a 'commandment in decree' but a 'commandment in promise'. Comparison should be made with Gal. 3.18, 21 for the contrast between promise and law, in a discussion also associated with filial duty and the Spirit that cries 'Abba, Father' (Gal. 4.6f.).

4 Fathers, do not enrage your children, but nurture them in the schooling and instruction of the Lord. The address to fathers alone (not mothers) ignores the intervening quotation, and this supports the view that the quotation was added by the editor. Fathers must avoid provoking their children to anger, for anger, as 4.26f. has already claimed, gives the devil room to incite even worse offences. Fathers will do this by making only reasonable demands of their children in line with the positive command that follows. They are to nurture them in the metaphorical sense (cf. 5.29) by schooling and instruction.

The word in Greek for **schooling** (*paideia*) when used by New Testament writers often picks up the Old Testament connotation of physical discipline and chastisement (see esp. Heb. 12.5–11); Paul uses it in this way at 1 Cor. 11.32 and 2 Cor. 6.9 and calls the Law a 'pedagogue', probably in this disciplinary sense, at Gal. 3.24f. But when it is combined with the verb 'nurture', the positive educational sense comes to the fore.

The noun **instruction** (*nouthesia*) may just be a synonym used for emphasis: if it adds a new thought at all, it is that of admonition, warning of dangers to be avoided. Paul uses it in reference to the admonishing function of Scripture at 1 Cor. 10.11 (cf. Titus 3.10) and the cognate verb of his own role as paternal educator of the Church at 1 Cor. 4.14, and at Rom. 15.14 of the whole congregation admonishing each other. The occurrence of the word in Colossians (1.28) is too far removed from the section on parental duty (Col. 3.21) to be the source here. The schooling and instruction which the father will give is 'of the Lord', the equivalent to the child's obedience 'in the Lord' at 6.1; but perhaps also with the additional nuance that those who function in a paternal way, in the Church as well as in the household, mediate the teaching of the heavenly Father (cf. 3.15).

C Slaves and masters   (6.5–9)

(5) Slaves, be obedient to your earthly masters, with fear and trembling in heartfelt sincerity on your part, as though to Christ, (6) not with the mere appearance of servility to win human approval, but as slaves of Christ, doing God's will from the heart and (7) serving with enthusiasm, as to the Lord and not human masters, (8) knowing that each, whether slave or free, if he does well, will receive a reward from the Lord. (9) And masters, do the same to them. Avoid threats, knowing that your Master and theirs is in heaven and shows no favouritism.

The third part of the code is longer and more verbose than the previous section. The similarity with Col. 3.22 – 4.1 is close but there are a number of divergences which make explanation in terms of direct borrowing difficult. The Colossians passage reads:

Slaves, obey your earthly masters in everything, not with the mere appearance of servility to win human approval but in sincerity of heart, fearing the Lord. Whatever your task, perform it from the heart, as to the Lord and not human masters, knowing that from the Lord you will receive the reward of inheritance; it is the Lord Christ you serve. For the wrongdoer will be paid back for whatever wrong has been done, and there is no favouritism. Masters, treat your slaves justly and fairly, for you know that you also have a Master in heaven.

The order of ideas in this passage of Colossians is neater – the basic injunction to slaves is followed by warnings and advice in a chiastic pattern (negative–positive; positive–negative). In Ephesians, this pattern is less clear and the final statement, with its 'whether slave or free', blurs it further. In both, the motif of fear occurs, but in Colossians it is fear towards God while in Ephesians it is fear towards masters. There is striking similarity in the phrases used to denote 'sincerity' and 'servility' but in Colossians they are in contrasting parallel to each other, while in Ephesians the former is linked with fear and the latter contrasted with service of God. Some words in Ephesians have no parallel – 'trembling', 'enthusiasm', 'whether slave or free'; and yet when Ephesians thus departs from the wording of Colossians, it still remains distinctly Pauline: 'fear and trembling', see 2 Cor. 7.15 and Phil. 2.12; 'whether slave or free', see 1 Cor. 12.13; and although enthusiasm (*eunoia*) is *hapax legomenon* here in the Pauline corpus, the idea is close to Rom. 12.11, 'serving the Lord, fervent in the spirit', where the word for 'fervent' is equally *hapax* and no one has for that reason doubted the authenticity of Romans.

The Colossians charge to masters to be 'just and fair' is stronger than the 'avoid threats' of Ephesians, which is 'rather colourless' as Lincoln admits (423). The exemplar of divine impartiality is appealed to by Colossians in reference to masters' treatment of slaves, but in Ephesians the same phrase applies to God's even-handed treatment of both masters and slaves. The divergences of Ephesians from Colossians are stylistically often for the worse; but in terms of content, the honours are more evenly distributed. It might be easier, therefore, if the verbal closeness is deemed to require an explanation in terms of literary dependence, to see Colossians as an improving version of Ephesians in this passage (see Munro 1983), were that explanation not ruled out when the letters are taken in their entirety. The verbal similarities are so numerous that separate use by two different authors of a common household code tradition is most unlikely (*pace* Best): the other instructions for slaves in deutero-Pauline literature, 1 Tim. 6.1, Titus 2.9f. and 1 Pet. 2.18–25, diverge widely from these passages. The most likely conclusion must be that the same person wrote the substance of both paragraphs, and used some of the same vocabulary in the freedom of a fresh composition.

There is no reason in terms of style or content to doubt that that person was Paul himself.

Domestic slaves in the Greek world were often allowed a considerable degree of freedom, including the freedom of religious association. If a Christian slave belonged to a pagan household, he or she would have to tread carefully, for the rhetoric of the new movement could appear to an outsider to be subversive of the established social and economic order. If, on the other hand, the master was a Christian while the slave was not (as at first was the case of Philemon and Onesimus) or both were Christian, then the temptation for the slave to exploit the situation to his or her advantage might have been hard to resist. Either way, the adoption and adaptation of the household code offered reassurance that the Christian movement posed no immediate practical threat to the *status quo*, despite its dreams of eschatological status reversal, and did not therefore warrant suppression or harassment.

It is often assumed by commentators that the household envisaged is uniformly Christian, and we have given reasons above for thinking that, especially in the husband–wife section, the post-apostolic author of Ephesians made that assumption. But of course it is quite possible that the underlying material, if it came from Paul, was meant differently, i.e. that the slaves and masters addressed do not necessarily belong to the same households. Only Christians are addressed, of course, but the possibility that they lived in mixed households is not excluded by the apparently reciprocal form. For an explanation of why relatively stronger emphasis falls on the moral injunctions to slaves than those to wives and children, leaving aside the added scriptural and theological elements in the earlier passages, see 'note on the household code' pp. 250–5 above.

5 Slaves. We should remember here the possible gap between the rhetorical situation of the text and the situation of the readers of a pseudepigraphon like Ephesians. Slave ownership might have been much less common than this passage at first seems to imply, especially in Jewish Christian households, in view of the severe restrictions on it laid down in the Mosaic Law. The interest of later readers would be, rather, in 'overhearing' Paul's teaching after a lapse of time and appreciating its wisdom and enduring spiritual relevance. As with the preceding section on children, the behaviour of the slave becomes a model and metaphor for the duty of obedience laid upon every Christian, more than a social problem faced by middle-class slave-owning families. This section, therefore, like the others, operates on two levels. It preserves Paul's statements about slaves, which were provoked by a particular historical situation, and allows an extra level of reference to discipleship as that slavery to Christ which is true freedom.

The slaves' **earthly masters** are in implied contrast to the heavenly Lord (see v. 9; the same Greek word (*kurios*) means both 'master' and 'Lord'). Some MSS, including P⁴⁶, place 'earthly' (lit. 'according to the flesh') after the noun in an ambiguous position where it might even qualify the verb, i.e. 'Obey your masters in a fleshly way' – clearly an unacceptable idea which most MSS avoid by harmonizing to the word order of the parallel at Col. 3.22. If P⁴⁶ and its allies have the correct reading, although they must indeed intend the same sense as Colossians, this would be a clear indication that the verse was not simply taken over from Colossians. Other changes support this: the omission of 'in everything' and the change from 'fearing the Lord' to 'with fear and trembling'. The latter is a standard biblical expression (9 times in the LXX) which occurs in Paul at 1 Cor. 2.3 (of Paul's trepidation on his first visit to Corinth), at 2 Cor. 7.15 (of the Corinthians' respectful reception of Titus), and at Phil. 2.12 (of working out one's salvation in general). It does not, then, imply craven subservience, as the following clause further demonstrates; true respect means heartfelt sincerity, i.e. pure motivation and single-minded effort.

As though to Christ is a recurring motif in this section, see 'as slaves of Christ' (v. 6) and 'as to the Lord' (v. 7). Slaves are to offer sincere service in the same manner as they serve Christ himself, though their duties as slaves do not of course exhaust their higher service as Christians to Christ. This notion of higher service, applicable to all the readers whatever their social status, begins to overshadow the literal address to slaves from verse 7 onwards (see below).

6f. Their service is to be rendered **not with the mere appearance of servility** (lit. 'not with eye-service' (*ophthalmodoulia*), a compound word which is not attested in Greek before this instance and the parallel at Col. 3.22). Moule (1947–8: 250) has argued plausibly that it is the sort of service a slave performs when the master 'has his eye on him'; but when his back is turned, he acts differently. This would then be an echo of the teaching of Jesus at Matt. 24.45ff. Lincoln prefers to understand 'eye-service' as a slave trying to 'catch his master's eye' and win approval from him by dissimulation, which he takes to be more of a contrast to the virtue of sincerity in verse 5. Ignoring its present context in which a negative sense is demanded, it would even be possible to take the term positively, of 'quick-eyed, attentive service'. The coincidence of the use of this unprecedented word in both Colossians and Ephesians is often taken as proof of literary dependence. But on reflection it could just as easily be an argument against it. If the author of Ephesians had only the text of Colossians to go on, he might well have rejected the word as too opaque and ambiguous. If, on the other hand, Paul had just coined the expression in writing to the Colossians, it would be natural for him to try it out on the Laodiceans too.

Some help is offered towards the interpretation of 'eye-service' by another Pauline compound, translated **to win human approval** (lit. 'as men-pleasers'). The word reflects Paul's own experience of being criticized for too much willingness to compromise (see 1 Cor. 9.22) – and too little (see Gal. 2.14)! At Gal. 1.10 he writes, 'If I were still trying to win human approval [lit. please men] I would not be the slave of Christ', implying that the slave of a human master could reasonably be expected to comply with his wishes but that slavery to the Lordship of Christ makes Paul rightly indifferent to human approbation. The radicalism of this statement, then, that slaves should not be men-pleasers but first and foremost **slaves of Christ**, bursts through the conventional morality on which the code is based, and that was, in part at least, Paul's intention.

Slaves of Christ are defined as those **doing God's will from the heart.** This is a characteristic Pauline idiom, see Rom. 13.11; 2 Cor. 5.6; Gal. 2.16. In neither of the two preceding sections has the duty to obey God above all other been expressed so clearly. Within the limits necessitated by the continuation of the slave-system, which Paul was in no position to abolish, he enunciates here a principle that is deeply subversive of it (cf. Gal. 3.28): the will of God, not the will of human authorities, is paramount (cf. Acts 5.29).

8 Knowing that each, whether slave or free, if he does well, will receive a reward from the Lord. The idiom that begins a clause with 'knowing that ... ', where it is the readers rather than the grammatical subject of the sentence that are being reminded of the basic content of Christian catechesis, is highly typical of Paul (e.g. Rom. 6.9; cf. 6.3, 6). The teaching about rewards at the last judgement (see 2 Cor. 5.10; Rom. 2.6; 14.10) is also part of Paul's way of preaching the gospel (see Rom. 2.16). The strongly Pauline idea, which has been toned down by the author of Ephesians in 2.1–10, that justification (acquittal) has already been achieved by Christ on the cross, made this 'eschatological reserve' (i.e. judgement according to works at the last assize) all the more necessary in Pauline catechesis if the charge of antinomianism was to be successfully rebutted (see Rom. 3.8).

The parallel at Col. 3.24 speaks of 'receiving from the Lord the reward of inheritance', which, although very different in wording, similarly takes for granted the basic teaching about a future inheritance in the age to come, to such an extent that it fails to notice the possible double meaning, i.e. 'receive from the slave-owner the inheritance of his property' – the sort of unworthy ambition that certain slaves might have fondly entertained. Paul shows himself to be naïvely innocent of the practicalities of slave-ownership, and this is one further reason for attributing the slave sections of Colossians and Ephesians to his own hand.

9 And masters, do the same to them. It is clear that the writer of these words was not in the slightest degree interested in laying down rules for the behaviour of slave-owners. No action of a slave towards a master has been mentioned in verses 5–8 which could reasonably be reciprocated by the master towards the slave. Presumably, what Paul meant to say was that slavery to Christ, doing the will of God from the heart and serving with enthusiasm, are common Christian obligations for masters and slaves alike.

Avoid threats. The word for threatening behaviour (*apeilē*) occurs only here in the Pauline corpus. It occurs twice in Acts: at 4.29 (cf. 4.21) of Peter and John standing up to 'intimidation' from the Sanhedrin; and at Acts 9.1 of Paul breathing murderous 'threats' against the Christians (i.e. the threat of death unless they recanted). In classical Greek the word, in the plural, often means merely 'boasts' and some LXX instances, e.g. Prov. 17.10, mean little more than 'rebuke'. It is difficult then to gauge the degree of severity associated with its use here, but it is something short of actual violence. Paul was hard pressed to think of a standard fault in masters, just as he was with fathers earlier, and the command to 'avoid threats' is unclear. Are threats to be avoided because the authority of a basically kind-hearted master unwilling to carry them out would be weakened? Or are mere threats to be avoided and replaced instead by instant punishment for offences? The ambiguity and impracticality of the advice shows that a different motive is operating. If Col. 4.1 were the source, it would be difficult to explain why its much clearer formulation, 'Treat slaves with justice and fairness', was rejected.

Knowing that your Master and theirs is in heaven and shows no favouritism. For the idiom 'knowing that', see on verse 8. The theme of the impartial justice of God is distinctively Pauline (see Bassler 1982). **Favouritism** ('partiality', *prosōpolēmpsia*) may in context be an allusion to the problem of 'favourite' slaves in a household, of whose privileges others would be jealous. But the word includes a wider connotation, that of making distinctions between people on grounds of social status; and in that light, the whole institution of slavery would be completely overthrown were the implications of this one word to be taken with full seriousness. Tragically, it took centuries for the Christian Church to realize the logic of its own discourse.

In the preceding sections, it is not said explicitly that wives have a husband in heaven and children a parent in heaven whose fairness, affection and care exceed all earthly analogies, though Paul, to an unrivalled degree perhaps in the early Church, dared to think so.

281

VII Christian warfare (6.10–20)

This section consists of two paragraphs, the famous allegory of the full armour of God, verses 10–17, and an intercessory prayer request, verses 18–20. They are usually taken together, because the verbs in v. 18 are participles, seen as dependent on the imperative in verse 17. However, the second paragraph could just as easily stand alone (see comment on v. 18), or be taken closely with 6.21–4 as part of the closing greeting; and the first paragraph could be taken as the last part of the so-called household code (see further below and on v. 10). In the present form of the text and in the mind of the editor they should perhaps be taken together, but these other possibilities are not thereby excluded.

The connection between the two parts of the section is none too close, in terms of either content or source. No piece of the Christian's armour is identified as 'the power of prayer', though it would have been appropriate to do so; and the military imagery gives way in the second paragraph to the contrasting image of 'an ambassador in chains'.

The sources also differ: the prayer request is similar to that in Col. 4.2–4 and its wording and content are entirely typical of Paul; the allegory, however, is a free-standing, carefully composed set-piece and at certain points, noted in the commentary, reflects the style of the editor. This is not to say that it is his own new composition; there may have been some basis for it in Paul's original letter, perhaps in connection with the warning against drunkenness at 5.18 (which is the context in which Paul uses military metaphors at 1 Thess. 5.7 and Rom. 13.12). And this in turn may have inspired the editor to incorporate a piece of tradition that had already worked up Paul's military metaphors. But while Paul's own practice was to subordinate the use of metaphor to his immediate specific purpose, here it is the other way round: the metaphor dictates to the exhortation in an almost literary way. It is not therefore difficult to see why the editor chose to reserve this impressive piece as the rousing conclusion to the letter.

Lincoln attempts to analyse this section as a *peroratio*, i.e. a summary of the preceding exposition, in line with classical rhetoric (432ff., and 1995). But this passage is not really a summary of what has gone before; quite late on in the letter it introduces a striking new image which is in some tension with the earlier material. This section fits even less comfortably into the category of speeches by generals before battle (*pace* Lincoln 433). It is more likely to be an allegorical paraenesis which was circulating in an oral, still fluid form in the community and was assumed to be Pauline. It could have been used on various occasions and for a variety of purposes.

The lengthy exhortation that constitutes the second half of Ephesians began at 4.1 with a reminder of Paul's imprisonment and a call to lowliness, meekness and patience (4.2). It ends here with a similar reminder (6.20), but also a contrasting call to the military virtues of strength, courage and perseverance. The contrast is surely deliberate. The whole armour of the God who won his pacific victory over the powers through the cross (see 2.14–16) is nothing less than the naked defencelessness of the crucified Christ. Colossians makes this same point when it daringly reinterprets the humiliation and torture of Jesus' crucifixion as the pinning up of a notice of slave release and a triumphal procession over disarmed principalities and powers (Col. 2.14f.). However, while throughout Colossians and in the earlier part of Ephesians Christ's victory is a past achievement, in this passage victory is awaited in the future and for the moment Christians still struggle against the forces of darkness. This paragraph of Ephesians singularly lacks any verbal echoes of Colossians, though it exhibits similarities of imagery and vocabulary with other letters of Paul, especially 1 Thess. 5.8; 2 Cor. 6.7 (cf. Rom. 6.13; 13.12). These observations pose a serious problem for the theory that Ephesians is based on Colossians. If our letter were consciously reworking Colossians, the differences both in omission and addition in this passage would invite the conclusion that they were deliberate contradictions, and yet there is no hint that Ephesians is intended to refute or replace Colossians, or that our author senses any tension between the affirmation of victory already won and the exhortation to fight on to the End. Here as elsewhere, Ephesians departs from Colossians in a carefree way and often becomes more and not less Pauline when it does so. Any theory of the composition of Ephesians that is to be satisfactory has to account for this feature.

The connection between this section and its immediate predecessor is at first difficult to follow. The change of tone, from quiet domestic harmony to the noise of battle, is very sudden. It is due, of course, to a change of focus from the qualities required within the Christian community – mutual submission, love and gentleness – to the need to face the external world with a stance of stern opposition. But the shift from wedding to warfare is so striking that further explanation of the writer's train of thought may be needed.

One explanation of the link, if there is one, between Christian warfare and the household code might be that, although most Christians by the time of the writer would come under one or more of the categories of the code, there is an important group who would not, namely young, independent and unmarried men. Free from family entanglements, they are eligible for recruitment as soldiers in God's army (see Deut. 20.5–9). When Paul calls Epaphroditus (Phil. 2.25) and Archippus (Phlm. 2) his 'fellow soldiers', it implies perhaps that they were unmarried like himself. Their experience, no less than that of the settled heads of households, is proposed in this section as a model for all Christians to follow. The author has perhaps hinted at certain reservations about the married state in his allegorization of Gen. 2.24 in reference to the Church (see on 5.32); and the gender-specific way he can speak of 'a perfect Man' (4.13; contrast 2.15) might also indicate his concern to provide an ideal of Christian discipleship for young adult males. The military images, like those of athletics (e.g. 1 Cor. 9.24ff.; Gal. 2.2; Phil. 3.13f.), would naturally serve that purpose.

A passage from the First Epistle of John supports this suggestion; in a heavily modified household code three classes are mentioned: children, fathers and young men (1 John 2.12–14). The first half of it reads:

> I write to you, children, because your sins are forgiven for his name's sake; I write to you, fathers, because you know the One who is from the beginning; I write to you, young men, because you have conquered the Evil One.

'Children' is the term used for the whole congregation (see 1 John 2.1, 18, 28 etc.), and fathers are plausibly identified with heads of households who take the lead in community life (such as Gaius and Demetrius in 3 John 1, 12, and contrast Diotrephes at 3 John 9). It is the additional category of young men which is something of a surprise. Attempts to understand them as assistant ministers or deacons are unconvincing; a social division seems more likely to most commentators (see Brown 1982; Houlden 1973a). The reasons given for singling out this group are relevant to our present discussion. The young men are addressed 'because you have conquered the evil one' (1 John 2.13) and, at greater length in the following verse, 'because you are strong and the word of God abides in you and you have conquered the evil one'. The themes of strength (6.10), the Word of God (6.17), and conquest of the evil one (6.16) all appear in this passage of Ephesians too.

A broader comparison may usefully be made with the Apocalypse, in which military images are all-pervasive (cf. 6.2, 4; 9.17 for bow, sword and breastplate) and the ideology of spiritual warfare is related principally to those who are represented in the vision as the 144,000 'male virgins who have not defiled themselves with women' (14.4). These Johannine texts, in the loose sense of the term, surely provide the most immediate background in Asian Christianity at the end of the first century for this clarion call to Christian warfare.

A   The armour of God   *(6.10–17)*

(10) Finally, be strong in the Lord and his mighty power. (11) Put on the armour of God, that you may face up to all the devil's tactics. (12) For our contest is not with human but with superhuman opponents, with principalities and authorities,

**with the powers of this dark world, with the spiritual forces of
wickedness in the heavenly realm. (13) Receive God's armour,
then, so that you can make your stand on the evil day, and be left
standing when it is all over. (14) Stand, then, with the belt of
truth around your waist, and justice as your breastplate, (15) with
the good news of peace as the shoes fitted to your feet. (16) With
all this take faith as your protective shield, with which you will be
able to extinguish all the burning arrows of the evil one. (17) And
take salvation as your helmet and the sword of the Spirit, which is
the Word of God.**

The structure of this paragraph is as follows: the basic exhortation to be
strong (v. 10) is spelled out in terms of putting on the armour ('panoply')
of God (vv. 11–12) and standing firm (defensively) in the fight (v. 13).
These injunctions are then developed in terms of, first, articles that are
worn (vv. 14–15) and, secondly, those that are carried (vv. 16–17), with
the helmet in the second category rather than the first.

This passage has often been read in a rather individualist way, so it is
important to point out that the imperatives in this section are all in the
plural (Kitchen 1994: 112–28); we should envisage not so much a lone
knight errant in full armour as a platoon of eager infantrymen.
Nevertheless there is no explicit reference to the themes of obedience
to a superior officer or solidarity in the ranks (contrast the centurion in
Matt. 8.9) – omissions which could point to the inner and essentially
individual struggle with sexual temptation as at least one of the purposes
for which this exhortation could have been employed. Sexual abstinence
is part of military discipline in Israel's Holy War tradition (cf. 1 Sam.
21.5); and the author has used material that underlined the danger of
sexual licence at several points in the earlier section on Christian conduct
(see 4.19; 5.3; 5.5; and possibly 5.12). The armour itself is allegorized in
relation to qualities which every believer needs. It self-evidently is not
the case that some members of the community are helmets and others
shoes (contrast the head addressing the feet in the body image of 1 Cor.
12.21). The armour all belongs to one individual but it is not thereby
individualist: the virtues to which it corresponds are communitarian
ones, as earlier references in the letter demonstrate: truth-telling (cf.
4.25, 'for we are members one of another'); righteousness (5.9); peace
(2.14); the unity of faith (4.13); and unity in the spirit (4.3).

There is, furthermore, a certain natural progression in the order in
which articles of clothing and weaponry are presented, not only in
relation to the image of a soldier preparing for battle but also in the
corresponding virtues of the Christian life. First comes the belt, which is
truth, i.e. initial acceptance of the gospel (cf. 1.13); then the breastplate
of righteousness, i.e. holy living (cf. 4.1); shoes are the gospel of peace,

i.e. the readiness to witness to others (cf. 6.19); and when faith is spoken of as a shield, it is not so much initial belief that is meant but faith as the means of becoming rooted in Christ (cf. 3.17); the last two images, the helmet of salvation and the sword of the Spirit ('which is the Word of God', understood as the word of judgement, see below on v. 17), may refer to the final goal of the Christian life. Thus the sequence is conversion–holiness–evangelism–endurance–salvation–judgement. While the separate elements in this allegory may be arbitrary (faith could just as well be the belt or the breastplate as the shield, for example), yet, as a set and in this particular sequence, the correspondences are not arbitrary.

10 Finally. This translation represents a Greek idiom (lit. 'of the rest' (in the genitive here) or 'as to the rest' (in the accusative)) which can be used either in a temporal sense, 'from now on' (e.g. Gal. 6.17), or in a logical sense, 'in conclusion' (e.g. Phil. 4.8). The temporal is not altogether inappropriate, for it could point forward to the future 'evil day' of verse 13. But the logical is more likely. It is less clear whether this 'finally' is the last main point of the letter as a whole (cf. 2 Cor. 13.11) or marks the conclusion of what has immediately preceded it in the household code (cf. 1 Thess. 4.1). Both may be implied.

Be strong in the Lord. The verb could be either middle or passive, literally either 'go on strengthening yourselves' or 'go on being strengthened'. The present tense and the preposition ('in' instead of 'by') tell slightly in favour of the middle, and that would point to the idea of gradual progress in Christian discipleship. But the passive receives support from the following reference to the power of God.

The idea of being strengthened by the Spirit has appeared already at 3.16 in an exhortation to grow towards maturity, and the encouragement to continue in good works featured at 2.10. Paul uses the same verb (*endunamousthai*) of his own apostolic empowerment at Phil. 4.11 and the confirmation of Abraham's faith at Rom. 4.20, but an even closer parallel to the thought is to be found at 1 Cor. 16.13: 'Keep awake, stand firm in faith, be courageous, be powerful', which extends the watchword of early Christian paraenesis, 'Keep awake' (Mark 13.33 etc.), in a way that could lead naturally into military imagery. Although Paul himself uses military metaphors only in passing (e.g. Rom. 6.13, 23; 1 Thess. 5.8) and does not develop them, it is easy to imagine how a preacher or prophet in the Pauline churches could latch on to the idea and build it up consistently into a Christian adaptation of the repeated injunction in Joshua 1 (vv. 6, 7, 9): 'Be strong and of good courage.'

The parallel at Col. 1.11, 'May you be strengthened with all strength according to his glorious might', is less significant than some commentators have claimed (e.g. Lincoln 434 and 442), for it occurs in the opening section, not in the ethical exhortations at the end, and there is no hint of a military metaphor.

His mighty power (lit. 'the strength of his might'). The author has used this combination already at 1.19, but it is especially fitting here.

11 Put on the armour of God is the military version of 'put on the new humanity' at 4.24. It can be compared with Col. 3.12, where, however, civilian clothing and less militaristic virtues are in view. Rom. 13.14 is the closer parallel, given the proximity of the reference to armour at 13.12. (REB at Rom. 13.14 goes so far as to make the connection explicit: 'Let Christ Jesus himself be the armour that you wear.') The imperative 'put on' here is followed by 'receive' at verse 13; both have armour as their object and one might have expected 'receive' to precede 'put on'. But the author is probably thinking first of putting on body-armour and then of receiving (from the hands of an assistant) weapons that are carried.

The Old Testament passages which have most affinity with this allegory and probably contributed to its development are both from Isaiah (11.4–5 and 59.17), though the picture of Yahweh as a warrior is widespread in Hebrew scripture, especially in the Psalms. Isa. 11.4–5 describes God's ideal king as one who will 'smite the earth with the rod of his mouth, and with the breath of his lips he shall slay the wicked. Righteousness shall be the girdle of his waist, and faithfulness the girdle of his loins'; and Isa. 59.17 describes Yahweh himself when it says: 'He put on righteousness as a breastplate, and a helmet of salvation upon his head; he put on garments of vengeance for clothing, and wrapped himself in fury as a mantle.' This imagery is taken up in the Wisdom of Solomon (5.16–23), where God, in the role of a divine warrior, will avenge the persecuted righteous man:

> The Lord will take his zeal as his whole armour, and will arm all creation to repel his enemies; he will put on righteousness as a breastplate, and wear impartial justice as a helmet; he will take holiness as an invincible shield, and sharpen stern wrath for a sword. (Wis. 5.17, 20a)

It is worth noting that, despite the encouragement that these texts provide, there is no explicitly christological elaboration of the image of the warrior in Ephesians or elsewhere in Paul (*pace* Yoder Neufeld 1997); the armour is provided by God, but it is worn by the Christian. For the classic discussion of the theme of *Militia Christi*, see von Harnack (1981). The Greek word for armour is *panoplia* (lit. 'whole armour'); it does not actually occur in either of the Isaiah passages (LXX), nor in any other letter of Paul. It is used at Luke 11.22, but of the devil (!) 'as a strong man *fully armed*'.

That you may face up (lit. 'that you may be able to stand'). To stand firm in battle is the prime duty of a foot-soldier. The idea is picked up again emphatically in verse 13. That it may also allude, as additional overtones, to standing for worship (Rev. 7.9), or prayer (see Matt. 6.5), or standing before a judge in a law-suit (Mark 13.9; Rev. 20.12) is not impossible. Standing ready to fight is, however, clearly the primary image and it contrasts the honourable combatant with the devil's underhand tactics, trying to trip up his opponent or set fire to his shield. Standing is a frequent metaphor in Paul (e.g. Rom. 14.4; Gal. 5.1) to describe Christian perseverance. The basic contrast here is between standing up and falling down (rather than standing one's ground and running away); to fall, in other words, is to lapse into sin (cf. 1 Cor. 10.12) rather than to lapse from the faith.

The Christian soldier is to face up **to all the devil's tactics**. The word for tactics (*methodeiai*) occurs only here and at Eph. 4.14 (in the singular) in the New Testament. In itself it is a neutral word ('method', 'technique') which has gathered negative connotations from context. The way that the devil's army wages war on God's people is graphically described in the Apocalypse (see esp. Rev. 12.17). The author does not specify what these tactics refer to in reality; we can only guess from the earlier exhortations what he might have in mind. He has mentioned at 2.14–18 the hostility between Jews and Gentiles, broken down within the Church, but perhaps still a threat outside it. The potential threat of the Roman state may be implied in the references to Paul's imprisonment but, if so, the use in positive symbolism of the equipment of the regular soldier would then need to be taken with a touch of irony. The moral degeneracy of pagan society has been emphasized earlier (see on 4.19) and these may be the principal allurements of the devil. Corruption infiltrates the Christian community through lies and especially through anger, which gives the devil his opportunity (see 4.26f. and cf. 4.32). It takes the form of sexual temptation at 5.3–5 and drunkenness at 5.18. The allegorical Christian soldier, then, is a model of self-discipline, resisting the temptations of sex, alcohol and violence rather more successfully (needless to say) than his literal imperial counterpart.

12 The struggle with the powers of darkness is described as **our contest** (*palē*) or wrestling match, presumably implying close, hand-to-hand combat (Gudorf 1998: 334). Carr (1981: 104–10) is forced to excise this verse as a later interpolation, because it conflicts with his theory that the principalities and powers are neutral or benign (see on 1.20f. above); this theory has been refuted by Arnold (1987: 71–87).

The contest is not with **human opponents**, literally 'blood and flesh' – the reverse order (cf. also Heb. 2.14) of the normal stock phrase (cf.

Matt. 16.17; Gal. 1.16; 1 Cor. 15.50). The reversal may be in response to a context that implies bloodshed in battle. Four terms for the **superhuman opponents** of Christians are mentioned, amplifying the reference to the devil in the previous verse: literally translated, they are 'principalities', 'authorities', 'world rulers of this darkness' and 'spiritual beings of wickedness in the heavenlies'. The first two terms, **principalities and authorities**, have been discussed at 3.10 and 1.21, where they were joined by 'powers', 'dominions' and 'every name that is named'. Two more of the names for the fallen angels who form the army of Satan are added. **Powers of this dark world** (lit. 'world rulers (*kosmokratores*) of this darkness') occurs only here in the New Testament but compare *Testament of Solomon* 18.2 (see Charlesworth 1983: 1.960–87). In magical papyri, the sun and the gods of the mystery cults are occasionally addressed as 'world ruler' (understood positively as a devotional title): Arnold (*DPL* 581) quotes the Hymn to Serapis (*PGM* 13.61.8–40): 'I call on you Lord, world ruler ... protect me from my own astrological destiny, destroy my foul fate, apportion good things for me in my horoscope.' The addition, 'of this darkness', is therefore crucial; it gives the term the necessary negative connotation – pagan deities are rejected as demonic (cf. also Paul at 1 Cor. 10.20).

The remaining title, **the spiritual forces of wickedness in the heavenly realm**, may be a summarizing description of all the preceding powers rather than a further category (so Lincoln 444). But it is equally possible that the text is working upwards from the evil geniuses that inspire oppressive political regimes ('principalities') or cause disruptions in the natural order ('authorities'), to the demonic deities worshipped in pagan cults and astrology ('world rulers'), and finally, with this phrase, to those who are the closest adjutants to the Prince of the Power of the Air (2.2). They are located 'in the heavenlies' (cf. 3.10; for this idiom, which is distinctive of Ephesians, see on 1.3) but, as the term suggests, there are many levels in the spirit-world, where evil angels have their own spheres of autonomous malevolent activity. If it is the case that the higher up in the hierarchy of evil (and the closer therefore to the throne of God) they are, the more arrogant these fallen angels become (see *T. Sol.* chs. 6, 8 and 18), then 'the spiritual forces of wickedness in the heavenly realm' of Eph. 6.12 could be identified with what the author of Col. 1.16 called 'thrones', the term which is missing from Eph. 1.21 (see above). The throne of God can be shared by Christ and the victorious Christian (see Rev. 3.21) and by the loyal council of God's prophets and apostles (see Rev. 4.4, cf. 4.11), but when the Prince of demons claims a throne of his own (cf. 2 Thess. 2.4) his treason becomes fully apparent as open rebellion.

13 Similar calls to **make your stand on the evil day** and resist the devil are found in 1 Pet. 5.9 and Jas 4.7. The present time was described as 'these evil days' at 5.16 and some commentators (e.g. Bruce 406) find the same meaning here, i.e. any moments of crisis or temptation confronting the individual Christian. But '*the* evil day' is more likely to belong to the Pauline inheritance of final eschatology (as Dibelius–Greeven 1953: 98; Houlden 339) referring to the last outbreak of Satan's apostasy (2 Thess. 2.3: 'Let no one deceive you in any way. That day cannot come before the final rebellion against God'; cf. 1 Thess. 5.2, 'The day of the Lord', and see further Rev. 20.1–10).

The soldier who makes his stand will be **left standing when it is all over** (lit. 'having done everything'). This may refer back to verse 11 and mean 'having put everything on' or 'having made every preparation' (cf. 2 Cor. 5.5). But if we are right to explain verse 13 as moving on from protective armour to offensive weaponry, then it is more likely that it means 'having resisted or withstood the assault'. The compound verb (*katergazesthai*) is frequent in Paul – 11 times in Romans alone – in the sense of 'to complete, accomplish or produce', with the prefix denoting thoroughness. Elsewhere, however, it can have the sense of 'to work against', i.e. 'to oppose' (cf. 1 Esd. 4.4) and some commentators appear to lean in this direction, e.g. Mitton (223): 'having won the day'. But the prospect for the Christian soldier on the evil day is not victory as such but simply resistance and survival. One might compare, in a similar apocalyptic context, Mark 13.13, 'he who endures to the end will be saved' and 13.20, 'If the Lord had not shortened the days no human being would be saved.' This is no achievement of one's own; victory is reserved for the last-minute intervention of the returning Christ (cf. 2 Thess. 2.8), the warrior Word of God (cf. Heb. 4.12; Rev. 19.11–16). To be left standing at the end and not carried off the field as a casualty of war is all that one can reasonably hope for.

14 Stand, then, with the belt of truth around your waist. The theme of standing is underlined again and the armour of God explained piece by piece. As noted above, the imagery here is drawn from Pauline and Old Testament literary sources mixed with some familiarity with the uniform of a Roman foot-soldier. The first item is taken from Isaiah (11.5 LXX), where the branch from the stump of Jesse (i.e. the Davidic Messiah) will have justice as the girdle of his waist and truth around his loins. Oriental flowing robes need to be hitched up for ease of movement on active service (Luke 12.35, cf. 1 Pet. 1.13). This might explain the priority given to the belt, for in Roman armour this would correspond to either the leather apron or the sword belt, but in neither case be worthy of such prominence (Oepke, *TDNT* 5. 303, 307). **Truth** could be God's truth, i.e. his fidelity (cf. 4.24), since the armour belongs ultimately to God; or the virtue of truth-telling, emphasized at 4.25, since the armour is worn by the Christian; or it could be the assured truth of Christian preaching (as at 1.13 and 4.21); or a combination of all three. The nature of the threat posed by the opposition is not described precisely – precision about the resources needed to oppose it is similarly unnecessary. The indeterminacy is probably deliberate: it allows for a variety of applications for the paraenesis.

And justice as your breastplate. Justice (or 'righteousness') is the belt at Isa. 11.5 but has become the breastplate of the Lord at Isa. 59.17. The identifications are somewhat arbitrary. At 1 Thess. 5.8 Paul identifies the breastplate as faith and love, while at 2 Cor. 6.7 justice is seen as the weapons in the right and left hand (which would be either sword and spear or sword and shield). Although, as we have seen, this author avoids the theological language of righteousness/justification by faith and translates it in terms of salvation (see above on 2.8), this does not mean that justice/righteousness here cannot be a property of God (see on 4.24) as well as a demand laid on the believer (compare the two uses at Rev. 19.11 and 22.11). For justice as the martyr's ultimate weapon against persecution, see 1 Pet. 3.14–16, cf. 2.23.

15 With the good news of peace as the shoes. Like the belt, shoes (or sandals) were not a major item of battle-dress for a Roman soldier. There could be an allusion here to his stout marching boots (Latin *caligae*), but the allegorical application is more likely to refer to Isa. 52.7: 'How beautiful on the mountains are the feet of him who brings good news' (quoted by Paul at Rom. 10.15), even though this text has no associated military imagery. Something like the mission charge in the gospel tradition may have been the catalyst for the development of this element of the allegory, especially the reference to sandals to be worn (Mark 6.9), the delivery of the message of peace (Matt. 10.13) and, for those who refuse to accept it, the shaking off of the dust from the feet as a sign of judgement (Matt. 10.14–15). It is relevant to compare the modification of these instructions at Luke 22.35–36, where a sword is added to the missionary's 'armoury'.

Shoes fitted to your feet (lit. 'be tied under as to the feet with the preparation of the gospel of peace'). There are two problems here: the meaning of the word 'preparation' and its grammatical relation to the following genitive. 'Preparation' or 'preparedness' (*hetoimasia*) only appears here in the New Testament, though the cognate verb is very common in a variety of contexts, occasionally military (e.g. Acts 23.23, of troops 'falling in', and Rev. 9.7 of the locusts like horses 'prepared for battle'). But whether this background is sufficiently determinative to translate the noun here as 'battle-readiness' (Lincoln 449) is less certain. For it would create a double level of metaphor: the soldier would have shoes which are 'preparedness to fight' and are in turn 'the gospel of peace'. But the other comparisons in the allegory have to do straightforwardly with the soldier's material rather than mental equipment. And if preparedness is not part of the metaphor but belongs to its application, what has prevented a direct correspondence between shoes and the gospel?

This leads us to the grammatical obscurity. The genitive might be epexegetic ('preparedness consisting in the gospel') or objective ('the preparing of the gospel'), which itself could be taken in either of two ways: 'being prepared to receive it for oneself' (so Schnackenburg 278) or 'being ready to preach it to others' (so Schlier 296). Both of the latter make perfectly good sense (Rom. 12.18 advocates readiness for peace; 1 Pet. 3.15 advocates readiness for evangelism). But given the author's proneness to weakly constructed phrases, the solution may be less complex. 'Preparation' may refer neither to the attitude of the soldier in the allegory nor to that of the Christian in real life, but simply to the feet, which have to be 'prepared' by being 'tied under', i.e. by the strapping up of footwear. This simpler interpretation, reflected in the translation above, would still retain the full force of the paradox involved in identifying the gospel of peace with an army jackboot (cf. Matt. 10.34).

16 With all this probably means 'in addition to all this', but 'in every situation' or 'at all times' are also possible renderings. That God himself is the **shield** of his people is a well-known Old Testament metaphor. God says to Abraham (Gen. 15.1), 'I am your shield' and the idea recurs frequently in the Psalms. The word used in LXX for shield is normally *aspis* – the small round metal shield designed for close combat. However, the word here is different, *thureos*, which also appears in the LXX (Ps. 34.2; 45.10); it denotes the long, curved wooden shields (metal would be too heavy) covered with leather which, placed edge to edge, formed a barricade during an assault. **Burning arrows** would be an obvious threat to this kind of protective armament. One precaution against incendiary attack, mentioned by Thucydides (2.75), was to soak the shields in water before an engagement. Whether the author was aware of these technicalities is uncertain, but not impossible. His description of the arrows as 'burning' (lit. 'burnt up', *pepurômena*) does slightly miss the point that they are *carrying* fire to their target (*purphora*, 'fire-bearing', would have been the more exact word). The Old Testament mentions fiery arrows (e.g. Ps. 7.13), but not as a hazard to wooden shields. So it may be that the notion of a wooden shield that extinguishes (rather than catches alight) is an idealistic projection – indeed, a nice inversion! – of the idea of the unquenchable fires of hell (cf. Mark 9.48 and Rev. 20.14).

Of the evil one. In the genitive case 'evil' (*ponêrou*) can be either masculine or neuter, an ambiguity which also affects the interpretation of the last clause of the Lord's Prayer (Matt. 6.13, 'Deliver us from evil';

NRSV, 'the evil one'). But since the cognate abstract noun (*ponêria*) has been used at 6.12 and the context implies personal agency, it is clearly here a title for the devil. As such, it is unique in the Pauline corpus. Elsewhere in the New Testament it is most characteristic of the Johannine writings (John 17.15; 1 John 2.13f.; 5.8f.). On the author's understanding of the hierarchy of evil, see on verse 12 above.

Faith may have the sense of saving faith (2.8), i.e. initial Christian commitment (1.15), but it is also a quality which may be possessed to a greater or lesser degree, i.e. faithfulness, which can grow and mature over time (see on 4.13). This ambiguity is not untypical of Paul himself (see Rom. 10.9, cf. 14.22; 1 Cor. 15.14, cf. 1 Cor. 12.9). Although the second of these meanings makes slightly better sense here, the first is not necessarily excluded. Which of them is heard more clearly would depend on the various settings in which the paraenesis could have been used in the Church's corporate life: at the commissioning of leaders, for example (4.11; cf. 4.8 for a military echo) or at the baptism of new members (cf. 5.14; and cf. also Ign. *Pol.* 6.2).

At 1 Thess. 5.8 faith was associated with the breastplate, which has a similar protective function to that of the shield. At 1 Pet. 5.8, the Christian resisting the devil, depicted this time as a wild beast rather than a military opponent, is similarly called on to be strong in faith.

17 And take salvation as your helmet (lit. 'the helmet of salvation') **and the sword of the Spirit, which is the Word of God.** The earlier items each have an imperatival clause to themselves; the last two, helmet and sword – which one might think were the most important – are hastily run together at the end. This is explicable if these two can only partially be received now, but are mainly eschatological gifts that will be granted in full measure on the last day (cf. also Wild 1984: 297). At 1 Thess. 5.8 Paul had identified the helmet specifically as the *hope* of salvation, in order to form a triplet with 'the breastplate of *faith* and *love*' (cf. 1 Cor. 13), and the same future reference may be implied here. The editor's use of 'salvation' to refer to what has already been realized in and for believers (see e.g. 2.5) does not exclude the hope that is still to come. Indeed, the whole thrust of this passage has been to offer reassurance that present warfare with the powers of darkness will end in God's final victory. In a certain sense, then, the helmet becomes less a piece of equipment for present conflict and more like a crown worn by the saints as a symbol of their future victory. Comparison with Rev. 2.10 is illuminating: 'Be faithful unto death and I will give you the crown of life'; and conversely, at Rev. 9.7, the golden crowns of the devil's army substitute for helmets in their arrogant and false anticipation of success. This interpretation is reinforced by the link with the sword of the Spirit, if that is not only a reference to what Christians may wield already but also an image of the instrument of divine judgement still to come; see below.

The word used for **salvation** here (*sôtêrion*, rather than *sôtêria*; see on 1.13) is found nowhere else in Paul, but is common in the LXX and in Luke-Acts among the New Testament writings. It may have been preferred to the alternative under the influence of Isa. 59.17 (see above on 6.11).

The final item in the armoury is **the sword of the Spirit, which is the Word** (*rêma*) **of God**. The relative pronoun is actually neuter, while 'sword' in Greek is feminine. Strictly, therefore, it should be the Spirit that is identified as the Word of God, but that would disrupt the allegorical pattern. Relative pronouns are often attracted to the gender of the nearest antecedent, so it is probably correct to see the sword as identified with the Word. The symbolism of the sword, of course, fits with the preceding military images, but it also goes beyond them into a more juridical metaphor (cf. Rom. 13.4). The thought is similar to that of Heb. 4.12, where the Word (*logos*) of God is said to be sharper than a two-edged sword that divides and judges. Similarly in 2 Thess. 2.8, where the Lord will slay the man of lawlessness with the breath (or spirit) of his mouth. In Revelation, the sword of future judgement is also frequently mentioned (1.6; 2.12, 16; and esp. 19.13–15, where one who is called the Word (*logos*) of God has a sharp sword issuing from his mouth and will rule with a sceptre of iron). It is unlikely that the Word (*rêma*) of God here has any christological connotation, since the context is too limited and not personal enough; it is more likely to refer to the pronouncement of final judgement.

Like the helmet of salvation, then, the sword is a symbol of the hope of victory and judgement to come, not just a weapon of present combat; it is an anticipation of the future in which the Christian will share the triumph of Christ (Rev. 2.27 and 1 Cor. 6.2), though within the community some may indeed wield the sharp sword of divine judgement already. On two occasions (1.13 and 4.30) when the Spirit was mentioned earlier, its role as guarantor of future hope was stressed; this may be a third.

The call to arms in Eph. 6.10–17 is understandably one of best known and best loved passages in the whole letter. It demonstrates rather clearly that allegory is not necessarily arid or artificial; in the hands of a master it can become a powerful technique for discerning the reality and mystery of religious faith.

B   Request for prayer   (6.18–20)

(18) Take every opportunity for prayer and intercession that the Spirit gives and be vigilant as well, persevering in intercession for

all the saints (19) and on my behalf too that I may be given the words to speak, to make freely known the secret of the gospel, (20) for which I am an ambassador in chains, so that I may speak freely as I ought.

If a new sentence begins at verse 18, then its participles should be taken as imperatives, as in this translation (see on 5.21); this section then constitutes a separate intercessory prayer request. The Colossians parallel (4.2–4) is also a separate section, and follows immediately after the household code, with none of the intervening allegory on Christian warfare. Ephesians is very close in substance but very different in wording, strangely so if it is dependent on Colossians. Yet some of the differences make the Ephesians version sound more, not less, like Paul. Prayer is linked to intercession (cf. Phil. 4.6); its constancy is emphasized ('every opportunity' cf. 1 Thess. 5.17 and Rom. 1.9f.); prayer is the gift of the Holy Spirit (cf., e.g., Rom. 8.15f., see Adai 1985: 237–43); 'the saints' is used in the regular sense of 'all Christians' – none of these thoroughly Pauline motifs figures in the Colossians passage. On the other hand, what would be the point of changing 'watchful' to 'vigilant', the verb 'persevere' (cf. Rom. 12.12) to the noun 'perseverance' (*proskarterēsis*, not found elsewhere in Paul), and the striking Pauline idiom of God opening the door of missionary opportunity (Col. 4.3; cf. also 1 Cor. 16.9 and 2 Cor. 2.12) to the unremarkable 'the opening of my mouth' (represented in the above translation by 'be given words to speak'), and yet at the same time greatly improving the rather dull 'to make clear' of Colossians to the stronger and more distinctively Pauline 'to speak freely' (or 'speak boldly', *parrēsiazesthai*, cf. 1 Thess. 2.2; Phil. 1.20, Phlm. 8)? So neither passage can be dependent in a literary way on the other, and both probably come from the hand of Paul, for there could be no reason for a pseudepigrapher to make such extensive minor alterations to his source yet to so little effect. If he was just about to copy in a whole paragraph word for word (6.21–2), why has he not done the same here?

By the time of writing, prayer for the success of Paul's ministry (v. 19) would no longer be a matter of urgency (or relevance). Nevertheless, the editor of Ephesians did have a motive for including here the original intercessory prayer request from Paul's letter, since it nicely complements the intercessory prayer report which he has included earlier (1.15–18).

18 The redundancy with which the verse begins (literally) **'Through all prayer ... pray at every opportunity'** probably means that the emphasis falls on the following phrase **'in the Spirit'**, referring not, therefore, to the spirit of the one who prays but to the Spirit (of God) who inspires all prayer (cf. Rom. 8.16, 26f.).

19 The secret of the gospel. On Paul's use of the word 'secret' see on 3.3; for the 'off-Pauline' usage see on 1.9.

20 Ambassador in chains. At Phlm. 9, Paul contrasts the two images of 'ambassador' and 'prisoner': an ambassador has greater freedom than the ordinary citizen, let alone a prisoner, and to imprison an ambassador would be a gross insult to the one he represented (Bash 1997: 132). Here the two ideas are paradoxically combined, for though the messenger is bound, the message is not (see also Acts 28.31). The 'chain' (*halusis*, singular in the Greek) may be a vivid synonym for 'bonds' (*desmioi*), Paul's regular expression (see Phil. 1.7, 13, 14, 17; Col. 4.18; Phlm. 10, 13; cf. also Eph 3.1 and 4.1). An imitator must be supposed to have given his imagination a little liberty (cf. Acts 28.20 and 2 Tim. 1.16), in spite of the consistent usage elsewhere. But it is more likely that the phrase is Paul's, born of his own linguistic creativity or, indeed, his own lived experience.

VIII Concluding message and grace (6.21–4)

(21) So that you also may know my situation and how I am faring, Tychicus, that dear brother and faithful assistant in the Lord, will fully inform you. (22) I have sent him to you for this very reason, that you may know of our circumstances and that he may heartily encourage you.

(23) Peace be to the brethren and love with faith from God the Father and the Lord Jesus Christ. (24) May grace with immortality be with all who love the Lord Jesus Christ.

The concluding section of the letter consists of two parts: a message about Tychicus, the supposed bearer of the letter, and a more or less conventional final 'grace' or benediction.

The much longer ending of Colossians at 4.7–18 also includes both of these elements: the first is almost identical in wording, except that it also mentions Onesimus, while the benediction is much shorter, to the point of being almost peremptory. Colossians, however, contains much else besides: references to Paul's fellow prisoners and prison visitors, in particular three Jews – Aristarchus, Mark and Jesus Justus – and three Gentiles – Epaphras, Luke and Demas. It commends Epaphras's earlier work among the churches of the Lycus valley. It sends greetings, via the Colossians, to the congregation in Laodicea and recommends they exchange letters, and it singles out the household church of Nympha or Nymphas and one Archippus; where they are located is unclear.

If a pseudepigrapher had wanted to give his work the air of verisimilitude by taking over from Colossians some of these circumstantial details, it is surprising that he fastened on to one name, Tychicus, which occurs nowhere else in Paul's own letters and becomes more prominent only in deutero-Pauline texts (cf. Acts 20.4; 2 Tim. 4.12;

Titus 3.12) which themselves may have been influenced by its appearance here; and that he turned down better known figures from Colossians, like Mark, Barnabas and Luke, and indeed Paul's own missionary assistant in Asia, Epaphras (cf. also Col. 1.7). Even more surprising on this hypothesis is the restraint and subtlety implied in an appeal to extra information about the apostle's circumstances to be supplied by Tychicus personally, details of which the author was himself presumably ignorant. These problems can hardly be solved by saying that the author here mechanically copied out a section of Colossians, for this is so obviously not his practice elsewhere. On the pseudepigraphical hypothesis, this passage, with 32 words in common with Colossians, is a remarkable exception to the general rule that Ephesians contains allusive echoes of the Pauline letters.

Mitton suggested that this circumstantial excerpt was the result of the writer consulting (presumably a rather elderly) Tychicus to receive his personal approval of this pseudonymous letter (1951: 268). But this is surely most improbable. Tychicus, unlike some other readers perhaps, would naturally have read this material as a reference to a historical fact which he was in the unique position to know was false. To suppose with W. L. Knox (1939: 203) that Tychicus was the actual author of the letter and casually dropped his own name into it in a different capacity strains credibility to breaking point. But at least these scholars have recognized the problem here.

According to the Goodspeed–Knox theory, the real author of Ephesians is not the one name left in from Colossians, but Onesimus, whose name has been deliberately left out. This suffers from a similar defect, for the author has modestly refrained from including his own name and yet has immodestly included in the collection of the apostle's letters, for which Ephesians is the intended preface, a personal note from Paul concerning himself.

Best, who, unlike most modern scholars, has realized the weaknesses of the case for the dependence of Ephesians on Colossians, is nevertheless in serious difficulty with this passage, which on the face of it refutes his view. He begins by pointing out the slight differences of 6.21–2 from Colossians 4.7: its first five words, which are a clumsy purpose clause that adds nothing to the sense, for it is already expressed in the second purpose clause in verse 22; the addition of the redundant 'how I am faring'; and the omission of the description of Tychicus as a 'fellow-servant'. Best concludes that it would be just as easy to see Colossians as dependent on Ephesians as the other way round, but this option he also rejects. 'Yet more probable than the use of one letter by the author of the other is their common membership of the same Pauline school; *they may have discussed together how they should end their letters* and decided to introduce the name of Tychicus as a messenger who would provide further information about Paul, thus creating a standard way of expressing such sentiments' (613, my emphasis). We agree with Best that this passage does not prove literary dependence on Colossians, but find far-fetched his explanation of its identical wording by appeal to conspiratorial conversations in the school of Pauline pseudepigraphy at Ephesus. If the two pseudepigraphers discussed in such close detail how to wrap up their letters, why did they not try to reach more of a common mind on their contents?

These theories well illustrate the dilemma posed by this passage. For Ephesians is at this point much too close to Colossians for comfort. If the author knew as much about Paul at first hand as either Tychicus or Onesimus, why is this ending to the letter so vague and unconvincing? But if the author was a later follower with only second-hand knowledge of Paul mediated through texts, why did he mention Tychicus and omit Onesimus (along with several other omissions), quote *in extenso* what he must have taken to be Paul's own words on such a trivial point, and yet avoid quotation elsewhere on points of theological substance? In terms both of literary dependence and historical chronology, the relationship between Eph. 6.21f. and Col. 4.7f. is 'so near and yet so far'.

The solution I have been defending in this commentary is that there are fragments in Ephesians of what Paul originally wrote (to the Laodiceans) alongside statements and omissions that he would not have made. So Paul himself wrote the words we have in this section at the same time as writing the similar conclusion to Colossians. From his prison cell in Ephesus he had commissioned Tychicus, himself an Asian (Acts 20.4) and probably, like Trophimus (Acts 21.9), a native of Ephesus, to carry his letters to Laodicea and Colossae. He did not refer to Onesimus in the letter to the Laodiceans, except perhaps obliquely (see on 4.28 and 6.5–9), because the slave came from Colossae. But he may well have mentioned by name others whom he wished to greet personally (for instance Nympha, though the wording of Col. 4.15 allows one to think of her as the hostess of a more isolated house-church, perhaps at Hierapolis; the omission of her name here would obviously then not be significant). It is possible that the letter to the Laodiceans included few personal greetings and that Paul was happy to leave it to Tychicus to do whatever was necessary. What greetings there were, of course, the editor was obliged to omit, for he had in mind a different setting from that of his Pauline source. Historically, Paul wrote from Ephesus to Laodicea; in this edited version Paul is writing from a more famous imprisonment in Rome to Ephesus.

21 So that you also may know makes good sense if the preceding sentence in the original letter mentioned some other group, i.e. the Colossian congregation. Otherwise 'you *also*' is very odd. If the variant word order in certain MSS is followed, 'also' could qualify the whole sentence, but the transposition is probably secondary and designed to avoid this very difficulty.

Tychicus will report on **my situation and how I am faring**, that is to say, Paul's state of health, the progress of his court case and the successes of his missionary work from prison. We do not know the details; neither did the editor. Tychicus is described as a **dear** ('beloved') **brother**. Ephesians does not use the common Pauline expression 'brother' to describe fellow Christians, except here and in the next verse (it has been inserted by later scribes in some MSS at 5.15 and 6.10). This supports the view that both verses come from the Pauline source.

22 I have sent him to you. This was originally an epistolary aorist (see above on 3.3), i.e. 'I *am sending* him' with this letter, but of course it will now be heard by the audience as a genuine past tense.

The phrase **our circumstances** (lit. 'the things concerning us') appears also in Colossians, where the first person plural pronoun is appropriate since Paul is writing in collaboration with Timothy (Col. 1.1), and this may well have been the case also with Laodiceans (see on Eph. 1.1). In the present letter the plural is presumably to be understood in a generalizing way, for the letter focuses exclusively on Paul as the unique prisoner of Christ (see on Eph. 3.1).

23–24 Peace be to the brethren and love with faith from God the Father and the Lord Jesus Christ. May grace with immortality be with all who love the Lord Jesus Christ. The concluding grace bears hardly any resemblance to that at Col. 4.18: 'I, Paul, write this greeting *with my own hand*. Remember my *bonds*. Grace be with you.' If the author were modelling his letter on Colossians, the omission of the references to Paul's imprisonment and particularly to his own authenticating signature (cf. 2 Thess. 3.17) would require some explanation. But no explanation is needed. For the form of the final blessing in Ephesians, wishing peace and love and the grace of Christ to the brethren, is consistent with the standard Pauline form: 'The grace of our (the) Lord Jesus Christ be with you (your spirit), brethren' (see Gal. 6.18; Phil. 4.23; 1 Thess. 5.28; Rom. 16.20). The inclusion of **peace** as well as grace, echoing the opening greeting (Eph. 1.2), is not too dissimilar from 2 Cor. 13.11 and Gal. 6.16 ('peace and mercy'); and '**all who love the Lord Jesus Christ**' is just the positive way of saying what the conclusion of 1 Corinthians puts negatively: 'If anyone has no love for the Lord, let him be anathema' (1 Cor. 16.22).

Paul does not usually elaborate on final greetings as he does sometimes on opening ones leading into a prayer report (see on Eph. 1.15–18). If the editor has done so (just slightly – and it is difficult to be certain) then the following features may be due to him.

(1) The addition **God the Father** produces a more theologically balanced final greeting. Paul's (see above) are normally expressed in an exclusively christocentric way.

(2) The third person form is not usual for Paul in a final greeting. **To the brethren** (rather than 'to you, brethren') might have been preferred by the editor as more general (like all who love the Lord Jesus Christ), allowing the audience, who were not, after all, the apostle's original addressees, to see themselves as included among the recipients of his benediction.

(3) The somewhat redundant and loosely attached references to 'love *with faith*' and 'grace ... *with immortality*' may be editorial. Peace, love and grace are standard blessings from God: **faith** is less obviously so. But this author has emphasized earlier that faith is to be understood as a gift of God (2.4–10), and faith, in the other sense of sound doctrine, is one of his concerns (4.5, 13). In a similar way grace may have been amplified by the reference to immortality (in the Greek it comes at the very end of the sentence). But this is a more complex issue and requires a longer note.

It is difficult to account for the phrase **with immortality** that concludes Ephesians. First, the grammar is ambiguous: it might be intended to be taken with the preceding participle: 'those who love with (or, 'in') immortality' (as RSV, 'with love undying'). Alternatively it could be attached just to the Lord Jesus Christ who is 'in immortality' because of his resurrection (so Martin 177 and Caird 94; cf. 1 Tim. 1.17). But it is more likely, given the parallelism with the earlier construction ('love with faith'), that it should be linked to grace at the beginning of the sentence, 'grace with immortality', i.e. forgiveness that leads to eternal life, for these are the ultimate blessings one might hope for from God.

The actual Greek word used for immortality (*aphtharsia*, 'incorruption') appears rarely in Paul and never in greetings. It is mainly confined to the discussion of the resurrection of the body in 1 Cor. 15.42, 50 and 54, where it is entirely appropriate. The only other use of it is in Rom. 2.7, where eternal life is promised to those who seek immortality, as opposed to the wrath that is in store for the disobedient. For Paul himself, therefore, immortality is a human longing or the condition of resurrection life, not a spiritual gift suited to a final blessing. In Ephesians 'immortality' occurs for the first and last time here, but along with its cognate adjective it is quite popular in deutero-Pauline circles (1 Pet. 1.4, 23; 3.4; 1 Tim. 1.17; 2 Tim. 1.10). Less certain of the imminent arrival of the age to come and the parousia of Christ as a public event in history, Christians at the end of the first century concentrated instead on the experience of eternity already (cf. John 17.3) in the heavenly realms.

APPENDIXES

A PSEUDO-PAUL TO THE LAODICEANS
(translated by W. Schneemelcher (1991–2: 2.131f.)

(1) Paul, an apostle not of men and not through man, but through Jesus Christ, to the brethren who are in Laodicea, (2) grace to you and peace from God the Father and the Lord Jesus Christ.

(3) I thank Christ in all my prayer that you are steadfast in him and persevering in his works, in expectation of the promise for the day of judgement. (4) And may you not be deceived by the vain talk of some people who tell (you) tales that they may lead you away from the truth of the gospel which is proclaimed by me; (5) And now may God grant that those who come from me for the furtherance of the truth of the gospel (. . .) may be able to serve and to do good works for the well-being of eternal life.

(6) And now my bonds are manifest, which I suffer in Christ, on account of which I am glad and rejoice. (7) This ministers to me unto eternal salvation, which (itself) is effected through your prayers and by the help of the Holy Spirit, whether it be through life or through death. (8) For my life is in Christ and to die is joy (to me).

(9) And this will his mercy work in you, that you may have the same love and be of one mind. (10) Therefore, beloved, as you have heard in my presence, so hold fast and do in the fear of God, and eternal life will be your portion. (11) For it is God who works in you. (12) And do without hesitation what you do. (13) And for the rest, beloved, rejoice in Christ and beware of those who are out for sordid gain. (14) May all your requests be manifest before God, and be ye steadfast in the mind of Christ. (15) And what is pure, true, proper, just and lovely, do. (16) And what you have heard and received, hold in your heart and peace will be with you.

[(17) Salute all the brethren with the holy kiss.] (18) The saints salute you. (19) The grace of the Lord Jesus Christ be with your spirit. (20) And see that this epistle is read to the Colossians and that of the Colossians among you.

B   PAUL TO THE LAODICEANS: A TENTATIVE RECONSTRUCTION

Greeting

1. (1) From Paul by God's will an apostle of Christ Jesus, and Timothy our brother to the saints who are at Laodicea, even the faithful in Christ Jesus, (2) grace to you and peace from God our Father and the Lord Jesus Christ.

Thanksgiving and prayer report

[A commendation of Epaphras and mention of his report to Paul about the Laodicean congregation may have been present here, omitted by the editor.]

(15) For this reason I also, when I heard of your faith in the Lord Jesus and your love for all the saints, (16) have not ceased to give thanks for you, making mention of you in my prayers, (17) that the God and Father of our Lord Jesus Christ might give to you the spirit of wisdom and revelation through knowledge of him, (18) so as to know what is the hope of his call, what are the riches of his glorious inheritance among the saints, (19) and what is the excellent greatness of his power towards you who believe.

Certain elements of 1.20–2.22 may have been present here but they have been so thoroughly reworked in Ephesians as to be irrecoverable.]

Paul's imprisonment and mission

3. (1) On this account, I, Paul, a prisoner of Christ for the sake of you Gentiles – (2) always assuming you have heard of the mission to you that God in his grace has given to me, (3) that by a revelation the secret was made known to me, as I have already written briefly. (4) As far as that is concerned, you can learn, when you read, the insight I have into the secret of Christ (5) which was not made known to other generations as it has now been revealed to his saints, (6) that the Gentiles should be co-heirs incorporate and shareholders in Christ Jesus through the gospel, (7) of which I have become a servant according to the gift which God in his grace has given to me, (8) the least of all the saints, to preach to the Gentiles the good news of the unfathomable riches of Christ (12) in whom we have boldness and access in confidence through faith in him.

A second prayer report and doxology

(13) Therefore I beg you not to be depressed by my afflictions on your behalf: they are your glory. (14) On account of this, I kneel before the Father of our Lord Jesus Christ (16) that he grant that you be strengthened with power through his Spirit in the inner person, (17) that Christ dwell in your hearts through faith, you being rooted and founded on love, (18) so that you may be able to grasp along with all the saints the breadth, length, height and depth, (19) and to know the love of Christ that surpasses knowledge. (20) To him who is able to do more abundantly, beyond everything that we ask or understand, (21) to him be glory in Christ Jesus for ever and ever.

Exhortation

4. (1) Therefore, brothers, I, a prisoner, exhort you in the Lord to behave in a manner worthy of your proper calling, (2) with total humility and gentleness, and with patience being tolerant with one another in love, (3) eager to preserve the unity of the spirit in the bond of peace. (7) For to each one of us grace has been given according to the measure of Christ's gift, (13) until we all attain to the unity of faith in the Son of God, to a perfect humanity, with a full stature measured by Christ himself, (14) so that we should cease to be infants (15) but should rather grow up in all things into him, (16) from whom the whole body, being constructed and assembled, builds itself up in love.

(17) So this is my instruction, as I bear witness in the Lord, that you are no longer to behave as the Gentiles do, in the futility of their minds, (18) darkened in their understanding, alienated from the life of God through their inherent ignorance with their hearts hardened, (19) who in their insensitivity have abandoned themselves to depravity, producing all sorts of uncleanness, with covetousness. (20) You did not so learn Christ, (21) assuming that you have heard of him, and were taught in him – as the truth is in Jesus!

(22) Put away the old humanity with its former behaviour, which is being destroyed through desire, (23) and be renewed in the spirit of your mind, and (24) put on the new humanity which has been created by God in true righteousness and holiness. (25) Have done with lying, then, because we are members one of another. (26) Do not let the sun set on your angry outburst; (27) do not give the devil any room. (28) The thief should not steal any longer, but be employed doing honest work with his own hands, in order to have something to share with the one in need. (29) Let no foul language come out of your mouth, but only what is good for edification as the occasion requires, in order that it may bestow

grace on those who hear. (31) Let all bitterness, rage, anger, shouting and slander be removed from you, along with all wickedness. (32) Instead, be kind to one another and compassionate, forgiving one another as God in Christ has forgiven you. 5. (3) But let fornication and all uncleanness or covetousness not even be named among you, as is fitting with saints, (4) and obscenity, frivolity and facetiousness which are hardly appropriate, but rather thanksgiving. (5) For you should know this, that no fornicator, unclean or covetous person, idolaters in other words, has any inheritance in the kingdom of God.

(6) Let no one deceive you with vain talk. (7) Do not have anything to do with such people. (8) Behave as children of the light (10) – approving what is well-pleasing to the Lord – (11) and take no part in the sterile works of darkness, (12) for what they do in secret it is shameful even to mention. (15) Therefore, watch out that you behave, not as fools but as wise, (16) making every moment count, because these are evil times. (17) Therefore do not be mindless, but understand what the Lord's will is; (18) and do not get drunk with wine – that way ruin lies – but be filled with the Spirit, (19) speaking to each other in psalms and hymns and spiritual songs, singing and chanting in your hearts to the Lord, (20) always giving thanks for everything in the name of our Lord Jesus Christ to him who is God and Father.

Household code

(22) Wives, submit in the Lord to your husbands. (25) Husbands, love your wives. 6. (1) Children, obey in the Lord your parents. (4) Fathers, do not provoke them. (5) Slaves, be obedient to your earthly masters, with fear and trembling in heartfelt sincerity on your part, as though to Christ, (6) not with the mere appearance of servility to win human approval, but as slaves of Christ, doing God's will from the heart and (7) serving with enthusiasm, as to the Lord and not human masters, (8) knowing that each, whether slave or free, if he does well will receive a reward from the Lord. (9) And masters, do the same to them. Avoid threats, knowing that your Master and theirs is in heaven and shows no favouritism.

Prayer request

(18) Take every opportunity for prayer and intercession that the Spirit gives and be vigilant as well, persevering in intercession for all the saints, (19) and on my behalf too that I may be given the words to speak, to make freely known the secret of the gospel, (20) for which I am an ambassador in chains, so that I may speak freely as I ought.

Closing greetings

[The names of Paul's companions and of leading church members in Laodicea, along with a reference to the congregation at Colossae, and perhaps an instruction to exchange letters, may have been present here; omitted by the editor.]

Commendation of the letter-bearer

(21) So that you also may know my situation and how I am faring, Tychicus, that dear brother and faithful assistant in the Lord, will fully inform you. (22) I have sent him to you for this very reason, that you may know of our circumstances and that he may heartily encourage you.

Grace

(23) Peace be to you, brothers, and love from God the Father and the Lord Jesus Christ. (24) May grace be with all who love the Lord Jesus Christ.

BIBLIOGRAPHY

FREQUENTLY CITED COMMENTARIES ON EPHESIANS, REFERRED TO BY AUTHOR'S NAME ALONE

Barth, M. *Ephesians 1–3*. (AB 34A) Garden City, NY: Doubleday, 1974. *Ephesians 4–6*. (AB 34B) Garden City, NY: Doubleday, 1974.

Best, E. *A Critical and Exegetical Commentary on Ephesians*. (ICC) Edinburgh: T. & T. Clark, 1998.

Bruce, F. F. *The Epistles to the Colossians, to Philemon, and to the Ephesians*. (NICNT) Grand Rapids: Eerdmans, 1984.

Caird, G. B. *Paul's Letters from Prison (Ephesians, Philippians, Colossians, Philemon)*. (New Clarendon Bible). Oxford: Oxford University Press, 1976.

Gnilka, J. *Der Epheserbrief*. (HTKNT) Freiburg: Herder, 1971.

Houlden, J. L. *Paul's Letters from Prison: Philippians, Colossians, Philemon, and Ephesians*. Harmondsworth: Penguin, 1970.

Lincoln, A. T. *Ephesians*. (WBC 42) Waco, TX: Word, 1990.

Mitton, C. L. *Ephesians*. (NCB) London: Oliphants, 1976.

Mussner, F. *Der Brief an die Epheser*. Gütersloh: Gerd Mohn, 1982.

Robinson, J. A. *St Paul's Epistle to the Ephesians*. 2nd edn. London: Macmillan, 1904.

Schlier, H. *Der Brief an die Epheser*. Dusseldorf: Patmos, 1963.

Schnackenburg, R. *The Epistle to the Ephesians. A Commentary*. Edinburgh: T. & T. Clark, 1991. ET of *Der Brief an die Epheser*. (EKKNT) Neukirchen-Vluyn: Neukirchener Verlag, 1982.

OTHER WORKS

Abbott, T. K. 1924. *A Critical and Exegetical Commentary on the Epistles to the Ephesians and to the Colossians*. (ICC) Edinburgh: T. & T. Clark.

Adai, J. 1985. *Der Heilige Geist als Gegenwart Gottes in den einzelnen Christen in der Kirche und in der Welt*. Frankfurt am Main: Peter Lang.

Aland, K. 1961. 'The problem of anonymity and pseudonymity in Christian literature of the first two centuries.' *JTS* N.S. 12: 39–49.

1979. 'Die Entstehung des Corpus Paulinum.' In his *Neutestamentliche Entwürfe*. Munich: Kaiser.

Allan, J. A. 1958. 'The "In Christ" formula in Ephesians.' *NTS* 5: 54–62.

Anderson, C. P. 1966. 'Who wrote the Letter to Laodicea?' *JBL* 85: 436–40.

1975. 'Hebrews among the letters of Paul.' *SR*: 258–66.

Anderson, R. D. 1996. *Ancient Rhetorical Theory and Paul*. Kampen: Kok.

Arnold, C. E. 1987. 'The "Exorcism" of Ephesians 6.12 in recent research.' *JSNT* 30: 71–87.

1989. *Ephesians: Power and Magic*. (SNTSMS 63) Cambridge: Cambridge University Press.

Aune, D. 1987. *The New Testament in its Literary Environment*. Philadelphia: Westminster.

Balch, D. 1981. *Let Wives be Submissive: The Domestic Code in 1 Peter*. Chico, CA: Scholars Press.

Bartchy, S. S. 1973. *ΜΑΛΛΟΝ ΧΡΗΣΑΙ First Century Slavery and the Interpretation of 1 Corinthians 7.21*. Missoula, MT: Scholars Press.

Bash, A. 1997. *Ambassadors for Christ*. (WUNT 2.92) Tübingen: Mohr (Siebeck).

Bassler, J. M. 1982. *Divine Impartiality: Paul and a Theological Axiom*. Chico, CA: Scholars Press.

Bauer, W. 1972. *Orthodoxy and Heresy in Earliest Christianity*. London: SCM Press.

Baumgarten, J. 1975. *Paulus und die Apokalyptik*. Neukirchen-Vluyn: Neukirchener.

Becker, J. and Luz, U. 1998. *Die Briefe an die Galater, Epheser und Kolosser*. NTD 8/1. Göttingen: Vandenhoeck & Ruprecht.

Beker, J. C. 1982. *Paul's Apocalyptic Gospel: The Coming Triumph of God*. Philadelphia: Fortress.

Best, E. 1955. *One Body in Christ*. London: SPCK.

1971. *1 Peter*. London: Oliphants.

1997a. 'Who used whom? The relationship of Ephesians and Colossians.' *NTS* 43: 72–96.

1997b. *Essays on Ephesians*. Edinburgh: T. & T. Clark.

Betz, H. D. 1979. *Galatians*. Philadelphia: Fortress Press.

Bitzer, L. 1968. 'The rhetorical situation.' *PhilR* 1: 1—14.

Bjerkelund, C. J. 1967. *Parakaló*. Oslo: Universitetsforlaget.

Blackman, E. C. 1948. *Marcion and His Influence*. London: SPCK.

Bockmuehl, M. N. A. 1990. *Revelation and Mystery*. (WUNT 2.36) Tübingen: Mohr (Siebeck).

1997. *The Epistle to the Philippians*. (BNTC) London: A. & C. Black.

Bogart, J. 1971. *Orthodox and Heretical Perfectionism in the Johannine Community as Evident in the First Epistle of John*. (SBLDS 33) Missoula, MT: Scholars Press.

Boismard, M.-E. 1999a. *La Lettre de Saint Paul aux Épîtres aux Laodicéens.*
Cahiers de la Revue Biblique 42. Paris: Gabalda.

1999b. *L'Énigme de la Lettre aux Éphésiens.* Études bibliques n.s. 39.
Paris: Gabalda.

Botha, J. 1994. *Subject to Whose Authority? Multiple Readings of Romans 13.*
(Emory Studies in Early Christianity) Atlanta: Scholars Press.

Bousset, W. 1921. *Kyrios Christos.* ET Nashville: Abingdon, 1970.

Bouttier, M. 1991. *L'Épître de saint Paul aux Éphésiens.* (CNT 9b)
Geneva: Labor et Fides.

Brown, R. E. 1966, 1970. *The Gospel according to John.* (AB 29 & 29a)
New York: Doubleday.

1979. *The Community of the Beloved Disciple: The Life, Loves and Hates of
an Individual Church in New Testament Times.* London: Geoffrey
Chapman.

1982. *The Epistles of John.* (AB 30) New York: Doubleday.

1984. *The Churches the Apostles left behind.* New York: Paulist Press.

1997. *An Introduction to the New Testament.* New York: Doubleday.

Brox, N. 1975. *Falsche Verfasserangaben: zur Erklärung des frühchristlichen
Pseudepigraphie.* Stuttgart: Katholisches Bibelwerk.

Bultmann, R. 1956. *Primitive Christianity in its Contemporary Setting.* ET
London: Thames and Hudson.

1971. *The Gospel of John.* ET Oxford: Basil Blackwell.

Byrne, B. 1979. *Sons of God – Seed of Abraham.* AnBib 83. Rome:
Pontifical Biblical Institute.

Cadbury, H. J. 1958–9. 'The dilemma of Ephesians.' *NTS* 5: 91–102.

Caird, G. B. 1964. 'The descent of Christ in Ephesians 4:7–11.' *SE* 2
(*TU* 87) Berlin: Academie Verlag, 535–45.

1969. 'The Glory of God in the Fourth Gospel: An exercise in
biblical semantics.' *NTS* 15: 265–77.

Campbell, A. R. 1994. *The Elders. Seniority within Earliest Christianity.*
Edinburgh: T. & T. Clark.

Campenhausen, H. F. von. 1972. *The Formation of the Christian Bible.*
London: A & C Black.

Caragounis, C. C. 1977. *The Ephesian Mysterion: Meaning and Content.*
Lund: C. W. K. Gleerup.

Carr, W. 1981. *Angels and Principalities.* (SNTSMS 42) Cambridge:
Cambridge University Press.

Chadwick, H. 1960. *Die Absicht der Epheserbriefes.* ZNW 51: 145–53.

Charlesworth, J. H. (ed.). 1983. *The Old Testament Pseudepigrapha.* 2 vols.
Garden City, NY: Doubleday.

Conzelmann, H. 1976. 'Der Brief an die Epheser.' In J. Becker, H.
Conzelmann and G. Friedrich, *Die Briefe an die Galater, Epheser,
Philipper, Kolosser, Thessalonicher und Philemon.* Göttingen: Vanden-
hoeck & Ruprecht.

Coppens, J. 1968. ' "Mystery" in the theology of St Paul and its parallels at Qumran.' In *Paul and Qumran*, 132–58. Ed. J. Murphy O'Connor. London: Chapman.

Coutts, J. 1956–7. 'Ephesians 1.3–14 and 1 Peter 1.3–12.' *NTS* 3: 115–27.

1958. 'The relationship of Ephesians and Colossians.' *NTS* 4: 201–7.

Cranfield, C. E. B. 1975. *Romans*. (ICC) 2 vols. Edinburgh: T. & T. Clark.

Cross, F. L. (ed.). 1956. *Studies in Ephesians*. London: Mowbray.

Crouch, J. E. 1972. *The Origin and Intention of the Colossian Haustafel*. (FRLANT 109) Göttingen: Vandenhoeck & Ruprecht.

Cullmann, O. 1953. *Early Christian Worship*. London: SCM Press.

Dahl, N. A. 1951. 'Adresse und Proömium des Epheserbriefes.' *TZ* 7: 241–64.

1975. 'Cosmic dimensions and religious knowledge in Eph 3.18.' In *Jesus und Paulus*, 57–75. Ed. E. E. Ellis and E. Grässer. Göttingen: Vandenhoeck & Ruprecht.

1978. 'Interpreting Ephesians: then and now.' *Currents in Theology and Mission* 5: 133–43.

1986. 'Gentiles, Christians and Israelites in the Epistle to the Ephesians.' *HTR* 79: 31–9.

Daniélou, J. 1964. *The Theology of Jewish Christianity*. London: Darton, Longman & Todd.

Davies, W. D. 1967. *Paul and Rabbinic Judaism*. 2nd edn. New York: Harper and Row.

Dawes, G. W. 1998. *The Body in Question: Metaphor and Meaning in the Interpretation of Ephesians 5:21–33*. Leiden: Brill.

Deidun, T. 1981. *New Covenant Morality in Paul*. (AnBib 89) Rome: Biblical Institute Press.

Dibelius, M. 1912. *An die Kolosser, Epheser, an Philemon*. (HNT 1) 3rd rev. edn. ET by H. Greeven, Tübingen: Mohr, 1953.

Dodd, C. H. 1928. 'Ephesians.' In *The Abingdon Bible Commentary*. Ed. F. C. Eiselen, E. Lewis & D. G. Downey. New York: Abingdon.

Doty, W. 1973. *Letters in Primitive Christianity*. Philadelphia: Fortress.

Duncan, G. S. 1929. *St Paul's Ephesian Ministry. A Reconstruction with Special Reference to the Ephesian Origin of the Imprisonment Epistles*. London: Hodder and Stoughton.

Dunn, J. D. G. 1989. *Christology in the Making*. 2nd edn. London: SCM Press.

1993. *The Epistle to the Galatians*. (BNTC) London: A. & C. Black.

Dupont, J. 1949. *Gnosis: La Connaissance religieuse dans les Épîtres de Saint Paul*. Paris: J. Gabalda.

Elliott, J. H. 1990. *A Home for the Homeless. A Social-Scientific Criticism of 1 Peter*. Minneapolis: Fortress.

Elliott, N. 1990. *The Rhetoric of Romans: Argumentative Constraint and Strategy and Paul's Dialogue with Judaism.* (JSNTSup 45) Sheffield: JSOT Press.

Ernst, J. 1970. *Pleroma und Pleroma Christi.* Regensburg: F. Pustet.

Faust, E. 1993. *Pax Christi et Pax Caesaris: religionsgeschichtliche, traditionsgeschichtliche und sozialgeschichtliche Studien zum Epheserbrief.* (NTOA 24) Göttingen: Vandenhoeck & Ruprecht.

Fee, G. D. 1987. *The First Epistle to the Corinthians.* (NICNT) Grand Rapids: Eerdmans.

Fischer, K. M. 1973. *Tendenz und Absicht des Epheserbriefes.* Göttingen: Vandenhoeck & Ruprecht.

Fitzmyer, J. A. 1971. *Essays on the Semitic Background of the New Testament.* London: Geoffrey Chapman.

1993. *Romans.* (AB 33) Garden City, NY: Doubleday.

Fleckenstein, K.-H. 1994. *Ordnet euch einander unter in der Furcht Christi: Die Eheperikope in Eph. 5,21–33: Geschichte der Interpretation, Analyse und Aktualisierung des Textes.* Würzburg: Echter Verlag.

Foakes Jackson, F. J. & Lake, K. (eds). 1920–33. *The Beginnings of Christianity: The Acts of the Apostles.* 5 vols. London: Macmillan.

Francis, F. O. and Meeks, W. (eds). 1975. *Conflict at Colossae.* Sources for Biblical Study 4. Missoula, MT: Scholars Press.

Furnish, V. P. 1968. *Theology and Ethics in Paul.* Nashville: Abingdon.

1979. *The Moral Teaching of Paul.* Rev. edn. Nashville: Abingdon.

1984. *II Corinthians.* (AB 32a) Garden City, NY: Doubleday.

Gärtner, B. 1965. *The Temple and the Community in Qumran and the New Testament.* (SNTSMS 1) Cambridge: Cambridge University Press.

Geoffrion, T. C. 1993. *The Rhetorical Purpose and Military Character of Philippians: A Call to Stand Firm.* Lewiston: Edwin Mellen Press.

Gese, M. 1997. *Das Vermächtnis des Apostels: die Rezeption der paulinischen Theologie im Epheserbriefe.* (WUNT 2.99) Tübingen: Mohr (Siebeck).

Gielen, M. 1990. *Tradition und Theologie neutestamentlicher Haustafelnethik.* (BBB 75) Frankfurt am Main: Anton Hain.

Goguel, M. 1935. 'Esquisse d'une solution nouvelle du problème de l'épître aux Éphésiens.' *RHR* 111: 254–84; 112: 73–99.

Goodman, M. 1994. *Mission and Conversion. Proselytizing in the Religious History of the Roman Empire.* Oxford: Clarendon Press.

Goodspeed, E. J. 1933. *The Meaning of Ephesians.* Chicago: University of Chicago Press.

1956. *The Key to Ephesians.* Chicago: University of Chicago Press.

Gordon, T. D. 1994. ' "Equipping" Ministry in Ephesians 4.' *JETS* 37: 69–78.

Goulder, M. D. 1991. 'The visionaries of Laodicea.' *JSNT* 43: 15–39.

Grelot, P. 1989. 'La structure d'Éphésiens 1.3–14.' *RB* 96: 193–209.

Grudem, W. 1985. 'Does κεφαλη ('head') mean 'source' or 'authority over' in Greek literature? A survey of 2,336 examples.' *Trinity Journal* 6: 38–59.

Grundmann, W. 1959. 'Die νηπιοι in der urchristlichen Paränese.' *NTS* 5: 188–215.

Gudorf, M. E. 1998. 'The use of παλη in Ephesians 6:12.' *JBL* 117: 331–5.

Hahneman, G. M. 1992. *The Muratorian Fragment and the Development of the Canon.* Oxford: Clarendon Press.

Hall Harris III, W. 1996. *The Descent of Christ: Ephesians 4.7–11 and Traditional Hebrew Imagery.* Leiden: E. J. Brill.

Hammer, P. L. 1960. 'A comparison of *kleronomia* in Paul and Ephesians.' *JBL* 79: 267–72.

Hanson, A. T. 1980. *The New Testament Interpretation of Scripture.* London: SPCK.

Hanson, S. 1963. *The Unity of the Church in the New Testament.* Lexington: American Library Association.

Harnack, A. von. 1910. 'Die Adresse der Epheserbriefes des Paulus.' *SPAW* 37: 696–709.

—— 1924. *Marcion: Das Evangelium vom fremden Gott.* Leipzig: Hinrichs'sche Buchhandlung. ET *The Gospel of the Alien God.* Durham: Labyrinth, 1989.

—— 1926. *Die Briefsammlung des Apostels Paulus, und die anderen vorkonstantinischen Briefsammlungen.* Leipzig: Hinrichs'sche Buchhandlung.

—— 1981. *Militia Christi.* Philadelphia: Fortress. ET of *Militia Christi: die christliche Religion und der Soldatenstand in den ersten Jahrhunderten.* Darmstadt: Wissenschaftliche Buchgesellschaft, 1963.

Harrison, P. N. 1921. *The Problem of the Pastoral Epistles.* London: Oxford University Press.

Hay, D. M. 1973. *Glory at the Right Hand: Psalm 110 in Early Christianity.* Nashville: Abingdon.

Hays, R. B. 1989. *Echoes of Scripture in the Letters of Paul.* New Haven: Yale University Press.

—— 1996. *The Moral Vision of the New Testament, Community, Cross and Creation: a Contemporary Introduction to New Testament Ethics.* New York: HarperCollins.

Hemer, C. J. 1986. *The Letters to the Seven Churches of Asia in their Local Setting.* (JSNTSup 11) Sheffield: JSOT Press.

Hengel, M. 1977. *Crucifixion.* London: SCM Press.

—— 1983. *Between Jesus and Paul.* London: SCM Press.

Himmelfarb, M. 1993. *Ascent to Heaven in Jewish and Christian Apocalypses.* Oxford: Oxford University Press.

Holtzmann, H. J. 1872. *Kritik der Epheser- und Kolosserbriefe auf Grund einer Analyse ihres Verwandtschaftsverhältnisses.* Leipzig: Englemann.

Hooker, M. D. 1964. 'Authority on her head: an examination of 1 Corinthians 11.10.' *NTS* 10: 410–16; reprinted in *idem*, *From Adam to Christ: Essays on Paul*. Cambridge: Cambridge University Press, 1990.

Houlden, J. L. 1973a. *A Commentary on the Johannine Epistles*. (BNTC) London: A. & C. Black.

1973b. 'Christ and the Church in Ephesians.' *SE* 6 (*TU* 112): 267–73.

Hübner, H. 1989. 'Glossen in Epheser 2.' In *Vom Urchristentum zu Jesus*, 392–406. Ed. H. Frankemölle & K. Kertelge. Freiberg: Herder.

Innitzer, T. 1904. 'Der "Hymnus" im Epheserbrief 1.3–14.' *ZKT* 28: 612–21.

Jeremias, J. 1964. *TDNT* 1.791–3) s.v. ἀκρογωνιαιος.

Johanson, B. C. 1987. *To All the Brethren*. Stockholm: Almquist & Wiskell.

Kamlah, E. 1964. *Der Form der katologischen Paränese im Neuen Testament*. Tübingen: Mohr.

Käsemann, E. 1967. New Testament Questions of Today, 'Paul and early Catholicism.' In 236–51 Philadelphia: Fortress Press.

1968. 'Ephesians and Acts.' In *Studies in Luke-Acts*. Ed. L. Keck & J. L. Martyn. London: SPCK.

1980. *Commentary on Romans*. London: SCM Press.

Keener, C. S. 1992. *Paul, Women and Wives: Marriage and Women's Ministry in the Letters of Paul*. Peabody, MA: Hendrickson.

Kelly, J. N. D. 1960. *Early Christian Creeds*. 2nd edn. London: Longmans.

Kennedy, G. A. 1984. *New Testament Interpretation through Rhetorical Criticism*. Chapel Hill: University of North Carolina Press.

Kenny, A. 1986. *A Stylometric Analysis of the New Testament*. Oxford: Clarendon Press.

Kern, P. H. 1998. *Rhetoric and Galatians*. (SNTSMS 101) Cambridge: Cambridge University Press.

Kilpatrick, G. D. 1990. *The Principles and Practice of New Testament Textual Criticism*. (BETL 96) Leuven: Peeters.

Kirby, J. 1968. *Ephesians: Baptism and Pentecost*. Montreal: McGill University Press.

Kitchen, M. 1994. *Ephesians*. (NTR) London: Routledge.

Kittredge, C. B. 1998. *Community and Authority: The Rhetoric of Obedience in the Pauline Tradition*. Harrisburg, PA: Trinity.

Kitzberger, I. R. 1986. *Bau der Gemeinde: das paulinische Wortfeld = oikodome/ep/oikodome*. (Forschung zur Bibel band 53) Würzberg: Echter Verlag.

Knox, J. 1935. *Philemon Among the Letters of Paul: A New View of its Place and Importance*. Nashville: Abingdon.

Knox, W. L. 1939. *St Paul and the Church of the Gentiles*. Cambridge: Cambridge University Press.

Koester, H. 1982. *Introduction to the New Testament. Volume Two: History and Literature of Early Christianity*. Philadelphia: Fortress Press.

Koester, H. (ed.). 1995. *Ephesos – Metropolis of Asia*. Valley Forge, PA: Trinity.

Kreitzer, L. 1997. *The Epistle to the Ephesians*. Peterborough: Epworth Press.

1998. ' "Crude language" and "shameful things done in secret" (Ephesians 5.4, 12): allusions to the cult of Demeter/Cybele in Hierapolis?' *JSNT* 71: 51–77.

Kroeger, C. C. 1987. 'The classical concept of *head* as source.' In *Equal to Serve*, 267–83. Ed. G. G. Hull. Old Tappan, NJ: Revell.

Kuhn, K. G. 1968. 'The Epistle to the Ephesians in the light of the Qumran texts.' In *Paul and Qumran*, 115–31. Ed. J. Murphy O'Connor. London: Geoffrey Chapman.

Lampe, G. W. H. 1951. *The Seal of the Spirit*. London: SPCK.

Lampe, P. 1985. 'Keine "Sklavenflucht" des Onesimus.' *ZNW* 76: 135–7.

Lightfoot, J. B. 1884. *Saint Paul's Epistles to the Colossians and Philemon*. London: Macmillan.

Lincoln, A. T. 1981. *Paradise Now and Not Yet*. (SNTSMS 43) Cambridge: Cambridge University Press.

1982. 'The use of the OT in Ephesians.' *JSNT* 14: 16–57.

1983. 'Ephesians 2.8–10 – a summary of Paul's Gospel.' *CBQ* 45: 617–30.

1995. ' "Stand therefore . . . ". Ephesians 6.10–20 as *peroratio*.' *BibInt* 3: 99–114.

Lindemann, A. 1975. *Die Aufhebung der Zeit. Geschichtverständnis und Eschatologie im Epheserbrief*. Gütersloh: Gerd Mohn.

1976. 'Bemerkungen zu Addressaten und zum Anlass des Epheserbriefes.' *ZNW* 67: 235–51.

1979. *Paulus im ältesten Christentum*. Tübingen: Mohr.

1985. *Der Epheserbrief*. Zürich: Theologischer Verlag.

Lohmeyer, E. 1926. 'Das Proömium des Epheserbriefs.' *TBl*: 120–25.

Lohse, E. 1971. *Colossians and Philemon*. (Hermeneia) Philadelphia: Fortress Press.

Luz, U. 1976. 'Rechtfertigung bei den Paulusschülern.' In *Rechtfertigung*, 365–83. Ed. J. Friedrich, W. Poehlmann & P. Stuhlmacher. Tübingen: Mohr.

Lyall, F. 1969. 'Roman Law in the writings of Paul: adoption.' *JBL* 88: 458–66.

MacDonald, M. 1988. *The Pauline Churches*. (SNTSMS 60) Cambridge: Cambridge University Press.

Martin, D. 1990. *Slavery as Salvation: The Metaphor of Slavery in Pauline Christianity*. New Haven: Yale University Press.

1994. *The Corinthian Body*. New Haven: Yale University Press.

Martin, R. P. 1968. 'An epistle in search of a life setting.' *ExpT* 79: 296–302.

Martyn, J. L. 1979. *History and Theology in the Fourth Gospel*. Rev. edn. Nashville: Abingdon.

Masson, C. 1953. *L'Épître de Paul aux Éphésiens*. Neuchâtel and Paris: Delachaux et Niestlé.

McKelvey, J. 1969. *The New Temple*. Oxford: Oxford University Press.

Meade, D. G. 1986. *Pseudonymity and Canon*. Tübingen: Mohr.

Meeks, W. A. 1967. *The Prophet-King: Moses Traditions and the Johannine Christology*. (NovTSup 14) Leiden: E. J. Brill.

1974. 'The image of the androgyne: some uses of a symbol in earliest Christianity.' *HR* 13: 165–208.

1977. 'The unity of humankind in Colossians and Ephesians.' In *God's Christ and his People: Essays Presented to Nils Alstrup Dahl*, 209–21. Ed. J. Jervell & W. A. Meeks. Oslo: Universitetsforlaget.

1983. *The First Urban Christians: The Social World of the Apostle Paul*. New Haven: Yale University Press.

1986. *The Moral World of the First Christians*. Philadelphia: Westminster.

1993. *The Origins of Christian Morality: The First Two Centuries*. New Haven: Yale University Press.

Merklein, H. 1973. *Das kirchliche Amt nach dem Epheserbrief*. Munich: Koesel.

Metzger, B. M. 1987. *The Canon of the New Testament*. Oxford: Clarendon Press.

1992. *The Text of the New Testament: Its Transmission, Corruption and Restoration*. 3rd edn. Oxford, Oxford University Press.

1994. *A Textual Commentary on the Greek New Testament*. 2nd edn. Stuttgart: United Bible Societies.

Meuzelaar, J. J. 1961. *Der Leib des Messias*. Assen: Van Gorcum.

Militic, S. F. 1988. *'One Flesh': Eph 5.22–24, 5.31: Marriage and the New Creation*. Rome: Pontifical Biblical Institute.

Miller, J. D. 1997. *The Pastoral Epistles as Composite Documents*. (SNTSMS 93) Cambridge: Cambridge University Press.

Mitton, C. L. 1951. *The Epistle to the Ephesians*. Oxford: Clarendon Press.

Moffatt, J. 1911. *An Introduction to the Literature of the New Testament*. Edinburgh: T. & T. Clark.

Morgan, R. M. with J. Barton. 1988. *Biblical Interpretation*. Oxford: Oxford University Press.

Moritz, T. 1996. *A Profound Mystery: The Use of the Old Testament in Ephesians*. (NovTSup 85) Leiden: E. J. Brill.

Morton, A. Q. 1978. *Literary Detection: How to Prove Authorship and Fraud in Literary Documents*. Epping: Bowker.

Morton, A. Q. 1980. *A Critical Concordance to the Letter of Paul to the Ephesians*. Wooster, OH: Biblical Research Associates.

Moule, C. F. D. 1947–8. 'A note on ὀφθαλμοδουλια' *ExpT* 59: 250.

1951. ' "Fullness" and "fill" in the New Testament.' *SJT* 4: 79–86.

1957. *The Epistles of Paul the Apostle to the Colossians and to Philemon*. Cambridge: Cambridge University Press.

1971. *An Idiom Book of New Testament Greek*. 2nd edn. Cambridge: Cambridge University Press.

1977. *The Origins of Christology*. Cambridge: Cambridge University Press.

Muddiman, J. B. 1987. 'The Glory of Jesus: Mark 10.37.' In *The Glory of Christ in the New Testament*, 51–8. Ed. L. D. Hurst & N. T. Wright. Oxford: Oxford University Press.

1994. 'An anatomy of Galatians.' In *Crossing the Boundaries. Essays in Biblical Interpretation in Honour of Michael D. Goulder*, 257–70. Ed. S. E. Porter, P. Joyce & D. E. Orton. Leiden: E. J. Brill.

Munro, W. 1983. *Authority in Paul and Peter. The Identification of a Pastoral Stratum in the Pauline Corpus and 1 Peter*. (SNTSMS 45) Cambridge: Cambridge University Press.

Murphy O'Connor, J. 1965. 'Who wrote Ephesians?' *TBT*: 1201–9.

1997. *Paul: A Critical Life*. Oxford: Oxford University Press.

Noack, B. 1952. 'Das Zitat in Eph. 5.14.' *ST* 5: 52–64.

Nock, A. D. 1934. 'A vision of Mandulis Aion.' *HTR* 27: 53–104.

Nordling, J. G. 1991. 'Onesimus Fugitivus: a defence of the runaway slave hypothesis in Philemon.' *JSNT* 41: 97–117.

O'Brien, P. T. 1977. *Introductory Thanksgivings in the Letters of Paul*. Leiden: Brill.

1979. 'Ephesians 1: an unusual introduction to a New Testament letter.' *NTS* 25: 504–16.

1982. *Colossians, Philemon*. (WBC 44) Waco, TX: Word.

1999. *The Letter to the Ephesians*. (PNTC) Grand Rapids: Eerdmans.

Odeberg, H. 1934. *The View of the Universe in the Epistle to the Ephesians*. Lund: Lund Universitets Arsskrift.

O'Neill, J. C. 1972. *The Recovery of Paul's Letter to the Galatians*. London: SPCK.

1975. *Paul's Letter to the Romans*. (Pelican NT Commentaries) Harmondsworth: Penguin.

Oster, R. E. 1976. 'The Ephesian Artemis as an opponent of early Christianity.' *JAC* 19: 27–44.

Overfield, P. D. 1978. 'Pleroma: a study in content and context.' *NTS* 25: 384–96.

Patzia, A. G. 1984. *Ephesians, Colossians, Philemon.* (NIBC) Peabody, MA: Hendrickson.

Percy, E. 1946. *Die Probleme der Kolosser- und Epheserbriefe.* Lund: Gleerup.

Perkins, P. 1997. *Ephesians.* (ANTC) Nashville: Abingdon.

Pogoloff, S. M. 1992. *Logos and Sophia: The Rhetorical Situation of 1 Corinthians.* (SBLDS 132) Atlanta: Scholars Press.

Pokorný, P. 1965. *Der Epheserbrief und die Gnosis.* Berlin: Evangelische Verlagsanstalt.

Porter, S. E. 1993. 'The theoretical justification for application of rhetorical categories to Pauline epistolary literature.' In *Rhetoric and the New Testament,* 100–22. Ed. S. E. Porter & T. H. Olbricht. (JSNTSup 90) Sheffield: JSOT.

⸻ 1994. *Idioms of the Greek New Testament.* Sheffield: Sheffield Academic Press.

Porter, S. E. (ed.). 1997. *Handbook of Classical Rhetoric in the Hellenistic Period 330 B.C.– A.D. 400.* Leiden: Brill.

Porter, S. E. & Tombs, D. (eds). 1995. *Approaches to New Testament Study.* Sheffield: Sheffield Academic Press.

Potterie, I. de la. 1977. 'Le Christ, plérôme de l'Église (Eph 1.22–23).' *Bib* 58: 500–24

Powell, M. A. 1993. *What is Narrative Criticism?* London: SPCK.

Ramasoron, L. 1977. 'Une lecture de Ephésiens 1,15 – 2,10.' *Bib* 58: 388–410.

Rapske, B. M. 1991. 'The prisoner Paul in the eyes of Onesimus.' *NTS* 37: 187–203.

Richards, E. R. 1991. *The Secretary in the Letters of Paul.* Tübingen: Mohr (Siebeck).

Robinson, J. A. T. 1952. *The Body: A Study in Pauline Theology.* London: SCM Press.

⸻ 1962. *Twelve New Testament Studies.* London: SCM Press.

Robinson, J. M. (ed.). 1988. *The Nag Hammadi Library.* San Francisco: Harper & Row.

Roetzel, C. J. 1983. 'Jewish Christian – Gentile Christian relations: discussion of Eph. 2.15a.' *ZNW* 74: 81–89.

Roller, O. 1933. *Das Formular der paulinischen Briefe.* Stuttgart: Kohlhammer.

Roon, A. van 1974. *The Authenticity of Ephesians.* (NovTSup 39) Leiden: Brill.

Rowland, C. C. 1982. *The Open Heaven: A Study of Apocalyptic in Judaism and Early Christianity.* London: SPCK.

Sampley, J. P. 1971. '*And the Two Shall Become One Flesh*': A Study of Traditions in Eph 5.21–33. (SNTSMS 16) Cambridge: Cambridge University Press.

Sanders, J. T. 1965. 'Hymnic elements in Ephesians 1–3.' *ZNW* 56: 214–32.

Schille, G. 1965. *Frühchristliche Hymnen*. Berlin: Evangelische Verlagsanstalt.

Schlier, H. 1930. *Christus und die Kirche im Epheserbrief*. (BHT 6) Tübingen: Mohr (Siebeck).

Schmithals, W. 1983. 'The *Corpus Paulinum* and Gnosis.' In *The New Testament and Gnosis*, 107–24. Ed. A. Logan & A. Wedderburn. Edinburgh: T. & T. Clark.

Schnackenburg, R. 1991. 'Ephesus: Entwicklung einer Gemeinde von Paulus zu Johannes.' *BZ* 35: 41–64.

Schneemelcher, W. (ed.). 1991–2. *New Testament Apocrypha*. 2 vols. Cambridge: James Clarke.

Schubert, P. 1939. *Form and Function of the Pauline Thanksgivings*. Berlin: A Topelmann.

Schweizer, E. 1982. *The Letter to the Colossians*. London: SPCK.

Scott, J. M. 1992. *Adoption as Sons of God*. (WUNT 2:48) Tübingen: Mohr (Siebeck).

Scroggs, R. 1966. *The Last Adam: A Study in Pauline Anthropology*. Philadephia: Fortress.

Stamps, D. L. 1993. 'Rethinking the rhetorical situation: the entextualization of the situation in New Testament epistles.' In *Rhetoric and the New Testament*, 193–210. Ed. S. E. Porter & T. H. Olbricht. (JSNTSup 90) Sheffield: JSOT.

Stead, G. C. 1969. 'The Valentinian myth of Sophia.' *JTS* N.S. 20: 75–104.

Stowers, S. K. 1986. *Letter Writing in Greco-Roman Antiquity*. Philadelphia: Westminster Press.

Strelan, R. 1996. *Paul, Artemis and the Jews in Ephesus*. (BZNW 80) Berlin: de Gruyter.

Stuhlmacher, P. 1974. ' "Er ist unser Friede" (Eph 2,14): zur Exegese und Bedeutung von Eph 2,14–18.' In *Neues Testament und Kirche* (FS R. Schnackenburg). Ed. J. Gnilka. Freiberg: Herder. ET ' "He is our Peace" (Eph. 2.14): on the exegesis and significance of Eph. 2.14–18.' In Stuhlmacher, *Reconciliation, Law & Righteousness: Essays in Biblical Theology*, 182–200. Philadelphia: Fortress Press, 1986.

Tachau, P. 1972. *'Einst' und 'Jetzt' im Neuen Testament*. Göttingen: Vandenhoeck & Ruprecht.

Theissen, G. 1978. *The First Followers of Jesus. A Sociological Analysis of the Earliest Christianity*. London: SCM Press.
    1982. *The Social Setting of Pauline Christianity: Essays on Corinth*. Edinburgh: T. & T. Clark.

Theissen, W. 1995. *Christen in Ephesus. Die historische und theologische Situation in vorpaulinische und paulinische Zeit und zur Zeit Apostelgeschichte und der Pastoralbriefe*. (TANZ 12) Tübingen: Franke Verlag.

Thomson, I. H. 1995. *Chiasmus in the Pauline Letters*. (JSNTSup 111) Sheffield: Sheffield Academic Press.

Tilborg, S. van. 1996. *Reading John in Ephesus*. Leiden: Brill.

Trebilco, P. 1991. *Jewish Communities in Asia Minor*. (SNTSMS 69) Cambridge: Cambridge University Press.

Trobisch, D. 1994. *Paul's Letter Collection: Tracing the Origins*. Minneapolis: Fortress Press.

Unnik, W. C. van. 1980. 'The Christian's freedom of speech in the New Testament.' In *Sparsa Collecta II*, 269–89. Leiden: Brill.

Wansink, C. S. 1996. *'Chained in Christ': The Experience and Rhetoric of Paul's Imprisonments*. Sheffield: JSOT Press.

Watson, F. 1986. *Paul, Judaism and the Gentiles*. (SNTSMS 56) Cambridge: Cambridge University Press.

Wedderburn, A. J. M. 1985. 'Some observations on Paul's use of the phrases "in Christ" and 'with Christ".' *JSNT* 25: 83–97.

Wedderburn, A. J. M. and Lincoln, A.T. 1993. *The Theology of the Later Pauline Letters*. Cambridge: Cambridge University Press.

Weima, J. A. D. 1995. 'What does Aristotle have to do with Paul? An evaluation of Rhetorical Criticism.' *BBR* 5: 177–98.

Wild, R. A. 1984. 'The warrior and the prisoner: some reflections on Ephesians 6:10–20.' *CBQ* 46: 284–98.

Wiles, G. 1974. *Paul's Intercessory Prayers*. (SNTSMS 24) Cambridge: Cambridge University Press.

Wink, W. 1984. *Naming the Powers*. Philadelphia: Fortress.

Winter, S. 1987. 'Paul's Letter to Philemon.' *NTS* 33: 1–15.

Yoder Neufeld, T. R. 1997. *Put on the Armour of God. The Divine Warrior from Isaiah to Ephesians*. (JSNTSup 140) Sheffield: Sheffield Academic Press.

Zuntz, G. 1953. *The Text of the Epistles: A Disquisition upon the Corpus Paulinum*. London: British Academy.

INDEX OF SCRIPTURAL
REFERENCES

INDEX OF MODERN AUTHORS

SUBJECT INDEX

Access 137f, 162f

Adam, last Adam 70, 77, 88–91, 113, 129, 133f, 203f, 219–21, 259–61, 268–70, (see also Anthropology)

Aeon 16, 96, 103, 110, 159, 161f

Adoption 68f

Ambassador 296

Anakephalaiosis, see Summation

Anthropology 66, 131, 182

Apocalyptic 18, 48, 66, 73, 75, 89–91, 103f, 133, 159, 171, 243, 246, 290

Apostles, apostleship 19, 39, 57–8, 75, 140–2, 146, 153–7, 190f, 198f

Armour 218, 234, 285–94

Artemis 35

Ascension 136f, 187–97

Authenticity of Ephesians 1–47 et passim

Baptism 14, 64f, 70, 115, 126, 146, 182–5, 218, 243, 265

Berakah, see Blessing

Blessing 62–76, 81, 97

Body of Christ, see Church

Boldness 162f, 295

Bride of Christ, see Church

Building metaphors, see Church

Captivity, captives 24, 136, 149, 188–92

Captivity letters, Paul's 12, 24, 57, 163

Catholicism, 'early' 14, 48, 200

Celibacy 51, 251, 283

Chiasm 64, 277

Children 204–5, 231, 273–6

Christology 33, 67f, 119f, 124, 201–4, 262 et passim; Christ as Beloved 70; as Head 76, 91, 208, 261; as One Lord 184; as Peace 125; as Son of God, 203 (see also Adam, last; Summation; Incarnation; Ascension)

Church, doctrine of 18f, 48f, 176 et passim; Church as Body 93f, 135, 182f, 200, 208, 225, 268; as Bride 18, 260f; as building 143f; as Eve 259, 262; as fullness of Christ 94; local and universal 19, 49, 93

Circular letter theory 5–7, 12, 17, 35, 60f, 143, 152

Clement, First letter of 34, 199

Collection for Jerusalem 24f, 83, 180, 201

Collection of Paul's letters 12–14, 27, 53, 56, 152

Colossae 21, 24–6, 31, 101, 227, 298

Cornerstone 142f

Covenant 36, 71f, 114, 118f, 121, 213

Creation, new creation 67, 112f, 133f, 159, 221

Credal formulae 5, 33, 82, 99, 181f

Cross 65, 73, 115, 131f, 134–6, 170f, 191, 210, 270 (see also Death of Christ)

Date of Ephesians 24, 32, 24f, 173, 206

Decalogue 225f, 272–5

Death of Christ 39f, 70f, 123, 191–3, 231, 264

Descent into Hell, see Underworld

335